A history of the Forest
during the New Zeala

FOREST RANGERS

RICHARD STOWERS

Forest Rangers' incised, silver cap badge (enlarged). This rare example, once owned by Corporal James McGuirk, is held by the Te Awamutu District Museum. Presented by Mrs Myra Pope, daughter of McGuirk, in 1956.

JOHN E. BINSLEY
Assistant Researcher of Biographical Section

The author gratefully acknowledges the assistance of John E. Binsley for his generous and unrelenting support and efforts throughout. John has kindly made available his unique and extensive research into colonial units which has proven an unrivalled source of information to me. Often he has struggled over questions where the answers have been difficult to verify.

The author also thanks the support and generous contribution made by Tim Ryan, renowned author and authority on uniforms and equipment. Tim is responsible for the splendid and accurate uniform illustrations.

Special thanks to Wayne McDonald for his tremendous support and access to rare rolls and research; to Ron Stewart for his specialist information on firearms; to Jennifer Smith for her meticulous editing; to Rose Young for her knowledge and information; to Hugh Keane for his knowledge and support; and Ian Anthony.

Acknowledgement is made to the staff of National Archives, museums and libraries throughout the country for their support.

First published in 1996 by Richard Stowers
29A Corrin Street, Hamilton, New Zealand
Phone or Fax: (07) 843 5371

Printed by Print House, 142 Kent Street, Hamilton, New Zealand

This book is available for quoting or photocopying and no prior written permission of the publisher is necessary

ISBN 0-473-03531-6

Also by Richard Stowers
Kiwi Versus Boer, the First New Zealand Mounted Rifles in the Anglo-Boer War 1899-1902. Published 1992.

GILLIAN & RICHARD STOWERS
5 HILLCREST RD, HAMILTON
PH/FAX: (07) 856-6133

Foreword

This book is a unique invitation to discover the history of a small but significant colonial military unit which saw service out of all proportion to its size and duration.

The corps was raised to challenge the Maori in their own environment, so its ranks were filled with men from many countries who were adept in the skills of bush warfare.

It has been said that these men were mercenaries fighting for a much higher pay than the British regular soldier, and with the promise of a confiscated land grant at the end of their service. However this is a simplification. To comprehend their motives one must understand something of the depressed economy of the North Island of New Zealand of the time, where settlers walked off or were driven off their land and the towns were filled with the disaffected unemployed. Other incentives to join were the protection of their vulnerable families in a bitter war that saw little distinction (by both sides), on age, sex, or civilian status. There must also have been the men who joined for the quest for adventure that brought many of these men half way around the world to the goldfields of New Zealand.

It is not the intention of the author to provide a history of the origins or political background to the campaigns he describes. These aspects of the New Zealand Wars have been covered in great detail in other books.

The politically correct will probably object to such terms as "natives" and "rebels". However this is not a political book and one should make no apologies for quoting the language of the time in context.

Richard Stowers is to be congratulated for researching and presenting such a specialised book, which was entirely self-funded, in today's tight publishing market.

This book will appeal to military historians, family history enthusiasts and militaria collectors alike, plus all those who have an interest in the history of this country.

Tim Ryan
Wellington. 1996

Contents

                                                                                                         Page

Introduction   **Bush-roving scouts** 1
    Origins and fighting qualities of the Forest Rangers.

Chapter 1   **Call for Forest Volunteers** 6
    Trouble in south Auckland; Recruitment of men; The promise of land; Roll of original company; Travellers' Rest Inn.

Chapter 2   **Hunua adventure** 15
    Expedition into Hunua Ranges; Operations in south Auckland.

Chapter 3   **Lusk's Clearing** 22
    First engagement for Forest Rangers at Lusk's Clearing; With the Flying Column; Further operations in south Auckland; Church parade.

Chapter 4   **Disbandment and re-enlistment** 33
    Jackson enlists men for new unit; Von Tempsky gets his own company; Roll at end of November 1863.

Chapter 5   **Jackson proves his worth** 36
    Paparata expedition and engagement; Von Tempsky's jealousy; Waikato campaign begins; Von Tempsky's relationship with his men; Rolls at end of December 1863 and January 1864; Rangiriri.

Chapter 6   **March to the front** 45
    Raglan diversion; No. 2 Company march to Tuhikaramea; Cameron's ability; On patrol near Te Rore; Fruit gathering foray; Sketching Paterangi fortifications.

Chapter 7   **Ambush on the Mangapiko** 58
    Bathing party ambushed at Waiari; Jackson's bravery; Despatches of Havelock, Jackson and von Tempsky; Roll for Waiari; Night attack on Paterangi.

Chapter 8   **Barbarity at Rangiaowhia** 70
    Night march to Te Awamutu; Engagement at Rangiaowhia; Brutal action around single whare; First Forest Ranger casualty.

Chapter 9   **Rout at Hairini** 80
    Engagement at Hairini; Widespread looting; Cameron's despatch for Rangiaowhia and Hairini; Roll for Rangiaowhia and Hairini.

Chapter 10   **In camp at Te Awamutu** 88
    Frontier life at Kihikihi and Te Awamutu; Skirmishes; Standoff at Pukekura.

Chapter 11   **Orakau – a desperate stand** 92
    Reconnaissance of Orakau village; Expedition south of the Puniu River; Fortifications at Orakau; Advance on Orakau; Battle of Orakau, the first two days.

Chapter 12   **Orakau – the massacre** 103
    Battle of Orakau, the final day; Pursuit across swamp; Carey's despatch; Forest Ranger casualties; Conclusions; Roll for Orakau; Operations at Ohaupo; Cameron's distaste for war.

Chapter 13   **Detachment at Maketu** 118
    Engagements at Maketu; Roll of detachment; Colville's despatch.

Chapter 14   **Broken promise** 121
    Jackson's efforts to secure land grants for his men.

Chapter 15   **The grant of land** 125
    Waiting for land; Land allotments; Hardships on the land; Call to Wanganui district; Roll of men travelling to Wanganui.

Chapter 16   **Von Tempsky in command** 134
    Engagement beside Patea River at Kakaramea; New Zealand's reaction.

Chapter 17   **Frustrations before Weraroa** 139
    Conflict between Cameron and Grey; Capture of Weraroa pa.

Chapter 18   **Relief of Pipiriki** 141
    Actions at Pipiriki; George leads Forest Rangers in relief.

Chapter 19   **Court-martial** 143
    Arrest of von Tempsky and loyal men; Westrup takes command; Roll of men on East Coast.

Chapter 20   **Fight in the rain** 147
    Engagements at Pukemaire and Hungahunga-toroa.

Chapter 21   **Seven day siege at Waerengaahika** 148
    Battle at Waerengaahika; Wilson's ambush; Fraser's despatch.

Chapter 22   **Chute's conquest of Taranaki** 155
    Roll at Camp Abraham, November 1865; Ammunition and boots; Actions at Okotuku, Te Putahi, Otapawa, Ketemarae; Encirclement of Mount Egmont; Action at Waikoko; Roll of men with Chute, December 1865 - February 1866.

Chapter 23   **Final disbandment** 168
    Roll of men returning to Te Awamutu from Wanganui; Roll of men remaining in Te Awamutu district; Events at Harapepe; Roll of men on fuel allowance.

Chapter 24   **Joining the Armed Constabulary** 172
    Roll of No. 5 Division; Disaster at Turuturu Mokai.

Chapter 25   **The Bird's Beak** 176
    McDonnell's last attack on Te Ngutu o te Manu; McDonnell's despatch; Faults at Te Ngutu o te Manu; Death of von Tempsky; Casualties at Te Ngutu o te Manu.

Chapter 26   **Disgrace and mutiny** 188
    Mutiny in the ranks of No. 5 Division; Whitmore's roll of infamy; Disbandment.

Chapter 27   **Frontier cavalry volunteers** 194
    Formation of Waikato Cavalry Volunteers.

Appendices

Forest Rangers – Biographical notes 195
    Introduction; Details of each Forest Ranger, including service and New Zealand Medal application details; New Zealand Cross citations included with details on George Hill and John Roberts.

Engagements 269
    Dates of engagements that included Forest Rangers and ex-Forest Rangers.

Weapons, uniform and equipment 270
    Descriptions of weapons, uniform and equipment carried by Forest Rangers; Bowie knife; Inventory for Chute's expedition.

Forest Ranger facts 288
Bibliography 289
Index 290

LIST OF PHOTOGRAPHS, ILLUSTRATIONS AND MAPS

	Page
Forest Ranger badge	Frontispiece
Major William Jackson	3
Major Gustavus Ferdinand von Tempsky	4
Great South Road as it crosses over the Razorback	8
Forest Volunteers recruitment advertisement	9
MAP: South Auckland, 1863	26
Flag captured at Paparata, 13 December 1863	39
Ngaruawahia, December 1863	45
Meremere, November 1863	46
Whatawhata camp, January 1864	48
Tuhikaramea, January 1864	50
Waipa River, January 1864	52
Te Rore camp, January 1864	54
MAP: Waiari engagement, 11 February 1864	60
Von Tempsky watercolour of Waiari engagement, 11 February 1864	62
Paterangi pa, February 1864	66
MAP: Waikato/Waipa delta, 1864	68
Engagement at Rangiaowhia, 21 February 1864	74
British troops at Rangiaowhia, February 1864	76
MAP: Rangiaowhia and Hairini engagements, 21/22 February 1864	78
E.A. Williams watercolour of Pukerimu landing, April 1864	90
Rewi Maniapoto	93
MAP: Orakau engagement, 31 March - 2 April 1864	98
Orakau pa, showing the British sap	100
Maori defenders at Orakau reject invitation to surrender	102
Colonial Defence Force Cavalry's pursuit at Orakau, 2 April 1864	112
Von Tempsky watercolour of Forest Rangers at Ohaupo, 1864	114
Cambridge, 1864	124
Surveyor's map of Harapepe township, March 1865	126
Von Tempsky's town grant	128
Von Tempsky's farm grant	130
A Forest Ranger in the Wanganui area, mid 1865	133
Captain Charles Westrup	144

	Page
MAP: East Coast	146
Major James Fraser	149
Ruins at Waerengaahika pa, November 1865	150
MAP: Waerengaahika engagement, 15-22 November 1865	151
Westrup's Forest Rangers in camp at Poverty Bay	152
MAP: South Taranaki/Wanganui	156
Von Tempsky watercolour of camp in front of Te Putahi pa, January 1866	160
Von Tempsky watercolour of the attack on Otapawa pa, January 1866	162
MAP: Otapawa engagement, 14 January 1866	163
Von Tempsky watercolour of Chute's column, January 1866	164
J. McDonald painting of Major von Tempsky	174
J. McDonald painting of Te Ngutu o te Manu, 7 September 1868	178
K. Watkins lithograph of von Tempsky's death, 7 September 1868	180
MAP: Te Ngutu o te Manu engagement, 7 September 1868	181
John Mackintosh Roberts	183
Inspector John Mackintosh Roberts and No. 6 Division Armed Constabulary, circa 1869	192
New Zealand Medal: Obverse and reverse	196
Major William Jackson	225
Private Ezra Smith	252
Major Gustavus Ferdinand von Tempsky	262
Jackson's Tranter revolver	271
Beaumont Adams 54 gauge revolver and example of holster	272
Callisher and Terry carbine	274
Von Tempsky watercolour of fully equipped Forest Ranger	275
Leather pouch with strap attributed to Charles Temple	276
Illustrations of Forest Ranger uniforms and equipment	277 - 279
Von Tempsky's bowie knife	282
Bowie knife of type used during New Zealand Wars	283

INTRODUCTION

Bush-roving scouts

The title "Rangers" can be traced back to the American Ranger companies formed during the Seven Years' War in North America, 1756-63. They were independent colonial troops who were paid directly by the British Government, but who were neither regular British soldiers nor provincial troops. Their task was guerilla warfare against the French and their Indian allies in the vast eastern woodlands of the American Colonies. The most notorious unit was Rogers Rangers formed in 1755.

Ranger units fought on both sides during the American War of Independence 1775-83. These units formed the model for the New Zealand Colonial Government when it wished to form a corps to fight the Maori on their own ground in the New Zealand forests.

To many New Zealanders the name Forest Rangers is associated with guerilla warfare during the Waikato War, 1863-64. There were many corps of rangers during the New Zealand Wars – Taranaki Bush Rangers, Patea Rangers, Opotiki Volunteer Rangers, Wanganui Bush Rangers and Wellington Rangers – but the most celebrated and notorious of these was the Forest Rangers, an elite corps of bush-roving scouts ... the eyes of the army.

James Cowan, a notable New Zealand historian, liked to romanticise, "There were the Forest Rangers, whose very name carries a flavour of adventure in the Dangerous Lands, suggests tales of scouting and skirmish and ambuscade, and bush marching and camping in wary silence."

They were enlisted originally by Lieutenant William Jackson at Papakura in August 1863, just prior to the Waikato War.

Later his second in command, the illustrious von Tempsky, had a company of his own, and the two went through the Waikato War together. Jackson and many of his commando-type soldiers became military settlers around Te Awamutu, Waikato, while others followed von Tempsky to South Taranaki and further campaigning.

The physical contrasts between the two were as striking as their leadership differences. Jackson, young John Bull, even to the short mutton-chop whiskers, and von Tempsky, swarthy, lean, a glint of fierceness in his dark eyes.

The end of both commanders was tragic. Von Tempsky fell in the bush fight at Te Ngutu o te Manu, near Hawera in 1868; and Jackson was lost overboard from a steamer on the West Coast many years later in 1889 when he was on his way home from parliamentary duties in Wellington.

Amongst the Maori, von Tempsky was known as Manu-rau, meaning "many birds", because of the rapidity with which he and his Forest Rangers moved through the bush, always surprising the Maori.

The men of the Forest Rangers (also known by separate companies as Jackson's Forest Rangers and Von Tempsky's Forest Rangers) were a collection of nationalities and occupations. There were bushmen, settlers, gold-diggers, sailors and professional soldiers, all young and self-reliant, ready for adventure. There were even two muscular

Jamaican Negroes – "as good as any white man," Jackson said, "and more sober than most". They were tough, free-ranging desperados, cast in the same mould as modern commandos; rough and ready but very effective at their task.

The total number of men that enlisted in the unit, established through extensive research of rolls and other sources, is about 365 (some claims of Forest Ranger service have been fabricated, making an exact number difficult to establish), but at any one time there would be no more than about 100 men. It is believed that many original records were destroyed by fire circa 1900, making a more accurate figure impossible. This high number emphasises the attrition of the unit by difficult conditions and the natural turnover of men as they found other attractive occupations to pursue in colonial New Zealand.

Men who were transferred to the Forest Rangers from other volunteer units were eager to escape the routine of redoubt building, marching on escort and guard duties. Many of them transferred from the Waikato Militia, as can be seen in the Biographical Notes section of the Appendices.

Eventually the Forest Rangers were the envy of other corps – they had a free-roving commission, did not bother much with drill, did no navvy work and were paid considerably more. They even received a double allowance of rum on account of the rough and often wet marching and camping, often without fires.

Moreover, they were armed with a handy breechloading carbine and revolver, while the regulars and militia still used clumsy, long and muzzle-loading Enfield rifles and had no revolvers.

Von Tempsky aptly summed up the early appearance of the Forest Rangers with a comment to Jackson after his first sighting of the men:

> I like the looks of your Rangers. Most of them seem used to the rough end of life, if I'm a judge of men.

He further described them on entering the Hunua Ranges, south of Auckland, in late 1863:

> Indian file was the order of march, and as we wound our way through the rich green undergrowth our long line of blue-shirted desperados, with their revolvers and breechloading carbines, and three days' provisions in haversacks, presented a most picturesque *coup d'œil.*

This is in definite contrast to their battlefield appearance a few months later at Hairini on 22 February 1864:

> Now, let me tell you that my men in the day of battle are not very confidence-inspiring objects to look at. What with dust, smoke, their wild dress, their armament and faces wild with excitement of the hour, a man would be quite justified in hesitating to trust his life altogether to their keeping, not being able to see the golden substratum of that desperado exterior.

The Rangers adapted well to the conditions in the field and seemed to thrive in barren environments. Much of the Forest Rangers' success is due to the fact that Jackson designed the unit to be self-sufficient in the field and encouraged the unit, as well as each man, to show individuality. According to von Tempsky, the bush-fighting unit had to "combine the advantages of the European soldier and the savage".

Major William Jackson.
Te Awamutu District Museum

It was these Forest Ranger qualities that the later Armed Constabulary was based upon. The organisation of guerilla fighting modelled on Jackson's design went some way toward the operational pattern of constabulary. Even the Forest Rangers' style of clothing and arms was adopted by the Armed Constabulary.

The term "guerilla" was well known to von Tempsky. It was a name coined from the Spanish word *guerrilleros* describing lightly armed irregulars operating behind enemy lines against the French in Spain from 1809 to 1813. Von Tempsky had much experience with guerilla fighters during his time in Central America.

Hamilton-Browne, in his book *With the Lost Legion in New Zealand*, describes their toughness in an 1866 expedition:

> These men, hardened by incessant exposure, during the summer months carried no blankets, packs nor rations, neither did they wear boots nor hats, but lived on what they could find, and when they halted just threw themselves on the ground and slept like animals. This unnatural training had rendered them capable of covering immense distances, and going for marvellously long intervals without food, sleep or rest. Yet they were born marauders, could and did steal everything and anything that came in their way.

Hamilton-Browne was an imposter who posed as a New Zealand Wars veteran. He joined the Armed Constabulary some months after the end of hostilities and never came under fire whilst he was in this country. He served with veterans and incorporated their bar and barrack-room reminiscences into his colourful books. These old soldiers' tales in many cases have a ring of truth to them and they must

Major Gustavus Ferdinand von Tempsky.
Te Awamutu District Museum

have provided him with excellent descriptions of the Forest Rangers.

The Forest Rangers had a reputation of giving their utmost to both battle and drunken debauchery. Hamilton-Browne gives a vivid description of camp life:

> In the meantime things were a bit quiet with us. When I say "quiet" I use the word in the sense that we had no fighting at least, with the Hauhau, for a time, for no one could call the Rangers' camp peaceful nor reposeful, nor was it a place in which a man given to sedentary pursuits would care to linger or dwell.
> I was now to experience the great curse of the colony, for I regret to say the majority of our men, rough and uncouth as they were, but who had been quiet and tractable enough in the field, now became a prey to the grog-seller, and the scenes of foul, drunken debauchery were disgusting to the last degree. This was only to be expected from the majority of our crew, as there were many among them who were the flotsam and jetsam of the South Seas and Pacific slope, but what surprised and disgusted me was that many of our worst cases were men who I knew to have been at one time gentlemen.
> ... here it was not even vulgar, it was bestial, and for days our camp was a pandemonium, filled with drunken, blaspheming fiends who, without any joviality, wit or humour, scarcely with even an attempt at a singsong, gulped down vile doctored rum till they collapsed and wallowed in their degradation.

This account could be an exaggeration to gain effect so the reader should use discretion. But the Forest Rangers were accustomed to long periods of hardship in the bush, cut off from society and many times separated from other units – operating independently in enemy territory. So when they touched on the fringes of civilisation, they were determined to find some relief from the drudgery of field work – and if allowed, usually pursued it till they ran out of money!

Private Carl Liebig, in a letter accompanying his New Zealand Medal application, touched on the spirit of adventure which drove many men from the Waikato Militia to join the Forest Rangers:

> I joined the 2nd Waikato's No. 10 Company commanded by Captain Davidson in 1863 – but seeing that there was no chance of any immediate engagement with the enemy I forthwith got myself transferred to Major von Tempsky's Rangers.

The very nature of forest ranging caused a high attrition amongst the men. The sense of constant alert to detect the first hint of ambush – for Maori at times lay completely concealed at almost touching distance – soon told on the Forest Rangers. So it was not surprising that men continually sought discharge from the unit. When the Forest Rangers were finally disbanded very few of the original men were still serving.

This century, the title of Ranger was reactivated by the American Army in 1942, when Ranger Battalions became the United States equivalent of British Commandos. The Canadian Army also has Ranger units such as the Queen's York Rangers of Toronto who are direct descendants of the Loyalist Queen's Rangers of the American War of Independence.

In June 1955 the New Zealand Army formed the Special Air Service attached to the British 22nd Special Air Service Regiment. The New Zealand Special Air Service became a separate corps in 1959 and, to commemorate the founding of the Forest Rangers 100 years before in 1863, was renamed the 1st Ranger Squadron, New Zealand Special Air Service on 1 September 1963. However, on 1 April 1978 the corps reverted to its original title of 1 NZSAS Squadron.

The same fighting qualities present in the modern units were inherent in the Forest Rangers. It was a force that acknowledged the self-reliance and individuality of the colonial New Zealander – qualities which proved effective against the Maori in the bush and produced a unique type of soldier that had a well respected record in later wars including the Anglo-Boer War of 1899-1902, First and Second World Wars, Korean and Vietnam Wars.

CHAPTER 1

Call for Forest Volunteers

Settlers of Auckland feared a Maori mass attack by sea across the Manukau Harbour and by land from the south. On 9 July 1863, the Government issued an order requiring all natives living in the Manukau district, on the Waikato frontier and north of the Mangatawhiri River, to take the oath of allegiance to Queen Victoria and surrender all arms. Otherwise they must retire south to the Waikato. Those who did not comply were to be forced from the area.

In a proclamation to the Maori Chiefs of the Waikato, dated 11 July 1863, Governor Grey asked them to stop the "evil acts" against "peaceable settlers". These settlers were pushing deeper and deeper into the bush south of Auckland with the intention of gaining free land. They also worked land in the delta district between the Waikato and Waipa Rivers and around Raglan.

Grey asked for the free passage of Europeans in the Waikato district, in particular for movement on the Waikato River. He also stated:

> ... Those who remain peaceably at their own villages in [the] Waikato, or move into such districts as may be pointed out by the Government, will be protected in their persons, property and land.
> Those who wage war against Her Majesty, or remain in arms, threatening the lives of her peaceable subjects, must take the consequences of their acts and they must understand that they forfeit the right to the possession of their lands guaranteed to them by the treaty of Waitangi; which lands will be occupied by a population capable of protecting for the future the quiet and un-offending from the violence with which they are now so constantly threatened.

It was obvious that whichever direction the Maori chose, they were to lose under the monopolistic mentality of the Colonial Government. They decided to continue their present course and ignored the proclamation. European settlers deep in the Waikato at this stage were not troubled by the Maori. Adding pressure to the possibility of war, the Colonial Government had already recruited the Waikato Militia with the promise of land after active service.

Condition No. 10 in the terms of enlistment for the Waikato Militia stated:

> Every settler under these conditions, who upon being relieved from actual service, receives a certificate of good conduct, will be entitled to one town allotment and one farm section.

The town allotment was one acre and the farm allotment varied from 400 acres for a field officer, 300 acres for a captain, 250 acres for a surgeon and subaltern, 80 acres for a sergeant, 60 acres for a corporal and 50 acres for a private. With such a heavy commitment to over 2000 volunteers, the easy option for the Government was the inevitable invasion of the Waikato.

An invasion suited Europeans living in Auckland, as they also desired the fertile land south of Drury, land they believed the Maori had little need for.

A slanted article, which appeared in the *Daily Southern Cross* (Auckland daily newspaper) on 6 October 1863, stated:

> If the lands are now taken from the Maori, through the fortune of war, it is a result for which the Maoris alone are responsible. They have had to choose between British citizenship and independence; and they have made their decision. They have rejected the conditions which might have incorporated them with the European colonists into one British community; and they can no longer plead the treaties made in their favour. They cannot be allowed to enjoy all the romantic part of the bargain, and to escape from its legal [European law] obligations. They are either British subjects in rebellion, or they are an independent nation, making war against England. In either character, they must take all the responsibilities.

These words sound like self-convincing efforts to justify an imminent invasion. The article continues:

> If they are rebels in arms against their legal Sovereign, then their lands are justly forfeited to the Crown. If they are belligerents de fare, then equally have we the right, if victors in the struggle, to confiscate their possessions [land], and to make them subject to our dominion. The right to conquest is a right, at least, which cannot be denied by the Maoris themselves, seeing that it is their own chief title to all property.
> … The right of a civilised nation to colonise a barbarous country is not worth disputing about. If necessary, it might be justified upon the very highest grounds. The earth was given to man at large, to use and to cultivate. It was not portioned out among various tribes or races, in separate lots and for eternal possession. Our right to New Zealand is precisely what our right was to New Holland [Australia], or to the continent of North America.

The choice of words might not be so strong had the powerful British regiments not been sitting in Auckland. Also the undertones of land confiscation must have been having some effect on Lieutenant-General Duncan Cameron's attitude to invasion of the Waikato.

Anticipating an attack, Governor Grey ordered Cameron to cross the Mangatawhiri River on 12 July 1863 with troops stationed at the Queen's Redoubt, Pokeno.

And so began the Waikato War. The first engagement was at Koheroa on 17 July 1863. This site can be found today on the hills overlooking Mercer.

After commencement of hostilities, roving bands of outlawed Kingite raiders entered the south Auckland rural district and were responsible for arson, theft and several murders.

But the Maori were aware of the impossible task of attacking Auckland, or attacking Cameron's far better equipped army. They took the easier option and harried troops along the military road leading south from Auckland (Great South Road). Cameron's line of communications, munitions and commissariat supplies moved along this road constantly. The Maori's actions were so successful that tenders were called for cutting back the bush along the sides of the road for the ten miles from Drury to Pokeno to lessen the risk of ambush.

A Commissariat detachment passes a road building party on the Great South Road where it crosses over the Razorback, just south of Bombay, south Auckland, late 1863. Note woven gabions in the foreground. Waikato Museum of Art and History

Neither the regular imperial soldiers nor the Auckland Militia were competent enough to pursue the raiding parties into the bush of the Hunua and Wairoa Ranges. It was also evident that the regular troops were not adequately armed for this duty.

Cameron wished to form a special corps to meet the Maori on their territory in the forests with the idea of ridding the bush immediately south of Auckland of hostile Maori.

William Morgan, a settler at Drury, stated in his diary on 4 August 1863:

> Scouring the bush has been pointed out as one of the most effectual means to drive the rebels into the interior, where, once they get there, they must be kept. Hitherto this scouring of the bush has been done very ineffectually, and therefore with very little advantage or success. In the future, this work should be done systematically and extensively, and, I think, a body of men should be raised for this most important duty. Accompanied by good dogs, armed with a revolver, a bowie knife, and a tomahawk, they would indeed strike terror into the hearts of the enemy. Take as an illustration the bushrangers of Taranaki, where for miles around a native dare not show himself.

Morgan's prophecy is quite uncanny in that he has hit upon the type of unit yet to be formed and the use of bowie knives and revolvers.

Even von Tempsky, then a journalist for the *Daily Southern Cross*, wrote:

A corps of guides would soon un-deceive the Maori and his admirers, formed from the men picked from the line, the volunteers and above all diggers experienced in Californian warfare, lightly equipped, armed with repeating rifles and well paid. They would soon prove the crack corps in the colony.

Under pressure from the Auckland public and settlers who lived along the forest edges, and after consultation with interested officers, the Government placed an advertisement several times in the *Daily Southern Cross* in the first week of August:

NOTICE

TO MILITIAMEN AND OTHERS

ACTIVE YOUNG MEN, having some experience of New Zealand forests, may now confer a benefit upon the Colony, and also ensure a comparatively free and exciting life for themselves, by JOINING a CORPS of FOREST VOLUNTEERS now being enrolled in this Province, to act as the Taranaki Volunteers have acted, in striking terror into the marauding natives, by operations not in the power of ordinary troops.

By joining this Corps, the routine of Militia life may be got rid of, and a body of active and pleasant comrades ensured.

Only men of good character wanted.

For further information, apply to the office of the DAILY SOUTHERN CROSS, O'Connell Street, Auckland, between the hours of 2 and 3 o'clock, and 8 and 9 p.m.

July 31, 1863.

Meanwhile, a young non-commissioned officer named William Jackson was serving in the Papakura Valley Rifle Volunteers (later called the Wairoa Rifles and belonging to the Auckland Militia). Previously he was farming his own land near Papakura.

On 22 July 1863 a Kingite Maori raiding party of about 45 warriors in the Papakura-Drury area shot a man named James Hunt, while he was cutting timber for his employer Mr Greenacre. However the party was disturbed by the arrival of a detachment of Auckland Militia from Papakura under Captain Clare – Sergeant William Jackson was a member of this detachment (Patrick Madigan, later a Forest

Ranger, was also present). The Militia were soon reinforced by a detachment of the 18th Regiment (about 100 men under the command of Captain Ring) and the engagement moved to nearby bush south of Kirikiri, about two miles from Papakura. The action became fierce with the arrival of more Maori and the tide only turned with the arrival of Lieutenant Rait and his mounted artillery troopers. These men, armed with swords and revolvers, dismounted before entering the bush (a technique later perfected by mounted infantry in the Anglo-Boer War, 1899-1902).

Rait's contribution to the engagement determined Jackson of the benefits of fighting the Maori in the bush on their own ground, and of commando-type fighting techniques. Already Jackson was training his men in the skills of bush fighting. After he made his feelings on the matter known to his superiors, the above newspaper advertisement appeared.

At an interview on 6 August 1863 between Jackson, the Governor, His Excellency Sir George Grey and The Honourable Mr Thomas Russell (the Defence Minister), there was discussion about the merits of a special bush-scouring corps and Jackson's personal involvement in that corps. He was especially suited to the challenge because of his resolute character, proven guerrilla techniques and personal knowledge of the frontier forests. But all was not in favour of Jackson. According to William Morgan, Jackson was not a popular choice with some of his former farming neighbours.

Shortly after, Jackson received his official authorisation:

> The Hon. T. Russell to Mr W. Jackson.
> Colonial Defence Office, Auckland, 6th August, 1863.
> Mr William Jackson, – You are authorized to raise a corps of men for the purpose of following up the natives in the bush, and scouring the Hunua Ranges, in the manner described this morning in conversation with His Excellency the Governor. The men will get 8s per day, with a commissariat ration. There will be one lieutenant and one ensign [subaltern or 2nd Lieutenant], whose pay will be 15s and 12s per diem, with allowances.
> The Government, in addition to the ordinary grant, will make a grant of land to any man who distinguishes himself, or the widow of any man who may be killed in action.
> Thomas Russell
> Any man now in any of the Colonial corps may leave to join this force.

The statement about a grant of land would later become a contentious issue for many years between Jackson, representing his men, and the Defence Office.

Jackson received his commission to be Lieutenant of a corps called the "Forest Rangers Volunteers", dated 14 August 1863. The corps name was soon abbreviated to "Forest Rangers". He was also given the entitlement to forage allowance for one horse, dated from 6 August 1863.

On 8 August Jackson took delivery of his first 24 Callisher and Terry carbines, transferred to him from the Colonial Defence Force Cavalry, Auckland. As well as these convenient bush guns, he was still expected to use long and clumsy Enfield Pattern 1856 Sergeants' Model rifles.

With the 24 carbines came 24 revolvers of mixed type and quality. Of these revolvers, only five were serviceable, the others being of obsolete type or ammunition, or in un-serviceable condition. Obviously these were discarded revolvers of the cavalry who were probably "dumping" them on the new Forest Rangers unit.

Over the next few days Jackson travelled on horseback to militia camps and settlements enlisting men for his new company. The terms of enlistment were only three month's service from 10 August to 10 November 1863 followed by disbandment. This was to be a specific unit for a specific job for a specific time, as the hostilities in the area were expected to be over in that time. Besides, the Government could not meet the high costs for a prolonged period.

The new company was raised mainly from local farmers who were used to working in the bush and more than capable of "roughing it" when pursuing Maori. He desired each man to show individuality, and the unit to be self-sufficient in the field. The unit contained many gold miners (the Coromandel goldfield was in difficulties with a lack of finance from backers because of the threat of Maori unrest) who were tough and self-reliant, the very material Jackson required.

Each new recruit had to swear an allegiance:

> I do sincerely promise and swear that I will be faithful and bear true allegiance to Her Majesty Queen Victoria and that I will faithfully serve in the Forest Rangers until I shall be lawfully discharged.

Colonel Nixon was most upset when Jackson endeavoured to seek new enlistments from the Colonial Defence Force. In an urgent letter to Russell he pleaded for Jackson to leave his force alone. Nixon feared that since the new Forest Rangers would perform similar duties to his own force, his would become redundant. Nixon ended his letter with:

> ... instruct Jackson that he is not to apply for men from my force.

Russell's answer was to restrict Jackson to a maximum of ten men from Nixon's force, stating it was imperative that Jackson get some of the "best men to be had". It is not known if any came across from the Colonial Defence Force to join the Forest Rangers. More likely Jackson, out of respect for a superior officer, and realising that he must fight alongside Nixon, decided to find his recruits elsewhere.

William Hay, being the first to volunteer, received the commission of Ensign dated 8 August 1863. Deprived of the chance of becoming an officer, John Mackintosh Roberts, the second man to volunteer, was made a sergeant.

Roll of original Forest Ranger company, September 1863:

Lieutenant (1): William Jackson

Ensigns (2): Hay, von Tempsky

Sergeants (9) (no more than eight at a time): Boyd, Bourke, Cole (guide), Dunn (deserted 26 September), McGregor (replacement for Dunn, promoted from private), McKenzie, Quinlan, John Roberts, Southey

Drummer (Bugler) (1): Skinner

Privates (52): Alexander, Richard Bell, Brerton, Buttle, Carran, Carrol, John Carter (surgeon), W.H. Carter, Cornes, Fahey, Finlay, Hendry, Alexander Hill, Holden, Huddleston, Henry Jackson, Kenna, Knowles, Long, McMinn, McNamara, Mahoney, Manning, Methven, Morgan, Muskett, Mutton (guide), Newcastle, Newton, Parr, Pollock (from 3 September), Raven, Ray, Reynolds, Richards, Rowden,

Rowland, Russell, Schumacher, Sherret (later promoted to sergeant), Ezra Smith, Peter Smith (guide), Steenson, Strong, William Taylor (later promoted to sergeant), Turner, Tyrell, Wakeford, George Ward, Watters, Wells, Westrup

Total number present was 65 all ranks.
It was Jackson's design to have no corporals in the unit.

Others who served with the original company:
Twelve other men served outside the month of September:
Appleyard (11-15 August), Barron (11-25 August), Beckham (11-25 August), William Burns (11-25 August), Garvey (11-25 August), Heffernan (11-28 August), Jacob (11-25 August), Napper (11-25 August), Parsons (11 October-11 November), Henry Roberts (11-28 August), William Smith (11-25 August), Warbey (11-25 August)

Eleven of the above twelve men sought their discharge between 25 and 28 August. Jackson must have offered a two week trial period to his men so as to keep only those who were dedicated to the unit and cause. These men, who obviously had misgivings about the arduous nature of Jackson's campaigning style, were lucky to have this opportunity.

Jackson also used the services of a man named Brassey, because of his knowledge of Maori habits and trails. For 15 years Brassey lived amongst various tribes after deserting from the British Army. He wedded a Maori and had children who were later taken from him by Maori at the outbreak of hostilities in south Auckland. Brassey set on a course of vengeance and joined up with the Forest Rangers. Being a deserter he never officially enlisted for fear of retribution, but just remained "attached" to the unit, casting doubt on his real name being Brassey. Jackson made Brassey an aide-de-camp but soon found him unmanageable when under the influence of alcohol. Later, von Tempsky took over responsibility of Brassey and after a little "roughing-up" made a good man out of him.

The new corps camped outside Papakura making the Travellers' Rest inn (about where Ardmore Primary School is today) on the Papakura to Wairoa (present day Clevedon) road, their headquarters. The inn was chosen because of its close proximity to the Hunua Ranges, and extensive outhouse accommodation. Jackson's farm was nearby. The inn was a combination of drinking-house, store and farmhouse, having been boarded up to about chest height by heavy planks with rifle slits to guard against attack. The host was a likeable character named Benjamin Smith – popularly called "Old Smith" – a former gold-digger and sailor. Some Colonial Defence Cavalry shared the accommodation. Jackson made his headquarters in an outhouse and the men camped across the road from the inn.

The inn was built on a 200 hundred acre farm. The house plan was a passageway in the centre with two rooms on each side. On both the right and left sides of the house were further passageways with extra rooms, and there were bedrooms upstairs in the loft. The front and back verandahs were boarded up and loopholed. Outside stables provided accommodation for men. (The inn eventually burnt down.)

Von Tempsky had recently given up gold mining at Coromandel and as a war correspondent for the *Daily Southern Cross* had moved to Drury to write stories of the frontier, especially about the newly formed Forest Rangers.

He stated in his manuscript:

> Having seen a good deal of savage warfare (*la petite guerre*), I was desirous of observing the same in New Zealand. As a preliminary thereto, I took an appointment as official correspondent in the Drury district for the [Daily] Southern Cross newspaper, and established my headquarters at the Drury Hotel. The headquarters of the 65th and 18th and Artillery were then at Drury camp; the latter was at this season one sea of mud, in which the damp and dreary tents stood like desolate islands. The Great South Road was in a frightful state, through the heavy traffic to the Queen's Redoubt [at Pokeno], and the officers on escort duty generally returned in a sad condition, from mud and rain.

Von Tempsky struck up instant friendships with Jackson, John Roberts and many other Forest Rangers, and was soon affectionately known as "Von" or the "Chief".

William Race, in his manuscript *Under the Flag*, wrote of Jackson's distinctive agricultural gait when walking:

> The No. 1 Company was officered by Captain Jackson, known [affectionately] to us as "the farmer" by the habit he had of using his sword as a walking stick on the line of march.

Jackson decided the best way to familiarise his men with the bush was to go into its depths. He kept his new command active with many expeditions in the Hunua and Wairoa Ranges. His first expedition commenced in mid-August.

John Roberts later narrated:

> A man had to get his bush legs, just as a sailor has his sea legs. We learned very early to look on a tree as a friend. If it could shelter a Maori, it could also shelter us.

By August 1864 the Waikato Maori tribes had been preparing for war for more than two years by making cultivations at Pukekawa (south of the Waikato River) and Paparata (south Auckland) as a ready source of provisions while engaged in warfare activities in the south Auckland area. They also established a large base in the bush between Papakura and Wairoa deep in the Hunua Ranges. This base was first sighted on 10 August by a scouting party of 35 men of the Wairoa Rifle Volunteers and No. 4 Company, Auckland Militia under Lieutenant Steele. Several smaller camps were also noted in the area.

The Forest Rangers ventured into the Hunua Ranges on Monday, 16 August. No contact was made with the Maori but Jackson's intentions were only to familiarise his men with the bush and train them in moving quietly through the undergrowth with a minimum of noise. He recorded the expedition in a report to Russell:

> We went out on Monday morning, and could not well take up the track. So under the guidance of Sergt Cole, went up on the ranges east of the Hunua opening, so as to get a full view of all the openings. After we got on the summit of the range, and mounted one or two large trees, we had a full view of all the country up to the Waikato.
> We saw a hill which had the appearance of being partially cleared and an

erection of some kind or other on the summit which Cole says was not cleared when he saw it last and also, that it lies in a northerly direction from Paparata.

The party heard several shots some two or three miles off, but could not determine the direction. However, after inspecting the clearing near Hill's house, they returned home for more provisions.

On this trip they took only bread which proved cumbersome. They resolved to take military issue biscuits in the future.

Jackson intended to destroy any Maori Kingite camps in the Hunua Ranges area. One of his many expeditions into the area was well recorded by von Tempsky, who was invited to accompany the expedition. He describes his first meetings with the Forest Rangers at the Travellers' Rest and preparations for the forthcoming adventure:

> ... I had often passed the headquarters of the Forest Rangers; these were established at a solitary inn by the roadside called the Travellers' Rest. When all other settlers had abandoned their homes, the proprietor of this place remained, strengthened and loopholed his home, and carried on his business, so he was a popular man with the military and all others who had to pass that way.
> This innkeeper, Mr Smith, had been a sailor and a gold-digger, and a sturdy cheery character he was. There one day I received a formal invitation from Lieut. Jackson to accompany him on a three days' expedition into the ranges. I jumped at the offer and promised timely attendance. I rode in the afternoon of the day previous to the appointment to Smith's to sleep there, as the expedition was to start at an early hour.
> Lieut. Jackson, Ensign Hay (son of Mr Hay, the settler near Papakura) and myself passed the evening in brilliant anticipation of our coming exploits, and to the whole an almost pathetic tone was given by the subdued presence of Mrs Jackson, who was spending this last evening before a perilous expedition in the company of her husband.

Mrs Jackson gave the party a rather pitiful touch. They had been married only a few months, and she had before her always the fear of a Maori bullet or a tomahawk blade for her venturesome husband.

Jackson, in a letter to Russell written early on the morning of 19 August, just prior to the next expedition, mentioned the poor quality boots the men wore in the bush:

> I may also add that the men are all I could wish as regards endurance, but the boots the men have got are perfectly useless for that particular work. They should be watertight and well nailed, otherwise the men will be continually falling.

Russell, in response to the boot problem, ordered that each man in the unit receive two pairs of adequate boots per year as well as extra clothing to combat the wet bush conditions.

In the same letter Jackson put in a request for a bugler, reasoning an appeal on a bugle could bring relief if they were overpowered by an enemy force. Russell responded by sending Skinner, who enlisted 26 August.

CHAPTER 2

Hunua adventure

Von Tempsky, as war correspondent for the *Daily Southern Cross*, accepted an invitation to accompany Lieutenant Jackson on one of his expeditions which commenced on 19 August 1863. Von Tempsky gives the following detailed account of conditions, tactics and equipment:

> On my way to the Wairoa I received an invitation from Lieutenant Jackson, commanding the Forest Rangers, to accompany him on an expedition through the ranges. I gladly complied, and we started the following day (Thursday) at 9 am – a delay in forwarding biscuit from Papakura prevented an early start. Smith's Inn being the headquarters of the corps, we proceeded thence in a southeasterly direction towards the Hunua. Passing the spot where Mr Cooper was shot [George Cooper, a settler in the Wairoa Ranges, was shot down and killed by marauding Maori when he went out to drive his cows up for milking, 24 July 1863], close to his house on the first slope of the range, we ascended through some clearings on to the first ridge.
> A narrow bush track led us after that down the other side, a luxuriant vegetation obscuring any chance of a fair view of the country. Towards 12 o'clock a sudden turn of the track brought the bright light of an open country across our forest-roof, and the Hunua opening, the old lair of the enemy, came in sight. Carefully we approached this neighbourhood, but, after a little scouting, were satisfied that the field was still unoccupied, and we had our dinner in the neighbourhood of Williams' hut. While the men were resting, Lieutenant Jackson, Ensign Hay, Sergeant Cole (the corps guide), and myself, went to scan the surrounding district with our glasses. A magnificent view of the valleys, ridges, fern and forest land lay before us – the heights of Paparata to the far southeast, and the thin line of our track towards the junction of the Tiara Keenu Block serpenting through the fern. No signs of anything new or unusual denoting an enemy's presence could be discovered, and the order for the march was given. We passed the blackened site of Williams' hut, burnt to the ground by the retiring enemy; and after turning a flanking height of the high forest ground, the abodes of the Hunua war party came in sight. They are still in good repair, as the attempt of Lieutenant Steele's party to fire them failed through the wetness of the thatch. Two hours' march through high fern brought us to the remains of Warner's hut, close on the forest; that was after having hit upon the enemy's track on his retreat, pointing evidently towards Paparata. This was an important discovery, and Lieutenant Jackson would have followed it up had his force been stronger, our whole complement consisting only of two officers, forty privates, eight non-commissioned officers, one volunteer, in all fifty one. We next entered the forest, intending to hit by a crosscut through the bush, a piece of unfinished road in the neighbourhood of the Mangawheau, a tributary of the upper course of the Wairoa. Up to this we had been guided

by men thoroughly acquainted with the neighbourhood, their knowledge being correct, and proving the inestimable importance of having such guides. Later in the afternoon the labyrinth of gullies and hills, interwoven by a most provoking network of supplejack, proved even too much for the most experienced, and we had to consult the never erring guide, the compass. During the struggle with supplejacks the judicious equipment of our party became apparent, the short carbines [only 23 carbines with the expedition] and the general light style of accoutrements, making it alone possible to wind our way through the interminable mazes. The capabilities of the men, too, were displayed in a most satisfactory manner. They carried a swag composed of one blanket, one great coat, twenty rounds of ammunition, all enveloped in a so-called waterproof, and a haversack containing three days' rations of meat and biscuit, half a bottle of rum, a revolver, cartridge box, carbine, some with sword-bayonets [hand-held only], others with tomahawks, and all these little items hanging from their bodies, made it a work of considerable difficulty to get along through the New Zealand forest without being thrown off one's equilibrium.

Darkness soon added to our difficulties, and after one's scramble down precipitous hillsides closely set with supplejack traps, a little stream invited us to encamp. No fires were lit; each groped his way to some lair, spread out the components of his swag, and a violent attack on meat and biscuit ensued. Sentinels for night-watch were told off, posted and appointed, and those not thus engaged threw themselves with hearty good will into the arms of the forest Morpheus, a rough but kindly deity, seldom disappointing his votary. Lieutenant Jackson, Ensign Hay, and myself, had, with the eye of connoisseurs, taken instant possession of the shelter of a most comfortable lair, tenanted probably the night previous by some knowing old boar. The rain that fell that night did not wet us much, as the slanting position of the old trunk and its forest parasites [epiphytes] proved a perfect roof, at least for two of us. Before daylight the sentinels were doubled, that time being the hour for Maori surprises.

At daylight we bolted biscuit and meat to our contentment, and, with belted swag and haversack, away we glided through the dripping forest with the rain rattling through the foliage. After a couple of hours our guides were nonplussed, confessed their helpless condition, and Mr Hay, compass in hand, took the lead – to some purpose, as it became apparent shortly after. By his guidance we hit upon the point we intended to make, proving thus the superiority of a general knowledge of country to that of a minute, though circumscribed, acquaintance with one locality. It rained heavily all day long. Of fern openings, we came upon two; the first is called Wharehinau Nue, the second Wharehinau Nuke – both old native plantations, and presenting the quintessence of rich volcanic soil.

Towards four in the afternoon, after traversing a third opening of an old plantation overgrown with dense scrub, we encamped on a hill at an early hour, to be enabled to erect some shelter for the night. Soon a little forest township springs into life, nikau and fern-palms being handy, and with eagerness we piled up shelter against the dropping rain. No fires were allowed till darkness had well set in, but all the wood was ready collected. At last the welcome word "fire" was heard, and here and there and everywhere through the thick forest gloom, carefully-tended sparks began to appear till the light of the fire, as it increased, shone upon men in all positions drying themselves with a grateful expression of countenance.

The night-watch was once more told off: and let me tell you young men so eager for the eight shillings per day for bushranging, that unless you have a sound, well-seasoned constitution to boast of, you had better think twice before you venture on such work; for night-watching after a hard day's scramble; night-watching with rain filling your boots, will give you a trial too costly if unsuccessful. In a small corps such night duty comes round from man to man very often, in fact, almost too often. With daylight we were on the march again, Mr Hay once more taking the lead.

After an hour's march we came at last upon the Mangawheau River – certainly in a roundabout way, but we hit it, anyhow, thanks to our intelligent ensign. The river contains a considerable quantity of water; we crossed it over some rocks above a small fall, and came thus, at last, into the mysterious precincts of one of our enemy's natural strongholds. Up to this we had seen no tracks; no traces of Maoris except at the Hunua, and some scattered cattle tracks. Now, however, the scene changed. Here and there nikau was found freshly cut, and soon a distinct track was come upon. Sergeant Henry Southey was placed at the head, and the track was followed up. Mr Hay had repeatedly told me that we would have to cross the track from Paparata to Maketu if we carried out our original intention of scouring all the openings down to Pokeno. He now believed that the track we did hit was the one referred to, and after a little it deemed advisable to follow it up in preference to crossing it, as the signs increased in freshness and number.

Temporary whares for war parties of 60 to 100 men were come upon; and spots with pigeon-snares for the summer season were passed. They consist of a hole – square or round – cut into some broad surface root of a large tree, filled with water and surrounded by snares attached to an adjoining little upright frame, and they are used in summer season when water gets scarce. We were traversing a magnificent forest, topping long and sharp-backed spurs, sloping to the southeast coast. Before descending a very marked one, however, we resorted to our usual mode of observation, that is in climbing some large trees. Two of our most expert climbers, Henry Southey and little Rowland – both of marine extraction – were this time assisted by Mr Cole, and the following result was obtained: a wide, open fern country stretched to the southeast; a broad distinct track led up a heavy fern hill; a large house or whare also visible in a hollow; a ridge due south and another northwest.

It was then decided, instead of proceeding to Pokeno, to follow this track at all hazard. Very silently and carefully our long blue-shirted Indian file wound through the green bushes, and considering the short time of enrolment, the men were careful enough in the all-important necessity of silence and stealthy step. Matters were becoming decidedly interesting now, and a little wholesome excitement tingling in one's blood gave spring and elasticity to the physical man. The signs became more and more pregnant with importance. We had seen soldier's trousers – two pairs – in one hut; remains of stretchers for the wounded, in another place; but now we came upon the most significant of all – a double track, one leading open to the right, and another hidden by artfully-laid branches to the left. Here was evidence of this path leading to something worth finding, and we slipped into it with eager curiosity and bated breath.

Traces of pigs abounded; and the track of a dog riveted our attention. Something like a distant bark had been heard previously, and the certainty of something being close at hand took possession of every one. The forest was dense in every direction around us – we could seldom see above 20 yards ahead – when suddenly, "Poaka, poak, poak", was heard ahead of us. Riveted with the excitement of coming events we halted. A distant voice began speaking to some audience – Henry Southey acting as interpreter for me. I heard one saying, "Ah! If we had the Pakehas before us now we would give it to them." Then followed a war dance. "Come on! Come on!" was shouted close at hand, and then we threw ourselves in ambush; when alas! A cap went off [percussion cap, but not the barrel charge] on the piece of some eager man struggling among supplejacks. A long silence ensued on the part of the hidden enemy, and Lieutenant Jackson thought it advisable to take up a position further back on the high ground. The talking could again be heard as we retreated as silently as we had come, halting once more on some eminence.

Here it was decided that as the exact locality was not positively known by our leaders, and as we knew that we were in the heart of the enemy's country, and were totally in the dark as to the number we might rouse by any engagement; and as the explosion of the cap without igniting the charge showed that, in spite of all possible precautions, perhaps many pieces were in a similar condition [wet powder], it was deemed necessary to retreat. By the same track we re-ascended the spur about half-past two in the afternoon, and pushed on through the forest till long after dark, when, losing the track, we retraced our steps to a clearing that we had passed, and camped for the night. The next morning we made an early start, and found that the track we had travelled was the one from Paparata to Maketu, as Mr Hay had expected.

Three hours' march brought us in sight of the old pa at Maketu. A woodland scenery of undulating ground appeared to the south; to the north were hilly gullies, where another pa and now abandoned huts were situated. To the west, right in front from Maketu village and plantations, appeared, and in the same direction, marking the distant South Road, rose the white peaks over the redoubt of Lieutenant Rixon, at the entrance to Shepherds' Bush – the whole with a bright gleam of the distant Manukau, forming a most beautiful landscape. A hearty tramp for a few hours brought us to the camp at Drury.

After three days in the bush hunger drove the men out! On arrival at Drury they all partook of a good meal at Mill's Hotel.

Later, Jackson complained to Russell about the inconvenience of using long rifles in the bush. Enfield rifles were proving totally unsuitable, getting caught in the undergrowth, reducing the Forest Rangers' momentum through the bush. In a letter to Russell dated 28 August, Jackson mentions:

> I have just returned from an expedition in the ranges behind Kirikiri and find the great inconvenience of having so many long rifles. They are continually catching in the supplejacks and impeding the progress of the men. We have at present in the Corps 23 carbines [originally 24 with one un-serviceable] and require 39 more. We suffer great inconvenience from the want of them so I wish you may let us have them as soon as possible.

Thirty-nine Callisher and Terry carbines were later forwarded to Jackson on 5 September. Russell obviously did not want to hinder the performance of the Forest Rangers, and met reasonable requests.

Von Tempsky and Jackson met frequently during August. Jackson soon recognised von Tempsky's wealth of military experience and ability in the bush and invited him to join Jackson's company of Forest Rangers (the original company). So Jackson travelled to Auckland to confer with Governor Grey about von Tempsky's ability. Soon after, Grey gave von Tempsky both British citizenship and a commission as ensign, dated 26 August 1863. The acceptance of Her Majesty's commissions required British citizenship. Germans in New Zealand at this time were generally unpopular so to get commissioned was a paramount achievement for von Tempsky.

The Forest Rangers were in the Pukekohe district from Sunday, 30 August to Wednesday, September 2. While they were in the neighbourhood of Tuakau an old Maori woman came out of the bush having been hidden there since the British troops took possession of the place some time earlier. She had been living on nikau and other bush foods, and was in a feeble state. She was fed by the Forest Rangers.

At this time an unknown member of the Forest Rangers corresponded in diary form to the *Daily Southern Cross* newspaper. The writer may have been Hay, Richard Bell or von Tempsky as they were all learned men. The style of writing seems too ordinary, lacking flourishes, to be credited to von Tempsky. Although incomplete, the excerpts give a first-hand account of conditions and movements. Only selected passages have been copied, each preceded by the date in bold type.

> **30 August:** We got orders to proceed from our headquarters on the Wairoa road to Pukekohe, a settled district, to the southwest of Drury. We arrived there after panning over a muddy road, in the afternoon, and encamped in a shed near the fortified church of the settlers.

> **31 August:** Today we proceeded west from this [church], in the direction of the house of Mr Scott, the unfortunate man who was lately shot at and dangerously wounded by a small party of Maoris. ... We returned without finding any more satisfactory evidence of late incursions of the Maoris, and shifted our camp to Mr MacDonald's farm. The latter is a delightful spot for an encampment, both in point of comfort, in dry ground, shelter, fire wood, and in a military point of view, as it occupies a commanding position, free of bush.

> **1 September:** It was intended this day to track the natives who shot Mr Scott. Four guides accompanied the expedition. The tracking led us in the

direction of Tuakau. ... We traversed Walter's opening, next Harris' opening; in the latter we found the homestead thoroughly sacked. Towards 12 am we descended into the fertile Tuakau valley, and traversed the now abandoned native settlement there. [They marched as far as the Alexandra Redoubt above the Waikato River.] ... On our return we took a wide sweep further to the east, and came back to camp at dusk, after passing through Nicoll's opening. In the neighbourhood of the latter we came upon a native trail of somewhat recent date, leading in the direction of Williamson's clearing.

2 September: Orders arrived during the night [probably carried by a trooper of the Colonial Defence Force] for us to proceed to Papakura, and patrol the neighbourhood. In the morning the unusual luxury of tents was once more dispensed with, and they were sent back to the Wairoa. The owner of our camping ground seemed quite distressed at our un-looked for departure, as our presence, by special and pressing invitation from him had furnished him with endless subjects for lectures to our men on cleanliness, honesty, and other virtues. ... We took on the trail we found yesterday, and scoured the bush in a southeasterly direction towards Razorback, but without result. Coming out on the Great South Road on Razorback, we proceeded to Martyn's farm, to await further orders.

They then proceeded on the east side of the South Road, near the camp at Martyn's, and travelled some five or six miles eastward scouring for Maori. They went down to Maketu, examining tracks on the way but discovering no evidence of Maori having been recently there. They visited an evacuated Maori settlement in the locality, and saw a large amount of crockery, tinware, old rags and other articles that presumably once belonged to settlers. They left the bush and arrived very tired in Drury on the evening of Thursday, 3 September. The Forest Rangers brought back three or four horses from Maketu, which belonged to Maori, and left them in charge of the officers at York Redoubt.

3 September: Got orders to range the bush east of the Great South Road. We penetrated about seven miles due east of Martyn's clearing, then turned northward, next westward – and after a long day's tramp came upon the rear of Maketu pa. ... As night was coming on fast we marched through Drury, and slept in a stable belonging to Mr Tanner.

4 September: Information had arrived during the night that some Maoris were supposed to be at the back of Kirikiri, so we started before daylight, and were in the cover of the bush before the enemy could observe our arrival. We took a northeasterly sweep through the densest part of the bush, to cut off the enemy, or come upon his tracks in his approach to Kirikiri. In the morning's work the perfect bushmanship of our men showed itself to great advantage. The labyrinth of supplejack and cutting grass no more impeded their silent and rapid progress than in the most ordinary bushtramp; and this coming on the sixth day of unceasing marching through more or less dense bush and broken country, showed the magnificent training now acquired by every man in the corps. We issued from the thick bush at the back of Sinclair's clearing without seeing any Maori trail. ... Thence we proceeded towards Captain Clare's house and the back of Kirikiri, but no tracks of anything came in our way. ... Once more we came upon the old Hunua encampment, where we dined *al fresco*, and afterwards gathered up our somewhat stiffened legs, and like the horse scenting the stable, tramped at a fine pace over the last eight or nine miles towards the Wairoa. I think that most of us were unmistakably glad to see in the far off plain the hospitable roof of Mr Benjamin Smith's Travellers' Rest inn. Rest, after six days of unceasing tramping through bush, is a luxury of such an exquisite sensation.

Jackson made a further request for revolvers on 5 September 1863, in a letter to the Colonial Defence Office:

I have the honour to acknowledge the receipt of your letter of August 31. We have only 5 revolvers for which ammunition can be procured easily — the rest being Colts of all sizes, the men can not replace their ammunition during bush travelling. Also, many of the Colts are not in a serviceable condition — we therefore require 57 revolvers of the same pattern, which I hope you will forward to us as soon as possible, as promised by the Honourable Thomas Russell. We expect that with the revolvers an ample supply of suitable ammunition will be forwarded at the same time. We contemplate starting on a new expedition as soon as the arms referred to arrive.

CHAPTER 3

Lusk's Clearing

The Forest Rangers, as a unit, experienced their first taste of action at Lusk's Clearing (today skirted by the main road between Pukekohe to Mauku), on Tuesday, 8 September 1863.

Imperial troops and the Forest Rangers had been sent to the Mauku area from Drury the previous day, with the imperial troops returning to camp that evening. Jackson and his men were using Walters' Hotel, situated at Lower Mauku on the Taikihi Inlet, for both their headquarters and camp when in the area.

On 8 September, the Forest Rangers and some Mauku Rifles started out to reconnoitre the area for the presence of Maori. They soon discovered that Maori had been scouring settlers' homesteads and after finding a distinct trail, they followed in pursuit. This trail was lost so they took the direction of Pukekohe Hill and were proceeding through bush when they heard gunfire coming from their rear. They made for the spot and found two of Mr Lusk's cattle had been shot.

It was at Lusk's Clearing, also known as Hill's Clearing, that many Forest Rangers were first under fire. Von Tempsky gives a good description of the action:

> We mustered about fifty men, including fifteen Mauku Rifles, under Lieutenant Lusk. From the lower Mauku, where the stockade of the settlement was erected, the houses of the settlers straggle along a wooded ridge running south; at about a mile and a half another ridge joins the former at a right angle, dotted with another set of settlers' houses, amongst them a little church with a white steeple, now made bullet-proof and garrisoned by settlers and militia. At the eastern end of that settlement the native village of Patumahoe commences; it had been abandoned long ago by the natives who had joined the cause of the fighting tribes.
> South of this about a mile or two lies the farm of Messrs. Lusk and Hill. We visited the house, and there at last we found fresh tracks. We followed them like sleuthhounds. They led through the corner of a large paddock, then entered the bush by a well-beaten path. We were about a mile from the paddock when we heard three, four, five, six shots fired, evidently in the paddock. We turned and hastened back. It was reported from the rear that Maoris could be heard shouting to one another. Jackson and Lusk decided that the party should divide, a process I did not believe in but had to assent to. One party under our ensign, Hay, guided by Mr Hill, was to look up the Maoris in our rear, as it was thought that they would be found the strongest number of enemies; thirty men, all Forest Rangers, were allotted to that party. The remaining twenty, under Jackson, Lusk, and myself, proceeded towards the paddock.
> Cautiously we sallied from the bush, reconnoitring the paddock. We saw no enemy. At last we saw a beast lying dead, evidently. That sign at least was satisfactory. We rushed up to it, found it warm yet, and with six bullet-holes in it. We looked around; nothing else was visible. The paddock was of great

length, about half a mile square, covered with burnt stumps and logs. The settlers set about skinning the beast while it was warm, and I reflected on the probabilities of our case and kept the men from lumping together, as I did not believe in the apparent serenity of the bush.

We had just scattered a bit when another shot was fired, towards the southwest corner of the paddock. There was no mistake in this; there were the Maoris, and thus they intended to draw us on. We pleased them to a certain extent, but not exactly the way they wanted us to go – across the open paddock right on to the dense bush where the shot was fired. We made for the bush immediately opposite to us and followed its cover along the edge towards the direction of the shot. We knew that at every step now we might come upon the Maoris, and I can assure you we kept a sharp lookout all around us; but we saw nothing; nothing moved except what we moved.

Thus we marched on. Where the deuce are the Maoris? Down comes a volley with a vengeance. The powder-smoke is blown into our faces; I rub my eyes – I can hardly see for the saltpetre fumes in them. "Give it to them, boys, right and left!" And away crack our carbines and rifles [the Mauku Rifles used Enfield rifles]. Over the din, the clatter and spatter of shots, you can hear the high-pitched voice of a Maori chanting an incantation. Our carbines answer. Ah, you hear a change of key now – you hear those two or three fellows singing "Miserere Domine" – and such a Miserere! – that one fellow in particular must have been hit in the spine, for his yells are abominable. Are none of our men hit? I cannot see one down yet – they are all behind trees, and blazing away for the very life of them.

What they can see, however, is an enigma to me, for all that I have seen, and see, are blue puffs of smoke from the green undergrowth. Once I saw a black head – had it on the bead of my revolver nearly, but it ducked. I have not fired a shot yet. Hang firing – I will try my old Mexican blade [sword]. A perfect labyrinth of fallen trees from the clearing, interlaced with a new green growth of creepers and old supplejack, is the accidental breastwork our friends have chosen as their fortress. I struggle into it, get hopelessly caught, and struggle out again. No advance that way, certainly. I join once more the skirmishers.

Jackson has fallen in with a new idea. He has drawn five rangers into the paddock behind some logs, and shouts to us to come to him. Of course it is a mistake; we remain where we are; but the Rangers commence blazing away, and we might get a friendly bullet by mistake, so we have to form in the paddock also, losing every chance of cutting off the retreat of the Maoris.

Von Tempsky was critical of Jackson's tactics – especially after proving to himself that bush movement was impossible. Jackson, sensing his men's baptism of fire, was more interested in giving his men a subdued introduction to bush fighting with a minimum of casualties. But it is evident even at this early stage of the campaign that von Tempsky was reckless in pursuit of glory.

There behind good cover, stumps and logs, a harmless exchange of shots is carried on for a while. Our thirty Rangers appear on our left wing, panting; they have found no Maoris, and, hearing our firing, have joined us.

I urge a charge. Not yet. Very well. I can see nothing to fire at, so I lie behind my stump and look at Lusk, who is in the same predicament. I have a dog with me who won't go under cover, and gets hit in the head – only a graze though, as I found out afterwards.

At last, while the fire of our opponents had grown slacker, for very good reasons, a party was sent from our right flank to cut them off. We were to charge when the cheer of this party was heard. We rushed with frantic valour into the bush. The bush was calmer than ever. We traverse and jump from tree to tree. Strange is this bush fighting – mysterious: blue smoke, green leaves, perhaps a black head: cries, defiant soul-rendering, you hear perhaps – yes, you can hear them talking next door to you, coolly familiarly, but you see nothing – nothing tangible to grasp, to wrestle with.

Our circumventive force still continued cheering in the depths of the wood, so that I began to think they had made a find of some of our game, but there they were dancing around a dozen extempore huts, the Maori encampment, revelling in retaken plunder and eating the Maori dinner cooking on the Maori fire. [The men found sugar, tea, plated ware, papers, mats, hats, a freshly cooked piece of pork and some jam!] There was no sign of a body anywhere. Yet there could be no doubt that several of them must have been hit, judging from the painful climax of howls they set up after our first meeting at 20 yards, where several of our men on the left flank must have seen the backs of several Maoris lying behind the stumps. We now know that five were killed, and that one hundred Maoris were opposed to us, mostly Patumahoe natives then engaged in plundering and destroying settlers' property in the neighbourhood. I believe that after our first close encounter no one on our side made any hits excepting perhaps Jackson and Hay, as both of them were crack shots and don't fire at the smoke, as the general run of excited combatants do.

We return to Mauku laden with spoil and intoxicated with our victory. The Forest Rangers and Mauku Rifles had fleshed their arms at last, and that is no small matter with young soldiers. In casualties Alfred Speedy [Mauku Rifles], son of Major Speedy, was shot through the cap, W. Worthington [of the Mauku Rifles; later killed on 23 October 1863 at Mauku] through the trousers, and Mr Wheeler [civilian] through the coat. This from a volley at 20 or 15 yards. Too much powder, ye Maoris!

The Forest Rangers, not being supplied with provisions, did not follow the Maori. They returned to the engagement site on the following day (Wednesday, 9 September) with some of the Mauku and Waiuku volunteers and followed the raiding Maori's tracks. They scoured a large extent of country over the Bald Hills, but came across no fresh tracks of the Maori. Presumably the raiders had returned to their base camp to administer mourning and burials for their dead; the five dead amounting to a tragedy for the Maori.

It was in such encounters that the Forest Rangers learned the art of taking cover skilfully and of darting from the shelter of one tree to the next after delivering a shot. Jackson and Lusk developed into very accurate shots with both carbine and rifle.

The force returned to camp and were out again searching on Thursday, 10 September – but to no avail. The men regretted missing a soldiers' ball held the previous night in a large room adjacent to Mills' Hotel (site of the today's Jolly Farmer Hotel, Drury).

The urgent need for handguns was accentuated by the lack of them at Lusk's Clearing. On 10 September Jackson sent a telegram to Russell urgently requesting the promised 57 revolvers:

> Sir, would you be kind enough to have sent up at once the revolvers as we are in great need of them. If you send them to Drury I will send for them. Also ammunition for them.

A footnote written on the telegraph form by Russell's office read:

> Capt. Mitchell sent 57 revolvers to Papakura the day before yesterday [8 September].

In the same telegram Jackson requests surgical instruments:

> Send me if you can a field case of surgical instruments. Also a tourniquet and forceps for extracting bullets.

Again an answering footnote (signed by a member of the office staff) was written on the telegraph form:

> I sent a surgeon's dressing case, a few days ago, and there are plenty of instruments at Papakura and at Wairoa. I will send a tourniquet and the forceps.

On 11 September the Forest Rangers took possession of 57 new revolvers – 21 Tranters and 36 Adams (or variety of Adams patents). Jackson selected a Tranter for his personal use. Up to now the unit had the use of only five serviceable revolvers. Effectively, by the issue of these revolvers (making a total of 62 serviceable revolvers), the unit more than doubled its fire-power in close combat. The men were eager to try their new handguns.

From Saturday, 12 September, the Forest Rangers worked in the Camerontown area for a few days but made no contact with Maori. From here they returned to Mauku.

Burtt's farm, about halfway between Papakura and Mauku at Paerata, was attacked on 14 September. Owned by Mr Burtt, an absent Auckland merchant, the farm was managed by Mr Watson who with his family bravely resisted the attack. The Forest Rangers moved into the homestead later on 14 September. The farm would often be used (as well as Walters' Hotel) as a field base by the Forest Rangers when doing scouting work in the Mauku area. The Forest Ranger's diary continues:

> **14 September:** A strange feeling comes over one when taking possession of some recently abandoned homestead, where the evidence of hurried departure and hasty packing up is to be seen. The fruitful garden is not yet in weeds, and this with the half-nailed up windows and barricaded doors, half-empty and half-furnished rooms, impresses you more vividly than anything else could do, with the sad consequences of war.

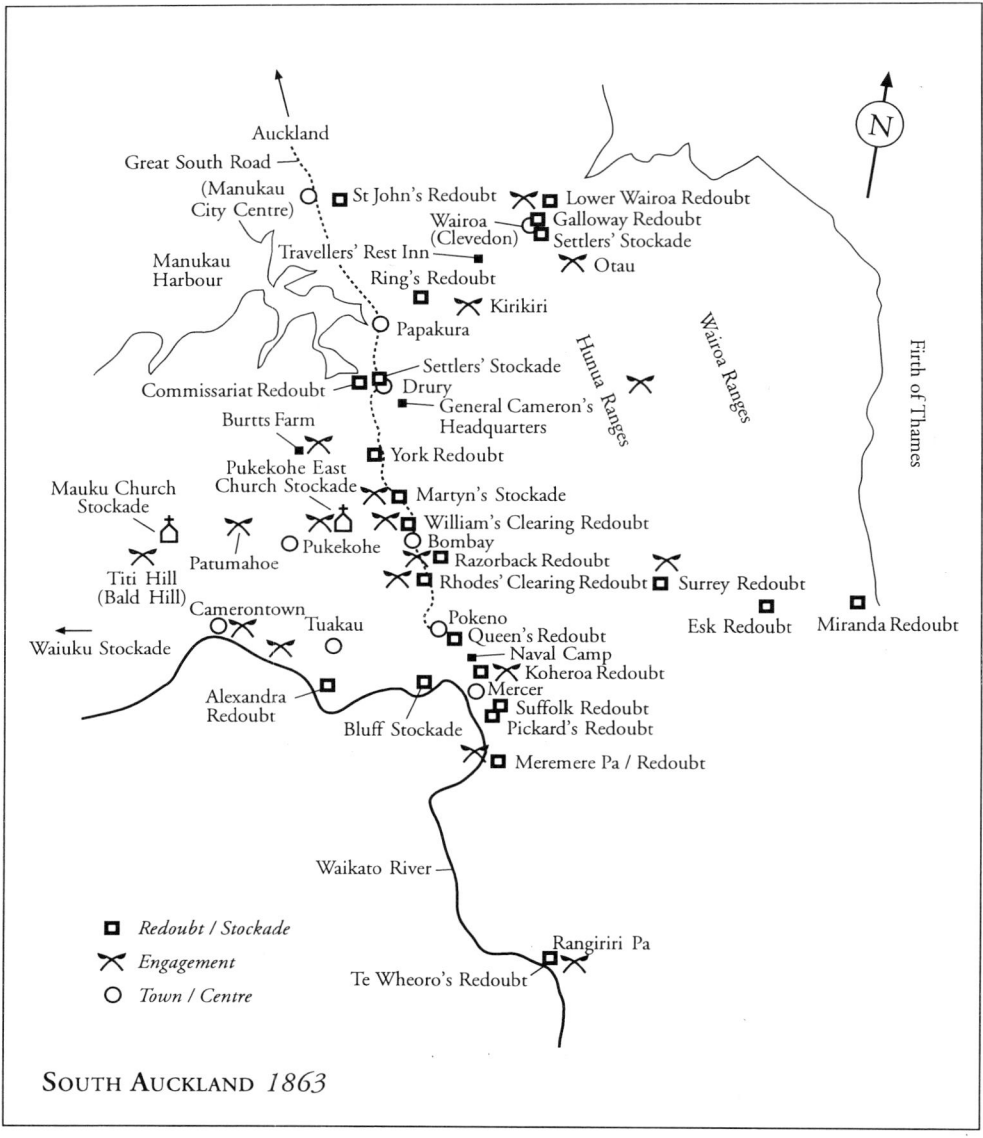

South Auckland 1863

15 September: This morning 50 men of the Forest Rangers, 20 of the Mauku Volunteers and special constables, were under arms to start for a visit to a native clearing to the south of this, in the neighbourhood of Pukekohe hill. ... Just as we were starting, information arrived through the roundabout way of friendly natives, regarding our last engagement on Messrs Lusk and Hill's farm [8 September]. ... The information was that reinforcements had come to the defeated party, and that they intended to pay us back the damage done to their feelings. [It seems the Forest Rangers had already established a reputation amongst the Maori in the south Auckland area.] ... Seventy, all counted, started off at our usual pace, guided by Mr Bragman, in a most scientific way, through the dense bush, where two years ago he made some marks for his guidance in the direction of the native clearing. This clearing is situated on the slope of an isolated hill bush, or at least scrub ascending the steep back of the elevation. Through the cover of the scrub we reached the crest and reconnoitred carefully. There at the bottom of the valley, encircled by the scrub lay the whares. We edged along the bush and rushed round the back of the houses – but found them empty. There was no doubt the whole place had not been visited for some time, and while grieving over our want of success, shots, single ones and volleys, were fired in the direction of Pukekohe stockade. We had but a scanty breakfast on account of the non-arrival of our commissariat cart, and we had nothing with us for the day, but drawing our belts tighter we made, by compass, for the shots, probably fired some miles distant from us. ... All along this route we found fresh native tracks in every direction, and as we approached the neighbourhood of Pukekohe stockade it became evident that a large force had passed that way not long before us. ... We crested a hill and saw Pukekohe stockade, about a mile from us, in peaceful condition, and nothing stirred around. It was then considerably past three in the afternoon and we had something like 11 miles before dinner could be got at. ... We turned our faces homeward marching as men march who go to their dinner after a 12 hour fast. About nine o'clock we arrived in camp where we had been anxiously expected.

18 September: Orders have arrived the night previous that we should join the "Flying Column" under Colonel Nixon. We marched this morning for Burtt's farm. To the west of the old Pukekohe road rises a bluff, with a back of gradual ascent sloping southward; on that slope lies the thriving farm of Mr Burtt. We encamped that night at the foot of the bluff, on Mr Luke's farm, nestled between copses of pretty bush. A row of tents cresting the ridge showed where the "Flying Column" was camped. The interior of Mr Luke's house, our headquarters, had just recently been converted from a comfortable bush residence into chaos, the operators being the Maoris of course.

Colonel Nixon of the Colonial Defence Force Cavalry, formed a large force called the "Flying Column" which included over 200 men from the 40th, 65th and 70th Regiments. Jackson and his men joined forces with Nixon's Flying Column on Saturday, 19 September at Burtt's farm. With ten days' provisions the new combined force intended to scour the surrounding bush for stray cattle.

19 September: Shifted up to Burtt's and started for a short tour through the bush, with detachments of the 70th under Captain Rutherford, the Defence Corps, under Captains Pye and Walmsley. The Pukekohe stockade was our destination. Nothing occurred or was seen on our road worthy of mentioning except perhaps that we saw, in the blackened site of Mr Hodge's house, the first indication of the wrath of the Maori getting the better of his policy. In vain we stole through the bush, along the back of Macdonald's house, in the hope of falling in with some of the enemy lingering near the scene of his latest exploit, but, as might have been expected, that locality had been abandoned for the time, according to Maori custom. The interior of Mr Macdonald's house was a piteous scene of destruction. The church and stockade, bullet marked as they were, were of course objects of interest. In the evening after our return, while we were at supper, the body of Hugh Maclean, shot through the heart, was brought into the apartment and laid out in a neighbouring one. ... News also arrived that the Mauku force had seen some 18 Maoris making their way from Mr May's house, at the Bald Hills, to the west and south of Patumahoe.

William Morgan in his diary (entry Friday, 25 September) describes events of the Flying Column:

In coming down from Pukekohe, I learned that the "Flying Column" had returned to headquarters at Burtt's [farm] yesterday, and a few particulars of its movements may be of interest. The force that left Burtt's last Sunday morning was upwards of 200 strong, consisting of detachments of the Defence Force, the 40th, 65th and 70th Regiments, and the Forest Rangers – the whole under Colonel Nixon. Captain Heaphy and Dr Carberry accompanied the expedition; also Messrs W. Nicholls and H. Harris as guides.

Burtt's house was left about half-past nine, and the column [carrying three day's provisions], with the guides and the gallant Colonel in command leading the way, went in the direction of Buckland's farm [and Walter's clearing]. On the way they camped in the bush and partook of refreshments. They then moved on through Buckland's land. The houses of Hodge [farm on Goldings Road, a mile or so east of present day Pukekohe], Harris and Buckland were found burnt down. Colonel Nixon ordered the force to camp in a dense bush until past midnight on Sunday. On Monday [September 21] morning at 1 o'clock, the column proceeded in the dark into Walter's flat, and getting on the track in the direction of Camerontown, proceeded towards that place, having some idea that they would fall in with the rebels. The importance of having guides was thus exemplified by a night march through the country – a great portion of which was bush – and with no possibility of being seen by the rebels.

On arriving at Camerontown, a scene of destruction presented itself. Whares were burnt to the ground, and large quantities of horse forage lay in heaps, spoiled by the weather [there being about three days of rain recently]. There were some whares, however, which were not destroyed. Blood was observed among some of the corn on the beach, indicative perhaps of tragical scenes. Finding no rebels in the vicinity, the force was moved forward to Purapura [on the right bank of the Waikato River], the men in the various detachments being most eager to come across some of the enemy. At Purapura fresh tracks were found leading down to the Waikato [River], as if there the rebels had crossed the river.

From this place, Nixon still leading the force, they proceeded to the district of Mauku. On the way several carcases of beasts were found on the ground, no doubt shot by the natives. The column arrived at Mauku on the evening of Monday, the 65th and the 40th taking up their quarters at the church, the 70th at Vickers', the Forest Rangers and Defence Force at Mr Crispe's, where Colonel Nixon and other officers also stopped.

The column remained, I believe at the Mauku all Tuesday. It being reported that the rebels were mustering in the neighbourhood of the Hermitage and in other places near Waiuku, the Colonel deemed it necessary, in the place of returning to headquarters, where he hourly expected, to retain the whole force, so that he might start out on an expedition on Wednesday morning. He divided his force into three detachments, and gave orders for them to take different routes, but ultimately to concentrate in one place. With guides knowing the locality, each detachment moved on, and ultimately met at the appointed rendezvous, but without coming across any of the rebels.

The force returned to headquarters last evening, Captain Rutherford commanding. Colonel Nixon started for Waiuku on Wednesday night, and returned to Burtt's last evening. I believe the column, or a portion of it, has started out this morning.

Captain Heaphy, Jackson and von Tempsky lodged in Burtt's farmhouse with the Watson family for about three weeks, and during their stay here von Tempsky spent his leisure time sketching the attack on the property. This would be the first of many watercolour sketches depicting the New Zealand War.

Private Richard Bell gives, in his unsuccessful bid for a New Zealand Medal, a detailed description of the Flying Column:

> I was called up in the militia when martial law was proclaimed in Auckland – doing duty at Wairoa South, now called Clevedon. From there I joined the late Major Jackson's Company Forest Rangers and was attached to the right wing of the Flying Column under Major Ryan of the 70th Regiment. There were about 200 Imperial soldiers in the column composed of men from the 40th, 65th, 12th [not clear if men from the 12th were present] and 70th Regts. Our duty was to keep the bush clear of natives from Wairoa to Pokeno and through to Pukekohe.

About this time Colonel Nixon, on advice from headquarters, decided the Flying Column would be more effective if it was split – one section operating to the east and the other to the west of Great South Road. Captain Rutherford commanded the west side while Major Ryan commanded the east. Nixon, stationed with the Colonial Defence Force, some British regulars and militia, was still in overall command based at Papakura. Likewise, the Forest Rangers were divided into two detachments (a sign of future developments); the east detachment under Jackson with von Tempsky in support at Wairoa and the west detachment under Ensign Hay at Mauku. The Forest Ranger's diary continues:

> **5 October:** This is a day of rest. Our forces came in from Waiuku yesterday afternoon, without having met with any natives. About 150 head of cattle were collected by the Defence corps.

Colonel Nixon left Burtt's farm on Tuesday, 6 October at 7 am with a force of about 200 men (including the Forest Rangers) and marched to Tuakau by way of Scott's, Hodge's and Nicholl's properties. The Alexandra Redoubt was visited, and the column encamped in the settlement. Immense fires were seen after dusk on the opposite bank of the Waikato River some two miles up river from the redoubt. Maori were also distinctly seen. A party of volunteers (including Forest Rangers) formed an ambush party for the night in case any of the Maori should cross the river. They positioned themselves in a suitable place but no Maori arrived. After another unsuccessful expedition the Flying Column returned to Papakura on Thursday, 8 October.

> **6 October:** ... It was then decided that an ambush should be laid on this side of the [Waikato] river near a landing place, a few miles above the [Alexandra] redoubt. Forty men – volunteers of the Defence corps and the Forest Rangers – under Captain Pye and Ensign von Tempsky started at dusk for the river. We were led by Private Newton of the Forest Rangers, who through his perfect knowledge of the country, had suggested the best possible locality for such an ambush. After the first mile it grew pitch dark, the little light remaining being effectually excluded from us by our dense forest roof. Newton guided us most admirably, in spite of darkness and denseness of bush. About half past 9 pm we issued with "bated breath" from the forest, and saw at our feet a glittering reach of the Waikato; on the dark ridge of looming hills on the opposite bank three lurid fires showed us where the enemy lay. ... About half past ten Newton reported from our extreme right flank that he could hear natives talking on the other side of the water. ... Hour after hour passed and there was no stir upon the river. ... About half past three Newton once more reported that he could hear the natives talking, in the same spot as before. ... Daylight came but with it a fog of such denseness that we could not see five paces ahead. ... The fog misled us and as we found that it would be hours before it was likely to rise enough for accurate shooting we decided upon returning to our main body which we had probably kept waiting already too long. By a sweep through the bush between the redoubt and the landing place we returned and arrived at half past nine am at Tuakau. An hour's rest for breakfast was granted us, and after that the whole column moved back to Burtt's where we arrived about 5 pm.
>
> **16 October:** We are now more than a week at Selby's [farm]. Daily tours through the bush in this neighbourhood have had no direct result whatever. ... The enemy is now concentrated in great force on three points in this neighbourhood; at Marshall's [farm], opposite Tuakau redoubt [across the Waikato River]; at Meremere opposite Whangamarino redoubt; and at Paparata, opposite the Koheroa ridges.

The Forest Rangers stayed on at Selby's farm near Tuakau and made their expeditions from there. Occasionally they went to the Waikato River hoping to sight a steamer which was expected. Their theory was that the Maori at Marshall's [farm] on the opposite would fire on the steamer giving the Forest Rangers targets to fire at. They had long range Enfield rifles with them for just that purpose. On 23

October they left Tuakau at 1 pm for Camerontown, Purapura, Mauku and then back to Tuakau. The last part of the trek was made in darkness with each of the men feeling for the man in front. They arrived after daybreak on 24 October and immediately had to report to Camerontown. Information reached there that a Maori force was on the Waikato River.

> **24 October:** ... Captain Rutherford of the 70th, who was in command of this expedition through Colonel Nixon's absence, moved us through the bush with the greatest precaution; for just as we were on the point of entering the bush we discovered two canoes coming towards our side of the river, and three shots were fired ahead of us. As we approached the landing place we could hear the Maoris talking quite plainly and unconcernedly. So soon as the bush thinned our force was halted and Captain Rutherford, with one of his officers, crept on hands and knees forward to reconnoitre. Nothing could be seen on the top of the bank nor below on the landing place, when some desperate donkey let his piece [rifle] off accidentally or intentionally. We thought our game spoiled, but as matters turned out, the thing was not so bad. The men on seeing the nature of the ambush destroyed, rushed down the bank through the dense forest, and fired volley after volley on the natives in the canoes.

By this stage the Maori had turned for the opposite bank and were half way across the river when the volleys commenced. Three of the eight Maori present were seen to be hit. After this the force continued on to Purapura finding a well-trodden Maori trail leading from the river in the direction of the Bald Hills. From here the force carried on to Mauku where the Forest Rangers fell exhausted at 6 pm.

The men occasionally had opportunities to relax from the rigours of bush marching. One such time was when the Forest Rangers returned from a long bush march with the Flying Column to Queen's Redoubt, Pokeno. Von Tempsky writes:

> The day following our arrival was Sunday and the first church parade of the Flying Column was held. We marched down to the redoubt and formed in the square with the troops for service. What a contrast our lot presented to the neat turnout of the troops of headquarters with their pipe-clayed [white] belts and polished boots, and tidy blue frocks! Even our Regulars had discarded pipe-clay and blacking long ago, and their blue jumpers looked decidedly seedy.
> But the strongest contrast was formed by the Forest Rangers. Such ragamuffins had never before been seen on church parade, and I fear the service was little attended to [probably because of the diverse religions practised by the Forest Rangers]; the troops were perfectly fascinated with such an unusual spectacle. Even the officers seemed overcome, particularly with the rig of our officers; but, heaven knows, a few months after that we looked all pretty much alike.

Von Tempsky with Thomas McDonnell (of Nixon's Colonial Defence Force Cavalry and later in command of an Armed Constabulary Field Force) volunteered to scout a Kingite position between the Waikato River and the Firth of Thames at Paparata, fourteen miles from Cameron's advanced post at Whangamarino on about

12 October 1863. They successfully reconnoitred the enemy's position and works at Paparata which was surrounded by outlying parties and scouts. The only track known was held by the enemy, and constantly used by them in moving from their stronghold at Meremere to Paparata. The two had to conceal themselves in a swamp close to Paparata during part of the night and the whole of the next day. Discovery by the Maori pig dogs was only prevented by their scent being destroyed by a timely shower of rain. On their return they took care that the Maori should know Europeans could penetrate into their sector by making their tracks obvious and leaving biscuit and empty preserve tins in their lair and along their retreat.

After putting themselves in some dangerous situations and obtaining the needed intelligence, the two returned safely. McDonnell was later to receive the New Zealand Cross for this and later actions.

CHAPTER 4

Disbandment and re-enlistment

On 9 November 1863, Jackson was informed that the Forest Rangers were to be disbanded as its term of engagement expired on 10 November. In an order to Jackson, dated 9 November 1863, Russell (Defence Minister) wrote:

> Your corps will be disbanded, as the term of your engagement expires on the 10th instant. You may, however, enlist one hundred men on the same terms as the Colonial Defence Force: viz., 5s per day, less charge of rations. They will probably form part of the Colonial Defence Force, not mounted, or may be attached to one of the Waikato Regiments.

The Forest Rangers, after many weeks of tramping in the Wairoa to Mauku area with only the odd sightings of Maori, as a rule took great pleasure to the approach of the day that was to release them from their three month's service. There were mutual feelings of relief when the men were paid off and parted from one another.

Jackson was now authorised to enlist one hundred men on the same terms as the Colonial Defence Force and would possibly form part of that force or would be attached to one of the Waikato militia regiments. The reason for the disbandment of the unit, followed by an immediate call for the formation of an even larger unit, was the shortage of Government funding. The Colonial Defence Office concluded in August 1863 that the hostilities south of Auckland and the Waikato war would be completed within three months. But because of the guerrilla tactics used by the Maori and the inability of the imperial troops to penetrate the bush in pursuit of the enemy, the war was to continue for about another four months. The cost of running the Forest Rangers was considered too expensive. The Forest Rangers had proven themselves beyond expectations during the short three month's service and their worth in the coming Waikato campaign was too valuable to dispense with, so the simple solution was to disband and reform with reduced rates of pay. In a letter from T.W. Lewis, Chief Clerk, Defence Office, to Mr G.S. Cooper as part of the land claims dispute by Major Jackson (dated 24 August 1871), Lewis stated:

> When the first corps of Forest Rangers was formed, the service was supposed to be one of peculiar danger, and, as stated by Major Jackson in one of his letters, it was thought that the Native disturbance would be quelled in a very short time. A specially high rate of pay (viz., 10s a day for sergeants and 8s. for privates) was authorized, in addition, as I believe, to a grant of land. ... the Government ... seemed to depart from the exceptionally good terms offered in the first instance to the Forest Rangers.
> ... the new corps was to form a part of the Colonial Defence Force (a corps without promise of land), or of the land-receiving corps, the Waikato Militia. The Forest Rangers under Major Jackson were, however, subsequently attached to (though afterwards separated from) the 2nd Waikato Regiment.

Jackson telegraphed Russell on 11 November 1863:

If the men cannot leave the Colony, many of them will rejoin; only ten or twelve have promised to do so yet. The detachment from the Mauku has not arrived yet. Am I to swear in what men I can get, and for how long? May I take men from Wairoa, Mauku, or Waiuku? I am awaiting an answer.

Obviously Jackson was confused in that he was not given enough information regarding the contract details for the new Forest Rangers. The answer from Russell soon dispelled any confusion:

You can swear in what men you can get. They must take service under the Waikato regulations for three years. You may take men from either of the places you name.

Jackson had the order to contract his new men under the terms of service for the Waikato Militia, but the problem now was the reduced rate of pay offered; it was the same as that already held by men in other units. With no extra incentive Jackson had trouble filling his company, and the task was even more difficult when von Tempsky later attempted to fill his company.

Von Tempsky's experience in bush fighting and his skill in the use of arms, particularly the sword, soon brought him into prominence and he received permission to form a second company of Forest Rangers on the same terms as Jackson's company. Although Jackson and von Tempsky were now of the same rank, Jackson remained the Commanding Officer of both companies of Forest Rangers. Von Tempsky never really came to terms with this, being often bitter and critical of Jackson's orders and tactics. Nowhere in von Tempsky's writings is there mention of Jackson's commanding authority, further evidence of his jealously and envy of superior officers.

The strength of each company was now to be up to sixty men. The scale of pay for the new Forest Rangers, issued on 25 November, was 5s per day less 10d for daily rations (for privates). This was far less than they had previously received.

On 27 November 1863 it was announced that both Jackson and von Tempsky were promoted to Captain. Jackson's promotion was backdated to 9 November and von Tempsky's to 10 November. Being senior by appointment, Jackson was in command of both companies of Forest Rangers. Their rate of pay was now set at 20s per day plus 4s daily as forage and contingency allowances, and less 10d for daily rations.

The reduction in pay convinced many to quit the unit thinking that their service could be more profitable elsewhere. Ensign Hay was one of these, allowing Charles Westrup to replace him as ensign. His commission was in the Auckland Militia, attached to the Forest Rangers, dated 26 November 1863.

The two new companies were required to take service under the Waikato Militia Regiments' regulations for three years, at the end of which term they would receive title to land grants in the Waikato.

Roll of Forest Rangers, November 1863:

Jackson's No. 1 Company: *Captain* (1): William Jackson. *Ensign* (1): Westrup. *Staff Sergeant* (1): (at a pay rate of 8s 6d per day) Bertram. *Sergeant* (1): (at a pay rate of 7s 6d per day) Holden. *Corporal* (1): (at a pay rate of 6s per day) William Taylor.

Privates (22): (at a pay rate of 5s per day) Alexander, Lawrence Burns, John Carter, Gibb, Grigg, Hendry, Henry Jackson, Johns, Long, McNamara, Madigan, Mahoney, Morgan, John Nolan, Rowden, Rowland, Temple, William Thomson, Thurston, George Ward, Watters, Wells.
Von Tempsky's No. 2 Company: *Captain* (1): Von Tempsky. *Ensign* (1): Roberts. *Staff Sergeant* (1): (at a pay rate of 8s 6d per day) Sherret. *Sergeants* (3): (at a pay rate of 7s 6d per day) Carran, Southey, Wakeford. *Corporal* (1): (at a pay rate of 6s per day) Sibley. *Privates* (7): (at a pay rate of 5s per day) Ballenden, Buttle, Bygum, Keena, McMinn, Mohr, Parsons.

This roll illustrates the frustrations faced by von Tempsky in filling his company after Jackson had a head-start. By the end of November he only had 13 men enlisted (excluding himself), compared to Jackson's 26 men. Since von Tempsky received his orders after Jackson, he was disappointed that the delay meant Jackson had been able to enlist a larger portion of the old Forest Rangers. However von Tempsky did manage to get some good men with bush experience gained in the original Forest Ranger company, such as Southey, a half-caste, who was appointed as a sergeant. Most of Jackson's men started on the first day of the payroll on 17 November.

Von Tempsky wrote of his first dozen men and the closeness he experienced with them:

> Besides I knew everyone of "my dozen". There was my old friend Southey, the half-caste, now sergeant with me; there was another sergeant, Carran, from the north, who had lived much in the bush and amongst Maoris – determined and daring; I knew every one of them from the old corps, they were reliable men, down to little Keena – a Welshman, small in body – but with a soul big enough to fill a house. Besides I had chosen a subaltern in whose character and pluck I had the utmost confidence – Mr Roberts.

The No. 1 Company was attached to the 2nd Regiment Waikato Militia and the No. 2 Company was attached to the 1st Regiment Waikato Militia.

Jackson established his headquarters in Papakura while von Tempsky established his in nearby Ramarama. Both continued to enlist men.

John Roberts was commissioned as Ensign in the Auckland Militia, attached to the Forest Rangers, dated 23 November 1863.

CHAPTER 5

Jackson proves his worth

At the commencement of operations, von Tempsky's No. 2 Company, Forest Rangers consisted of two officers and twelve men. Their first expedition in mid December was back to the Paparata valley to ascertain Maori positions. They left from Ramarama and followed old Maori tracks to the abandoned stronghold of Paparata but saw no Maori other than a few women. On reaching the Paparata valley von Tempsky set up a camp for his men and then visited the nearby Surrey Redoubt which lay on the rim of the valley. (Since his scouting expedition with McDonnell to this area in October, a line of redoubts had been established between the Waikato River and the Firth of Thames.) At the redoubt von Tempsky met up with Thomas McDonnell and the two friends arranged a return visit to their "famous swamp lair" the following day. Ensign Roberts accompanied them on their pilgrimage while the remainder of von Tempsky's Company was given a day of rest, which included swimming and gathering wild honey in the warm sun.

Meanwhile Jackson's No. 1 Company's first operation was also in the Paparata area bringing them in surprise contact with hostile Maori resulting in many Maori being killed.

On Friday, 11 December 1863, soon after midday (1.15 pm), Jackson's No. 1 Company, Forest Rangers, started out from Papakura camp to reconnoitre land in front of the Wairoa and Hunua Ranges. Captain Jackson was in command with Ensign Westrup in support and Alexander Hill (local settler) as guide.

On the road east towards Wairoa, in the vicinity of Buckland's Clearing, they discovered tracks, probably from some Maori scouting party, leading south towards the bush. Immediately they followed the track and camped that night in the forest. On the Saturday, 12 December, they pushed on through the forest, following fresh tracks in a south to southeast direction and camped in the forest for a second night. Again no fire was allowed.

Jackson pushed his men forward on the Sunday, 13 December, the track now in the vicinity of Paparata. The corps came upon an enemy encampment of an estimated 40 Maori engaged in cleaning their firearms, bathing and other activities. Jackson thought them to be the same party that had been murdering and plundering settlers in the Wairoa district recently. The sound of a cow-bell swung by a child alerted the Forest Rangers. George Ward, who was first to emerge from the bush, found a Maori bathing. The alerted Maori, thinking Ward a Maori because of his black skin, beckoned Ward to approach him – but Ward shot him dead. Taking the Maori totally by surprise, a murderous volley was fired by about eight Forest Rangers led by Westrup and John Smith (Wairoa Smith), who had followed the stream. After the volley the Forest Rangers rushed the Maori with their revolvers causing the survivors to flee into the forest. A few Maori had fought desperately in hand-to-hand confrontations.

With the enemy were several women who assisted in getting the wounded away. One warrior who rushed back to defend his wounded comrade was killed instantly by a bullet in the forehead. The wounded brother's wife emerged from the forest shortly after the attack and tended to her husband until he died several days later.

Seven or eight Maori were killed and more were wounded. Jackson's men collected the articles left behind by the Maori. These consisted of three flags, rings, watches and other items, many of which were spoils from Maori raids on settlers. From here the Corps returned to Papakura camp.

Apparently the Maori party that left the Wairoa district split into two groups in the forest on the advice of a Maori named Timoti te Amopo who had powers of second sight. He warned the party of possible danger from Pakeha soldiers. So at the time of the attack some had already left the party the previous day.

In his official despatch of the expedition and engagement, Jackson reported:

> Papakura, December 14, 1863
> Sir, I have the honour to report for the information of the Lieutenant-General Commanding, that in accordance with your instructions, I started on Friday, the 11th December at 1.15 pm, with a force of my company of Forest Rangers, on an expedition towards the Wairoa River.
> [Not all No. 1 Company was present. Those present were: Officers: Captain William Jackson, Ensign Westrup; Non-Commissioned Officers and Privates: Alexander, Staff-Sergeant Bertram, Robert Bruce, William Bruce, Lawrence Burns, Coghlan, Cole, Fitzgerald, Gibb, Grigg, Hendry, Alexander Hill, Holden, Henry Jackson, Corporal Johns, Long, Madigan, Mahoney, Morgan, Peters, Rowden, Rowland, James Smith, John Smith, Temple, William Michael Thomson, Vaughan, George Ward, Watters, Wells, James Williams.]
> At 6.30 pm on that day, I camped on the Hunua River, and started from thence at 4.30 next morning; at 6.30 am we struck native tracks which appeared to be quite fresh; at 10.30 am we found a camping ground, which was capable of accommodating 30 or 40 natives. One of the fires here was still hot. At 4.30 pm we got to another camping ground, the fires at which were quite hot; we had evidently gained a day's march on the enemy. I continued our march until 6.15 pm, when finding we had overrun the track, I camped for the night. On Sunday, 13th December, I broke camp at 5.30 am and turned back to re-examine the path, and found tracks diverging to the left. I then posted some men to look out for smoke [tree climbers], which we soon discovered rising out of the ranges. We went very quietly towards it, and by using great caution succeeded in surprising the enemy about 8.40 am. We had got between their sentry and their camp.
> When about twelve or fifteen yards from the enemy, I halted my men on an eminence, to give them breath, and gave the orders that they should first attack the enemy with their carbines, and then rush them with their revolvers. The Maoris were then cleaning their guns. The surprise was complete. After our carbines were discharged, the enemy apparently expecting we had only empty pieces, turned upon us with their guns and tomahawks, but the revolvers soon sent them to the right-about. Several of the enemy who were wounded by the discharge of the carbines were assisted away by the women, who were very busy removing arms, dead and wounded. I saw two or three natives hit who were immediately helped away by women. I had directed my

men not to fire at the women, and I am happy to say they did not, though it is very possible that some of the women and children may have got hurt in the affray, but I only know of one instance, a woman I believe was wounded in the leg by a stray shot.

The affair lasted only four or five minutes. I saw three dead men taken off, and four of their dead were left in our hands. Two of the natives, when surrounded, endeavoured to stab my men, one using a bowie knife and the other a large carving knife, but the revolver made short work of them. One native at great risk returned and attempted to carry away a small tin box, but a bullet made him drop it and run off. Many of those who escaped were wounded. Had my party been larger, I think I could easily have surrounded the enemy and taken them all prisoners. None of my men was hurt as only those of the enemy who were on the outskirts of the camp could find time to load and fire on us, and they were just as likely to hit their own men as mine. I estimate the number of the enemy to have been over 40 men. One of the natives, before he died, told me there were 28, and on being asked said there were 28 double, holding up two of his fingers. He also said his tribe was the Ngatipaoa. He would not tell me his own name, but said the next man was a chief named Matariki.

The scene of the engagement was in the ranges, about five miles north of Paparata. The natives retreated in an easterly direction. One of the sentries I had posted informed me, some time after we had left the place, that a broad track led easterly from near where he was posted, and that he saw a man on horseback go up it. The enemy appeared to have plenty of provisions; we found a good deal of tea and sugar and some flour; there was abundance of fern-root, three or four iron pots had meat in them, and a good quantity of pork was hanging up. In the box which the native tried to secure, mentioned above [captured by Corporal William Johns], were three flags, one a large red flag on which was embroidered a white cross and star and the word "AOTEAROA" in white letters. It is made of silk and is neat and handsome. Another flag is a large red pendant with a white cross, the remaining flag is a handkerchief, of the Union Jack pattern.

The other spoils are a double-barrelled gun, a large horse pistol, and a smaller pistol, three or four cartridge boxes, a great deal of property which had belonged to settlers, such as scarlet hangings, fancy window blinds, small work boxes, some papers belonging to Mr Richardson of Wairoa and a coat belonging to Mr Johnson of the same place, several articles which had been stolen by the natives from Mr McDonald at the time Trust's children were murdered near Howick. I therefore conclude these natives were of the party who committed those murders. One of my men has two small packets of hair, I think European. They are evidently relics. He will give them up to any one who may claim them. We could not bring away much of the "loot" as we were heavily loaded with our arms, blankets etc., but I think I brought away sufficient to prove the character of the party we fell in with. We destroyed several packages and tins of gunpowder, and threw a great number of bullets into the creek.

I have great pleasure in reporting that my men behaved with great coolness

Illustration of one of the flags captured by the Forest Rangers at Paparata on 13 December 1863. The original flag, now in the Auckland Institute and Museum collection, is in poor condition.

and courage. There was no firing at random. I am anxious to bring to your special notice the brave and cool conduct of Ensign Westrup, who was foremost in the attack, and made every shot of his revolver tell; also of Private John Smith, who had a severe hand to hand struggle with a powerful native.
William Jackson
Captain Commanding Forest Rangers

The exact location of this skirmish is near the headwaters of the Wairoa and Mangatawhiri Rivers, nearer to Ararimu than to Paparata. They bivouacked the first night by the Hunua River then followed a trail through the Kohukohunui Range towards Wharekawa where enemy contact was made.

The three flags captured by Corporal William Johns were put on show in Papakura. The large red flag on which was embroidered a white cross and star and the word "AOTEAROA" in white letters was made by Heni te Kiri-karamu (later known as Heni Pore or Jane Foley and who gave water to Colonel Booth at the battle at Gate Pa) for her chief Wi Koka. In 1913, on the 50th anniversary of the taking of the flag at Paparata, it was presented by representatives of the Jackson family and the surviving members of No. 1 Company to the Auckland Old Colonists' Museum. The flag was displayed in the foyer of the Auckland Public Library for many years. It was still looked upon with reverence by Maori. The flag is now in the Auckland Institute and Museum, but is not on display owing to deterioration. It is believed the red dye in the silk has chemically reacted with the silk threads, breaking them down. Efforts are being made to halt the damage.

At the time of the presentation of the flag in 1913, a nephew of Jackson wrote a colourful and gruesome account of the Paparata action. He describes the initial contact with the Maori raiding party:

> Approaching the Maori camp the Rangers had split into two parties and one of them had come across a log over a ravine upon which was a Maori sentry. Among Jackson's party were two Negroes [George Ward and James Watters], formerly man-o-wars men from the West Indies. A Maori mat and other gear had been picked up at an abandoned whare, and it was suggested that one of the black men, George Ward, should dress as a Maori, and endeavour to dispose of the sentry. He was able to come up without arousing suspicion, and then, drawing his bowie knife, disembowelled the sentry and toppled him into the stream, without making any noise to arouse the camp. Apparently some of the Rangers were younger men and one of them, Private Charles Coghlan, nicknamed "Steve", looked over at the body with its innards trailing off down the fast running stream and was sick. After that of course he had to stand a great deal of chaff from the tough Rangers.

Von Tempsky's more detailed account conflicts with this when he says George Ward shot the sentry first and used the knife afterwards.

This contact with the enemy and the following successful action consumed von Tempsky with jealousy. On joining the Forest Rangers he at once pitted himself against Jackson in the pursuit of glory. Jackson was probably unaware of the rivalry at this early stage, being too engrossed in doing his job and doing it well!

Von Tempsky wrote on seeing Jackson return from his expedition:

> ... my first emotion, was a strong pang of jealousy. That my rival, particularly one to whom I felt myself superior in experience and knowledge, should have thus outstripped me ... For a moment the green eyed monster became rampant within me – but I recollected in time that I was a white man and that our foes had received a lesson.

It is a pity that von Tempsky should want to silently compete in serious rivalry within the same unit, and possibly take the Forest Rangers down a path of fragmentation and ill-harmony – thus threatening its combined strength. From this time till the disbandment of the Forest Rangers the two companies were often openly competing against each other in petty rivalry, consumed by the jealousy instilled in them by von Tempsky.

William Race commented on the rivalry:

> There was no harmony between the two corps [Companies], although organised on the same lines, and together.

Jackson's Paparata expedition arrived at Wairoa on Sunday night, 13 December, and came on to Papakura on the Monday.

Immediately both companies returned to the site of the action in the hope of tracking down Maori who had escaped the engagement, but no contact could be made. To von Tempsky's surprise and humiliation, a track his company had come upon but not followed, would have taken them to the same party of Maori.

There was a lot of public controversy about the cold-blooded murder of the Maori at Paparata. Many think the Maori were killed while taking prayers (being also Sunday) but Jackson states that the Maori were cleaning firearms.

An article in the *Daily Southern Cross*, dated 17 December, states that the action:

> ... has not met with the unqualified approval of all parties, and more especially of some of the military. Among the various accusations brought against the Rangers for the very smart and admirable affair of Sunday last, is that of cold-blooded murder, in attacking natives who were, it is said, entirely unprepared for their approach. It is said that the natives, or some of them were at prayers.

This action clearly illustrates the success of a small well-trained and hard-hitting unit over the larger cumbersome Flying Column. The latter was far too large to steal through the bush especially when accompanied by mounted troops – probably explaining why they never caught up with raiding Maori.

At about this time a young non-commissioned officer, Sergeant Whitfield, was getting a memorable sendoff from his old unit, No. 4 Company, 2nd Regiment Waikato Militia, to join the Forest Rangers. A correspondent for the *Daily Southern Cross* recorded the event at Camp Kirikiri on 12 December.

> The monotony of this camp was agreeably relieved this morning, in consequence of a presentation by the non-commissioned officers and men of No. 4 Company, 2nd Waikato Militia, to Sergeant Robert Whitfield of that company, who has been transferred to Captain Jackson's Corps of Forest Rangers. At seven o'clock, a.m., on parade, the men having been formed into square, Captain Freer passed some very high encomiums on Sergeant Whitfield's conduct as a non-commissioned officer during the time he had been under his command, commenting on the kindly feeling displayed by the company to a comrade on the eve of departure, and handing the testimonial, consisting of a revolver, with case and pocket compass, to him, read the address, which was as follows:
> Camp Kirikiri, December 12. To Sergeant Robert Whitfield.
> We the undersigned non-commissioned officers and privates of No. 4 Company, 2nd Regiment Waikato Militia, stationed at Kirikiri, desirous of giving expression to the feelings of esteem we entertain towards you, beg (on the eve of your leaving our company to join Captain Jackson's Forest Rangers), your acceptance of a patent revolver pistol by "Tranter", and a pocket compass, which we trust you will find useful in the more exciting and dangerous field of action that you are about to enter. We sincerely regret to part with you, and wish you success and happiness in your future undertakings.

There followed 42 signatures.

On Thursday, 17 December, both companies of the Forest Rangers and part of the Flying Column under Major Ryan, started another expedition into the Hunua Ranges with three days' provisions in pursuit of Maori. Major Ryan and his force separated from the Forest Rangers and emerged from the bush on Saturday, 19 December. That same day the Forest Rangers walked 30 miles from the vicinity of Paparata to Maketu and then to Drury, arriving in the evening. The objective of the expedition was to ascertain if any of the raiding Maori had returned with reinforcements to the scene of their late encounter with the Forest Rangers. They also searched for plantations of potatoes or grain, but no Maori or plantations were discovered.

By the end of December the No. 2 Company had gathered forty men including ten men already enlisted in the 1st Waikato Militia Regiment.

As General Cameron pushed south into the Waikato he had effectively bypassed the Hunua Ranges and other forest land just south of Auckland. But these areas still harboured raiding Maori who continued to make hit and run raids in his rear. So he maintained the Forest Rangers presence in the area as a deterrent to any prospective raids.

Both companies remained in Papakura to continue training and patrolling the south Auckland forest areas. Training included frequent silent marches through the bush and learning to respond to von Tempsky's whistle. Von Tempsky's concern was that his men be outfitted and prepared for action in the bush and conditioned to trekking and fighting.

By this stage No. 2 Company had two black men, Germans, a Dane, a Canadian, an Italian, Prussians, and men from Ireland, Scotland, Wales and England. Many of them had come to New Zealand in search of gold. Many of the men referred to their unit as Von Tempsky's Forest Rangers echoing the hero status von Tempsky desired so much.

Von Tempsky commented on the mixture of men:

> Like Jackson, I had two black men, former man-o'-war's men; one had also been a prizefighter. I had men of splendid education, and men as ignorant as the soil on which they trod.

Even Race commented on the international flavour of the company:

> And the corps was a mixed one too, no less than 12 different nationalities in 50 men. Russia, Germany, Poland, Dane, Prussia, English, Irish, Scotch, Austria, France, one half-caste Maori [Southey] and two blacks, and one baronet. Such was the composition of the No. 2 Company.

Von Tempsky enjoyed the new degree of freedom enabling him to eliminate many of the disciplines associated with militia forces such as lights out at a stated time and daily drill. He exercised his own strategies in the field, giving his men considerable freedom but still showing strict discipline when required. His men were described as rough and lawless with adventurer spirit, but they obeyed his orders. Von Tempsky was known to mete out instant punishment in the field.

Von Tempsky was determined to create an elite corps and made every endeavour possible to improve the fighting ability of his men. He was also untiring in his efforts on behalf of his men and this soon won him considerable personal loyalty. They began to worship and idolise their leader, so much so that many found it impossible to serve under any other commanding officer – a fault which was to have serious repercussions after von Tempsky's death at Te Ngutu o te Manu.

By the end of the year further enlistments in both companies boosted Forest Ranger numbers making them a more formidable fighting unit. The unit was also nearing the maximum number of men allowed on the roll.

Roll of Forest Rangers, December 1863:

Jackson's No. 1 Company: *Captain* (1): William Jackson. *Ensign* (1): Westrup. *Staff Sergeant* (1): Bertram. *Sergeants* (3): Holden, James Williams, Whitfield. *Corporals* (3): Coghlan, John Smith, William Taylor. *Privates* (42): Alexander, Benson, Black, Robert Bruce, William Bruce, Lawrence Burns, John Carter, Cole, Costello, Fitzgerald, Gallie, Gibb, Grigg, Haines, Hannah, Hannay, Hendry, Henry Jackson, Johns, Long, Hugh McDonald, Madigan, Mahoney, Morgan, Murray, John Nolan, Martin Nolan, Osborne, Peters, Rowden, Rowland, James Smith, Thomas Smith, Stephenson, Temple, William Thomson (different from the William Thomson in No. 2 Company), Thurston, Vaughan, George Ward, Watters, Wells, William Williams.

Lawrence Burns did not appear on this company's roll for December, after being present in November. Perhaps he left the unit over December, a clerical error occurred or he stayed at headquarters. McNamara was transferred to No. 2 Company and promoted to corporal. James Smith, Fitzgerald, Hugh McDonald and Peters enrolled in Otago 10 November, sailing to Auckland and joining the corps on 1 December (receiving pay from 10 November).

Von Tempsky's No. 2 Company: *Captain* (1): Von Tempsky. *Ensign* (1): Roberts. *Staff Sergeant* (1): Sherret. *Sergeants* (3): Carran, Southey, Wakeford. *Corporal* (3): McMinn, McNamara, Sibley. *Privates* (20): Ballenden, Bochow, Burry, Buttle, Bygum, Donovan, Fallon, Hartland, Hellkessel, Keena, Mohr, Parsons, Pohlen, Race, Ross, Shine, Stanley, Sumsion, Toovey, Wheeler.

Von Tempsky's No. 2 company was still numerically behind Jackson's No. 1 Company. But during January 1864, before moving south to the Waikato, No. 2 Company increased its roll to be on a par with Jackson's. During January 1864 Jackson enlisted only a further two (Privates Thorpe and Torpey), with Private John Smith being promoted to Corporal. During this same period von Tempsky enlisted 25 privates.

Roll of Forest Rangers, January 1864:

Von Tempsky's No. 2 Company: *Captain* (1): Von Tempsky. *Ensign* (1): Roberts. *Staff Sergeant* (1): Sherret. *Sergeants* (3): Carran, Southey, Wakeford. *Corporals* (3): McMinn, McNamara, Sibley. *Privates* (45): Albin, Anderson, Ballenden, Bidgood, Bochow, Burry, Butter, Buttle, Bygum, Clifford, Cochrane, Collins, Donovan, Fallon, Freeman, Harris, Hartland, Healas, Hellkessel, Higgins, Jones, Keena, Liebig, Lindsay, McClymont, Magole, Mohr, Mulligan, Neil, Parsons, Pohlen, Race, Ross, Scally, Shine, Simmons, Stanley, Sturmer, Sumsion, James Taylor, William Thomson (not the William Thomson in No. 1 Company), Toovey, Tubby, Wheeler, Woods.

General Cameron realised that the country his force must pass through to reach the fertile lands of the Waikato interior – especially the delta lands between the Waipa and Waikato Rivers – was virtually impassable to a marching army. From Pokeno to Rangiaowhia the land was interrupted by numerous swamps and kahikatea forests, making land travel difficult and dangerous, as the opportunities of ambush were too many. Cameron experienced this in the ten miles of road from Drury to Pokeno. So following the Maori example of a river fleet, he constructed shallow-draughted steamers that could be used as both gunboats and cargo carriers.

Then came the calamitous and costly attack on the Rangiriri pa on 20 November 1863. Cameron made a complete blunder of the whole affair. He persisted with frontal attacks, did not attempt to surround the pa to cut off any escape or reinforcements of the garrison, and completely underestimated the ability of the Maori to construct and defend a formidable earthwork. On top of all this he failed to correctly reconnoitre the position. He paid the price dearly with 47 killed and 85 wounded. The Maori casualties are estimated at 50 killed and about the same number wounded, as well as 180 prisoners being taken. The outcome was twofold – firstly, Cameron did not wish to commit his forces to another frontal assault on a pa, and secondly, the Maori still saw advantages in well constructed defences, enough to make them try again on several occasions before the Waikato campaign finished.

While the British Regiments and No. 1 Company, Forest Rangers moved south, the No. 2 Company, Forest Rangers continued their training at Papakura.

William Race joined No. 2 Company on 24 December 1863. He describes camp life at Papakura from December 1863 to January 1864:

> At the time of being enrolled we occupied tents on a flat close to the little village of Papakura, as also the first portion of the mounted men known as Postal Orderlies afterwards Defence Corps [Colonial Defence Corps Cavalry]. For several weeks we were encamped there for acquiring efficiency in drill, mostly with the bowie knife, as a defence against the tomahawk in any hand to hand encounter that might take place. Von Tempsky himself drilling us, with a muffled tomahawk at one hand and a spear or lance termination [head joined] to an eight foot handle. Our accoutrements were 1 Colt revolver, 1 Callisher and Terry breech loader and the redoubtable bowie knife about 18 inches long blade and some four inches wide.

Either Race is out to impress the reader with his exaggerated dimensions or he was suffering from memory loss as his manuscript was written about some 30 years later. Race continues:

> Our uniform consisted of serge jumper and trousers, haletights and leggings, and one red blanket only [memory loss again as the colour was blue], water bottle encased in leather, and a forage cap with "FR" in German silver in the front.

Race relates the tedium of garrison duty:

> For some weeks we did a sort of short duty at night at an old mill in the village [Drury] which was situated close to the river and which had been converted into a store protem [temporary] for the ammunition etc. and clothing. A small redoubt was in this village and the militia who occupied it relieved our men, eight of them in the mornings, and on Sundays we created quite a sensation when marching to the little church, with our revolvers on and in charge of Ensign Roberts, his relatives living in the vicinity.

CHAPTER 6

March to the front

The battle at Rangiriri did not involve any Forest Rangers, but the No. 1 Company was present with the military build-up at Ngaruawahia and along the Waipa River after 8 January 1864.

Early in January 1864 Cameron, now Sir Duncan (rewarded for his bungled victory at Rangiriri), sent his force forward from Ngaruawahia along the Waipa River to Whatawhata to set up a new base camp. Soon after, he pushed forward a short distance to set up another camp at Tuhikaramea. Cameron used the steamers *Avon* and *Rangiriri* to convey tents and stores via the Waipa River to the two new camps. Tuhikaramea was chosen because opposite, across the Waipa River and over the divide, was the Waitetuna Valley and Raglan.

Cameron, being a cautious commander, decided to reduce the vulnerability of his supply routes by opening up another line of communication with Auckland. Raglan seemed the logical route as supplies could be shipped there from Auckland, then transported by packhorse across the Kapamahunga Range to Cameron's army dispersed along the Waipa River.

On 20 December 1863, General Cameron despatched from Auckland a force of about 750 men consisting of the 50th Regiment and a detachment of the 2nd Regiment Waikato Militia to Raglan on the west coast. Included in the 2nd Waikatos was Captain Jackson and the No. 1 Company Forest Rangers. The force was under the command of Colonel Waddy of the 50th Regiment.

The steamers *Alexander* and *Kangaroo* were used to carry the force. It arrived off Raglan on the afternoon of 20 December, but due to heavy weather the Raglan bar was impassable. The troops were not landed until the following day, and the horses and drays two days later.

Colonel Waddy's orders were to establish road communications between the upper Raglan Harbour and the Waipa River as quickly as possible. First, a fortified post

Ngaruawahia, December 1863. Spencer Collection, Hawke's Bay Museum

Meremere, November 1863. *Spencer Collection, Hawke's Bay Museum*

was established as far up the harbour as stores could be taken by boat. The site chosen was on Captain Johnstone's land near the mouth of the Waitetuna River. Here an earth redoubt was constructed, large enough to garrison up to 200 men. Another redoubt was constructed at the end of William Naylor's road from Raglan, about at the junction of today's Hamilton-Raglan road and Old Mountain Road. Across the Kapamahunga Range and through about two and a half miles of bush ran a narrow Maori track – virtually Old Mountain Road of today. Army fatigue parties proceeded to make this track passable for both troops and packhorses. Contact was soon made with Cameron's army at Tuhikaramea.

During this period the No. 1 Company Forest Rangers offered protection to the road makers by scouring the bush in search of Maori, and at times venturing as far as Ngaruawahia to meet with Cameron. As soon as a camp was set up at Tuhikaramea, Jackson shifted his company's base there but continued operations along the dividing range between Raglan and the Waipa River.

At Tuhikaramea the Royal Engineers, with two canoes, scaling ladders (last used at Rangiriri) and planks, constructed a pontoon to float troops and supplies across the Waipa River. To ease the strain on river transport, the 70th Regiment and 140 men of the 40th Regiment were rafted over the river and marched to the Waitetuna end of the track where they were fed from the new supply depot at Raglan. Later, extra supplies were transported along the new track to relieve the pressure caused by the sinking of the river boat *Avon* in the Waipa River.

A two-storeyed, loopholed, wooden blockhouse was constructed in Raglan township and garrisoned by members of the No. 2 Regiment Waikato Militia.

Von Tempsky also received orders from General Galloway on 28 December 1863, to prepare his unit in readiness for the advance to Raglan by sea. This order was obviously withdrawn as the No. 2 Company eventually proceeded south on foot.

In January, No. 2 Company Forest Rangers proceeded from Papakura to join the main advance at Tuhikaramea. After the drudgery of camp life at Ramarama, the men were pleased to be going to the front. Many of them had enlisted for the adventure and at last their chance had arrived. They marched out of Papakura on 23 January 1864.

Race mentions the move from Papakura to Tuhikaramea:

> We received orders to join the imperial forces, then stationed at Tuhikaramea, as speedily as possible and both companies were in high spirits at the chance of seeing something more stirring than the ceaseless monotony of camp life. ... On the day we received marching orders, we left the hospitable little village of Papakura situated about three miles from Drury in the direction of the fort; our baggage following in the transport drays supplied for that purpose. It was very warm weather and the Great South Road had about two or three inches of dust, yet with our accoutrements and one double blanket, we managed to make some 23 miles that march and halted for the night in a cosy grassy spot close to an inlet by the Waikato River known then as Sailors' Creek, from the fact that the men of war and Water Transport Corps used to take in stores etc. preparatory to conveying to commissariat departments stationed higher up at Ngaruawahia or Rangiriri where the troops then were.

Whatawhata camp, above the Waipa River, January 1864. *Spencer Collection, Hawke's Bay Museum*

March to the front

Von Tempsky had a magnificent degree of fitness which kept him out-striding his men. On routemarches, right up to the time of his death, he often carried on when his men rested, often staying overnight at some forward location in the company of officers, to involve himself in intelligent conversations. This peculiarity gave him an advantage in military intelligence when rejoining his unit, adding to his importance and ego. Race describes von Tempsky's continued walking on the first day's march from Papakura:

> It was after this first day's march that von Tempsky went some nine miles further on that night to Meremere which was then in the hands of the British. The next day we picked up our "Chief" and halted at night in the vicinity of Rangiriri which had been the scene of the terrible hand to hand fight.

Race describes their arrival at Cameron's camp:

> ... some two nights after we reached our destination of Tuhikaramea. [Von Tempsky's company actually arrived at nearby Whatawhata camp.] We had covered more than 70 miles beneath a burning sun and very little water to be had, unless we left the route and penetrated some deep bush swarming with mosquitos, and which was only known to our guide Sergeant Southey, a brave and intelligent half-caste. It was quite dark when we reached the forces then under General Cameron, too dark to recognise them; an extra rum was served out to us and we had to turn into our blanket in a potato field.

The No. 2 Company Forest Rangers arrived at Whatawhata army camp on the evening of 26 January 1864.

Cameron's force on 27 January moved from Tuhikaramea towards Pikopiko and the upper Waipa. A correspondent for the *Daily Southern Cross* wrote:

> About four o'clock, the soldiers crawled out of their tents, and busied themselves packing up their tents, rations, and little etceteras, the whole force on the east side of the river being under orders to move off at five o'clock. The morning was somewhat dull and misty, – the sun just appearing over the ranges, but the rays not having acquired sufficient strength to dispel the sea of mist, which lay in the camp valley. The regiments took up their positions in the following order, in mass of columns, at quarter distances: 40th, under command of Colonel Leslie; 50th, under Colonel Waddy; 12th, under Colonel Hamilton; 65th, under Colonel Young; 70th, in charge of Colonel Mullock; Jackson's Forest Rangers, under command of Captain Jackson. The packhorses followed in the rear, conveying the officers' baggage. On the order being given for marching, the troops were formed fours deep, and so proceeded a short distance, but ultimately fell into single file, as the narrow path would not permit two to walk abreast without being retarded considerably by fern and tea-tree.

Jackson's company of Forest Rangers soon moved to the front, keeping a short distance in advance of the first imperial troops. The correspondent continues:

> The [return] route to Whatawhata was traversed for some distance, until a

Tuhikaramea, near the Waipa River, January 1864. *Spencer Collection, Hawke's Bay Museum*

track running eastward and in the direction of Pikopiko was struck, when this road was taken. At the junction of the two tracks 291 men of the 12th from Whatawhata joined the force, also 40 mounted artillery [Lieutenant Rait's men], 50 of the Colonial Defence Force, and 25 Cavalry Volunteers under command of Colonel Nixon.
Von Tempsky's company of Forest Rangers did not join here, being detained as an escort for the three 12-pounder Armstrong guns to be brought from Whatawhata.
The force followed the Maori track along high ground and occasionally glimpsed the distant enemy positions around Pikopiko where three Maori flags could be seen flying.

Von Tempsky, escorting the Armstrong guns, remembered the proceedings of the same day in his writings:

> On the 27th January, 1864, the two columns from Tuhikaramea and Whatawhata started on the main road to Pikopiko. For miles and miles now there was an unbroken stream of soldiers, bullock-drays, artillery, packhorses and orderlies meandering over the plains and fern ridges of the sacred Maori delta [land caught between the Waikato and Waipa Rivers]. Yellow clouds of dust hovered along our road, to the great disparagement of our faces, sight, and clear speech.
> We had the special honour to escort on the first day some Armstrong guns dragged by bullocks. On a low backed ridge of considerable width, near a deserted village, the army encamped under their blanket tents. I saw Jackson's blue-blanket tents [No. 1 Company] in the Tuhikaramea column. We [No. 2 Company] discarded even that trouble and slept in the fern, in the line of battle, at the most exposed flank, opposite the bush.

There would not be much "special honour" in escorting slow bullock-drawn guns, especially for von Tempsky, who would rather be at the front of the column. Maybe it was a case of "last in, last out".
The sleeping arrangement clearly illustrates von Tempsky's urgency to get into battle before anyone else. By sleeping on the edge of camp, close to bush where Maori may have been lurking, they would be the first into action and possibly first to be heroes. Jackson on the other hand probably read the Maori's intentions better and decided that any pending actions were still to the front of the column. Von Tempsky continues:

> On the following morning [28 January] we sighted Pikopiko, and one's heart began to beat as soon as the General [Cameron] began to mass his troops in columns before the Maori stronghold [Paterangi].
> There they lay. No despicable object even in the eyes of the greatest ignoramus of works of defence. There were the Maoris – at least their black heads visible on the parapet; here and there sentries walking on the parapet, and again, some fellows dancing on it and waving to us and shouting "Come on!"

Falling back from pa to pa the Waikato and Ngatimaniapoto Maori at last concentrated their forces in a great series of entrenchments at Pikopiko, Rangiatea

Waipa River. This photograph clearly illustrates the open country covered with fern, grass and scattered clumps of mature kahikatea. January 1864.
Spencer Collection. Hawke's Bay Museum

March to the front 53

and Paterangi – all protecting the fertile land and villages around Rangiaowhia. The major fortification was at Paterangi with its elaborate system of earthworks. The Maori had predicted the main line of Cameron's advance from Ngaruawahia to Rangiaowhia was down the east bank of the Waipa River – all other routes being hampered by swamps.

General Cameron had seen service in the Crimea War. His concept of battle tactics differ little from those used in the Crimea and even earlier at Waterloo in 1815. He still believed in the square formation and massed attack in conventional lines. He could relate only to open ground where artillery and rifle fire had clear fields of fire. So as soon as he came up against the Maori and the New Zealand jungle-like bush he was at a distinct disadvantage.

Governor Grey was much annoyed at what he considered unnecessary delay, and pressed Cameron to assault Paterangi immediately. Cameron refused. The Governor became more urgent and finally ordered Cameron to make the assault. Cameron bluntly told Grey to "go to hell". According to witnesses present, these were the exact words, and they had a deeper meaning in 1864 than at present. This is the first noticeable rift in the relationship between the two.

For more than an hour the battle-ready soldiers were kept in suspense awaiting orders from Cameron. With Rangiriri still fresh in his mind, Cameron showed some intuition and plain old common sense.

Von Tempsky continues:

> Our suspense was broken at last by the columns filing away to the west, past Pikopiko, towards the Waipa, and this night we camped unmolested near Te Rore. Our encampment extended nearly a mile from the banks of the Waipa to the hills opposite Paterangi. The headquarters were pitched in a grove of fruit trees on an eminence isolated by gullies on three sides, and at the foot of it the two companies of Forest Rangers were ordered to pitch their camp [entrusted to be the General's personal bodyguard].
> We also had charge of a picket guarding the entrance to a valley on the Waipa where all the commissariat stores and munitions of war were kept.
> We were, moreover, to be ever ready to move at any one point, be it night or be it day; we felt proud of this kind of honour, and to the last man in the two companies our alertness was never found deficient.

Daily life could be observed in the Maori stronghold on Paterangi from the advanced post. A small battery of three Armstrong guns fired occasional rounds into the pa to keep the Maori on guard and guessing, while snipers fired into the earthworks from another advanced post.

The Forest Rangers were occupied stockpiling supplies, scouting and fern burning. Parties of Forest Rangers were constantly roaming the surrounding district in anticipation of meeting hostile Maori and gathering important intelligence for Cameron's command. They had a standing order to proceed along both banks of the Waipa River for some distance to meet the steamers as they arrived, to prevent hostile Maori firing upon the vessels from the banks where the river narrows.

Maori gathered in ambush one day where the Mangaotama Stream enters the Waipa. But as the Forest Rangers moved into the open to skirt a swamp, Maori

Te Rore camp west of Paterangi, above the Waipa River. Late January 1864. Spencer Collection, Hawke's Bay Museum

signallers in the Pikopiko defences spotted them and fired guns as a warning to the waiting ambush.

A party of Forest Rangers spent a day in the bush on the Pirongia mountain foothills, having started about midnight on Tuesday, 2 February, and returning late Wednesday afternoon. They discovered many Maori tracks leading between the Waipa River and the mountain.

Another party of Forest Rangers were fortunate to discover, during one of their excursions, a large Maori canoe which had been concealed up a small creek, a few miles from camp. A quantity of stolen potatoes and peaches from Maori cultivations was placed in the bottom as ballast and the Forest Rangers then paddled down the river with their prize to a tumultuous reception at camp.

Scarcely a day passed in camp at Te Rore that the Maori did not attempt to shoot soldiers and others who had ventured a short distance from camp on foraging expeditions. On Friday night, 5 February, the Forest Rangers turned out about midnight and fired several volleys at a number of Maori who ventured somewhat close to the sentinels.

While out scouting for cattle for the commissariat department one day, a group of 11 No. 2 Company Forest Rangers under Sergeant Henry Carran were surprised by a Maori patrol near a swamp to the east of Te Rore. William Race writes of the incident:

> ... some dozen were out cattle hunting and no officer with them, when some 100 Maoris surrounded the Rangers in a swamp. One whare happened to be there, and the flax being high [nearby]. Under the directions of the sergeant they all made for it, and determined to sell their lives dearly. Plenty of ammunition they had but none thought of escaping. One of the men was on horseback and he was told to ride for his life to the camp [at Te Rore] some four miles off for assistance. The Maoris fired at the horseman and saving, as was discovered afterwards, his horse's ear was shot through, escaped to camp.
> In the meantime not knowing how the rider had fared, the little party of 10 hoped to hold out in the whare till succour arrived. The door was barricaded as best it could, on came the Maoris dancing and whooping preparatory to finishing them off. About 100 yards distant they stopped to perform a war dance. It was then that the sergeant proved his superiority to the best in that dilemma.
> They were surrounded by tall flax, and said the sergeant "Our only chance is to clear out at the back and hope to get away unseen, it is our only chance." And while they [the Maori] were in a state of excitement in consequence of their being sure the Rangers were caught in a trap, they [the Forest Rangers] with their bowie knives soon forced a hole into the raupo sides [of the whare] and one by one got out and under the cover of the thick flax actually passed the Maoris [within] about 30 yards (for their route home was in that direction) unnoticed. ... after crossing a river about four feet deep some two miles from the whare, they [entered camp].

They received a hero's welcome on entering camp. Ensign Roberts embraced each in turn, showing his great affection for his men.

Construction commenced on a redoubt some half a mile from camp and went on for some weeks. The soldiers occupied themselves with games and sports under the hot sun. Fruit was found in abundance, especially by the Forest Rangers who often left camp on patrol leaving the imperials behind.

William Race relates the pleasures of camp life:

> In the meantime much mirth was to be found on the level banks of the river, such as improvised cricket matches between the Blue Jackets [Royal Navy sailors] and a scratch team of mounted men and Forest Rangers, also athletic games in which the officers of each corps heartily joined in. No other duty was ours except reconnoitring expeditions into the surrounding locality, and as it was the season for water melons and peaches, we were indeed welcomed on our returning for the luscious fruit we brought with us.

On one of these fruit gathering forays while reconnoitring, a detachment of the No. 2 Company Forest Rangers met with trouble from a group of Maori who were also on patrol. William Race, who happened to be present, relates the episode:

> I remember one sultry afternoon we had secured a considerable lot of peaches, so many that we all took off our shirts (ten of us) and tied them with the sleeves into a fair sized bundle; von Tempsky too, for he was with us that day.
> We had discovered a peach grove un-gathered, close to a bend of the [Waipa] river, and being as I have stated a sultry day, after securing the fruit thought we would have a bathe to wash off some of the dust, and whilst sporting in the water a sentry, that was previously posted (catch our captain forgetting such precaution!), sang out "Quick, the Maoris are on us!" And sure enough, some 300 yards off, about 50 of the beggars were coming as fast as they could, whooping and evidently making sure of us.
> Fortunately for us the river at this bend was not very wide, some two chains. Immediately Von realised the position and said "Across the river boys as fast as we can, take your clothes if possible but make sure of your revolvers". For we mostly only carried them when on short expeditions and also only those that could swim went.
> There was to be seen a hurry skurry. We managed to tie our clothes in bundles and sling them around our necks, falling or resting on our backs, and the belt and revolver resting on each bundle in the same way. Even two or three men took over their bundle of peaches.
> Von Tempsky took some peaches, and one man in the water had to let go his, it was too near choking him. The actual swimming was only 15 yards as the approaches on each side of the river ran out some distance with not more than four or five feet [of water]. But before we had crossed the river, the Maoris had reached the spot we left and fired a few shots or rather slugs at us, but as they generally fired from the hip, [the shots] passed too high to hurt.
> We turned back for a moment to look at them, but saw only a huddled mass of dark nakedness gesticulating and shouting at us. We lost no time in getting under cover on the other side and, making a detour, crossed the river again

at a shallow spot, reaching camp at dusk, minus only five or six shirts but a good many beautiful ripe peaches.

Von Tempsky was obviously very cautious about who went on patrols, requiring that they all could swim. He also saw the advantage of travelling light with no carbines and accessories, although ten Forest Rangers could have made a good show with their quick loading carbines against 50 Maori. Von Tempsky was lucky not to come under too much pressure with the Maori whooping and rushing at them rather than keeping concealed until within rifle range.

In Te Rore camp, von Tempsky, tired of waiting for action, decided to create some of his own. He took a select group from his unit and proceeded to a forward position before Paterangi to sketch. Von Tempsky describes what happened:

> I had a great desire to make a sketch of Paterangi, so, getting leave from the General [which seems surprising or maybe Cameron wished to gift the sketch to his superiors to illustrate the formidable nature of Paterangi and exonerate him for his procrastination], I took five men with me and started. I had chosen five of my best shots to keep heads below the parapet while I made my sketch, and I had also chosen them from amongst the new men to see what effect the whistle of a bullet would have upon them.
> I passed the picket hill, and leaving my men with Roberts in some fern, I advanced to see how far the Maori sharpshooters would allow me to come. An Enfield bullet striking the ground at my feet soon convinced me that I was far enough.

While he was sketching, more Enfield bullets gradually closed on him, forcing him to move to the left. While the men fired away from behind, von Tempsky soon completed the sketch he intended gifting to Cameron. This wanton display of courage is little more than stupidity; at any moment von Tempsky could have been killed, the colonial forces losing a valuable officer. One wonders if von Tempsky was convinced of his immortality – he, a conceited Prussian could not be struck down by a "savage's" bullet! Did he see himself above all other officers in the field? It was this arrogance and total disregard for danger that eventually did cause his death at Te Ngutu o te Manu in September 1868.

Cameron and his army stayed at Te Rore for several weeks. He had no intention of mounting a frontal attack on Paterangi as the cost in lives would be too high.

CHAPTER 7

Ambush on the Mangapiko

While at Te Rore Cameron's force was involved in an engagement along the banks of the Mangapiko Stream, a short distance northeast from present day Pirongia.

About one mile south of the fortifications on Paterangi, the Mangapiko Stream, which flows west to the Waipa, doubles back and forms a loop pointing to the north. At the "neck" of this loop is an ancient Maori earthwork fortification called Waiari, comprised of three large parapets with ditches, which were overgrown with thick manuka and fern.

The loop is quite large encompassing about 18 acres. Each parapet runs from side to side across the "neck" of the loop at right angles to the river. The river banks around the "neck" are steep, dropping about 50 feet to the water. Today the three parapets are still well formed with the southernmost being the highest, measuring about 20 feet from its base in the neighbouring ditch to the top of the parapet. The three parapets are spaced at about 80 yard intervals and 100 yards further north is a 25 foot natural bluff which divides the loop. North of this bluff, within the loop, is a river flat which gently slopes away to the river on all three sides.

The three ditches have been partially filled in to provide a modern farm track access to the loop which is now in pasture. The whole land mass forms a formidable, natural fortress, well chosen by pre-European Maori.

Just upstream from this loop the stream is narrow and a Maori-constructed bridge of a tree trunk cut flat on top crossed where the banks are about fifteen feet apart. At the northern end of the loop was a swimming hole frequented by parties of soldiers on the hot summer days. On 11 February 1864 one such bathing party from the 40th Regiment arrived from the camp in front of Paterangi for a mid-afternoon swim.

Meanwhile a Maori raiding party, concealing themselves in the undergrowth near Waiari in preparation for a night attack on Colonel Waddy's advance camp that evening, were surprised to see an under-protected swimming party approach them. They could not resist the temptation of firing on the bathers and the small detachment of covering soldiers. The sound of shooting soon brought reinforcements from the 40th and 50th Regiments' camp along with Captains Jackson and Charles Heaphy (Auckland Rifle Volunteers). Jackson immediately skirmished with his revolver in and beside the river at the northern end of the loop before sending for von Tempsky and the Forest Rangers at the more distant camp at Te Rore, about two miles away. The rest of the Forest Rangers under Ensigns Westrup and Roberts (about 40 men) were on duty burning fern on the outer perimeters of the camps in the direction of Mount Pirongia.

William Race recalls the news coming into camp:

> Like wildfire the news spread through the camp. "The 40th are attacked in the ravine by scores of Maoris and the soldiers are frightened to go down to them," are almost the exact words that our Captain [von Tempsky] said as

he came running down to our lines, he happening to be in the quarters of the imperial troops at the time [as usual], which was some chain or so from our position on the low bank of the Te Rore River. Hastily putting on his sword and revolver, singing out at the same time "Come on some volunteers", he and a score of them departed quickly to the scene of the fight.

Colonel Havelock was directing operations and soon ordered the arriving Forest Rangers along the west side of the loop to a position opposite Waiari pa. Here they were ordered to cross the river and clear Maori hidden in the overgrown breastworks of the old fortification.

Von Tempsky noted:

> A ditch of the breastwork of an ancient pa sloped down to the river. It was densely covered with scrub, as well as the bank of the river. My men bounded down into it like tigers. On our hands and knees we had to creep, revolver in hand, looking for our visible foes. The thumping of double-barrel guns around us announced soon that we were in the midst of the nest. I had in all about thirty men. Some were stationed on the top of the bank, others in the very river, and the rest crawling through the scrub. There were strange meetings in that scrub. Muzzle to muzzle, the shot of despair, the repeating cracks of revolvers and carbine thuds, and the brown bodies of Maoris made their appearance gradually, either rolling down the hill or being dragged out of the scrub.

In one instance, a Forest Ranger carbine, after being discharged, proved of eminent service in knocking down an advancing Maori. The stock was broken away from the barrel by the force of the blow.

The ancient fortification was cleared in the late afternoon, and the soldiers returning to their respective camps. The retreat was orderly with the Forest Rangers covering the rear.

Lieutenant-Colonel Havelock stated in his report of the Waiari engagement to Colonel R. Waddy, commanding the advance camp near Paterangi:

> ... about 2:30 pm, on an alarm that a bathing party had been suddenly fired on from an ambush by apparently 100 Maoris detached from the Paterangi pa, the inlaying pickets of 40th and 50th Regiments, at this camp, turned out promptly, and hastened to the scene, being reinforced immediately by parties of both regiments as fast as the men could seize their arms.
> The Maoris retired along the left bank, and a sharp running fight soon commenced between them and the foremost pursuers.
> Finding themselves so readily met, they took post, while endeavouring to gain their pa, on the site of an ancient entrenchment called Waiari, where the high mounts and deep ditches of an old fortification, densely overgrown with thick cover, gave them, together with their intimate knowledge of the ground, great advantage.
> On reaching the level plain under Paterangi, after crossing the Takoutu Stream, I found that the pursuit and fight had gone to my right. But as there were threats of large bodies sallying out to cut off those of our men whose eagerness had carried them farthest to the front, I collected every available

WAIARI ENGAGEMENT *11 February 1864*

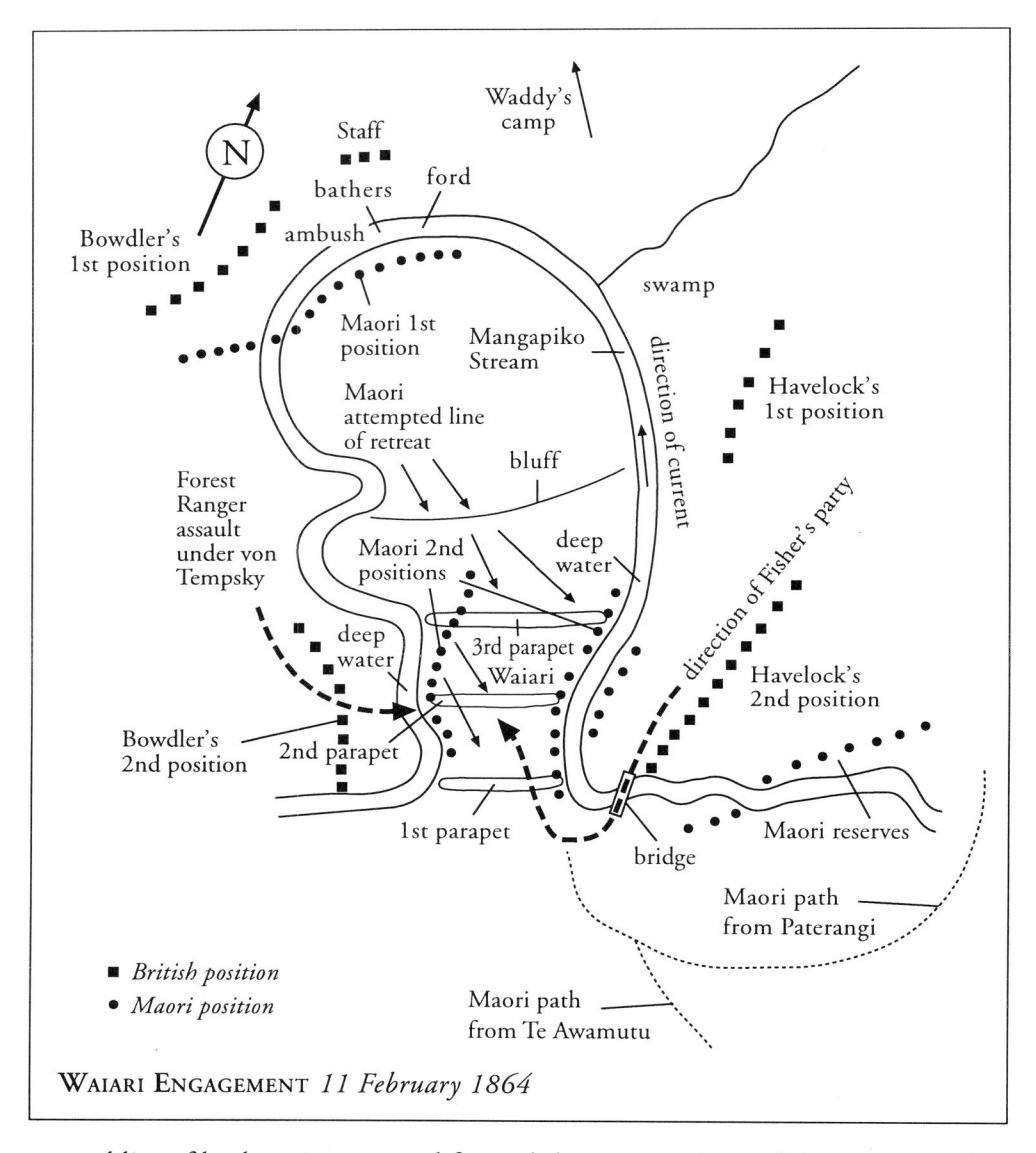

soldier of both regiments, and formed them up in chain of skirmishers and supports to watch this flank.

Soon after, a considerable party under Captain Trench, 40th [Regiment], having assured our left and rear, I moved rapidly down to where our leading men were hotly engaged and pressed. They were commanded by Captain Fisher, 40th, who had hastened here earlier with a few men.

Captain Heaphy, Auckland Rifle Volunteers, and Captain Jackson, Forest Rangers (both accidentally on the spot), had lent their services, and reinforced him with some 30 men of the 40th and 50th.

These parties, that which myself brought up, and one under Ensign King, 40th, united, had now the happiness to come full on the main body of the Maoris, retiring towards Paterangi. We turned them back to the shelter of the ancient earthwork above mentioned, which is singularly placed in a double loop of the Mangapiko [Stream].

Major Bowdler's party of 40th, who had moved down the right bank, were firing on the front of the Maoris from across the river. Our arrival on their rear effectually hemmed them in, and sealed their fate.

After much hot firing we were able to dash across the river into the entrenchment, over a bridge formed of a single plank [flattened tree trunk]. The banks are here from 40 to 60 feet high, precipitous, and densely wooded. A series of hand to hand encounters here took place, between the Maoris crouching secreted in thick bush, and our men, who displayed, if anything too keen an eagerness to dash at and close with their lurking enemies whenever visible. This forwardness cost some valuable lives, but the punishment inflicted on the Maoris was sharp and telling, and read them a severe lesson. At the time some 20 men of the Forest Rangers (both companies) arriving from the head-quarter camp, materially assisted in hunting out and destroying the enemy.

Eventually, every Maori that could be discovered being either killed or wounded or made prisoner, the work of removing our wounded (most difficult from the narrowness of the planked bridge) and of securing their dead commenced.

Two large parties [reserves] of the enemy now approaching through thick bush, endeavoured to intercept this. It became necessary to throw Captain Fisher's party, with which were Lieutenant Simeon and Ensign King, again on the right bank, where they most steadily covered this operation under a sharp crossfire.

Finally, near dark, all our wounded having been removed, and as many as possible of the Maori dead brought in, the skirmishers were gradually withdrawn, file by file, across the plank bridge, and the troops moved slowly, taking every advantage of ground, towards camp.

This very successful affair cost the Maoris 28 men killed (counted), and two wounded prisoners in our hands. Both these are said to be chiefs. Our loss was five killed and six wounded (one since dead).

Indeed this unintentional engagement on behalf of the imperial soldiers proved a deterrent to the Maori for future ambushes. Although the swimming party had bathed in close proximity to dense bush with an obviously inadequate picket, they fared well as a consequence. Once again the Maori overloaded their firearms with powder and fired high, minimizing casualties amongst the imperial soldiers.

The action was a great boost to British morale in the forces camped before Paterangi, as they hadn't a victory for some time, having lost many lives at Rangiriri on 20 November 1863. The imperial soldiers again displayed their unwillingness to penetrate dense bush to engage the enemy, leaving this task to the experienced, bush fighting Forest Rangers.

Because of the bravery shown by Captain Charles Heaphy (Auckland Rifle

Von Tempsky watercolour depicting Forest Rangers engaging Maori at Waiari, 11 February 1864. Von Tempsky can be seen giving orders with sword in hand.
Auckland Institute and Museum

Volunteer and Staff Surveyor) in this action, he received the Victoria Cross, the only Victoria Cross awarded to a colonial soldier in the New Zealand Wars. Early in the action, Heaphy, while trying to rescue a wounded soldier, received a volley from very close range – five bullets grazing and contusing him.

The British suffered six dead and five wounded while the Maori suffered 41 dead and about 30 wounded. The Forest Rangers are believed to have killed at least eight enemy, collecting their bodies and returning them to camp. Two Forest Rangers received injuries; one was wounded in the eye and the other received a flesh wound on the hip.

Both Jackson and von Tempsky are mentioned in Havelock's report:

> Captain Jackson, Forest Rangers, gave great assistance; and Captain von Tempsky, when I directed him to relieve the soldiers, who had been skirmishing for hours, covered the extreme rear of our march with much coolness and judgement.

Von Tempsky and ten of his men covered the rear of the stretcher parties while crossing the Mangapiko Stream at dusk, being the last to retire. With them was Charles Heaphy. Still a few desultory shots came from the Maori with one ball passing between the rear Forest Rangers and striking a man of the 40th Regiment further up front in the wrist.

A corporal of No. 1 Company, Forest Rangers, recalled many years later the ire of Lieutenant-Colonel Havelock at the inattention displayed by the Forest Rangers to bugle calls at Waiari:

> It was getting dusk and still all our Rangers had not come out of the scrub, and we could hear their carbines cracking in reply to the heavy banging of the double-barrel guns. Captain Jackson was standing alongside Colonel Havelock, A.D.C. – the son of the famous hero of the Indian mutiny – who asked why the Rangers had not returned. Jackson replied in his blunt fashion that he didn't know; he supposed they'd come out when they had finished their job. The "retire" was sounded again, but still our fellows kept popping away in the dusk. At last, Colonel Havelock, swearing that he would turn out the 40th Regiment and fire on the Rangers if they did not obey orders, called up all the buglers that could be found and told them to sound the "retire" all together. Presently our boys came out of the manuka and joined us, as pleased as kings with their afternoon's hot work.

This quote illustrates the subtle defiance and insolence of the Forest Rangers towards imperial officers. They seemed to take great delight in extracting pompous reactions from their imperial counterparts. But although they dressed roughly and performed camp duties casually, they were well respected in action both by the enemy and the imperial soldiers.

Captain Jackson in a report to Captain J.D. Baker, Acting Assistant Military Secretary, wrote:

> Camp Te Rore, February 12th, 1864.
> Sir, In accordance with instructions, I have the honour to report, for the information of the Lieutenant-General commanding, that yesterday morning,

in company with Captain Heaphy, I started to look at the enemy's position at Paterangi [old abandoned pa]; that, whilst in Lieutenant-Colonel Havelock's tent, we heard some heavy firing on the Mangapiko [Stream]. We immediately proceeded to the scene, and I led a party of soldiers to the rear of the enemy [along the east side of the loop towards the bridge], and thus cut off their retreat. Whilst there we shot several natives. Some of them drifted down the river, and three I pulled on shore. One of the natives snapped both his barrels at me, and I shot him with my revolver, took his gun [kept by Jackson as a trophy], and brought him across the river. Whilst there, I noticed several natives concealed in the thick scrub on the edge of the river, and thought that a few of the Forest Rangers would be useful in driving them out of it. I therefore, with the permission of the Lieutenant-General, sent for all who were in camp, about thirty-five, and they arrived about four or five o'clock pm, under the command of Captain von Tempsky. I took them [through Bowdler's position] to the place where the enemy were concealed, and instructed them to go down and search for the natives, which they did, and in about ten or fifteen minutes they brought up five natives, whom they had killed, and two who were wounded. The wounded were carried to the nearest camp.
William Jackson,
Captain Commanding Forest Rangers.

Captain von Tempsky in a report to Captain J.D. Baker, Acting Assistant Military Secretary, stated:

Camp Te Rore, February 12th, 1864.
Sir, I have the honour to report, for the information of the Lieutenant-General commanding the Forces, that on the 11th instant, at three pm, an orderly arrived in camp with orders for the Forest Rangers to proceed immediately to the front. Forty men of the two companies being absent on duty (burning fern), and Captain Jackson being at the front already, I proceeded with 35 men of both companies to the scene of action on the Mangapiko creek. On arriving at the extreme right flank of our position, I met Captain Jackson, who informed me that there were natives in a thicket on the river bank [forward of Bowdler's position]. Colonel Havelock then ordered me to dislodge these natives. My men, with promptitude, surrounded the thicket, and entering the same, revolvers in hand, extracted in a short time seven natives which they had killed at close quarters, after a good deal of a resisting fire from those same natives. We carried seven bodies up to the bank, laying them in a heap. Two of the same number, showing signs of life, were carried to our nearest redoubt, one of them dying on the road; the latter was laid with nine bodies brought in previously by the regulars. My men behaved with coolness, judgement, and alacrity, particularly in covering the orderly retreat of the forces.
G.F. von Tempsky
Captain Forest Rangers, No. 2 Company.

The above report demonstrates vividly the jealousy experienced by von Tempsky towards Jackson and to superior rank. He claims the Forest Rangers collectively as "my men" cutting out any authority of Jackson's – especially as the Forest Rangers present were a mixture from both companies. Von Tempsky mentions his orders before Waiari came from Havelock, when they actually came from Jackson. His report went directly to Baker and not via Jackson – any report he made probably should have been addressed and forwarded direct to Jackson. Both Jackson and von Tempsky were captains, but Jackson was commanding officer of both companies of Forest Rangers, as the title at the end of his report indicates. Remember Jackson's commission out-dates von Tempsky's by one day.

Secretly, von Tempsky was certainly out for glory, not wishing to share this with others – a characteristic that first became apparent after Jackson's successful expedition into the Hunua Ranges. Jackson comes across in his report as being humble, careful and correct whereas von Tempsky's writing demonstrates more flourish, excitement and probably arrogance – all characteristics of the man.

Much can be learnt from von Tempsky's watercolour painting of the engagement (shown on page 62). The patches of low bush and scrub that hid the Maori seem to be confined to the river banks with the tops covered with grass and low fern. The parapet with ditch shown is the southernmost of the three because of its height. Since the ditch is shown to the right of the parapet, von Tempsky depicted his painting from the west side (forward of Bowdler's position) looking toward the east, as the ditches today are found on the south side of each parapet. Forest Rangers can be seen carrying Maori corpses up the ditch to another corpse guarded near the top. From here they were carried to the far side, across the log bridge and into camp. As the action took place during the height of summer, the water level is low allowing the Forest Ranger at the front to stand in the river. Some men are shown on the tops with their carbines at the ready, obviously looking to snipe at targets in the bush and scrub below.

Roll of Forest Rangers at time of Waiari engagement, 11 February 1864:

Jackson's No. 1 Company: *Captain* (1): William Jackson. *Ensign* (1): Westrup. *Staff Sergeant* (1): Bertram. *Sergeants* (3): Holden, Whitfield, James Williams. *Corporals* (3): Coghlan, John Smith, William Taylor. *Privates* (44): Alexander, Benson, Black, Robert Bruce, William Bruce, Laurence Burns, Carter, Cole, Costello, Fitzgerald, Gallie, Gibb, Grigg, Haines, Hannah, Hannay, Hendry, Henry Jackson, Johns, Long, McDonald, Madigan, Mahoney, Morgan, Murray, John Nolan, Martin Nolan, Osborne, Peters, Rowden, Rowland, James Smith, Thomas Smith, Stephenson, Temple, William Thomson (different from the William Thomson in No. 2 Company), Thorpe, Thurston, Torpey, Vaughan, George Ward, Watters, Wells, William Williams.

Von Tempsky's No. 2 Company: *Captain* (1): von Tempsky. *Ensign* (1): Roberts. *Staff Sergeant* (1): Sherret. *Sergeants* (3): Carran, Southey, Wakeford. *Corporals* (3): McMinn, McNamara, Sibley. *Privates* (45): Albin, Anderson, Ballenden, Bidgood, Bochow, Burry, Butter, Buttle, Bygum, Clifford, Cochrane, Collins, Donovan, Fallon, Freeman, Harris, Hartland, Healas, Hellkessel, Higgins, Jones, Keena, Liebig, Lindsay, McClymont, Magole, Mohr, Mulligan, Neil, Parsons, Pohlen, Race, Ross, Scally, Shine, Simmons, Stanley, Sturmer, Sumsion, James Taylor, William Thomson (different from the William Thomson in No. 1 Company), Toovey, Tubby, Wheeler, Woods.

Paterangi pa after it was evacuated. This major earthwork was bypassed by the British force. February 1864. Spencer Collection, Hawke's Bay Museum

Charles Westrup (No. 1 Company) was promoted from Ensign to Lieutenant dated 11 February 1864, the day of the action at Waiari.

Robert Whitfield (No. 1 Company) was commissioned as Ensign dated 18 February 1864.

After the Waiari engagement and before the rush for Rangiaowhia (20 February), a night attack was planned on the Paterangi fortifications. The redoubt was almost completed and convoys could still be seen supplying the Maori positions.

General Cameron knew that the Maori vacated the rifle pits attached to the pa at night and slept in the safety of the pa proper. Von Tempsky seized upon this opportunity to create some action and, after consultation with Cameron, decided on a plan of surprising the Maori at night by the Forest Rangers taking possession of the rifle pits. Then, after a signal, Cameron would follow up with a body of soldiers.

Von Tempsky used all his available men from No. 2 Company. Jackson was in Auckland at the time so von Tempsky decided to take along those he considered the best of Jackson's No. 1 Company. This obviously met with some grievance in the No. 1 Company as all that company were hand-picked by Jackson and probably all should have been involved.

So one night at about 9 pm the select group of Forest Rangers left camp fully equipped. It was a very dark night as they moved out in single file under order of strict silence. They followed a native road, and at about 200 yards from the pa von Tempsky halted and divided the men – half to the left side of the road and half to the right. He moved along the lines telling the men to be ready for a low whistle, the command to fall quietly into single file again when they reached the steeper climb. They all had their revolvers at the ready in case of immediate contact with the Maori.

William Race writes of what happened next:

> On we marched or rather stole stealthily up the sides very quietly, we had ascended about some ten yards when bang went a shot, not from the enemy but from one of us, and we knew it too, as well as our commander. He thundered angrily out:
> "Get under cover of the fern and out of the way of the Maori guns!"
> We did not want telling twice, every one then for himself. We knew too well our plan was spoilt for us and discovered to the enemy, and in less than a minute a Forest Ranger was not to be seen.
> ... there was nothing to be seen but fern, even if it had been daylight. Several shots were fired in our direction from the pits but had no effect.

The untimely shot was possibly a good omen, for the outer rifle pits were occupied, though it was not known by how many, and the whole affair could have been a massacre. The men in No. 2 Company were quick to point the finger at Jackson's men as being responsible for the shot. William Race continues:

> Two things we were the wiser that night. First and most important to us was that the Maoris slept or rather kept [watch] in their pits, second that it was one of Jackson's corps [who] fired the shot. Supposed to have been jealousy on that company's part owing to their officer not being there to reap the

Forest Rangers

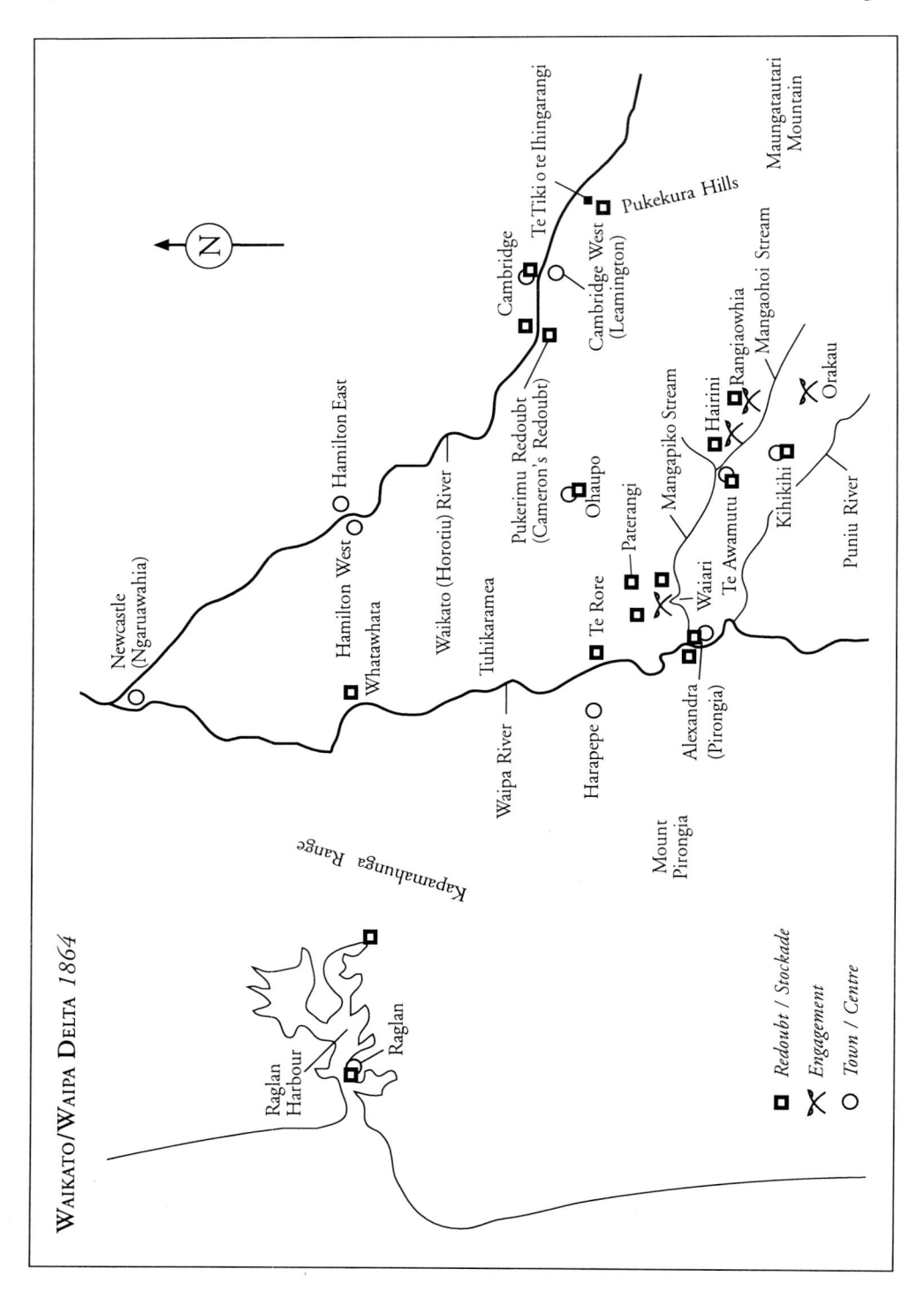

Waikato/Waipa Delta 1864

- ■ Redoubt / Stockade
- ✗ Engagement
- ○ Town / Centre

honour of success had it been obtained.
... but for that shot we should have walked into the Maoris' arms.

William Race may have missed the point about the reason for the jealousy. Jackson's men, if they deliberately fired the shot, probably had had enough of von Tempsky's self importance and arrogance and decided to ruin his clever plan. If Jackson was present, would he have seen problems with the plan from the start and never accepted the fact that the rifle pits were empty? Whatever the reason, it is obvious that jealousy was rampant between the two companies.

CHAPTER 8

Barbarity at Rangiaowhia

After the tragic loss of life at the taking of the position at Rangiriri, General Cameron was reluctant to storm any further pa by a frontal attack. He believed that if the Maori pa at Paterangi and Pikopiko were bypassed and the source of food at Rangiaowhia was captured, then the two fortresses might fall without a fight. Having procured guides, Cameron decided on a night march. Preparations were made and a large force of over 1200 men – both on horse and foot – left Te Rore on the Saturday evening of 20 February 1864 after darkness had fallen. The rest of the force was to follow with the luggage the next day.

The strictest silence was enforced as they moved off parade with the General commanding in person. No bugle had sounded, the tents remained standing, and the cover of the moonless night was perfect for a night march.

Von Tempsky led the advance guard, composed of No. 2 Company, Forest Rangers, and 100 men of the 65th Regiment under Lieutenant Tabuteau. Next came the Colonial Defence Force Cavalry under Colonel Nixon and the Mounted Artillery under Lieutenant Rait. The rest of the 65th, 70th and 50th Regiments followed. Lieutenant Westrup with No. 1 Company, Forest Rangers, formed the rear guard. Captain Jackson had recently gone to Auckland and had not yet returned.

The road to Waiari allowed the men to march in fours; from there the column moved in single file. Once past the redoubt at Waiari, the column crossed fern ridges in the direction of Te Awamutu. The high fern had to be trodden down by the advance guard. James Edwards, a half-caste guide, rode ahead with Captain Greaves of the 70th Regiment. Edwards' loyalties to the unit were a bit dubious, as he had relatives at Rangiaowhia.

It was not known whether the old pa of Otawhao, closer to Te Awamutu, was occupied. The Forest Rangers scouted on ahead but found it empty. By now they could hear the cocks crowing in Te Awamutu, and the steeple of the church came into sight.

The sun rose on a glorious morning as they reached the village of Te Awamutu. It was Sunday 21 February 1864. The Colonial Defence Cavalry was ordered to the front and after passing the mission station at Te Awamutu, the order was given to advance and capture the village of Rangiaowhia, two miles ahead. "Forward! Trot!" was the order. Major Nixon rode near the front as the cavalry approached the village. By this time all the men on foot had fallen behind.

As they approached Rangiaowhia the route became easier. There was an extensive cultivated area on which the Ngati-Apakura and Ngati-Hinetu people grew potatoes, wheat and maize. Provisions of kumara, potatoes, cooked pigs and chickens for the garrisons at Paterangi and Pikopiko lay within the village.

On sighting the village, Nixon ordered "Charge!" The troopers galloped ahead. A few natives rushed out of whare firing on the attackers. The cavalry pursued them over the kumara and corn plantations.

Captain Wilson of the Colonial Defence Force later wrote:

> I mention that in the pursuit, before the whare was attacked, the Maoris,

men and women, were jumbled together, running away, and being dressed much alike, the women were in great danger of being killed, and as I had command of the advanced guard, I called to the women, telling them to sit down, "E kotou, e nga wahine a noho ki raro, kei mate kotou." They obeyed, and when we passed them they then got up and ran on.

By this time the first foot soldiers had arrived. Von Tempsky narrated:

Kahikatea forest straggled up to the village, here and there, and when we approached it nearer a succession of ridges with some swamp intervening showed us that we had been somewhat deceived in the distance.
The rapid crack, crack of revolvers and carbines announced to us now that the troopers [Colonial Defence Cavalry followed by Rait's Mounted Artillery] had not forgotten their spurs in getting ahead of us. We listened eagerly for the sound of double-barrel guns, and that sound also was soon heard.

The Forest Rangers got to the engagement considerably ahead of the main body – mainly because of von Tempsky's eagerness to engage the enemy. A mounted civilian with some of the artillery troopers met von Tempsky and said that there was nothing for the Forest Rangers to do in the forward direction and that they should proceed to the Catholic church which was believed to be crammed with armed Maori.

The Forest Rangers with about 100 men of the 65th Regiment in support, moved forward in extended order, past several rows of deserted whare from which an occasional shot came past them. They continued on to the church crowning the mound at the north end of the village, ignoring the whare en route.

On reaching the church, von Tempsky ordered Lieutenant Roberts round the right flank of the church and the encirclement was completed slowly.

Maori could be seen at the windows and soon a white flag was shown.

Von Tempsky recounted:

"Very well, lads," I thought, "then I shall take you prisoner." We advanced still nearer. Roberts' signal announced to me that the church was surrounded, when I heard Captain Greaves' voice calling to me from the rear:
"The General does not want you to press the Maoris any further."
"Not take them prisoner, even?"
"No."
I obeyed, though I was fast consuming my tongue by merciless mastication. But this is due to the order of a man like General Cameron, so I ordered my men off and marched to where the firing continued.

It is possible that occupants of the church were mainly women, children and elderly men.

William Race's description of the episode is different, saying that von Tempsky at first (when approached by Captain Greaves while still some distance from the church) ignored Captain Greaves' orders to "right about turn and leave the rebels alone" and then proceeded up close to the church. William Race writes:

… then our Captain [von Tempsky] halted us a moment and said "Loose your revolvers and be in readiness for the double," which meant to rush

them with cocked revolvers before they could get in the open to attack us. Just as those orders were to have been carried out, up gallops furiously the Captain [Greaves] again and in angry tones expressed these very words to our chief "It is the imperative orders of General Cameron you report immediately, and leave these Maoris alone Sir."
Von on receiving those orders swung his naked sword from over his shoulder and it stuck in the grass, exclaiming at the same time "I have a good mind never to lift it again for New Zealand!"
… the Maoris came crowding out of the church, some mounting their horses which had been tethered outside and some footing it. But all joined in calling us a cowardly lot of pakehas and come on and fight.
These are all facts as witnessed by myself.

Von Tempsky's account is quite different from William Race's. Obviously von Tempsky was humiliated by the affair and decided to rewrite history in his favour. He would not take too kindly at being called a coward, especially after proving himself quite the opposite in the field. The Maori could not resist the opportunity to mock him with their remarks on leaving the church.

Von Tempsky did not have the patience for some of General Cameron's policies on the treatment of Maori, considering them all the enemy at the scene of an engagement. Cameron's order was probably a reaction to the aftermath of Rangiriri where prisoners were taken and sent to Auckland, causing more concern amongst the Maori than the actual battle. Cameron was probably trying to settle the action with the minimum of aggravation, thinking about the massive task of protecting his drawn out supply lines. He also saw the Waikato campaign as a means for the colonial government to grab fertile Maori land. A rift between Cameron and his colonial officers was now becoming visible.

It is said that von Tempsky insisted on searching the church. When resisted by the Reverend Father Vinay, he blew the door lock with his revolver, only to find that the church sheltered women and children and no Maori warriors. If this is true, then von Tempsky used Cameron's order to cover his tracks.

Von Tempsky continues in his narration:

> The two churches lay more towards the left flank of the village. The firing continued more to our right near the centre of the village. As we approached that point we got a few long-range shots from distant whares, but took no notice of them.
> In passing a boarded house, however, one more like the building of a European than a Maori, two shots were rapidly fired at us from the verandah. I did not believe my eyes when I saw there a woman coolly sitting on the verandah and hiding a still smoking double-barrel [in Maori, tupara] underneath it. She was decently dressed in semi-European style adopted by influential Maoris. She was oldish, and not very fair to look at, particularly as her timeworn features were bent into one concentrated expression of hatred – such a hatred as Johnson revered and you read of occasionally in old plays. I went up to her and had the gun taken away, looking at her all the time, not knowing whether I should laugh or feel pathetic – the coolness, the ugliness, and reckless hatred of this specimen of Maoridom puzzling my choice of

sentiment exceedingly.

Von Tempsky, at the point of warning her, was informed by some passing officers that she had actually fired at them and wounded a man of the 65th Regiment and had already received a warning. The Forest Rangers took her prisoner but soon after let her slip away unnoticed.

As the unit started to move again another couple of shots came from inside the same house. They surrounded the house and as von Tempsky related:

> Just as Roberts got to the back part, another woman burst from its door, and, running with the fleetness of a deer, dropped her gun just in time to have her sex recognised and respected. I was glad that her fleetness saved me from another female responsibility, and proceeded onward.

In the meantime, the mounted men, having done their work, turned about and were taking prisoners as they came along. Their attention was drawn to a whare with a one-on-one struggle beside it. Corporal Thomas Little of the Colonial Defence Force Cavalry was wrestling with a large Maori. Little secured the Maori and Private Edward McHale of the same unit was ordered by Captain Wilson to make prisoners of the men heard talking inside the whare. Six men and a youth were earlier seen to enter the whare. (Little was mortally wounded in his thigh on the following day at Hairini).

McHale entered and was met with two shots fired by the occupants. Wilson, thinking McHale was firing on the Maori, jumped from his horse and entered the doorway clouded with gun smoke. He found McHale's body lying face down, with feet nearest the door. Wilson quickly backed out and ordered the troopers to fire their carbines into the sides of the whare which was built of wooden slabs. The floor was sunken being about two feet below ground level. McHale's two guns and ammunition were taken from his body and used by the occupants.

Soon men from other units arrived, followed by General Cameron and his staff. After the whare was surrounded, Colonel Nixon sent Lieutenant Thomas McDonnell and Ensign William G. Mair (interpreter) to ask the Maori to surrender, assuring them of good treatment. The Maori, probably remembering the prisoners taken at Rangiriri, answered with a volley.

The firing into the whare recommenced, but the occupants were relatively secure because of the sunken floor. A private of the 65th Regiment, Charles Askew, rushed forward to ascertain the fate of the trooper, but his blanket roll on his back became stuck in the door, was subsequently shot in the head (the bullet entered his right eye and passed out behind his left ear).

The firing on the whare intensified, with even the officers firing their pistols. Colonel Nixon stepped from behind a neighbouring whare to fire and was mortally wounded in the chest by a bullet fired from the doorway. Nixon later died on 27 May 1864 at his home in Mangere.

Captain Bower caught up with von Tempsky and his men and informed him that Nixon had been shot. They hurried to the scene and found a circle of soldiers of all regiments surrounding at some distance a nearly solitary whare with a very narrow and low door. In the doorway still lay the body of Private Askew. A constant firing of rifles into the whare was carried on with little regard for crossfire.

Again the occupants were called upon to surrender. After no response, some of the surrounding whare were set alight in the hope that the flames might jump to

British and colonial troops fire into a whare at Rangiaowhia, 21 February 1864. Auckland Public Library

the occupied whare.
Von Tempsky instantly decided on a course of action. He wrote:

> So looking round at my nearest men, I said, "We will rush the whare boys." "Aye! Rush it, Rush it!" was echoed, and with one "Forward!" about a dozen of us were round the door in an instant. Sergeant Carran had got ahead of me, and had poked his head into the low doorway. I stood impatiently behind him, just on one side of the door, thinking that we ought to take the body of the 65th man out of the way first. Carran then drew back his head and said to me: "There is only one dead man inside, sir."
> I could not quite understand this, though I could see that it was pitch black inside, and so Carran might have been mistaken.
> At this moment Corporal [Horatio] Alexander, of the Defence Corps [Colonial Defence Force], had pushed his way between myself and Carran, and, squatting down in the low doorway, commenced to arrange his carbine for taking aim, evidently puzzled by the darkness – I urging him either to make room for us or jump in.
> A double-barrel thunders, discharged from the interior of the house, a bullet knocks through Alexander's brain, and he drops backward. The doorway was now completely chocked with the two bodies. My men dragged away Alexander, and, after firing five shots of my revolver quickly into the corner from which I had heard the last report, I dragged the 65th man out of the door myself. At that moment, also, one of my men got shot in the hip – a fine young fellow, John Ballenden. He staggered forward and dropped, never more to rise, though he lingered for months in hospital.

Von Tempsky now debated the benefits of assault. By now flames were lapping over the nearest whare and were touching the roof of the occupied whare. The occupants must have heard the approaching fire, but still no surrender.

Soon, an old Maori emerged from the whare and quickly approached the surrounding soldiers. He was unarmed and held up his arms in a gesture to surrender. Von Tempsky's account continues:

> "Spare him! Spare him!" is shouted by all the officers and most of the men. But some ruffians – and some men blinded with rage at the loss of comrades, perhaps – fired at the Maori.
> The expression of the Maori's face, his attitude on receiving the first bullet, is now as vivid before my mind's eye as when my heart first sickened over the sight. When the first shots struck him he smiled a sort of sad and disappointed smile; then, bowing his head, and staggering already, he wrapped his blanket over his face, and, receiving his death bullets without a groan, dropped quietly to the ground.

William Race writes of this brutal killing and how a Forest Ranger who was present contradicted an officer and got away with it. But such boldness and straightforward attitude was typical of the Forest Rangers who delighted in bringing an officer down. William Race writes:

> ... he commenced speaking and gesticulating very loudly above the din around, but it was a short lived speak for in less than two minutes he was

British troops (possibly of the 50th Regiment) take in the sun at Rangiaowhia, late February 1864. *Spencer Collection, Hawke's Bay Museum*

riddled with bullets and fell in front of the whare a corpse. Just at this moment up rides Lieutenant St. Hill, one of the General's aide-de-camps and stooping from his saddle bow seized hold of the collar of the jumper of a Forest Ranger. Shaking him roughly he said "You cowardly scoundrel, how dare you shoot an unarmed man like that," he having seen the Ranger let drive with his revolver at the Maori being only a few yards from him.

For answer the Ranger pulled up his sleeve and showed the officer a nasty jagged flesh wound on the arm, received a few minutes before from one of the amazons before captured. Tit for tat, Von's man said "The woman tried to kill me and I tried to kill him, that's all." The lieutenant rode away muttering about having him punished and there it ended.

The flames now caught the roof. After a tense wait another Maori emerged from the door, stood upright, and fired his last two shots at the troops. He died in a hail of answering bullets.

When the whare was near to collapsing, yet another man emerged but was shot down while taking aim at the soldiers.

The charred bodies of seven Maori and McHale were taken from the whare. There were ten defenders originally. McHale was identified only by the buckles on his uniform.

Maori later claimed that the soldiers murdered them at Rangiaowhia, especially the group surrounded in the whare. Officers argued that McHale, who was sent in to take them prisoner, was first to be fired on.

The fact that many officers actually took part in this action, rather than just looking on, indicates their desire to maintain discipline, so minimising Maori casualties.

Bishop Selwyn was present with the British force. After he was spotted very early in the campaign riding with Cameron, many Waikato Maori condemned Selwyn and Christianity, even though his presence in the force was humanitarian. Further, the choice of a Sunday to attack women and children at Rangiaowhia went against Maori missionary teachings.

In the written accounts about Rangiaowhia, discrepancies indicate that some undesirable incidents may have occurred. There may have been more casualties amongst the Maori, and maybe the killing of some women and children. Official accounts are vague and noncommittal as the later official despatch shows. See Cameron's combined report for engagements at Rangiaowhia and Hairini under the chapter titled "Rout at Hairini".

William Race commented of the engagement at Rangiaowhia:

It was magnificent, but it was not war. What could be said of this achievement.

The Maori at Rangiaowhia displayed an indomitable fearlessness of death. They certainly were admired by the troops for their nobleness, spirit and resolve not to become prisoners, preferring death to confinement.

Later, about a dozen whare were burnt with some of the occupants (between 20 and 30) moving north through the village and making a short stand in the Catholic church. The Forest Rangers returned and skirmished with the armed Maori who fired from the windows. The Maori found that the walls were not bullet-proof. After some Forest Rangers and regulars charged the church the occupants made

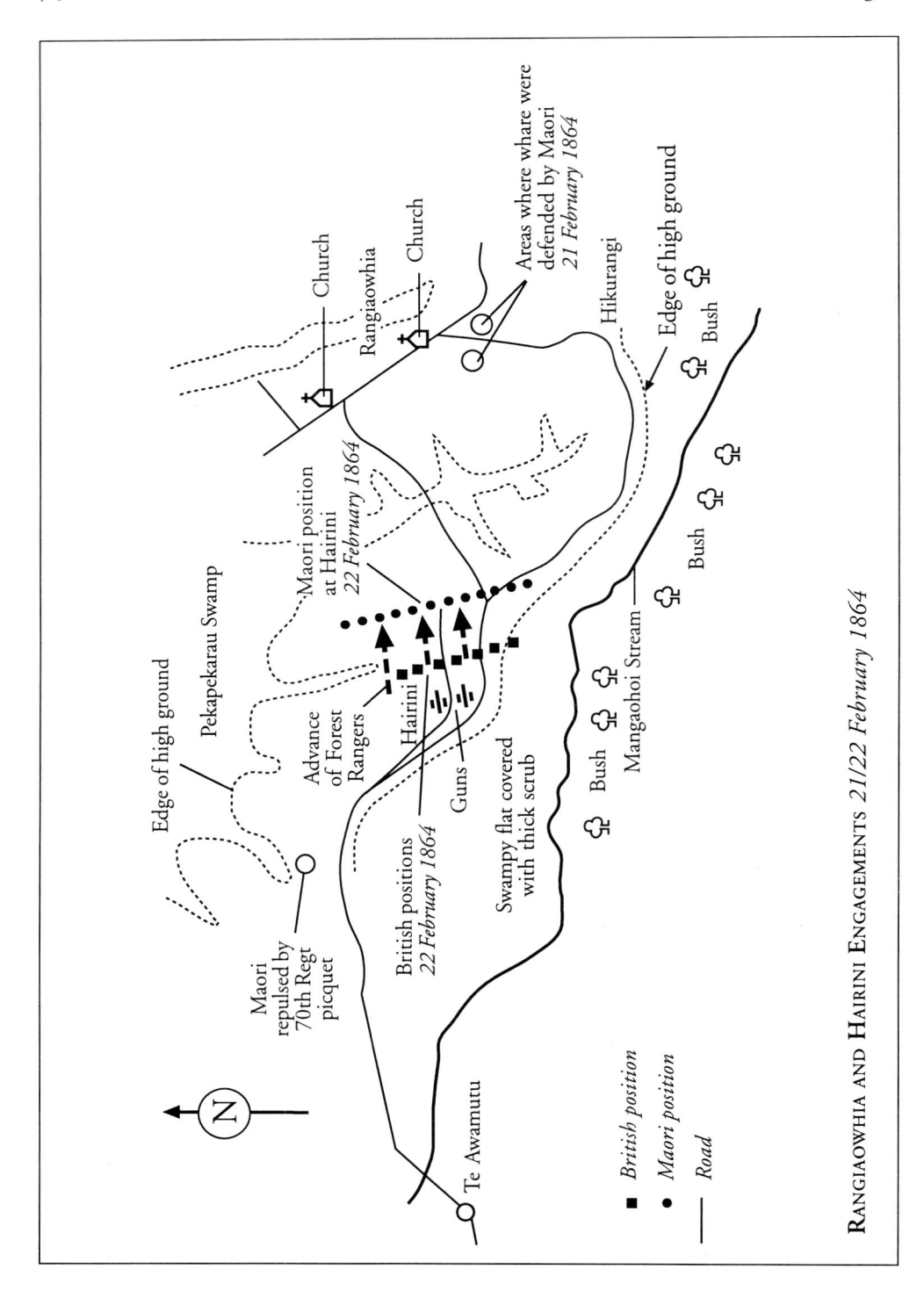

RANGIAOWHIA AND HAIRINI ENGAGEMENTS *21/22 February 1864*

their escape through the north facing door and fled to the nearby swamp.

Cameron decided to fall back to Te Awamutu with most of his men, and set up camp there, leaving the 50th Regiment and two guns under Colonel Weare, near the Catholic Church at Rangiaowhia.

The only Forest Ranger casualty at the Rangiaowhia engagement was Private John Ballenden (No. 2 Company), who was dangerously wounded when a bullet entered near his hip. He died after some months in hospital. The *Daily Southern Cross* reported him as being in a critical condition on 28 February 1864.

This was a terrible blow to the men of the Forest Rangers, as Ballenden was well liked and held in the highest regard. William Race writes of him:

> The wounded Forest Ranger's name was Ballenden, I think from Inverness, but as a volunteer he had endeared himself to the corps by reason of not only his social qualities but as the life of the party. The best athlete, cricketer, and master of all kinds of games that helped to break the monotony of camp life. He was too, a slight fellow yet well built at 5 foot 6 inches only, and so dark we used to in fun question his being a Scotsman, but rather a half caste.

Just prior to Rangiaowhia, Ballenden would go into periods of depression with sudden loss of all his vitality. As he was a favourite of the officers, von Tempsky decided to ascertain the reason for his moods. Apparently he was just under 21 years old and before leaving Scotland a gypsy had informed him that he would never live to see that day.

After Ballenden was wounded, von Tempsky had him sent to Queen's Redoubt hospital at Pokeno to ensure the best possible care. Still not 21 years old, Ballenden convinced himself of his fate and died. The doctor later stated "despondency killed him, not the Maori slug".

In all, five soldiers lost their lives as a result of the action at Rangiaowhia.

Private William Johns of No. 1 Company, Forest Rangers, at a later date, sums up events at Rangiaowhia:

> About a dozen whares were burned in the village. The fight extended from the head of the swamp, where Colonel Nixon was shot, right up to the Catholic church, whence we drove the Maoris over the crest into the swamps, next to the Maori racecourse. Some shots were fired at us from the English church; some Maoris were inside the building. It was an open skirmish from then right along. There were not more than 200 Maoris altogether in Rangiaowhia that day, but they fought well, and had plenty of ammunition. After one of our fellows had been shot, my commanding officer said to me, "Private, take two men and see if there are any Maoris in the whare there," pointing to a house about twenty yards away. I posted the two men outside and stooped to enter the house, which was sunk into the ground, with a low entrance. As I entered I was felled by a terrific blow on the side of the neck, but deflected somewhat by the edge of the doorway. I lay there stunned for some moments, and when I recovered I saw a Maori weapon, a long taiaha, lying beside me. My men told me that the inmates of the whare had escaped by bursting through the thatch at the back, and got clear away. It was a very narrow escape for me, and I took the taiaha as a memento of it. I took no further share in the fight that day, but I was able to march back to Te Awamutu.

CHAPTER 9

Rout at Hairini

On the morning of Monday, 22 February 1864, the day after the capture of Rangiaowhia, the Forest Rangers went on a fruit stealing foray to Bishop Selwyn's orchard but met with resistance from imperial soldiers with bayonets fixed.

William Race recalls the episode:

> That day [22 February] was employed in pitching tents for the time being to await what next.
>
> ... the Forest Rangers availed themselves of their liberty as having a "roving commission" and being very hungry having eaten their 24 hours' ration issued the previous night, came across Bishop Selwyn's orchard and for half an hour secured in "paradise". It was in full serving, every fruit almost was there, down to filberts [hazel nuts]. The Rangers' haversacks never before or again contained such delicacies as on that eventful morn – orlean plums, nectarines, figs, luscious pears, passionfruit, golden pippins, russets, greengages, damsons – every taste was gratified.
>
> And just as their bags were full, four armed sentries drove us forth from our Eden not with a flaming sword but with the bayonet's point or at least would have done so but we left gracefully. And well we might for we kept our loot, and never again was a soldier allowed in.

That same afternoon, a much sharper action occurred very near the site of the battle of the previous day. This was the action of Hairini (or Hairini Hill). It took place not far from the present road between Te Awamutu and Cambridge, about one mile from Te Awamutu.

When the Maori fortified at Paterangi realised that they had been outflanked on the morning of 21 February, they hastily travelled to Hairini determined to avenge the storming of Rangiaowhia.

Earlier, in the morning, an outlying picket was fired upon on the north side of the Mangaohoi Stream. A request came back to camp in Te Awamutu for reinforcements. The Forest Rangers (79 all ranks), Colonial Defence Force Cavalry, Mounted Artillery, 50th Regiment, detachments of the 65th and 70th Regiments and small detachments of Royal Artillery and Royal Engineers were all despatched.

The Forest Rangers received orders to march about 1 pm. They hurried past all the other troops to be in front on the approach to Hairini. They saw no sign of an engagement until they reached a commanding fern ridge on which the line of battle was formed. Firing had been going on already between British skirmishers and the Maori.

The enemy position could be seen clearly. Rangiaowhia was behind on top of a rise on which were some of the outlying whare. The brow was crowned with a long stake fence, ditch and low parapet. This position had been strengthened by Maori during the night and morning and many Maori could be seen behind the parapet.

At the foot of the hill, the main road skirted a swamp and curved towards the British right flank. The Maori were protected on their right flank by the impassable Pekapekarau swamp, and on their left flank by a dense forest.

Artillery began firing on the Maori position. The 50th Regiment, under Colonel Waddy, and the Colonial Defence Force Cavalry, now under Captains Pye and Walmsley, were on the extreme right of the Forest Rangers. The 50th Regiment fixed bayonets and advanced on the main road in a frontal attack – predictable and typical of the British army for the period. Von Tempsky, deciding not to get involved in the advance and not as yet having any direct orders, moved to the left and attacked the Maori right flank.

An ex-Forest Ranger (unknown), years after the battle, remembered the firing of artillery over their heads:

> It was as pretty a bit of hot firing as I have ever seen. The Armstrongs were sending their shells screeching over us, and the Maori bullets were cutting down the fern near me with as even a swathe almost as you could cut it with a slash-hook. We were lying down within 300 yards of the enemy. At last the "Charge!" was sounded, and away we went, the whole of us, we Rangers making for the Maoris' right flank, and the 50th Regiment, on our right, for the centre. With a great cheer the 50th swept splendidly up to the parapet with bayonets at the charge.
> We on the left stormed the Maori line on even terms with them; we had no bayonets, but used our revolvers for close-quarters work.

The 50th Regiment stormed over the Maori parapet. At this point the defence broke and fled. The cavalry pursued them and caused many casualties.

Meanwhile the Forest Rangers' attack continued on the Maori right flank, as described by von Tempsky:

> We had to cross several little gullies and rises; at each place affording the least shelter I breathed my men for a moment, and then dashed them again over the next exposed space. Three severe instalments of a lead shower rattled, thumped and whistled round us; each time I put the men under shelter till the shower passed, and then rushed on again. As yet I had seen only one of my men hit [Private James Taylor with a gunshot wound to the finger]. As we got into the swamp we just saw the gleam of the bayonets of the 50th close upon the left flank of the Maoris [to the far right of the Forest Rangers]. We heard the British cheer, echoed it, and rushed on to the right of the position, where I also saw a peach-grove that might be of use to us.
> Of a sudden, while panting up the hillside, with an upper stratum of lead travelling over our heads towards our friends we had left behind us, I saw that long black line of heads waver. I heard confused cries and shouts presaging disorder – and lo! – it broke and fled – some to the right, where I saw the Defence Corps [Colonial Defence Force Cavalry] after them; and some to the left; to these we lent our company.

The fleeing Maori headed for the Pekapekarau swamp. The Forest Rangers reached the peach grove which commanded the swamp to their left. From here they fired upon the Maori making their escape through the raupo and flax.

Some soldiers of the 70th Regiment had followed the Forest Rangers and were present in the peach grove. However, after the arrival of Lieutenant-Colonel Carey of the staff, they were despatched back to their regiment.

Some Maori were seen between the Forest Rangers' position and the part of Rangiaowhia where the two churches stood, so they moved off in that direction. Occasionally they saw a Maori or heard a bullet. They happened upon a wounded Maori propped against a stump, his left leg stretched out with a large pool of blood around it. He surveyed the Forest Rangers' approach without a start or a movement.

Von Tempsky made a gesture of friendship and proceeded to examine the wound. An Enfield bullet had shattered the left leg below the knee and he was fast bleeding to death. A bootlace was used as a tourniquet and the man's shirt used for a bandage. They left some water with him before moving on.

Thinking that the Catholic church might again be used to hide Maori, von Tempsky had the lock blown away by a carbine shot. But the church was found to be empty. On leaving they re-fastened the door the best they could.

Lieutenant-Colonel Carey again arrived and gave orders to guard the adjoining dwelling-house of the priest and allow no one to enter. Von Tempsky gave his men permission to plunder nearby whare. The whole of the loot was put on the verandah of the priest's house and a sentry placed over it. The men moved off to plunder again while von Tempsky personally guarded the house.

Colonel Weare of the 50th Regiment appeared and said he had orders to take over the guard of the house – and nothing, including the loot, was to be removed. Von Tempsky objected, but to no avail. Weare placed a picket under a subaltern and left.

Von Tempsky relates the events that followed:

> I recalled my Rangers by my whistle, drew them up outside, and carried out myself every individual article belonging to them, not forgetting one or two articles of loot belonging to Colonel Weare, accidentally mixed with ours, considered already as safely acquired by right of seniority. It was to me about as interesting an interlude as could be found amongst the sad realities of higher interests around me. And I look back to my struggle with Colonel Weare for the loot of my men probably with the same amount of amusement as he does himself by this time. He put me under arrest. I took no notice of it, nor did General Cameron, who joked with me the next day about it.

The Forest Rangers returned to camp at Te Awamutu with their loot. The sight must have caused a spectacle amongst the soldiers present; von Tempsky writes:

> There were men representing a walking museum of fowls strung and hung all over their persons. There were men having the carcases of pigs strapped to their bodies; one even carried a live young sow, baby-wise in his arms, restraining its desperate struggles and screams by the strength of a powerful arm. There were men mounted on Maori horses, one of them my half-caste Sergeant Southey, decorated with feathers used at the Maori war dance. The whole two companies bristled with Maori spears, tomahawks, double-barrel guns and so forth. I myself had a magnificent long-handled tomahawk, given to me by one of my men, who picked it up on the battlefield. I gave it to General Cameron.

This episode typifies von Tempsky's attitude to his men — making an extra effort for their sake — even at his own expense. He tried to make light of disobeying orders and actually got away with it, not even damaging relationships with fellow officers. He had the incredible ability of reading a person or situation immediately — on and off the battlefield — and choosing an appropriate path to follow. The giving of the tomahawk to General Cameron was a clever gesture.

The Forest Rangers' entry into Te Awamutu created not only admiration but envy. Apparently loot was fairly scarce in the New Zealand Wars and usually the British troops — especially the Naval Brigade — scored the lot. Von Tempsky must have taken great delight in his men's conquests and antics.

Von Tempsky spoke highly of his men's bravery in the field after Hairini:

> In dismissing my men that evening, I could not but testify to their gallant conduct, particularly No. 1 Company, under Lieutenant Westrup, who had followed me when I went a considerable pace, and when my own men, being in high fern, could not keep up with me.

General Cameron acknowledged the efforts of the Forest Rangers by allocating an extra ration of rum to be served out to them that night.

An ex-Forest Ranger (unknown), many years later, gives his version of the victorious entry into Te Awamutu camp:

> We had found great stores [meant for the Maoris defending the earthworks at Paterangi] of potatoes, pigs and fowls lying ready to be carted to the big pa at Paterangi. The stuff was stacked here and there along the middle of the village between the two churches. When we marched back to Te Awamutu that night one of our fellows was leading, or rather driving, a pig by a rope. As we came near the mission station gate at Te Awamutu we saw General Cameron standing there with Bishop Selwyn. The Ranger called out, "Make way for the Maori prisoner!" The General ordered, "Arrest that man!" But the Ranger dropped the rope, left the pig, and bolted. All the same, he had a fair whack of that porker for his supper.

The Forest Rangers obviously had a reputation for misbehaviour and looting, but even so must have provided some entertainment for the soldiers. The imperial officers must have looked on with disdain and contempt, the Forest Rangers' behaviour going against all their principles of good soldiering. The comedy at the close of this day is best illustrated by William Race:

> On the Forest Rangers' chief [von Tempsky] obeying orders to scour the district after the charge, we on returning came across a small kind of mission school or house recently vacated by the Maoris and to our joy discovered a few fowls, some turkeys and about a dozen tame rabbits in hutches. Also a Maori pony and last but not least a well worn Bishop's hat, with a few priestly clothes. Well, you can imagine short work was made in disposing of them, and as we had only some two miles to reach camp, carried our loot in an imposing manner.
> The half caste [Southey] guide we had, made a flax bridle and backed the pony, clapped on the hat, and some sort of a long black coat and took the

lead followed by about 30 successful plunderers. Turkeys or fowls or rabbits were slung over their shoulders and thus in the evening they reached Te Awamutu.

We had as we thought left the Bishop [Selwyn] at Te Rore, but to increase the fun just as we approached the church near to our camp there he was as we passed, of course he recognised the hat at once, as also the rest of the captured articles, and the sight so enraged him that he stepped into the road and facing us called us all "A parcel of thieves and robbers," quite forgetting the old adage "All is fair in love and war". Then too he somehow insulted some of the artillery I think, and they threatened him. They had taken some old fencing [from round the mission] for their camp fires.

The naval men came into camp that evening with their six-pounder gun loaded with pigs and potatoes.

These pillaging actions are only a fraction of the total damage to property and theft carried out by the advancing troops, both imperial and colonial. A Compensation Court in 1865 heard a total of 372 claimants in the Auckland Province for a total of £136,000. This court was headed by Thomas Beckham of the Royal Marines, as Commissioner for investigating claims for compensation for losses occasioned, subsequent to 11 July 1863. Only £71,000 was paid out by the Government, as it was desperately short of funds. The forty Maori claimants did not fare so well, receiving only £2432 or about a third of their £7400 claim.

For some, being in the army was an excuse to plunder with no repercussions and considered their prizes as "the spoils of war". These actions constitute a despicable crime that some Maori were also guilty of. From the above pillaging descriptions, the mercenary-like Forest Rangers were probably the most guilty of all the British units.

The only Forest Ranger casualty at the Hairini engagement was Private James Taylor (No. 2 Company) who received a slight gunshot wound to his finger.

In his official despatch to the Governor, Sir George Grey, Lieutenant-General Cameron mentions the march from Te Rore to Te Awamutu, and both actions at Rangiaowhia and Hairini:

> Headquarters, Te Awamutu, 25 February 1864
> Sir, I have the honour to report, for your Excellency's information, that at 11 o'clock on the night of the 20 February, I marched with a force [Royal Artillery Mounted Corps (41 all ranks); Colonial Defence Force (47 all ranks); Royal Engineers (26 all ranks); 14th Regiment (5 all ranks); 18th Regiment (7 all ranks); 40th Regiment (4 all ranks); 65th Regiment (456 all ranks); 70th Regiment (398 all ranks); Forest Rangers (1 captain, 2 subalterns, 4 sergeants, and 95 men inclusive of corporals– totalling 102 all ranks); Navy and Marines (155 all ranks); a total of 1241 all ranks] from Te Rore towards Te Awamutu, by a track which crosses the Mangapiko at Waiari.
> I left Colonel Waddy at Te Rore in command of the remainder of the troops, with orders to continue in the entrenched camp in front of Paterangi pa until the following night.
> I arrived at Te Awamutu at daybreak on the 21st, and immediately pushed on to Rangiaowhia, which I found nearly deserted. The few natives who

were in the place were completely taken by surprise, and refusing to lay down their arms, fired on the Mounted Royal Artillery and Colonial Defence Force, whom I sent on in advance of the column. The natives were quickly dispersed, and the greater part escaped, but a few of them taking shelter in a whare, made a desperate resistance, until the Forest Rangers and a company of the 65th Regiment surrounded the whare, which was set on fire, and the defenders either killed or taken prisoners.

I regret to say that several casualties occurred on our side, and amongst them Colonel Nixon, commanding the Defence Force, who was severely wounded in endeavouring to enter the whare. Our loss was two killed and 6 wounded. About 12 natives were killed and 12 taken prisoner.

I have detained 21 women and children who were found in the village.

Immediately after the settlement was cleared I marched the troops back to Te Awamutu.

At 4.30 o'clock in the morning of the 21st, a large convoy, escorted by the 50th Regiment, under Colonel Weare, left Te Rore, and followed the track through Waiari, which I mentioned above, arrived at Te Awamutu at 2 o'clock in the afternoon.

Early on the morning of the 22nd, the officer of the advanced picket reported that he had seen 700 natives passing along the road from Paterangi to Rangiaowhia, where they halted. Natives were also seen on our right at Kihikihi. I therefore determined to march on Rangiaowhia the following morning, and in order that my force might be sufficient to occupy that place as well as Te Awamutu, I ordered Colonel Waddy to march the same evening from Paterangi with a force [18th Regiment (148 all ranks); 40th Regiment (392 all ranks); 50th Regiment (110 all ranks); Colonial Defence Force (6 troopers); a total of 656 all ranks]. But as it was reported to me about noon the same day that a considerable body of natives had advanced on Rangiaowhia, and were fortifying themselves on the site of an old pa called Hairini – a position extremely strong by nature, and blocking the road between Te Awamutu and Rangiaowhia – I determined to attack them immediately.

At 1.30 o'clock pm I advanced on their position with a force [Royal Artillery Cavalry (37 all ranks); Colonial Defence Force (49 all ranks); Royal Artillery (28 all ranks); Royal Engineers (11 all ranks); 50th Regiment (506 all ranks); 65th Regiment (222 all ranks); 70th Regiment (296 all ranks); Forest Rangers (1 captain: Von Tempsky, 2 subalterns, 4 sergeants and 72 men including corporals – totalling 79 all ranks); a total of 1228 all ranks].

Small detached parties of the enemy, who were posted about a mile in front of Hairini, having been driven back by the skirmishers, which were composed of companies of the 50th and 70th Regiments. I brought up the two six-pounder Armstrong guns, under the command of Brevet Lieutenant-Colonel Barstow, to a commanding height about 500 yards from the position.

After several rounds had been fired from these guns with good effect, I ordered Colonel Weare with the 50th Regiment to carry the position at the point of the bayonet, having the 65th in support and the 70th in reserve, while the cavalry were formed up on the right, behind the brow of the hill, ready to pursue the enemy.

The 50th were exposed to a very heavy fire in advancing towards the position, which they carried with great gallantry.

The natives fell hurriedly back before the leading files of the 50th could reach them with the bayonet, and retired through a swamp in the direction of the Maungatautari Road. The cavalry had an opportunity of charging them as they retreated, and did some execution. They no further stand, but fled precipitately towards Maungatautari, leaving almost everything but their arms behind them.

I enclose returns of our casualties on this occasion and on the day previous. I estimate the number of natives who defended the position at Hairini at 400. Their loss I have not been able to ascertain, but they must have had at least 30 killed.

Leaving the 50th Regiment and two guns under Colonel Weare, near the Catholic Church at Rangiaowhia, I withdrew the remainder of the troops to Te Awamutu, where Colonel Waddy arrived with his force at 11 o'clock that night; having; before he left Te Rore, taken possession of the Paterangi pa, which, as well as the one at Pikopiko, was deserted by the enemy in the morning.

I cannot praise too highly the admirable conduct of all the troops, regular and colonial, during the fatiguing night march of the 20th, and the operations of the two following days; but particularly of the Mounted Royal Artillery, under Lieutenant Rait; of the Colonel Defence Force, under Lieutenant-Colonel Nixon, and afterwards under Captain Walmsley; and of the 50th Regiment, under Colonel Weare.

I deeply regret that the severe wound received by Lieutenant-Colonel Nixon has deprived me, though I trust only for a short time, of his valuable services. The state of discipline and efficiency of the Colonial Defence Force, and the eagerness which they invariably manifest to come into contact with the enemy, are chiefly due to the example and exertions of that able and zealous officer.

I beg to bring under your favourable notice the invaluable services rendered to the force under my command by Mr Edwards [guide], of the Native Department, whose information regarding the roads and tracks of this part of the country I have always found most correct. Without his assistance to guide the column, the night march of the 20th could not have been undertaken.

Roll of Forest Rangers at the time of Rangiaowhia and Hairini engagements, 21-22 February 1864:

Jackson's No. 1 Company: *Captain* (1): William Jackson (on a visit to Auckland at time of engagements at Rangiaowhia and Hairini). *Lieutenant* (1): Westrup. *Ensign* (1): Whitfield. *Staff Sergeant* (1): Bertram. *Sergeants* (3): Holden, John Smith, James Williams. *Corporals* (2): Coghlan, Taylor. *Privates* (43): Alexander, Benson, Black, Robert Bruce, William Bruce, Burns, Carter, Cole, Costello, Fitzgerald, Gallie, Gibb, Grigg, Haines, Hannah, Hannay, Hendry, Henry Jackson, Johns, Long, McDonald, Madigan, Mahoney, Morgan, Murray, John Nolan, Martin Nolan, Osborne, Peters,

Rowden, Rowland, James Smith, Thomas Smith, Stephenson, Temple, Thomson, Thurston, Torpey, Vaughan, George Ward, Watters, Wells, Williams.
Von Tempsky's No. 2 Company: *Captain* (1): Von Tempsky. *Ensign* (1): Roberts. *Staff Sergeant* (1): Sherret. *Sergeants* (3): Carran, Southey, Wakeford. *Corporals* (4): McMinn, McNamara (demoted to private 21 February), Parsons (promoted from private 22 February), Sibley. *Privates* (46): Albin, Anderson, Ballenden, Bidgood, Bochow, Burry, Butter, Buttle, Bygum, Clifford, Cochrane, Collins, Donovan, Fallon, Freeman, Harris, Hartland, Healas, Hellkessel, Higgins, Jones, Keena, Liebig, Lindsay, McClymont, McNamara (demoted from corporal 21 February, probably for drunkenness), Magole, Mohr, Mulligan, Neil, Parsons (promoted to Corporal 22 February), Pohlen, Race, Ross, Scally, Shine, Simmons, Stanley, Sturmer, Sumsion, Taylor, Thomson, Toovey, Tubby, Wheeler, Woods.

CHAPTER 10

In camp at Te Awamutu

Rewi Maniapoto was at this time at Kihikihi, a village about three miles south of Te Awamutu. The British attacked the village on 23 February and the Maori fell back to the south and southwest over the Puniu River. The British soldiers burnt the carved meeting house before returning to Te Awamutu. The Maori, realising the position was not held, returned and reoccupied Kihikihi.

So the British once more decided to capture Kihikihi. Colonel Waddy was given the task, and von Tempsky led both companies of Forest Rangers as the advance guard of the attacking force. Von Tempsky writes:

> As we approached Kihikihi, I went somewhat in advance, and seeing the Maoris near the bush adjoining the village, we gave chase, and sent back word to that effect. We skirmished through some maize-fields, with a dense forest to our left, to which bush I gave a wide berth. But we could not get well at them as they had the start of us, and we were suddenly brought up by a swamp. We skirmished with them across the swamp, but got little good out of it. I saw them retreating into some distant whares, and making themselves quite comfortable, proving to me thereby that they were now supported, and that position was strong. As we found the swamp altogether impassable without making a detour for miles, I returned, having formed, however, my plan already to look after these gentlemen.

That night the Forest Rangers entered the bush with the intention of surprising the whare. After an arduous night march through a swampy kahikatea forest, they were opposite the whare at daybreak. But after a rush across the open space they found the whare empty and everything inside smashed.

Sergeant Carran reported to von Tempsky that he saw Maori in nearby bush beyond a swamp. When the Forest Rangers moved from the whare they were fired on by the Maori, but nothing came of the action because the intervening swamp prevented either side from attacking.

The Forest Rangers settled down at Kihikihi for some rest after a hectic few days. They enjoyed the late summer heat and the supplement of fresh food from Rangiaowhia to their meagre army rations.

Camp life must have been like any frontier town, with its abundance of men and few women. With little or no alcohol available and an abundance of army pay in their pockets, the men would have to invent their own entertainment. Cricket and athletics broke the monotony. William Race gives a picturesque view of day to day proceedings:

> It will be understood that no canteens were there, and neither at the Paterangi [Te Rore] encampment before this one [Te Awamutu camp] was established. Consequently the imperial troops were flushed with several months' pay, and therefore it changed hands amongst themselves at their favourite game of brag or poker and various groups daily and nightly gambled pretty freely

at those games. Piles of coppers, silver and sometimes some notes or gold were mixed plentifully in those heaps.

This brought down the censure of the good Bishop for when straying about he too often witnessed [the games].

Another outlet for the circulation of the coin was the grog (rum) which was bought and sold at times at fabulous prices. And those who were the vendors could have reaped a pretty harvest if they had liked. Half a crown a tot, which means about two ounces, was the usual price or one pound or even two was often given for a bottle, which would be about a week's allowance per soldier.

But the threat of surprise attack from the Maori caused General Cameron to maintain constant pickets on the perimeter of the town.

Part of the large mission house at Te Awamutu was converted into a hospital for the wounded and sick. Typhoid fever was prevalent at the time. The other part of the mission held Maori prisoners. At one time up to 30 women were there, but they were soon afterwards liberated.

Ensign John Roberts (No. 2 Company) was promoted to Lieutenant, his commission dated 10 March 1864.

With the onset of winter and frosty nights, von Tempsky corresponded with Thomas Russell of the Defence Office on 17 March 1864 requesting greatcoats for his men. He further showed his concern for his men's welfare, by trying in the same letter, to have the 10 pence a day charge for rations reduced to the three and a half pence, which the militiamen paid.

Von Tempsky went on to say:

> ... or better still that they may get their rations gratis in consideration of their hard work and good conduct.

The fact that they paid more than their counterparts in the Waikato Regiments of Militia for rations was a source of grievance. They believed that because they were paid a higher rate to compensate for the arduous and dangerous nature of their service, that the authorities were trying to get some of it back by overcharging them for rations.

They got their greatcoats, but there was no reduction in the cost of rations.

During March 1864 while in camp at Kihikihi, Jackson took the opportunity to requisition ammunition for both companies of Forest Rangers. Practice shooting and the result of recent engagements had drained their supply of ammunition. As the calibres of their firearms were different from those used in the British column, his request went to the Deputy Adjutant General, Militia and Volunteers (Lieutenant-Colonel Balneavis), in Auckland. Jackson wrote:

> Camp Kihikihi, March 14th 1864
> Sir, Would you be kind enough to send as soon as you can (6000) six thousand rounds of Terry Carbine ammunition. We have only one case of spare rounds. Also 1500 rounds of revolver ammunition [54 bore].

Balneavis has countersigned the letter on 17 March 1864 with the note "Send the quantity." A quartermaster has noted with the letter "The within named supply

E.A. Williams watercolour depicting the landing at Pukerimu Redoubt, near Cambridge, April 1864. Pukerimu was used by Forest Rangers as a base in 1864.
Waikato Museum of Art and History. © Hocken Library, Dunedin

of ammunition forwarded to Captain Jackson this day" – this day being 28 March 1864.

So it is likely that the ammunition arrived in time either for Jackson to issue to his company before they moved on Orakau, or for the Quartermaster stationed at Te Awamutu to forward directly to Orakau in von Tempsky's absence (for Jackson was at Ohaupo just prior to the engagement at Orakau). The ammunition would be anxiously needed by both companies at Orakau.

Cameron considered attacking two Maori pa at the foot of the Pukekura Range, a few miles south of Cambridge. The two positions were close to each other, with the eastern most pa lower on the slope and immediately above the rapids on the Waikato River. These sites can still be observed today, above the Waikato River where the Karapiro dam is situated.

Cameron first moved against these fortifications from his new camp at Pukerimu on 2 March. With about 1000 troops, Cameron concentrated on the stronger and lower Te Tiki o te Ihingarangi pa. The troops halted about 1200 yards in front of the modified ancient earthwork. The defenders raised their red battle flag, followed by a few defiant rifle shots. The flag was then lowered and some Maori performed a haka on the parapets.

Cameron had no intention to attack immediately as he didn't know the ground immediately before the pa and experience had taught him to expect obstacles. He deployed his troops – the 50th Regiment on the right, the Colonial Defence Force cavalry on both flanks, the Forest Rangers in the centre, and the marines, sailors 70th Regiment in reserve.

Six Forest Rangers moved off to reconnoitre the smaller, upper pa. When they approached to within 400 yards they were fired upon from that position.

Cameron was now satisfied with his survey of both positions and moved the column back to Pukerimu redoubt. This upset the Maori who again make loud demonstrations on the parapets, firing more shots. Cameron was convinced that the two positions were strong and well designed. Unlike Paterangi, these two positions would be difficult to outflank, with the Waikato River immediately to the left and the steep slopes of the Pukekura Range and Maungatautari mountain to the right.

In late March 1864, Jackson took his No. 1 Company to Ohaupo, to patrol and protect the Maori track that passed through Ohaupo, skirting the northern edge of the swamp between Te Awamutu and Pukerimu Redoubt, near Cambridge.

CHAPTER 11

Orakau – a desperate stand

A large number of Kingite Maori under Rewi Maniapoto constructed a strong earthwork at the village of Orakau – meaning in Maori: the place of trees – about three miles east from Kihikihi, and made a historic stand against the British troops.

Situated on a gentle rise, the village of Orakau had unobstructed views to the north down gentle rolling fern-covered slopes. To the south and east lay kahikatea forested swamps separating Orakau from the hills at Pukekura and Maungatautari mountain. Half a mile to the north was the Mangaohoi Stream, while two miles to the south was the Puniu River, both flowing to the northwest and the Waipa River. The surrounding area was fertile with fruit trees and cultivated fields. The variety of fruit the Maori grew at this idyllic location included peaches, almonds, cherries, apples, grapes and quinces. Vegetables included potatoes, kumara, maize, melons, pumpkins and marrows. The gentle rolling northern slopes were cultivated with wheat.

Before the war, this rich growing area, along with the area at Rangiaowhia, supplied wheat and produce to markets in Auckland, transported by canoe on the Mangapiko Stream and Waipa and Waikato Rivers.

On 29 February 1864, a military expedition led by Colonel Waddy of the 50th Regiment left Te Awamutu. They moved in a easterly direction to reconnoitre Maori activity in the vicinity of Orakau village. No. 2 Company, Forest Rangers, under von Tempsky, formed the vanguard. About a mile before Orakau, coming from Kihikihi, the Forest Rangers encountered on a small hill a newly made stake fence with a high bank rising to the rear. This looked suspicious to von Tempsky, who decided to collapse a section of fence and rush the bank. On the brow they discovered un-manned rifle-pits hidden by manuka branches pushed into the earth to hide the defensive works. Von Tempsky recounts:

> "Listen, men," I said, "We must make one broad rush at that place – one long, strong, all-together push – and that fence must go down. Then up the bank like lightning." Thus arranged – thus it was done. With a cheer a wave of sprightly fellows dashed against that fence. Down it went – up the bank we flew. There were masked rifle-pits just dug and just deserted. They had stuck sprigs and branches of tea-tree into the newly-thrown-up earth to hide the presence of those pits.

A few long-range shots were fired at them here by Maori who were observed to fall back on Orakau. The Forest Rangers then went through Orakau village in skirmishing order but found the position deserted, the inhabitants having retreated to the east and the swamps. When the imperial troops came up, some of the whare were torched before the force returned to Te Awamutu.

Jackson, who had recently arrived back from Auckland, returned there on leave with von Tempsky. While in Auckland both received accolades for their

Orakau – a desperate stand

Rewi Maniapoto.
This Ngatimaniapoto chief opposed the siting of the Orakau pa believing it would be too exposed to British artillery.

Copied from early Joshua Firth photo

accomplishments in the Waikato campaign. This was in contrast to the cool reception they had received from imperial officers prior to Christmas 1863.

Meanwhile Roberts and Westrup were left in command of the Forest Rangers at Kihikihi. On what appeared to the imperial officers to be a routine patrol in the immediate neighbourhood, the party of Forest Rangers then slipped quietly across the Puniu River and camped the night on a summit of a wooded hill above the large Maori village at Wharepapa. They were not yet detected by the Maori.

At daybreak, while the Maori were preparing breakfast, the party of Forest Rangers charged down the slope and completely surprised the Maori, who fled leaving their meal for their attackers. After eating their fill the Forest Rangers returned to Kihikihi.

However, on hearing the report of this skirmish their commanding officer at Kihikihi was far from pleased. The Forest Rangers were immediately ordered back to Te Awamutu camp. The were virtually confined to camp with no chance of any further ventures.

This sort of initiative is what quick and decisive actions with low casualties are made of. Instead of being praised for their enterprise they were punished and banished from the front line. The affair displays the constant jealousy from the imperial officers towards their counterparts in the colonial forces. With Jackson and von Tempsky in Auckland, the imperial officers took advantage of their absence to take immediate punitive action.

But word soon got to Auckland where Jackson and von Tempsky both showed their displeasure at the treatment handed out to their men.

Meanwhile, after agreeing to continue the war with a new initiative, the Maori decided to construct an earthworks pa north of the Puniu River at the seemingly strategic location of Orakau. Rewi believed the position would be too exposed to British field guns and argued for a site closer to the Mangaohoi Stream and the kahikatea forests, which would afford them an easy escape if needed. But he succumbed to the pressure from other chiefs. Orakau was well situated for the supply of food and water to the garrison.

The chosen site was on a gentle slope called Rangataua, amongst the peach trees at Orakau. The main work measured about 80 feet long and 40 feet wide with the narrow sides facing east and west.

The pa design was an earthwork with external ditch and broad parapet. Inside was another ditch well traversed against enfilading fire. Many of the traverses were converted into burrows partly covered as protection against artillery fire. The outside parapet was about six feet thick and about six to eight feet above the ditch. This was laminated using alternate layers of soil and fern, giving it added strength against artillery fire. At strategic positions long horizontal rifle loopholes were constructed and surrounded on the sides and top by timber.

A short trench led out from the northwest angle to a small outwork. At the time of the first assault this outwork was not completed being only three feet deep.

No palisading (tall secured wooden pole perimeter fencing) as on other pa was used. Instead, the pa was surrounded by a post and three rail fence. This proved to be a serious obstacle to attackers as it was partly obscured by fern, flax-bushes and peach trees. In profile, the pa was low, enabling the Maori to complete the construction without being noticed by the British. The surrounding fruit trees also helped to hide the construction. The low profile did not increase the vulnerability of the earthwork as events proved it to be one of the most difficult positions assaulted by the British and colonial forces throughout the New Zealand Wars.

Another work was planned for the neighbouring rise called Karaponia (meaning in Maori: California) about three hundred yards to the west of the Orakau earthwork. It was proposed to construct another pa here with connecting parapet and double trench, but due to the rapidity of the British advance this never eventuated and the ridge was used by the British staff headquarters during the engagement.

Most of the Ngatimaniapoto people from the village decided to leave the area rather than stay and fight.

The defenders consisted of about 50 Maori of the Ngatimaniapoto tribe, but the bulk of the defenders came from the Urewera tribe – who had come 150 miles to fight the Pakeha – and from the Ngatiraukawa and Ngati te Kohera and other west Taupo tribes.

Only about 310 Maori defended the pa, including about 20 women and children, presumably caught in the pa when hostilities started. Some of the women who remained wanted to be with loved ones and to help supply food and water within the pa, showing the Maori confidence in the impenetrability of the position. Rewi Maniapoto was placed in supreme command.

The defenders were poorly armed. Most had double-barrelled guns; there were a few flintlocks and some modern Enfield or similar rifles taken from Europeans during earlier hostilities. Fifteen such weapons were brought from Taranaki. Some Maori warriors carried only tomahawks and traditional weapons. There was a shortage of powder in the pa, as most of it was still in nearby Orakau village when the British attacked. There was also a shortage of food and water inside the pa once the siege began, although some young men stole out on the first night and returned with provisions. But well before the siege ended the defenders were to run out of water — an important factor in the ending of the siege.

Had the construction of the pa been allowed to run its full course, and with a full supply of food and water, the outcome would probably had been the same but the shortages may have protracted the siege a further three days, or until all the defenders were killed.

The first sighting of the construction was made by two surveyors on the morning of 30 March 1864. They were positioned on a hill near Kihikihi and observed the pa through a theodolite telescope. The position was also noticed by Lieutenant Lusk (Mauku Rifles), attached to the Commissariat Corps. A rider carrying the information was sent immediately to Lieutenant-Colonel Haultain, commanding the Kihikihi Redoubt, then to Brigadier-General Carey stationed at Te Awamutu camp. An immediate reconnaissance was made by Carey on horseback in the early afternoon. Realising the significance of the pa and the benefits of an early engagement, Carey hurriedly returned to camp and organised a three-pronged advance on Orakau for that night.

This display of urgency was because General Cameron was only a few hours away at Pukerimu camp, near Cambridge, and Carey wanted to control the attack personally, fearing Cameron's intervention before the battle commenced. He had already noticed Cameron's admiration for the Maori cause and feared Cameron might procrastinate and stall the attack.

Carey's plan was to surround and cut off the pa by dawn so as to minimise the number of defenders and the amount of supplies held in the pa. More importantly, an attack on the pa before construction was completed would minimise the number of British casualties. Carey did not want a repeat of the heavy casualties they had suffered at Rangiriri.

The right-flank column left Te Awamutu at midnight under the command of Major Blyth of the 40th Regiment. This column consisted of von Tempsky with about half of his No. 2 Company, Forest Rangers (28 men all ranks), as the advance guard, a detachment of the 40th Regiment (109 men all ranks) and a detachment of the 65th Regiment (138 men all ranks) — totalling 275 all ranks. At the time, the No. 1 Company, Forest Rangers, and Jackson were in camp at Ohaupo. From Te Awamutu they marched past Kihikihi, then turning south, they crossed the Puniu River and headed along the south bank to Waikeria before re-crossing the Puniu River and heading north. This eventually brought them to the southeast corner of the pa. On arrival von Tempsky took up a position to the east, the direction from which he expected a relieving force of Kingite would appear (and actually did the following day).

The centre column left Te Awamutu at 3 am on 31 March under the command of Brigadier-General Carey. This column consisted of Lieutenant Roberts with about half of the No. 2 Company, Forest Rangers (26 men all ranks), as the advance guard, detachment of Royal Artillery (two 6-pounder Armstrong guns, 35 men all ranks), detachment of mounted Royal Artillery (32 men all ranks), Royal Engineers (6 men all ranks), one lieutenant of the 12th Regiment, detachment of the 18th Regiment (153 men all ranks), detachment of the 40th Regiment (285 men all ranks), detachment of the 65th Regiment (42 men all ranks) and a detachment of the 1st Regiment Waikato Militia (Colonel Haultain and 151 men all ranks) – totalling 732 all ranks. The centre column marched along the dray road to Kihikihi, joining Haultain and the 1st Regiment Waikato Militia who were based at the Kihikihi Redoubt and continuing along the dray road (virtually the Kihikihi-Arapuni road of today) to Orakau.

The left column left the redoubt at Rangiaowhia about 3 am under the command of Captain Blewitt. This column consisted of a detachment of the 65th Regiment (58 men all ranks) and a detachment of the 3rd Regiment Waikato Militia (55 men all ranks) – totalling 113 men all ranks. They had the more difficult task of crossing the Mangaohoi Stream and passing through kahikatea bush and swamp to reach Orakau in roughly a straight line from Rangiaowhia.

Blyth's column passed close to the old pa site at Otautahanga after dawn, a little more than a mile southeast of Orakau. Here von Tempsky and his men fired on five Maori encountered to the right of the track. Corporal Toovey killed one man. Soon firing could be heard from Orakau so the column moved quickly in extended order.

Meanwhile the centre column were the first to reach Orakau, arriving at dawn. On entering the village they were fired by Maori skirmishers hidden in the peach groves. As Von Tempsky states, it was still unclear to the advance exactly what they were up against:

> There was an old stockyard fence visible, but as to the nature of any defences no one had any idea of what was before them. The word for assault was then given, and Captain Ring and Roberts leading gallantly ...

Immediately Roberts and his 25 Forest Rangers and 120 men of the 18th Regiment attacked. Parts of the earthwork were still unfinished, these being the east side parapet and post and rail fence and the outwork from the northwest corner. Many Maori were in a prayer session outside the pa when soldiers were first seen. The attack advanced in skirmishing order on the west and northwest sides, with the Forest Rangers on the left. Captain Ring of the 18th Regiment was mortally wounded. The Maori held their fire until the attackers were within 50 yards, then fired volley after volley. A few Forest Rangers had tried to get into the outer ditch around the parapet but were not supported. Unfamiliarity with the ground immediately in front of the pa and heavy volleys from the defenders caused the attack to falter and retreat.

Roberts described the attack:

> We could hardly believe it was the main position at first. Suddenly, as we advanced, the whole west face of the pa, the front we were approaching, opened fire. Puffs of smoke and gun flashes ran along the front of the entrenchment and back again, the rain of bullets from the Maori tupara came over our heads. We were hunting down cover in an instant.
> We lay down on the edge of the cultivation and went to work as hard as we could with our long knives, each man digging a shallow shelter for himself

and throwing up the earth in front; the bullets were coming over thick that day.

Again the charge was sounded but this attack, which included reinforcements from the 40th Regiment, was just as unsuccessful as the first. Roberts and his men came within a few yards of the defenders in the parapet (the outwork now being abandoned) and a few Forest Rangers actually got into the outer ditch before the recall was sounded. Again Roberts saw he was not sufficiently supported and was forced to retire.

These two attacks illustrate the failure to reconnoitre the pa before the troops were rushed against it in premature assaults. The imperial soldiers paid the price by losing a gallant officer and some men.

Carey realised by now that the pa was a formidable fortress and decided to besiege the site (now that the other two columns were on the battlefield) and soften it with artillery fire. The two Armstrong guns were positioned on the Karaponia ridge about 350 yards distant and fired into the pa. Being well constructed with fern and soil the pa proved most resilient to shellfire.

Lieutenant Hurst of the 18th Regiment (acting engineer officer) convinced Carey to approach the pa with a sap (protected trench used to approach an enemy's position). This eventually came near to the northwest corner of the pa. Gabions (woven baskets to contain soil) were brought from Te Awamutu, and later made on site, to protect the parapets of the sap from enemy fire.

The east side of the pa was covered by von Tempsky and his detachment of Forest Rangers. They took cover in a hollow area between the pa and the swamp. Von Tempsky describes events of the first day:

> For two hours we lay under what cover the inequalities of the ground afforded, with a heavy and well-directed fire upon us. We could see the Maoris strengthening their works as busy as bees, firing away also with rifles from two or three embrasures with most unpleasant comparative accuracy.

Some of the firing from the pa was accurate enough to keep the troops pinned down. This fire was made worse on the first day of the siege as the soldiers were close to the pa – the command still considered a general assault which never came.

Here they were joined by the rest of the No. 2 Company Forest Rangers and Lieutenant Roberts. Meanwhile, the Forest Rangers' position in front of the pa was uncomfortable as bullets fired from the far side to protect the sap's construction landed in their vicinity. Using their bowie knives they quickly dug shallow rifle-pits for protection.

Von Tempsky describes their predicament:

> We could not even fire, as the danger of a crossfire was then too imminent, and I must confess that I was heartily glad when we were removed at last from that uselessly-exposed position to a point further back, where the sudden fall of the ridge gave a comparative shelter from bullets.

At midday von Tempsky observed Maori reinforcements in the distance coming from the east and making for the forest between Orakau and Rangiaowhia. At the time he was stationed in a hollow near the road which ran from Orakau towards

98   *Forest Rangers*

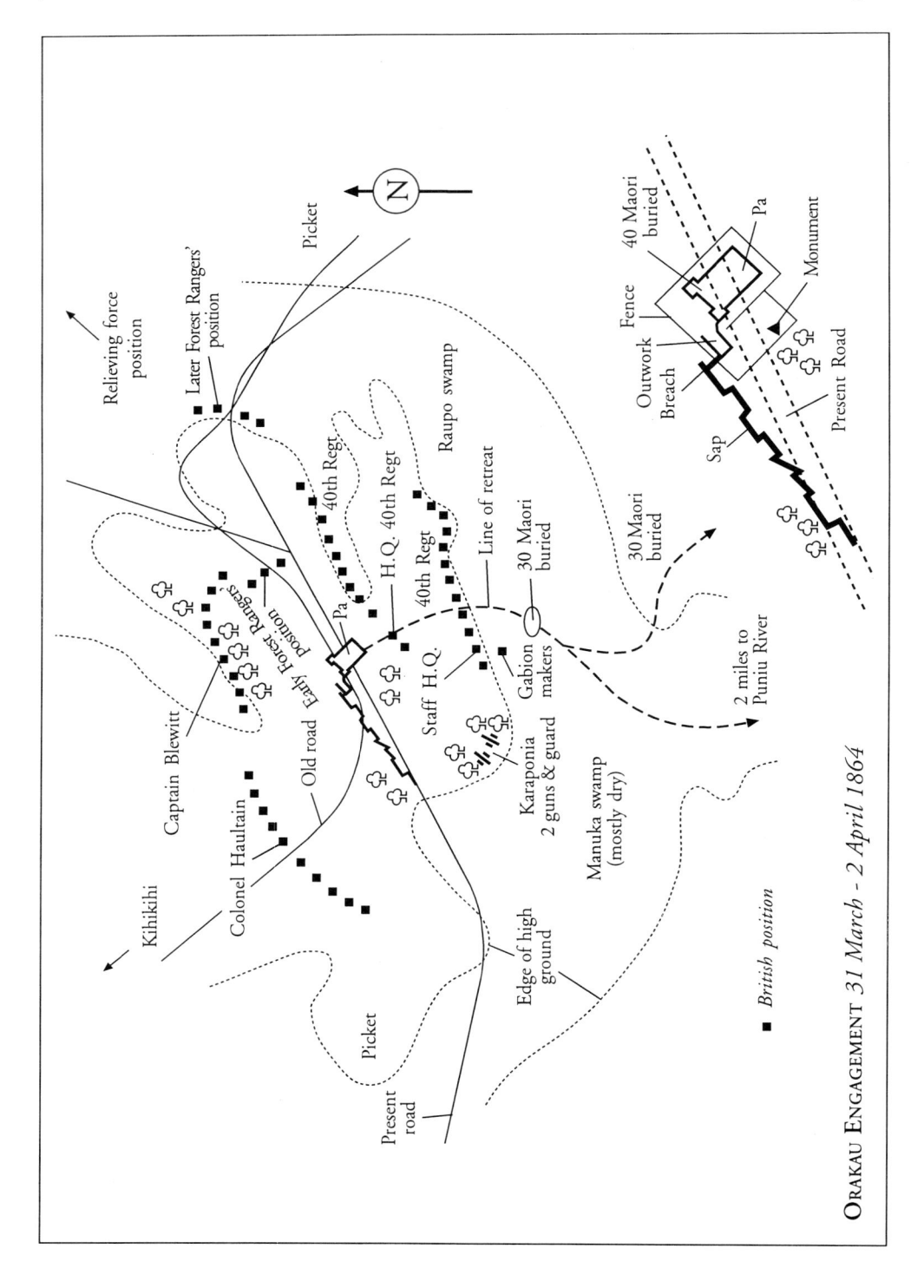

Orakau Engagement 31 March – 2 April 1864

Otautahanga, Parawera and Maungatautari, crossed the swamp at his rear and led up an adjoining ridge, on which stood a large weatherboard house. Von Tempsky had previously placed a picket near the house as intuition of Maori reinforcements prompted him. The view the picket had from near the house commanded the very point of the forest where the reinforcements were gathering.

A Maori in the pa communicated in high-pitched yells with the new arrivals across the swamp – obviously giving instructions. Von Tempsky crossed the swamp to the picket with reinforcements and extended the line along the brow of the hill in some manuka scrub. There was open ground between them and the forest holding the 300-400 Maori reinforcements. Then the Maori started chanting and war dancing, building up to a frenzy. Twice it subsided and the skirmishers appeared, firing into the Forest Rangers, but the cracks of their carbines sent the attackers back into the bush. There they remained, firing ineffectually at the Forest Rangers at long range.

A force under command of Captain Inman arrived at Orakau in the afternoon. This consisted of a detachment of the 12th Regiment (98 men all ranks) and Jackson with his No. 1 Company, Forest Rangers (50 men all ranks), arriving from Ohaupo – totalling 148 all ranks. Some of Jackson's men, many of them diggers from the gold fields, had volunteered to work in the sap. They did excellent work, and were left under the direction of Ensign Whitfield.

Jackson immediately positioned his men with von Tempsky's on the east perimeter. Von Tempsky was pleased to see their arrival at such a crucial time.

In von Tempsky's writings he mentions the arrival of Jackson and his men on the morning of the second day. In Carey's official despatch, written immediately on the conclusion of the action, the time of the arrival is during the afternoon of the first day. Carey includes the No. 1 Company's strength with that of Inman which supports to their arrival on the first day. It is possible Jackson stayed near the sap on the first night and joined von Tempsky on the east side early on the second day. Von Tempsky did not write his account until a few years later so the mistake is possibly an oversight.

As dusk fell von Tempsky gave Lieutenant Roberts command of the picket and fell back to the Orakau side of the swamp.

Von Tempsky recalls:

> I gave Roberts charge of the picket. It could not be in better hands. That day his behaviour before the pa, and on previous instances, had borne me out in my preconceived idea of the young man that he was as true as steel. I ranged all my men on one side of the road, lying down close to one another in the fern, with strict orders not to stir from their positions until I gave the word – to let the Maoris [the pa defenders escaping rather than the reinforcements entering the pa] run the gauntlet of their fire – and then, when Roberts had barred the narrow pass across the swamp, to charge them, bowie-knife and revolver in hand.

The Forest Rangers had an anxious time, listening to the firing going on all night on the sap side of the pa. Von Tempsky states:

> Hour after hour I listened to the firing and to the pinging of bullets whistling over our heads and dropping amongst us the whole lifelong night.

Orakau pa, showing the British sap. Engraving from Illustrated London News, 1864. Waikato Museum of Art and History

> ... I went to the picket several times, and returned each time in great haste, fearing the Maoris might break cover during my absence.

The mounted Royal Artillery gunners under Lieutenant Rait patrolled on horseback along the whole perimeter throughout the night. On passing von Tempsky, Rait would stop and discuss the possibility of a Maori break-out.

And so ended the first day of the battle at Orakau with no prospect of an early conclusion.

Day Two – 1 April

Early on the second morning (1 April) further reinforcements arrived under command of Captain Greaves. These consisted of a detachment of the 18th Regiment (123 men all ranks) and a detachment of the 70th Regiment (97 men all ranks) – totalling 220 all ranks.

The defenders began running out a counter-sap to outflank the besiegers' sap. The firing from each covering party became fierce.

Artillery fire continued all day. A party of defenders rushed the east perimeter (the opposite side from the sap) and were repulsed by strong fire from the Forest Rangers.

Some artillery shells were lobbed into the Maori reinforcements across the swamp preventing any attempt of theirs to break the siege.

The particularly hot day made conditions within the pa difficult because of the lack of water and a mounting list of wounded and dead. By the end of the second day the supply of lead was also running short.

During the evening the Forest Rangers had their first casualty at Orakau and subsequently their first death of the Waikato campaign. (Ballenden was mortally wounded at Rangiaowhia but had not yet died.) Corporal Charles Coghlan, when casually placing a gabion above the sap, was mortally wounded by a bullet to the abdomen. He died the following day.

A more colourful description of Coghlan's death was given in an account written by a nephew of Jackson in 1913. He stated that Coghlan had to avenge his humiliation of being sick at the sight of Maori innards at Paparata:

> However he retrieved his reputation at Orakau, where having had his share of rum ration, he jumped up and cried, "I'll teach you Maoris whether I'm afraid", mounted on the sap and yelled defiance at the enemy only a few yards away. He was immediately fatally shot with a bullet through the head.

And so ended the second day of the engagement at Orakau. That night Rewi Maniapoto instructed his men to fire short lengths of fruit tree branch during the hours of darkness to conserve the lead supply. Also, under cover of darkness, one warrior courageously stole through the British lines to retrieve a calabash of water for the wounded.

Maori defenders at Orakau reject Ensign Mair's invitation to surrender. A.H. Messenger

CHAPTER 12

Orakau – the massacre

Day Three – 2 April

In the early light of the third day, another hot day, the Maori held council and decided to abandon the pa due to the lack of water. But the recommencement of rifle and artillery fire soon stopped the breakout.

A rush by some Maori at the sap in the morning was turned back.

The Forest Rangers were weary from the constant barrage of spent bullets fired from the opposite side of the pa. Von Tempsky commented:

> There was no excitement to compensate for the constant annoyance of bullets flying about you for three days and two nights.

False reports that the final assault was about to happen also drained the unit of enthusiasm. Von Tempsky, thinking there was still a need for volunteers in the sap, took 16 volunteers from No. 2 Company and marched around to the sap. But on meeting Captain Baker they were ordered to return immediately. Crestfallen, the men returned to their perimeter position.

Being an expert shot with a carbine, Jackson himself joined the men in the sap, firing into the pa at close range.

Soon after noon, when General Cameron arrived from Pukerimu Redoubt with his staff and an escort of Colonial Defence Force Cavalry, an attempt was made from the head of the sap to request a surrender from the defenders.

Ensign William Gilbert Mair of the Colonial Defence Cavalry, who acted as staff interpreter, and Mr Mainwaring were sent to the sap with a white flag to invite the defenders to surrender and promise safety for the garrison. Accounts of what was actually said on the day differ slightly. Mair's account is generally accepted as the most accurate. The answer came a few minutes later from the defenders, "E hoa, ka whawhai tonu ahau ki a koe, ake, ake!" ("Friend, I shall fight against you for ever and ever!"). Then Mair requested that the women and children come out. There was a short deliberation and the answer came, "Ki te mate nga tane, me mate ano nga wahine me nga tamariki." ("If the men are to die, the women and children must die too.")

Other words were also exchanged. Finally a bullet grazed Mair's right shoulder. Mair then reported back to Cameron, who was greatly impressed by the stubborn devotion of the Maori.

The Maori preferred to risk death rather than face the horrors of seemingly permanent detention in a coal-hulk anchored off Auckland. Governor Grey mentioned the lasting damage to Maori being kept prisoners on the *Marion* (the fate of Maori capture at Rangiriri) in a letter to the authorities in London:

> The natives distinctly state that the reason why they would not accept the terms offered to them by General Cameron at Orakau was because they feared they would all be taken to Auckland, as prisoners were from Rangiriri, and perhaps never be liberated.

To show how incongruous some wartime activities can be, at about midday on the third day mail arrived aboard drays from Te Awamutu and these returned in a few hours bearing anything to be posted. It seems a dangerous thing to do, as the battle reached a climax, for soldiers to crouch and scribble letters to loved ones back home in Britain. The distribution of letters must have caused problems.

One Armstrong gun was pulled into the sap in the early afternoon to pound the parapet from close range. Because the sap was now close to the post and rail fence (about 30 yards from the parapet), hand grenades could be tossed into the pa. Captain Jackson continued firing his carbine into the pa from the head of the sap.

Soon the sap joined the outwork and the battle entered its final stage.

As the small party of Forest Rangers helped to push the sap toward the enemy's position, a Waikato militiaman was shot down about half way between the head of the sap and the pa – a distance of about twenty yards from the pa – and was left lying wounded and exposed to heavy fire from the enemy. The party of Forest Rangers under Ensign Whitfield determined to recover the wounded man. But sending two or more men to bring him in would result in more men being killed or wounded.

After an exchange of ideas, it was determined the best method to extract the wounded man was to make a sudden rush across the open space thus causing a diversion by taking possession of the enemy's outwork. In going across the open space the Forest Rangers exposed themselves to the fire of the Maori facing the sap. Because of the suddenness of the movement, they were almost across the space before shots were fired and being close under the front of the pa they were somewhat protected as the Maori had to raise themselves to fire on a lower elevation. During the diversion the wounded man was brought in and handed over to medical staff.

Some time later Major Herford (3rd Regiment Waikato Militia) and others were shot down in two attempts trying to join the Forest Rangers. The Forest Rangers continued to clear the outwork of Maori. Others soon joined them and a party carrying hand grenades was now able to get into position immediately below the pa wall.

The throwing of grenades into the pa caused great confusion and consternation amongst the defenders.

Each time a party rushed forward to join the Forest Rangers a "Hurrah!" went up from the British perimeter, each side of the sap. On hearing this, von Tempsky immediately took a group of Forest Rangers to investigate. He states:

> Along the slant of the hill the fern is high, and the level of the ground scarce shows our heads.
> ... The Maoris saw us first just on cresting the hill, and sent a heavy fire at us.
> ... I saw some heaps of rubbish under some trees, with a half-broken-down pig fence, at 30 yards from the pa. That was a good halting place to breathe my men and count them. Alas! there was not above a dozen. There were my two sergeants, Carran and Toovey, Magole and little Keena, and a few of Jackson's company – but we had lost our tail by the velocity of our flight forward. Well, the place had a very tenable look about it, so, seeing that every man lay well covered, I sent Sergeant Carran back for reinforcements,

and saw that my men kept the Maoris' heads well down the parapet. Our arrival there had in the first instance driven back a few Maoris attempting to escape from the angle I expected they would make use of.

Von Tempsky's modest description of the events does not bear much resemblance to a description by Thomas Gudgeon in *The Defenders of New Zealand:*

> During the action it was necessary for von Tempsky and a group of his men to take up a position commanding an angle of the enemy pa so as to dislodge the occupants. In doing so he was compelled to lead his men between a heavy crossfire from the Maoris at almost point blank range. Exposed to a shower of bullets, they worked their way forward – lying flat till the shower of bullets passed – then dashing forward – then falling flat again to avoid the next shower. Once they gained their objective the Forest Rangers open fired on the Maoris making their position untenable, thus helping to force the Maoris to retreat.

Soon Carran returned. Von Tempsky continues:

> Carran returned in a little while, and said that Captain Baker wanted me immediately at my post, so nolens volens [willy-nilly], I had to return, seeing that a dozen men were not enough with which to assault 300 Maoris behind a high parapet. During my return I was informed by my men that one of those following me had been hit, and was lying in the very path to the pa. ... This poor fellow had chosen the main track to walk upon, probably scorning the fern, and had so come by his death. It was Corporal Taylor [recently promoted to Sergeant], an old soldier of the 70th.

Apparently the well-liked Taylor had been in the sap serving out a ration of rum to the detachment from Jackson's company and had stayed behind to store away the surplus rum. Having done so he made his way back to von Tempsky's perimeter and thoughtlessly wandered down the section of road exposed to Maori view. He was shot in the throat and fell face down. It is possible that Taylor had had more than his share of rum. To retrieve the body, a few Forest Rangers formed a human chain by holding the legs of the one in front while flat on the ground. When Taylor was reached they were pulled to the cover of high fern beside the road. Jackson later rewarded the two foremost men by presenting them with Taylor's watch and chain. Von Tempsky continues:

> Sadly we carried our burden to our post, where I found my mentor Captain Baker charged to the muzzle with military reprimands for me. While he and I and Major Blyth were arguing on this subject a tremendous shout arose from the pa.
> ... At last the Maoris had broken cover.

The defenders (including women and children) massed and rushed the southeast perimeter. Immediately soldiers rushed from the sap into the pa and fired into the last of the retreating Maori. Sergeant Southey was the first to enter the pa.

An old warrior lay dead with his gun pointing over the parapet. One leg had been shattered earlier in the siege and he had it bound up with flax leaves and sticks for splints, so that he could prop himself up against the parapet and go on fighting.

The surviving Maori headed south towards the swamp pursued by all the soldiers in the vicinity. Soldiers lining the perimeter could not fire at the Maori as they passed for fear of crossfiring along the neighbouring perimeter.

Von Tempsky describes the chase:

> Giving hurried orders to Westrup to watch the forest side of the picket hill, and taking Roberts with me, we went off at full speed along the ridge to cut off the Maoris whom we saw now ascending the furthest extreme of that ridge.
> "Run, men, run! Cut them off! Cut them off!" And the Rangers bounded over the ground as if their feet had wings.
> The Maoris had a tremendous start of it, but the passage of the swamp and scrub in the bottom of the gully had delayed them somewhat. We came within shot of them, and as their long, irregular mass ascended the next rise our fire began to tell. Still we had to use the utmost exertion to keep within sight and shot of them, and would probably have lost half had not Rait with his troopers and some of the Defence Corps headed them by a daring breakneck ride across country.

The Forest Rangers, mounted Royal Artillery and some Colonial Defence Force troopers pursued the Maori for a distance of about six miles. The Forest Rangers, led by von Tempsky and Roberts, and the cavalry tried to head off the retreat by keeping to high ground on the southeast side of the swamp. The Forest Rangers soon caught up with the Maori and shot many with their carbines. The mounted men were soon left behind (due to the difficulty of negotiating horses through flax and soft ground). In von Tempsky own words:

> There was Roberts ahead of us all with Torpey, of Jackson's company, and two or three others, the fleetest of the corps. That day I christened Roberts Deerfoot as I panted behind him, bellowing my lungs out in shouting to the men and directing the pursuit.
> ... But the Maoris, seeing only these troopers after them, and from the other side of the swamp commenced to give them some ugly shots, killing in a moment two horses and wounding some of the men. Now, Rait's troopers had only revolvers, which were utterly useless at that distance, so they began to be rather doubtful what to do with their Tartar, when the Rangers made their appearance, and the presence of their carbines became soon painfully evident to the natives. Off they started again, now at a lesser distance they began to drop under our fire very fast; also some of them had outrun their fleetness, and, our wind and stamina beginning to tell after the first three miles, many a laggard was shot down after giving us the last desperate shot of his barrel.

Some Forest Rangers even crossed the Puniu but at the sound of the recall they returned to Orakau. Von Tempsky states in his journal:

> Most of the troops abandoned the pursuit at the Puniu River, but several of us Forest Rangers and two or three men of Rait's Artillery crossed the river

and went on in chase for a little distance. We caught up with one Maori, who repeatedly turned and deliberately knelt and levelled his single-barrel shotgun (he was endeavouring to cover the retreat of some of his wounded). I and the Ranger who was near to me took cover among the wiwi rushes and scrub, fired, and were reloading as we lay there. The Maori retreated a few yards, then turned and presented his gun at us as before. Several shots were fired at him, but he did not reply. At last one of us shot him dead. We went up to the plucky fellow as he lay there in the rushes, and we found that his gun was empty; he had not a single cartridge left. On the middle fingers of his left hand he wore a little bag which held a few percussion caps. I was terribly grieved – we all were – to think that we had killed so brave a man. Of course we did not know he was pointing an unloaded gun at us; we had to save ourselves from being potted, as we thought. Had he dropped his useless gun, and stood up and shown that he was unarmed and helpless, we would have been only to glad to have spared him. But at that time none of us knew enough Maori to call upon him to surrender.

One reason why the Forest Rangers were so far in front of other pursuers during the pursuit was that they could reload their carbines at the trot rather than stop and reload as soldiers with muzzle loading rifles were forced to do.

Soon the pursuit ended with von Tempsky noting:

> ... The last natives we saw were three or four trotting along the top of a distant ridge.

Von Tempsky and Roberts re-crossed the Puniu River and found Colonel Havelock collecting the scattered squads of pursuers. He marched them back to Orakau in a body, leaving von Tempsky behind to wait for some Forest Rangers who had not yet made their appearance. When these men arrived they also returned to Orakau.

All the wounded defenders (including a few women) were carried into the imperial camp. One of the captives was a half-caste girl who had an arm shattered by a bullet.

And so ended the dreadful rout that was attributed mainly to the Forest Rangers and some of the mounted men. It was not until the next day that the soldiers fully realised the terrible outcome of the pursuit. Probably fewer than 50 out of about 300 Maori escaped unscathed. About 160 Maori were killed or died of wounds. Rewi Maniapoto managed to escape un-wounded escorted by a protecting ring of devout supporters. The British casualties were 17 killed and 51 wounded.

In the initial charge into the pa two women are known to have been bayoneted by imperial troops hungry for revenge – although it has been said that the women were hard to distinguish from the men. Most of the native women were saved from slaughter by the protection of a few Forest Rangers, one being Southey. One women was found dead clasping a Bible to her breast. Bibles were found on several dead and wounded Maori.

Most of the Maori dead were buried near where they fell in several mass graves. Nearly 40 men and women were buried in their trenches. The exact spot today is just to the north side of the road opposite the memorial. The soldiers just tumbled the parapet in over the bodies. One eyewitness described how a clenched hand of a

Maori protruded above the ground, and a soldier trampled on it till it was below the surface.

The pa when captured contained about three tons of raw potatoes and a little cooked Maori bread. There was no water in the pa nor any vessel to hold water.

For their gallantry in this battle, officially described as "the very able services rendered", Jackson and von Tempsky were both promoted to the rank of Major. Jackson's commission was dated 3 April 1864 (named to the 2nd Regiment Waikato Militia) and von Tempsky's the day after (named to the 1st Regiment Waikato Militia), maintaining Jackson as senior in appointment by one day. This further contributed to von Tempsky's jealousy of Jackson.

It was estimated that about 40,000 rounds of ammunition were fired by the troops during the three days' fighting at Orakau.

Although fatigue parties went out on the day after the battle ended to collect the dead Maori, not all of them were found. About a fortnight later Forest Rangers were reconnoitring in the area of the swamp and noticed the fetid smell of rotting bodies.

In his official account of the battle to the Assistant Military Secretary, Headquarters, Brigadier-General Carey wrote:

> Camp Te Awamutu, April 3, 1864.
> Sir, I have the honour to state, for the information of the Lieutenant-General commanding the forces, that about midday of 30 March 1864, it was reported to me by Lieutenant-Colonel Haultain, commanding the Kihikihi Redoubt, that Maoris were seen in force at the village of Orakau, about two and a half to three miles distant from his post.
> I immediately rode over [from Te Awamutu camp] and made a reconnaissance. Found that the natives were engaged building a pa, and as it was then too late in the day to attack at once, I returned to this camp and made arrangements to march on the enemy's position during the night. Captain Baker, 18th Royal Irish (Deputy Assistant Adjutant-General), fortunately found two men in the camp – Messrs. Gage and W. Astle – whom from their local knowledge I at once engaged as guides, which circumstance enabled me to determine on a combined movement.
> My plan of attack was to advance with the main body along the dray road to Orakau; to detach a force of 250 men under Major Blyth, 40th Regiment, who would take a circuitous route through a somewhat difficult country, crossing and re-crossing the Puniu River, and, marching on my right flank, to take the enemy's position in reverse; and thirdly, to draw a force of 160 men from Rangiaowhia and Hairini under Captain Blewitt, 65th Regiment, who would march across to the enemy's position on my left, the three bodies of troops arriving, if possible, simultaneously before the enemy's stronghold shortly before daylight.
> At midnight Major Blyth, 40th Regiment, marched with 250 men, with directions to take the road to the right, cross and re-cross the Puniu River, and to gain the rear of the enemy's position before daylight, halting there until he should hear my attack, and then to dispose of his force so as to cut off the retreat of the enemy.
> The road from Rangiaowhia to Orakau I found on enquiry to be very difficult,

being intercepted by deep swamp and thick bush. However, having every confidence in Captain Blewitt's energy, I directed that officer, who commands at Rangiaowhia, to march during the night and endeavour to form a junction with me before daylight on the proper right of the enemy's position, bringing with him 100 men.

At 3 o'clock on Thursday morning, the 31st, I marched with the main body along the dray road to Kihikihi, taking on Lieutenant-Colonel Haultain and 150 men from that post, and then proceeded by the same road to the village of Orakau, which I reached without opposition as the day dawned. The enemy, evidently taken by surprise, open fired on the advance guard – composed of 120 of the Royal Irish and twenty of the Forest Rangers, gallantly led by Captain Ring, 18th Royal Irish, and supported by 100 of the 40th Regiment, who immediately rushed forward to the attack in skirmishing order. The position being found very strong, an earthwork with strong flank defences, deep ditches with posts and rails outside, and nearly covered from view with flax bushes, peach trees, and high fern – this party was forced to retire; but it at once reformed, and, being reinforced by another company of the 40th Regiment, again tried to take the place by assault, but with no better success. Here, Captain Ring, 18th Royal Irish, fell mortally wounded, and Captain Fischer, 40th Regiment, severely so, besides four men killed and several wounded. On Captain Ring's falling, Captain Baker, 18th Royal Irish (Deputy Adjutant-General), most gallantly galloped up, dismounted, and, calling for volunteers, again endeavoured to carry the place by assault. This also failed.

Finding that there was no chance of taking the pa in this manner, from the immense strength, and other men having fallen, I determined to desist from the mode of attack; and having heard that both Major Blyth, 40th Regiment, and Captain Blewitt were at their appointed posts, I decided on surrounding the place and adopting the more slow but sure method of approaching the position by sap, which was shortly after commenced under the very able direction of Lieutenant Hurst, 12th Regiment, attached to the Royal Engineers Department. At this time Lieutenant Carre, Royal Artillery, endeavoured to effect a breach in the enemy's works, but could make no impression on it.

A further supply of entrenching tools and gabions (which latter had most fortunately been prepared at the neighbouring posts for service at headquarters on the Horotiu [Waikato River]) were immediately ordered up with the men's blankets, food etc. and every possible precaution taken by the proper disposition of the force to prevent the escape of the enemy.

During the afternoon a reinforcement of some 150 or 200 of the enemy, from the direction of Maungatautari, appeared in sight, evidently determined on relieving the place. They advanced to a bush situated about 900 yards in rear of our outposts, but seeing that it was scarcely possible to break through the line formed by our troops, they halted and commenced firing volleys, at the same time exciting the men in the pa to increased energy, by dancing the war dance, shouting, etc.

The wounded were sent on to Te Awamutu and Kihikihi. The sap was pushed forward vigorously, and the troops so posted as to prevent any possibility of escape by the natives during the night.

Heavy firing was kept up by the enemy on the troops both in the sap and around the place during the day and night, causing but few casualties, the men contriving to cover themselves in temporary rifle pits, dug out with their bayonets and hands. [In the case of the Forest Rangers – with their bowie knives, if they had one.]

A reinforcement of 200 men, under the command of Captain Inman, 18th Royal Irish, reached me from headquarters during the afternoon.

Having reported my proceedings to the commander of the forces in the morning, I was glad to receive a reinforcement sent by him (148, of 12th Regiment), and guided by Captain Greaves, Deputy Assistant Quartermaster General, which arrived about daylight on the morning of April 1, and which enabled me to relieve the men in the sap more constantly, and therefore to carry on the work more quickly. Captain Greaves ever afforded me material assistance in the duties of his department. This day was spent in working at the sap and making rifle pits around the pa, few casualties occurring. Captain Betty, Royal Artillery, arrived during the day and assumed command of the Royal Artillery, which enabled Lieutenant Carre to render some assistance to Lieutenant Hurst in constructing the sap, he having been at it without intermission.

During the night a few of the enemy were perceived trying to effect an escape from the pa, but, being immediately fired upon, returned to their earthwork. I omitted to mention that Captain Betty, Royal Artillery, threw some well directed shells at the Maori reinforcement in the bush and on the hills, which evidently disconcerted them considerably.

At an early hour on the morning of 2nd April Lieutenant-Colonel Sir Henry Havelock, Bart (Deputy Assistant Quartermaster General), arrived with the hand grenades, which were at once thrown into the enemy's position with great effect by Sergeant McKay, Royal Artillery, who thus rendered good and gallant service at great personal risk, under a galling fire.

About noon I ordered Captain Betty, Royal Artillery, to have a six-pounder Armstrong gun carried into the sap, an entrance having been made. It open fired on the enemy's work, destroying the palisading, making a considerable breach and silencing in a great measure the fire of the enemy on the men engaged at the head of the sap.

The commander of the forces [General Cameron], with his staff, etc., arrived on the ground at this time, and witnessed the remainder of the operations. Colonel Mould, C.B., Royal Engineers, coming up with General Cameron, gave his able assistance towards the completion of the sap into the enemy's work. As it was known that women and children were in the pa, the enemy was called upon to surrender previous to the concentrated fire of the Armstrong gun and hand grenades on their work. They were told that their lives would be spared, and if they declined they were requested at least to have compassion on their women and children, and send them out. They replied that they would not do so, but would fight to the last. The pa was then carried. The enemy, effecting his escape from the opposite side of the work, dashed through a space from which the troops had been thrown back under cover, to enable the [Armstrong] gun to open. They were, however, speedily followed up, and suffered a severe loss during a pursuit of nearly six miles, Lieutenant Rait, Royal Artillery [mounted], with his troopers, and Captain Pye, Colonial Defence Force [cavalry], with a small detachment, having headed them and kept them back until the infantry [including Forest Rangers] came up. I regret to say that in the pa and in the pursuit some three or four women were killed unavoidably, probably owing to the similarity of dress of both men and women, and their hair being cut equally short, rendering it impossible to distinguish one from the other at any distance.

The troops were recalled about sundown, and bivouacked round the enemy's late position.

At an early hour this morning I caused diligent search to be made for the killed and wounded of the enemy. Their loss was considerable, amounting to 101 killed, besides 18 to 20 reported by native persons as buried in the pa; 26 wounded and taken prisoners, and 7 un-wounded taken prisoners. In addition to this number, the natives were seen to be engaged carrying off dead and wounded early in the morning at the most distant point of pursuit, and fresh tracks showed that they had been similarly occupied during the night.

I bring to the special notice of the Lieutenant-General commanding the forces the gallant bearing of Captain Baker, 18th Royal Irish (Deputy Assistant Adjutant-General), during the whole of the operations, but more especially on the occasion already mentioned of the fall of that brave and lamented soldier, Captain Ring.

Also, the determined bravery of Captain Herford, Waikato Militia, who was very severely wounded (loss of eye), and the gallantry of Lieutenant Harrison, Waikato Militia, both of whom remained at the head of the sap nearly the whole time, keeping down the fire of the enemy by the well directed balls of their own rifles. Likewise to Sergeant McKay, Royal Artillery, who, as before mentioned, under a galling fire, threw, with the greatest precision and coolness, hand grenades from the sap and from the lodgment made in the outer work of the enemy into his stronghold.

The wounded received the greatest possible attention on the field from the senior medical officer, Dr White, 65th Regiment; ably seconded by Assistant-Surgeons Spencer, 18th Royal Irish, Jules, 40th Regiment, and Hilston, R.N., until the arrival of Dr Mouat, C.B., V.C., the P.M.O., who left nothing undone in providing for their comfort, etc.

I trust the conduct of the officers and men under my command during this long operation of three days and two nights, without cover and constantly under fire, may meet with the approval of the Commander of the Forces. The casualties on our side – 16 killed and 52 wounded, of which I enclose a return – are, I regret to say, severe.

George J. Carey,
Brigadier-General.

The Forest Rangers had two casualties at Orakau. They were: Corporal Charles Coghlan, No. 1 Company, who was mortally wounded by a bullet penetrating his abdomen; Sergeant William Taylor, No. 1 Company, who was instantly killed by a

The Colonial Defence Force Cavalry in pursuit of Maori after their break-out of Orakau pa, 2 April 1864. Picturesque Atlas of Australasia

bullet to his upper chest and throat.

From the Maori perspective, Orakau was a defeat. Historians, when looking back, behold the Maori's bravery and stubbornness against the might and far superior numbers of the imperial and colonial soldiers present. The Maori's scornful defiance was further accentuated by the devoted role of the women who remained to share the ordeal with their husbands and brothers. Through the eyes of the New Zealand government of the day, the defenders were rebels holding stubbornly to nationalism and a broken cause.

Generally speaking the imperial soldiers regretted having to fight such a courageous and dedicated foe desperately defending their homelands, holding much respect for them. It was the colonial soldier who wanted the enemy vanquished so they could get at the "booty" – the fertile land round Te Awamutu promised to them in the terms of their enlistment.

General Cameron had by now developed a distaste for fighting the Maori, seeing the only benefit was to provide land for the colonial "settler" soldiers. He had already displayed his distaste at Rangiaowhia where he ordered the immediate release of Maori captives held in the church.

In his despatch dated 7 April 1864 from Pukerimu, Cambridge, he wrote:

> It is impossible not to admire the heroic courage and devotion of the natives in defending themselves for so long against overwhelming numbers. Surrounded closely on all sides, cut off from their supply of water, and deprived of all hope of succour, they resolutely held their ground for more than two days, and did not abandon the position until the sap had reached the ditch of their last entrenchment.

There is a lament of the Ngatimaniapoto for their dead in Taranaki battles of 1860, that they also applied to the battle at Orakau:

> *The land is swept and desolate,*
> *Mournfully rolls the tide of Puniu,*
> *The waters sob as they flow.*

James Edward Fitzgerald, one of the founders of the Canterbury settlement, wrote an editorial article in the *Christchurch Press* on 16 April 1864:

> No human situation can be conceived more desperate or more hopeless – their lands gone, their race melting away like snow before the sun, and their own turn come at last, with the enemy surrounding them on all sides, and nothing but certain death staring them in the face ...
>
> They will say it was not a war for safety or for law, or for truth or liberty, but it was a war dictated by avarice and prosecuted by spoliation. It was war to remove a neighbour's landmark, to destroy a race that we might dwell in their tents ...
>
> But if there be anything in the whole miserable story to excite the admiration of a generous mind, it is this sad spectacle of those grim and tawny figures, gaunt with the watching and weariness, the wounds and nakedness of a long campaign in the bush, staring over their ragged palisades on the hosts of the conquerors from whom escape was impossible and wailing out their last chant of death and defiance "Ake! Ake! Ake! – for ever! for ever! for ever!"

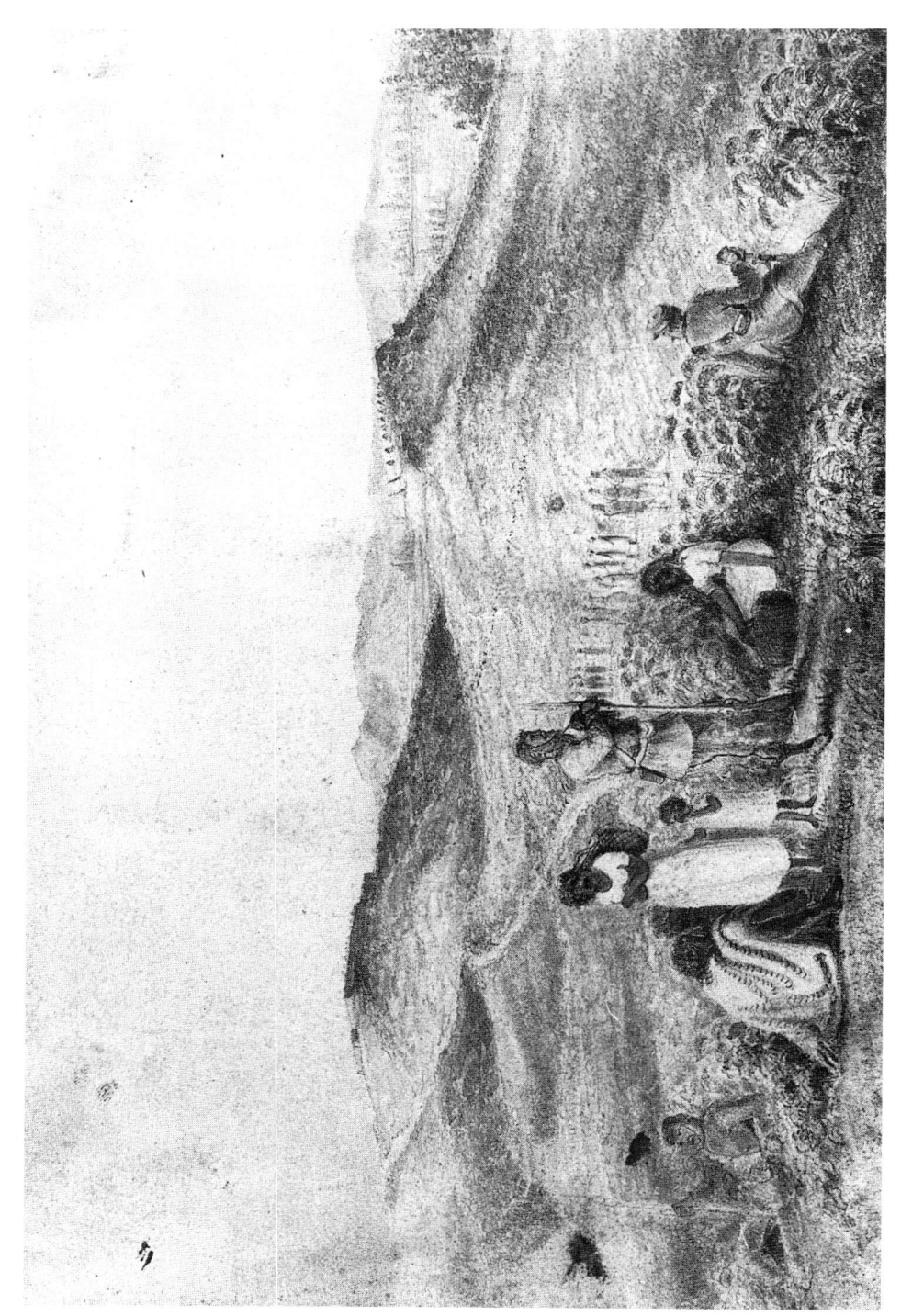

Von Tempsky watercolour of No. 2 Company, Forest Rangers in camp at Ohaupo, 1864. *Waikato Museum of Art and History*

Roll of Forest Rangers at time of Orakau engagement, 31 March - 2 April 1864:

Jackson's No. 1 Company: *Captain* (1): Jackson. *Lieutenant* (1): Westrup. *Ensign* (1): Whitfield. *Staff Sergeant* (1): Bertram. *Sergeants* (3): James Cunningham, John Smith, Taylor (killed at Orakau by a bullet to upper chest). *Corporals* (4): Coghlan (mortally wounded at Orakau with bullet penetrating the abdomen), Long, Morgan, James Smith. *Privates* (44): Alexander, Babington, Benson, Bindon, Philip Bond, William Bond, Robert Bruce, William Bruce, John Burns, Laurence Burns, Cole, Costello, Robert Cunningham, Davis (joined during battle on 1 April), Duggan, Evans, Findlay, Frost, Gallie, Gibb, Grigg, Hannay, Hendry, Jennings, Johns, McEnany, Madigan, Mahoney, Murray, John Nolan, Martin Nolan, Osborne, Rowden, Thomas Smith, Stephenson, Thomson, Torpey, Temple, Tucker, Vincent, Vaughan, George Ward, Wells, Williams.

Von Tempsky's No. 2 Company: *Captain* (1): von Tempsky. *Lieutenant* (1): Roberts. *Ensign* (1): Sherret. *Staff Sergeant* (1): McMinn. *Sergeants* (3): Carran, Southey, Wakeford. *Corporals* (3): Parsons, Sibley, Toovey. *Privates* (51): Albin, Anderson, Ballenden, Bidgood, Bochow, Burry, Butter, Buttle, Bygum, Clifford, Cochrane, Collins, Conrad, Donovan, Fallon, Fraser, Freeman, Harris, Hartland, Healas, Hellkessel, Higgins, Jones, Keena, Liebig, Lindsay, McClymont, McNamara, Magole, Lawrence Mitchell, Mohr, Mulligan, Neil, Owens, Pohlen, Quinn, Race, Ross, Rush, Scally, Schacht, Shine, Simmons, Stanley, Sturmer, Sumsion, Taylor, Thomson, Tubby, Wheeler, Woods.

On 3 April the Forest Rangers were moved from Orakau, the main body of British troops having left the previous day.

The Waikato campaign came to an end with the taking of the two Maori pa at the foot of the Pukekura Range, the lower and stronger being Te Tiki o te Ihingarangi pa.

On the morning of 5 April 1864, a force of 300 men of the 70th Regiment and a few men of the 18th Regiment, under Lieutenant-Colonel Havelock marched from Pukerimu south along the east bank of the Waikato River. They observed the two Maori positions at Pukekura to be abandoned and immediately occupied them without casualties.

It is believed the Maori only had about 400 men to defend the two positions so they decided to fall back to Porewa pa, near Horahora, at the foot of Maungatautari mountain.

Colonel MacNeil, Aide-de-Camp to General Cameron, had been ambushed near Ohaupo at the time of the battle at Orakau. So a permanent post was positioned on a commanding ridge a little south of present-day Ohaupo. A redoubt was built by the 40th Regiment under Major Blyth while von Tempsky with his company patrolled the road and scouted the bush – generally making travel safe between Te Awamutu and the Pukerimu Redoubt near Cambridge.

William Race describes their short stay in Ohaupo:

> It was a very desolate looking place at an elevation of several feet above the main road and about 200 yards from the bush. Consequently we had to sleep under arms for fear of a surprise from the rebels via that bush.
> ... [It was at Ohaupo] that von Tempsky received an official indication of his promotion to a major.

... One day the orderly Corporal [actually Staff Sergeant] McMinn brought with the daily rations (biscuits) three loaves of newly baked bread, one for the chief [von Tempsky], one for Lieutenant Roberts and one for Ensign Sherret, explaining that the commissariat had established ovens. So soft tack was the order of the day, for officers only. Von Tempsky simply said on hearing this explanation "Well Corporal, take ours back and draw biscuits as usual, when my men can get it too, we'll draw ours", and biscuits they had.

Another time, about a quarter of a mile from us down on the flat was a large redoubt occupied by some 100 men of the 40th under Major Blyth. These men were engaged with pick and shovel, levelling the Maori pas. One morning a sergeant came to our camp with a requisition signed by the Major [Blyth] for 20 men of the Forest Rangers to assist the regulars in their work of levelling.

Von read the requisition and told the sergeant to give his compliments to the Major, and that a party of his men were going out reconnoitring and he could not spare them. After the sergeant departed he ordered Roberts to fall in the men. ... [Von Tempsky] came out of his tent and told us ... "Men, you stood by me when I wanted you, now I'll stand by you, it shall never be said my Rangers are transformed into navvies to do pick and shovel work." Then turning to Lieutenant Roberts, said take 20 or 30, let them put on their revolvers, and take their books if they have any, and go out a mile or two, out of sight, and picnic for a hour or two.

This was the order for three consecutive mornings. The Forest Rangers took great delight in passing the regulars at their toil but never let on their scheme.

Von Tempsky by this proved himself either a great leader of men or patronising and manipulative. He seemed to look for the opportunities to impress upon the men his greatness and fairness. But obviously he did feel for his men and enjoyed contact with them on their level, a far cry from the treatment imperial soldiers received from their superiors.

Another example of von Tempsky's compassion for his men was when one of his men contracted typhoid fever and was placed in hospital at Te Awamutu. Three days later he visited the Forest Ranger and found him nearly dead in an old tent lying on some wet fern. He was supposed to be under the care of Doctor Demster of the Imperial Army Hospital Corps. Von Tempsky sent for Demster and expressed his profound opinions of Demster's lack of care, threatening to bring the case to General Cameron's attention. After telling Demster to leave, von Tempsky then immediately sought out Doctor Spencer (a highly respected and clever doctor attached to the 18th Regiment), and begged him to take over the care of the Forest Ranger, who after a bad bout of the disease did recover.

Von Tempsky and his No. 2 Company were at Ohaupo till June 1864.

With the Waikato campaign at an end, General Cameron pondered on its success. Throughout the campaign Cameron, as General commanding the Imperial Army, represented the British attitude to New Zealand's wars and to the rights of the Maori. Governor Grey on the other hand, as head of the colonial government represented, through the pressure of his Ministers, the interests of the settlers and their impatience to get possession of Maori land. The relationship between the two started to deteriorate. Previously letters from Cameron to Grey were headed "My dear Sir George", but later slipped to the impersonal opening of just "Sir".

On arrival in New Zealand Cameron had only wanted to fight the Maori. But through the Maori chivalry he learned to admire them. Incidents in the campaign strengthened Cameron's distaste for the war in which he believed the New Zealand Government was using the Imperial Army merely to obtain land for the settlers. He strongly believed that the settler soldiers, the Waikato Militia for example, were seldom willing to fight for themselves. He once wrote to Grey that the settler soldiers were:

> ... expecting to have nothing to do but enrich themselves by the presence of the [imperial] troops without any trouble or inconvenience to themselves.

Later, after the first battle at Kakaramea or Te Ngaio (15 March 1865), Cameron asked a wounded Maori:

> Why did you resist our advance? Could you not see we were an overwhelming force?

The Maori's reply was:

> What would you have us do? This is our village; these are our plantations. Men are not fit to live if they are not brave enough to defend their own homes.

Cameron's view was also shared by many of his officers. Colonel Greer once wrote of:

> ... the gallant stand made by the Maori at their rifle pits. They stood the charge without flinching and did not retire until forced out at the point of the bayonet.

Another matter that upset the imperial soldiers was the arms and ammunition the Maori used against them; these being sold to the Maori by colonials. This commerce was lucrative with large sums of money changing hands. The effect was to protract the war and provide the colonials with more trade opportunities. The trade also caused more British casualties.

Cameron later wrote:

> I shall be required to carry on this miserable war for the profit and gratification of the Colony.

A total of 1,217,437 acres was confiscated from the Maori in the Waikato. Of this, 224,080 acres was designated native reserves (obviously un-arable land) and 50,000 acres were returned to tribes. The rest stayed in the colonial Government's control. About 150,000 acres were used for military settlements. The largest block of 446,978 acres was put up for sale. The Government's intention was to sell the land to cover the cost of the campaign but revenue fell well short of their target. Later, a further 214,000 acres were confiscated at Tauranga.

CHAPTER 13

Detachment at Maketu

A strong force of Ngatiporou Maori moved along the coast from the Matata region towards Maketu, in the Bay of Plenty, on 21 April 1864. Their advance guard surprised two Officers – Major Colville (43rd Regiment) and Ensign H.F. Way (3rd Regiment Waikato Militia) – who were duck-shooting in a canoe on the Waihi lagoon, about 2 miles east of Maketu. The two men had a lucky escape and returned to Maketu. Stationed at Maketu was a detachment of 14 men of the Forest Rangers and Colonial Defence Force under Major Drummond Hay (Waikato Militia) and Captain Thomas McDonnell. Skirmishing followed for the next few days with the British getting support from two boats, the gunboat *Sandfly* and the warship *Falcon*. The Maori entrenched below the Maketu fort and Pukemaire redoubt (both built on old pa sites). But after cannon fire from the two boats and Pukemaire redoubt on 27 April the Maori retreated across the lagoon and occupied the sandhills on the east side.

This position was gallantly stormed by Hay and McDonnell with a small force consisting of Forest Rangers (8), Colonial Defence Cavalry (6) and the friendly Arawa Maori ("Friendly Natives"). The enemy Maori were then pursued along the beach with the help of gunfire from the two boats following off the coast. The final stand of the enemy was made near the Pua-Kowhai Stream, about two miles west of Matata, where the Arawa Maori rushed about 400 of the enemy who broke and fled. The enemy then were hotly pursued along the beach by the Arawa, Forest Rangers and Colonial Defence Force, as far as Matata. About 50 of the enemy were killed but only one Arawa Maori was killed.

The eight Forest Rangers from No. 1 Company and members of the Colonial Defence Force Cavalry had been sent on 18 March 1864 to Maketu by Captain Jackson from Pukerimu Redoubt, Cambridge, at the request of General Cameron. They were a token force to reinforce the Arawa with a European presence. The detachment, under command of Sergeant Thomas Holden, travelled by Maori tracks via Matamata and the Kaimai Range to reach Maketu in the Bay of Plenty.

The Forest Rangers present were removed from Forest Ranger acquittance rolls (not receiving pay) from 16 March 1864. They were possibly placed on McDonnell's payroll for the friendly Arawa Maori.

Roll of Forest Ranger detachment at Maketu, 1864:

Sergeant (1): Thomas Holden. Privates (7): John Carter, Richard Fitzgerald, Henry Jackson, Hugh McDonald, James Peters, Henry Rowland, James Watters.

Jackson possibly expected all eight of the detachment to return to the Waikato and rejoin the Forest Rangers on completion of their duties at Maketu, but only three, Sergeant Holden and Privates Carter and Watters, eventually rejoined on 3 November 1864. These three received back pay for the two unpaid days before they left Cambridge (17-18 April 1864).

Major Colville (43rd Light Infantry, commanding at Maketu) stated in his official

Detachment at Maketu

despatch from Maketu on 21 April 1864:

> Sir, I have the honour to report to you an engagement with the East Coast Natives at Waihi, two miles from the fort at Maketu, in which about 110 men of the force under my command were engaged.
> An ambuscade was laid near the ford at Waihi this morning; and at least 50 rebels opened fire on Ensign Way, 3rd Waikato Regiment [Militia]; Private Key, 43rd Light Infantry, and myself, when we were crossing the river at 10 am in a canoe.
> The rebels were certainly not above fifty yards distant at the time, and I consider our escape as most providential and wonderful.
> They pursued us across the ford, on our jumping out of the canoe into the water, and followed us yelling and firing till we got into the bush and escaped.
> On arrival at the fort, I immediately ordered out a party of 50 men of the 43rd Light Infantry and 3rd Waikato Regiment [Militia], under command of Captain Smith, 43rd Light Infantry, to drive the enemy across the ford.
> They found on arrival that the enemy had re-crossed the river, and had established themselves about 400 yards distant on that side, and kept up a constant fire from the sand hills and bush around, which we returned with interest.
> Finding the enemy mustering strong, I sent for a further reinforcement of 30 men, under the command of Captain Harris, 43rd Light Infantry, and Ensign Way, 3rd Waikato Regiment. Major Drummond Hay [Waikato Militia] and Captain [Thomas] McDonnell also arrived with the Forest Rangers (14 men); and a number of the friendly Arawa tribe also joined. I requested Major Hay to cross the river with his Rangers and all the native allies.
> This he did; but as very few of the natives would follow him, he was reluctantly compelled to retire after remaining engaged for some time.
> My orders are so very stringent not to go far from the settlement of Maketu, that I was compelled to content myself with lining the side of the river, and firing at 400 yards and more at the rebels.
> The East Coast natives, apparently 300 strong, are now entrenching themselves at the position they occupied today, and I hear they are receiving further reinforcements.
> I have, therefore, requested Major Hay to attack them across the river in the morning, if he can induce the native allies to follow him.
> At dusk I withdrew my men and returned to the fort, leaving a strong party of natives to protect the village of Waihi, and give the alarm in the event of the rebels coming on.
> My best thanks are due to Captains Smith and Honourable A.E. Harris, 43rd Light Infantry, for the able manner they led their companies into action. Also to Ensign Way, commanding the detachment of the 3rd Waikato Regiment.
> I have the honour to enclose a list of wounded [only 4 were wounded: 2 severely and 2 slightly], which I am glad to say is but small, considering we were under fire between six and seven hours. Besides the enclosed, Captain

McDonnell, of the Forest Rangers, was slightly wounded in the hand.

I consider I am strong enough to hold the settlement provided more ammunition is sent me as soon as possible, as I expect to be engaged again tomorrow.

From the nature of the country and from our being unable to cross the river, it is impossible to estimate the loss of the enemy. They were, however, seen carrying off killed or wounded men on several occasions during the day.

Major George Drummond Hay mentioned in his despatch of the operation:

> On the morning of the 27th the enemy had fired heavily at Fort Colville [Maketu], commencing at 4 am. Subsequently, HMS *Falcon* and the *Sandfly* having arrived, they were shelled out of their position and retreated across Waihi [lagoon], the men of war [boats] following them up the coast for about twelve miles.

And of the final push and engagement:

> The men of the Defence Force and Forest Rangers attached to the Native Contingent, were so fatigued with the march, having far more than the natives to carry, that they were only able to join in the pursuit.

CHAPTER 14

Broken promise

Major Jackson entered into a dispute in a series of dialogues between himself and the Honourable Thomas Russell and later Major Atkinson, both Colonial Defence Ministers. The dispute was over land claims for himself and for the original company of Forest Rangers (raised in August 1863 and disbanded in November 1863).

Jackson believed that the terms of service with the original Forest Rangers included land and extra land for distinguished service. Jackson, in a letter to Russell dated 17 October 1864, stated:

> ... several men who served in the first company of Forest Rangers, under my command, have written to me concerning the land which was promised to them.

His prompt answer from the Colonial Defence Office was that:

> ... the men of the old company who took their discharges, and have not joined the existing company of Forest Rangers, are not entitled to land.

Many men re-enlisted in the new Forest Rangers and so were entitled to a land grant under the conditions of service of the Waikato Militia, so only a few applicants were refused. Jackson believed he, personally, was entitled to separate claims – one for the first term of service and the one for the second. The Ministry did not look too kindly on Jackson, considering him to be greedy.

Jackson fought back with a letter to Russell stating:

> The men were to have each a grant of land, and to any man who might distinguish himself, a special grant. With reference to myself, I was given to understand that I should have a large grant of good land.
> ... His excellency also said he thought the war would be over in three or four months. Mr Russell instructed me to swear in the men only for three months.
> The men were particular about the land, which was promised to them without any condition, it merely called the ordinary grant. I may also state that the men were disbanded at the end of three months; also that they did all the work required of them, which was sometimes of a very harassing nature, being almost continually in the bush day and night in a wet winter.

Jackson was admirable in that he pursued the claims to the limit, putting himself in an unfavourable light with his superiors. He believed the Ministry had fallen well short of their promises. A pending change of Government at this stage disrupted proceedings.

On 12 November 1864, Jackson wrote to Russell requesting that the Forest Rangers be separated from the Waikato Militia, requesting that his company of Forest Rangers:

... be detached from the 2nd Waikato Militia, for the following reasons, namely: – That I consider my company entitled to a special section of land, which it will not get whilst attached to the 2nd Waikato Militia, as each company will have to draw lots. That, whilst I am in the 2nd Waikato Militia, some officers command me who otherwise would not. That I have great difficulty in getting men discharged, in room of substitutes. I have to get a particular class of men, and when I have found them I have to wait, from one week to one month, as the papers and etc., have to pass through so many offices, which would be obviated were I made independent of the regiment.

Jackson's wish was granted on 31 January 1865 in the reply:

The Forest Rangers will be detached from the 2nd Waikato Militia, and made into a separate corps. They will be located at Rangiaowhia.

Rangiaowhia was also where land grants were given. The Government still refused land grants to those enrolled in the original Forest Ranger company, but granted land to those in the No. 1 and No. 2 companies.

A few years later, Jackson continued his pursuit of the matter.

The Ministry began to believe a personal attack on Jackson would quieten his anger. An internal memorandum within the Government dated 30 July 1870 referred to Jackson as:

... becoming so common as to amount to a positive nuisance, and ought to be discouraged.

But the Government did have a good argument against Jackson, stating in another internal memorandum dated 27 January 1871:

Major Jackson has done good service, and he has been very handsomely treated. He has the best piece of land in Waikato. He was kept on full pay for many months after the time of his location upon his land, and he received from the Government besides, £209, in compensation for losses on his farm at Wairoa [Clevedon], which he had left whilst he was on service.

In a letter from T.W. Lewis, Chief Clerk, Defence Office, to Mr G.S. Cooper dated 24 August 1871, summing up the whole land claim business, Lewis stated:

And here I remark that it would appear that the claims to land, under the first conditions of service, of Major Jackson and others of the first [original] company of Forest Rangers (who joined the second corps) were waived, or, more properly speaking, merged into their claims under the Waikato Regulations.

... and that those men who belonged to the first company of Forest Rangers, and who, on their disbandment, did not re-enrol for the completion of the period of service, which alone could entitle them to the "ordinary" grant of land, cannot now claim it.

With this statement the land claims matter was drawn to a temporary close. The Government pointed out that if the extra grant of land was given to Jackson, it would set a precedent, allowing other similar claims, resulting "in the loss to the Colony of upwards of 4000 acres of land". The Forest Rangers who missed out on a land grant must have been greatly disappointed.

Under new pressure from Hay and others, Jackson made a last pitch for the claims. When the Naval and Military and Local Forces Lands Claim Commission sat in 1882, Jackson applied for two separate grants of 500 acres each, and one for Hay of 200 acres. It is unclear why he applied for 500 acres, his rank only entitled him to 400. The claims were rejected.

Jackson again tried in 1887 with a new claim of only 400 acres. In addition, Hay, and now Roberts, claimed for 200 acres each. The answer was the same, "No". Roberts was only a sergeant at the disbandment of the original company, so he was not entitled to a 200 acre claim.

Finally the Government relented on a repeat claim dated 9 June 1890 from the above three. Roberts received 80 acres and a remission certificate for £40 (10s per acre). Jackson and Hay both received 200 acres and remission certificates of £100 each. But Jackson was never to receive his entitlement – he was lost overboard from the Steamship *Rotorua* between Wellington and New Plymouth on the night of 29 September 1889, while returning from parliamentary duties in Wellington.

Cambridge, 1864, looking southeast at the confluence of Karapiro Stream and the Waikato River. Both companies of Forest Rangers were based at Cambridge during 1864. *Cambridge Museum*

CHAPTER 15

The grant of land

Von Tempsky and his No. 2 Company were sent in June 1864 from Ohaupo to Ngahinapouri, on the Waipa River, between Te Rore and Whatawhata. It was feared that Maori had returned to the Kapamahunga Range across the Waipa. The alarm however proved unfounded. Nevertheless they remained at their new post and had to pass the winter in tents after having built wintering huts at Ohaupo. The Forest Rangers occupied the west bank while a company from the 12th Regiment occupied the east bank. The men had a happy time here, but the weather restricted training and exercise – von Tempsky was concerned about the men losing their combat fitness.

During idle time here von Tempsky started to write the manuscript *Memoranda of the New Zealand Campaign*, an autobiography of his involvement in the Waikato campaign.

As the weather improved in September, No. 2 Company scoured Mount Pirongia and the Kapamahunga Range for hostile Maori. These expeditions continued into December.

Towards Christmas the company moved to Pukerimu Redoubt, near Cambridge.

Meanwhile Jackson with his No. 1 Company were posted to Pukerimu Redoubt. By mid August 1864, only the Forest Rangers and a few detachments of British troops occupied the redoubt.

Jackson was daily expecting his unit to be called to Kihikihi to take possession of their land grants.

On the night of 30 August a disastrous fire broke out in the Pukerimu camp. Most of the huts and buildings were constructed of raupo (swamp reeds), so the fire spread quickly. Only the hospital, officers' quarters and Forest Rangers' huts survived the flames. Jackson displayed great coolness and leadership throughout, saving many buildings from the inferno.

Von Tempsky, after his arrival at Pukerimu Redoubt, wanted to enlarge the company strength of the Forest Rangers to 100 men, including an orderly sergeant and an extra corporal.

Major Atkinson thanked von Tempsky for his suggestions but it seems little came of them.

At the same time von Tempsky also tried to improve conditions of service for his men. During December 1864 he wrote to Major H.A. Atkinson, Defence Minister, suggesting changes be made. Up to then Forest Rangers could leave the unit provided they found a "substitute" to replace them. Von Tempsky believed this regulation lost good men only to be replaced by not-so-good men. He suggested also that the geographical area of service outlined at their enlistment should be extended from the Auckland Province to cover the whole of the North Island. Another change sought was that those who wished to leave the Forest Rangers should have the right to join the 1st Regiment of Waikato Militia (to which No. 2 Company, Forest Rangers, was attached) if they wanted to complete three years of service to get a land grant.

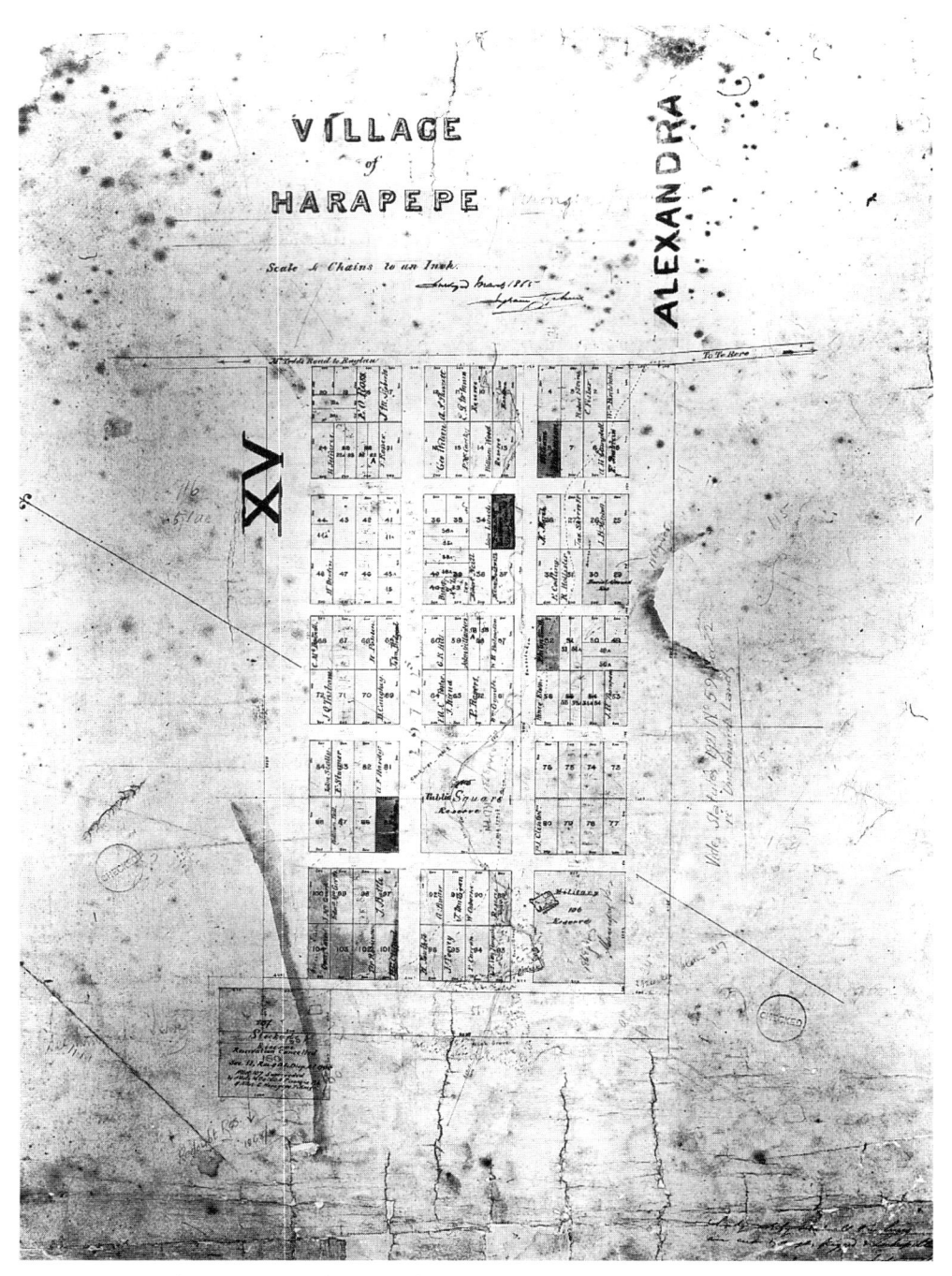

Surveyor's map of Harapepe township, March 1865. Each town lot measured one acre. The township never developed and even today the site is part of an open field. Waikato Museum of Art and History

Von Tempsky attempted to have John Roberts promoted to Captain and Sherret to Lieutenant, both promotions within the Forest Rangers. Haultain settled the matter by declaring a captain was not necessary in such a small unit.

Garrison duty in the Waikato provided little excitement for the Forest Rangers, many of whom enlisted for adventure. They became frustrated and bored while waiting for the surveyor parties to complete their work of dividing the land into lots.

Tired of waiting, a few Forest Rangers are believed to have deserted at this time. Others waited for their land only to sell it to the first land hawker who came along. Offered a choice between coastal lands at Tauranga and the attractive inland Waikato district, von Tempsky and his company chose Harapepe (earlier spelling of Harapipi) and the northeastern foothills of Pirongia mountain.

Von Tempsky must have influenced his men in choosing Harapepe rather than Tauranga. In retrospect, Harapepe was the lesser option. Von Tempsky was annoyed with the authorities and their slowness in preparing land for grants at Tauranga, and in a reflex action chose the foothills of Pirongia, possibly to spite the authorities. Bordering the confiscation line and considered the more dangerous sector on the frontier, Harapepe appealed to von Tempsky in his search for glory. In a letter to his wife (dated 8 February 1865 from Cambridge) he writes:

> I dare but to propose to my men the choice of two locations – one the old Tauranga plan – the other a place near Ngahinapouri, called Harapepe. The land question at Tauranga being in a unsettled state and the position of Harapepe offering the advantages of the great centre of Waikato industry, made me recommend Harapepe to the men, particularly as there is excellent land in that neighbourhood. The majority therefore was in favour of Harapepe and that has settled the matter.

The physical attractiveness of the land also helped to sway him. In a following letter dated 15 February, von Tempsky writes:

> It's a sweet piece of land – fertile – picturesque and favourably situated for traffic [meaning the planned further road to Raglan]. The centre of an old Maori settlement, covered with peach groves, laden with fruit, grass throughout the valley – two beautiful streams with pebbly bottoms run through the valley.

At Harapepe, on the track between Alexandra (Pirongia) and Raglan, a 100 acre site had been surveyed for a township in the centre of the settlement. On 16 February 1865 von Tempsky and his company boarded the steamer *Pioneer* at Pukerimu and travelled north along the Waikato River to Ngaruawahia then south up the Waipa River, landing opposite Te Rore the next day. They soon had a tent settlement on the town site. The men where allotted 50 acres in the country around Harapepe at the base of Mount Pirongia, and a one acre section within the town site. Jackson and von Tempsky were allocated 400 acres in the country.

At this time the Government was desperate to lessen its financial commitment, choosing to have soldiers struck off pay as quickly as possible and place them on their land. By April 1865, nearly half the Forest Rangers had been settled on their land. The Government also decided to delay the building of the promised blockhouse

Town grant for von Tempsky's one acre lot in the township of Harapepe. This is a typical title to a military land grant in the Waikato.

The grant of land

at Harapepe to protect the settlement.

A condition of accepting the land meant that each Forest Ranger must personally occupy the land or lose the right to it. If he could find a buyer who would take over the liability for military service, he could sell his allotment but most probably receive only a pittance for all his hard work to date. Alternatively he could just walk away in a form of desertion.

Unencumbered ownership was only possible after three years of enlistment in the Forest Rangers, or after August 1866.

For most there was no home, no wife or women, no school, no church and no roads. The task ahead of them was daunting in the least, a lifetime of toil to change their land into a farm. They had no capital to buy stock and materials or to employ labour. Another real problem was the threat of Maori attack, especially to more isolated farms.

Many surveyed farm sections were rejected as unsuitable. The main reasons for rejection were the lack of access and the lack of drainage (many farms were laid out on swamps). As there were many unsuitable farm plots, a working rule emerged that if no more than half of the farm was in swamp, the farm had to be accepted.

Consequently many Forest Rangers chose to continue their military service until their three years were completed.

At the end of March 1865 Brigadier-General Carey, in command at Te Awamutu, moved a body of Forest Rangers and Waikato Militia to the Wanganui district in response to an order received from the Minister of Colonial Defence.

The body comprised a company of Forest Rangers (Major von Tempsky, 1 captain, 2 subalterns and 53 men), and a company of Waikato Militia (Captain F. Nelson George, 2 subalterns and 50 men).

Carey stated in a communique delivered by von Tempsky to the Deputy Quartermaster-General at Wanganui (dated 30 March 1865):

> ... The company of Forest Rangers is composed of thirty volunteers from Major von Tempsky's men, made up to fifty by volunteers from those under Major Jackson at Kihikihi. The other company under Captain George [3rd Regiment Waikato Militia], is made up by volunteers from the 2nd, 3rd, and 4th Regiments Waikato Militia, in about equal proportions.
> As the remnant of Major von Tempsky's company [a total of 33 men] would scarcely be sufficient to hold the new post at Harapepe, I have requested Colonel Haultain [commanding officer of the Waikato Regiments of Militia] to make up the strength to fifty rank and file.
> The maintenance of this post I hold to be important, being on the road to Raglan and strengthening the right flank of the frontier.

It was felt that some incentive should be offered to the men to encourage them to serve in the Wanganui district rather than remain in the Waikato. Special conditions of service were drawn up for the force travelling to Wanganui. Von Tempsky proposed to the Defence Office:

> 1. That all men, Forest Rangers and Waikato Militia, composing this detachment under my command, shall receive a crown grant for their land in the Waikato district after four months service in the south (dating

Von Tempsky's 400 acre military land grant title for land bordering the Waipa River at Harapepe.

The grant of land 131

from the day of formation of detachment).
2. That the Waikato Militia under my command, performing the same service as the Forest Rangers shall be paid at the same rate as the latter (four shillings, twopence per day) from the day they volunteered for this service.
3. That an efficient surgeon be attached to my detachment, a man capable and willing to accompany us in our expeditions.

The only change made by the Defence Office to these proposals was to No. 1, namely that service:

> ... will be rated during this winter as double time, so that six month's service at Wanganui during the winter season will count as one year's service towards the attainment of their Crown Grants for their land in the Waikato district.

These conditions led many of the Waikato Militiamen in the detachment to believe they actually were being transferred to the Forest Rangers. Indications of this are evident in their later New Zealand Medal claims.

Roll of Forest Rangers to travel to Wanganui, April 1865:

(Company No. given in bracket after name): *Major* (1): Von Tempsky (2). *Lieutenant* (1): Westrup (1). *Ensign* (1): Whitfield (1). *Sergeants* (2): Ross (2), William Bond (1). *Corporals* (4): Butter (2), McGuirk (1), Osborne (1), Watters (1). *Privates* (48): Thomas Anderson (2), Beetham (1), Benson (1), Best (1), Birchfield (2), Philip Bond (1), John Burns (2), Lawrence Burns (1), John Campbell (1), Carter (1), Clinton (2), Clotworthy (1), Codling (2), Colton (2), Cullinan (1), Curran (2), Duggan (1), Elston (2), Fischer (2), Foster (2), Hardy (2), Hartland (2), Hearfield (2), Hennessey (2), George Hill (2), Jones (2), Lee (1), Liebig (2), Lloyd (1), McCarthy (2), McCulloch (1), Moses McDonald (1), McGrath (2), McHerron (2), Martin (1), Lawrence Mitchell (2), Moylan (2), Owens (2), Scally (2), Shuker (1), Simmons (2), Colin Smith (2), William Stephenson (2), Amelius Taylor (2), Treadwell (1), Usher (2), Woods (2), Wright (2).

Elijah Codling was enlisted on 15 April en route to Port Waikato, and Usher discharged on 18 April at Port Waikato.

About this time von Tempsky applied to the Defence Minister to have Roberts promoted to Captain, but this request was refused. Roberts accepted his land grant (town section No. 17 in the proposed Harapepe village and 200 acre country property – Nos. 9, 10, 11, 13), and was struck off pay on 31 July 1865. Roberts handed over command of the Harapepe based No. 2 Company to the remaining non-commissioned officer, Sergeant McMinn.

Carey was concerned by the reduction of forces on the frontier at Te Awamutu as the Maori near the frontier (confiscation line) seemed in an unsettled state.

Thirty-two men of the No. 2 Company, including two officers, elected to remain behind at Harapepe and other members of the 2nd Regiment Waikato Militia were sent to Harapepe to keep numbers there up to strength until the Wanganui-bound men returned.

With hostile Maori just across the confiscation line, and well-worn bush tracks connecting Harapepe to Kawhia and the south, it was decided to make the settlement more secure. The most urgent task was to build a redoubt.

The force under von Tempsky left the Te Awamutu district on 5 April 1865, proceeded from Port Waikato aboard a steamer on 18 April to Wanganui. They then proceeded to Kakaramea Redoubt. Von Tempsky felt the urgency to weld his recruits into one body, so immediately started reconnoitring the surrounding district.

Von Tempsky enlisted new Forest Ranger recruits in the Wanganui district. These new men did not come under the terms of service of the Waikato Militia and did not qualify for land grants.

General Cameron, who had been in the district for nearly one year, deliberately avoided direct contact with the Maori after his sharp defeat at Nukumaru. He had decided to keep his forces near the coast and not venture into the bush. This decision caused heated debate in the Government as to his effectiveness. He was soon dubbed "the Lame Seagull" for his lack of action. Cameron marched 2,300 troops 54 miles in 57 days – a reflection not on their courage but on the injustice of the war. Imperial officers and men had no stomach for continued plunder after the massive confiscation of Maori land in the Waikato. His regimental commanders were increasingly unenthusiastic about warfare, which they regarded as unnecessarily prolonged by greed for land.

A Forest Ranger private at the time von Tempsky was operating in the Wanganui district, mid 1865. Presumably, because of his total lack of issued uniform and equipment, he enlisted in Wanganui and as yet had not received any uniform. Museum of New Zealand

CHAPTER 16

Von Tempsky in command

Von Tempsky, with a party of eighty men, both Forest Rangers and Waikato Militia, entered the bush north of Patea and followed a track along the Patea River on the lookout for a Maori encampment believed to be in the area.

General Cameron had shown reluctance in bush fighting thinking that the Maori might surprise attack his men at any time – so when von Tempsky and the Forest Rangers showed the initiative, they afterwards received instant recognition from the nation. Von Tempsky wanted to prove to the Maori and General Cameron that the Maori could be found, however safe they thought their secret encampments were. Von Tempsky also wanted to attack and inflict heavy casualties on the Maori.

In the early morning of 13 May 1865 the Corps came upon a Maori hideout near Kakaramea, and immediately mounted a surprise attack. The site was an easily defendable position with steep gullies to the sides and a bluff and river in the rear – very typical of planned Maori strongholds.

The resulting Kakaramea engagement is best described in von Tempsky's detailed official report:

> Wanganui, May 16th, 1865
> Sir, I have the honour to report for the information of the New Zealand Government, that on the 13th instant I had an engagement with rebel Maoris, encamped on the Patea River, four miles north of Kakaramea.
> On the 9th of May I had sent out two parties of my detachment at Kakaramea to scout along the right and left bank of the Patea River. One party under my command found a track leading along the right bank of the river, it descended a steep cliff, furnished with ladders of poles and supplejack; it had many of the intervening streams bridged. I concluded therefore that considerable importance was attached by the Maoris to this track, and decided upon exploring its course for some distance. Having dogs with me that day I could not expect to surprise the natives, and not wishing to leave my tracks too far on the road I returned, resolved to use it on the following night.
> The second party, under Captain George and Ensign Whitfield, were fired upon by natives; shots were exchanged, and our men chased the natives for some distance, till they disappeared. It appeared therefore that the natives were to be found after all on the left bank; so that night at 1 am I started with my whole detachment, crossed the river, and was before dawn opposite the native encampment, but the river intervened, and we had to content ourselves with listening to the Pai Marire morning hymns and watching the smoke rise. Dense bush prevented us from seeing a single Maori, and prudence forbade any attempt of an attack from our side of the river.
> We returned early on the 10th, with the intention of following the track on the right bank the coming night; but three scouts [rebel Maori] made their appearance at dusk, coming evidently from the track, where our footprints of the 9th must have revealed our intentions, and making a surprise that

night anything but feasible.

On the 11th ten scouts on foot and one on horseback [rebel Maori] were seen coming from the same direction as the first three; so that night also was passed over as un-propitious, particularly as the continued smoke of the Maori encampment proved their determination of stopping where they were. On the night of Friday to Saturday at 1 am, I started with a force of forty-eight Forest Rangers and sixteen Waikato Militia officered by Captain George, Lieutenant Westrup, Ensign Whitfield and Irwin, leaving Lieutenant Malone [2nd Regiment Waikato Militia] with twenty additional Waikato Militia to guard the pass over the cliff, as ten determined men could have prevented there the return of hundreds. We got over two-thirds of our way without incident, though the road [track] was of the most difficult nature, and the time was night. Arrived at an extensive clearing, however, we lost the track. Two different tracks we ran down bootlessly – one ended in a precipice and eel-weir – the other in a place of steeping corn, at the bottom of a deep gorge. With infinite labour, through a dense forest, we found at last the right track and hurried along it. We came upon a row of large whares on the top of a commanding hill, but daylight was dawning already. On investigation the whares proved to be deserted, though the ashes of recent fires were still warm. While pondering over the probability of the natives having deserted the neighbourhood, large volumes of smoke ascending from a neighbouring hill below us settled that question completely.

A deep wooded ravine separated the native encampment from the hill we were on – beyond the encampment was the [Patea] river. There seemed to me no chance of a surprise now – but having brought a new detachment face to face with the enemy for the first time, I deemed it necessary to attack, even at some risk. We rapidly descended the ravine and ascended the hill; a sudden turn in our road on the top brought us to a slip-panel gate, and there, in the centre, or nearly so, of a large clearing, was the native encampment.

We could see the Maori sentry and other Maoris walking about. I extended the men along the clearing, but found that the edge of the clearing was barricaded. It was necessary to break through this barricading; the noise caused thereby and the distance to the huts gave the Maoris time to grasp their guns and receive our charge with a heavy volley. We drove them, however, from the huts into the bush, Ensign Whitfield and Captain George conspicuous in their gallantry; but this was the time when we suffered the most lost, as Ensign Whitfield was hit by two shots, one breaking his arm and one entering his side; Private MacBean [McBain] of No. 1 Company, Forest Rangers, was hit in the head while close to the bush. We took what cover we could get in front of the bush within twenty yards of it. A heavy fire continued now for some time. The Maoris danced Pai Marire hymns and danced the war dance behind their barricading and had harangues for the purposes of inducing a charge; once or twice we heard them advance a little, but stop short at the first fire at any visible member of their party.

I sent Lieutenant Westrup to outflank them in the bush, but it was soon found that their flanks were protected by gullies. A frontal charge on our part would have been quite as good a piece of folly as on their part. I had enough, even with two men *hors de combat*, to convey them back to camp over the frightful road we had before us. As the Maoris before us were evidently calling in all directions for assistance, and, moreover, as I heard their calls answered, I deemed it at last necessary to draw off the men before some reinforcement took us at a disadvantage. I sent Lieutenant Westrup to take possession of the gate once more, forwarded the wounded and gradually drew off my men in small parties, without the Maoris perceiving our retreat. At half past nine I left my position in front of the bush with the last five men, and left the clearing which we had entered precisely at half past six.

Six or eight Maoris were *hors de combat* at that time. We determined finding an easier route for the transport of the wounded. For about a mile we cut through a dense bush in a gully till a precipice of 150 feet closed our retreat in that direction. We returned towards our old track, but found that a party of Maoris had taken possession of the big whares on top of the hill. As we had approached the whares carefully, my advanced guard, under Sergeant Ross, shot three incautious Maoris [the first being shot by Sergeant Ross] who were peeping round the corners of the whares.

To force our way past these whares would have added considerably to our wounded, whatever other advantage might be gained; the day was advancing fast, so I sent another exploring party under Captain George to look after the possibility of heading the gully, while I kept watch on the Maoris in the whares. The gully was at last reported passable; we drew off gradually once more, and entered the bush unmolested. Three distinct forest gullies had to be traversed, and a road [track] cut through them for the transport of the wounded, till we reached the fern ridges and our camp at 4 pm, having been on our legs for fifteen hours without rest, food, or drink.

I have to bring to your special notice the conspicuous gallantry of Ensign Whitfield, who I grieve to say, died of his wounds at Patea, the 13th, at 11:30 pm; also the gallantry of Captain George in leading his men across the clearing, getting several bullets through his clothing and the tip of his thumb blown off. The soldierly management of Lieutenant Westrup was beyond all praise, as well as the usefulness of Ensign Irwin and Lieutenant Malone, the latter in command of the reserve at the cliff.

Above all, however, I must mention the unflinching conduct of all my non-commissioned officers and men, who performed their arduous duties on that long day without a murmur, and with courageous alacrity.

Private MacBean [McBain] died on the road home, was buried there temporarily, and conveyed to camp on the following day. On that day Lieutenant Westrup went out with a party of volunteers to look for a man of his company who had lost his way in the bush. That man (Private Best, No. 1 Company, Forest Rangers,) was not found on the 15th instant.

G.F. von Tempsky, Forest Rangers

After hearing rifle fire, Lieutenant Doveton of the 50th Regiment went with twenty men to von Tempsky's assistance but made no contact with the Forest Rangers due to the labyrinth of tracks.

Von Tempsky showed great skill in retreating without further contact with the enemy. In the engagement the Forest Rangers lost two men, and the Maori lost an estimated seventeen. Both Forest Ranger casualties were eventually carried out of the bush and given proper burials.

Private Carl Liebig later stated (in July 1871):

> At the battle of Kakaramea as Major George can testify I almost without any assistance had to cut a new track through the bush for a distance of two miles in order to carry our wounded men through as we could not get back again over the Gentle Annie with our wounded.

This "successful" engagement received much publicity from the press – increasing colonial morale and making heroes out of von Tempsky and his men. Von Tempsky had proven that a colonial officer (as opposed an imperial officer) with a handful of well-trained men could venture into the bush and engage the enemy in a decisive manner.

At the time of the Kakaramea engagement about 6000 imperial troops in the same district were in a state of inactivity.

Apart from skirmishes, the engagement at Kakaramea was the first and only large engagement where von Tempsky was in overall command.

The Prime Minister ordered that von Tempsky's Kakaramea report should be published in full in the *New Zealand Gazette*, an uncommon practice at the time. He also commented:

> Major von Tempsky should be cordially thanked for his gallant and well-planned attack upon the rebel encampment near Kakaramea; he has shown that it is possible to surprise natives in their own fastnesses; it is understood that the natives have since evacuated their position.

This may be an overreaction to the relatively minor action but the comments are surely pointed at the inactive Cameron and the Whitehall Government.

On the strength of his new fame von Tempsky travelled to Wellington to met the Prime Minister and attend a dinner on his behalf.

The search party led by Lieutenant Westrup returned without finding Private Best. Whilst on this search the party exchanged shots with rebel Maori on the neighbouring ridge known as Gentle Annie. Private Francis Eldred Best is listed as dying on 14 May 1865.

Sergeant Ross was promoted to Ensign, the commission dated 25 June 1865.

During the period of May to July the Forest Rangers and Waikato Militiamen were based at Nukumaru under the overall command of General Waddy.

On 11 June, 15 new circular tents were issued to the Forest Rangers at Nukumaru from quartermaster stores in Wanganui. These would be adequate to sleep about 80-90 men.

On 17 July three Callisher and Terry carbines were reported lost by the Forest Rangers.

This loss was not favourably received by the Colonial Defence Office.

A return of "average monthly expenses incurred by the colony in military operations" at Wanganui for the three months ending 30 June 1865 sets out the cost of pay per month for the Forest Rangers (107 men all ranks):

Major	1	£30	0	0
Captain	1	£30	0	0
Lieutenants	2	£42	0	0
Ensigns	2	£36	0	0
Sergeants	5	£56	5	0
Corporals	8	£72	0	0
Privates	88	£549	10	0
Total cost		£815	15	0

The reason for the seemingly enlarged unit is that the Waikato Militiamen attached to the Forest Rangers received the same pay for the duration of their stay in the Wanganui district, and were included on the Forest Ranger pay sheets.

At about this time, the Forest Rangers residing at Harapepe, after taking up land, celebrated the formation of the corps by attending a second anniversary dinner at the Settlers' Arms, Papakura, now kept by Clotworthy. John Roberts officiated at the function.

CHAPTER 17

Frustrations before Weraroa

Late on the night of 19 July 1865, intelligence was received from the Wanganui command of the critical position at Pipiriki. It became evident that the strong and menacing position at Weraroa pa had to be resolved immediately so that a relief force could be despatched to Pipiriki.

Weraroa pa was constructed on a high headland formed by the confluence of the Waitotara River and the Koie Stream. The pa stood atop very precipitous banks about 300 feet above the river flats below. It was believed that Weraroa was the Hauhau headquarters for the region, making its capture essential. In January 1865 General Cameron had dismissed the idea of its capture, stating that the operation would require more men than the approximately 6000 he had at his disposal.

Some of the Native Contingent (Kupapa under Major Thomas McDonnell) had contact with members of the Hauhau garrison at Weraroa and there were murmurs that the garrison would be prepared to enter negotiations to surrender. This was because a few Hauhau chiefs were considering making peace with the Government following the example of Wiremu Tamehana (William Thompson) in the Waikato. Von Tempsky had made this information known to the Prime Minister while on a recent trip to Wellington, and had suggested that a small force might be able to obtain a surrender.

Von Tempsky returned to Wanganui and Kakaramea where he and McDonnell started to plan an operation. But any troop movements did not go unnoticed by the imperial officers, namely Lieutenant-Colonel Logan, who opposed the operation. He did not openly stop the force from proceeding towards Weraroa, but tried to hamper the movements of the Native Contingent. Logan ordered them to Woodall's Redoubt, but realising how essential they were for negotiations, McDonnell ordered them to Okehu and then to Pakaraka. Logan reacted by cutting off their commissariat.

Von Tempsky and McDonnell persevered in their task despite the indirect opposition coming from Cameron. The force camped at Maeneene between Weraroa and Nukumaru. McDonnell attempted to negotiate a surrender with a delegation of the Weraroa pa garrison, who agreed to surrender to McDonnell and run a white flag up in the pa. Von Tempsky stated:

> I sent my men into the bush – waited for McDonnell, but the night coming on and the natives not making their appearance, we rode up to the palisading of the pa, where a messenger from McDonnell awaited me to say that in the morning he would settle everything.

But this was not to be. During the night some Hauhau came to McDonnell's camp to say they would give up the pa to him. In the morning Lieutenant-Colonel Logan arrived with his own messengers. The Hauhau became suspicious and stalled surrender negotiations. The Native Contingent wanted to attack, but Logan refused them permission.

Von Tempsky, who was completely frustrated by this stage, tendered his resignation. Cameron fully supported Logan and protested to Governor Grey as to the Native Contingent's complete disregard to his authority. He condemned the Defence Minister for:

> ... directly authorising subordinate officers of the Colonial Forces to deal with the enemy, in utter disregard of their duty to the service, and the common respect due to the Brigadier-General in command.

At last the imperial command came head-to-head with the Colonial Defence Office. Cameron did not mind McDonnell and von Tempsky displaying bravery and initiative against the Maori at Paparata, but now did not like that same initiative aimed against himself. He did not like his go-slow tactics exposed before the colony, at a time when heavy costs of the imperial army was heading the colony towards bankruptcy. The Attorney-General moved to have Cameron court-martialled for incompetence and deliberate neglect of his instructions.

Seeing the Government was now powerless in its command of the forces and the colony in the hands of an imperial military dictatorship, the Prime Minister, Frederick Weld, resigned. Finally Cameron resigned.

So it seems that von Tempsky and the Forest Rangers, together with McDonnell, were instrumental in removing Cameron from office. Cameron had virtually brought the colony's efforts to end the war to a standstill.

However, before Cameron's resignation, Governor Grey personally led the troops in the field in an effort to resolve the stalemate before Weraroa. With negotiations now proving useless, Grey prepared to attack.

On 20 July a force of Forest Rangers, a small detachment of Wanganui Yeomanry Cavalry (dismounted) and the Native Contingent and friendly natives, under Major Rookes, completed a skilful turning movement in bad weather. They marched under cover of the bush along the Karaka plateau, to the rear of Weraroa, and during the night took positions commanding the Hauhau villages of Perekama and Areiahi. The operation was successful, capturing Areiahi and all its inhabitants. About 60 warriors were taken prisoner.

The force opened fire on Weraroa pa from the Karaka plateau at a range of 600 yards. Ensign Ross, considered an excellent shot amongst the Forest Rangers, assisted. A night attack was planned. A force set out via Perekama village intending to scale the cliff in the rear of the stronghold. Just prior to the ascent, news was brought to them that the pa had been abandoned. Apparently the capture of Areiahi village had convinced the garrison that the fortress was untenable. In the morning the pa was occupied by the force. The final capture was a bloodless one.

Von Tempsky was not present at the end, being stricken with rheumatism. All those cold wet nights sleeping in the open must tell on a man's health. In a letter to his wife dated 24 July he explained:

> I was suddenly stricken down with a violent attack of rheumatism in the back.

Von Tempsky retired by wagon to Wanganui to convalesce.

Although Cameron suffered from inactivity, he finally achieved his goal in taking Weraroa pa without a fight. This supported his wish to avoid frontal and costly confrontations with the Maori and not to inflict heavy casualties on the Maori.

With the problem of Weraroa resolved, the colonial force was now disposed to relieve the siege at Pipiriki.

CHAPTER 18

Relief of Pipiriki

A military post at Pipiriki, 55 miles up the Wanganui River, under the command of Major Willoughby Brassey, was formed in late April 1865. Brassey's garrison consisted of the Nos. 8 and 9 Companies of the Taranaki Military Settlers under Captains T. Wilson and Pennefather, and a company of Patea Rangers under Lieutenant J. Hirst. Captain W. Newland was also present with the Patea Rangers. This European force of about 200 strong was joined by 60 warriors of the Wanganui Native Contingent. Their position was on the west bank of the Wanganui River (directly opposite the present township), and consisted of three earth redoubts close together. After some weeks the Native Contingent was called away to help in the operations against the Weraroa pa on the Waitotara River.

The Hauhau considered the Government force at Pipiriki a threat to their wellbeing and positioned about a thousand warriors in camps nearby, their headquarters being Pukehinau pa. After Brassey received information from friendly Maori living nearby of an imminent attack, he removed the guard picket on the river bank to safety on 18 July.

On the morning of 19 July, Lieutenant Chapman of the Patea Rangers was attacked near the river's edge but escaped to the safety of a redoubt. Hauhau took up nearby positions and started sniping at troops in two of the redoubts. This was the beginning of a twelve day siege. Lieutenant Clery with about twenty men stormed the Hauhau positions with a bayonet charge. The Maori retreated with the loss of a few warriors and repositioned themselves on a nearby hill.

Meanwhile the Patea Rangers and Taranaki Military Settlers withstood a general attack. Losing a few men, the Maori dug in. The redoubts came under persistent sniping from several directions. In a move to conserve ammunition, six sharpshooters were ordered to return an accurate fire on the well concealed Hauhau. This strategy held the enemy to their positions.

Each night the Hauhau dug new rifle-pits closer to the redoubts. On the third morning of the siege Captain Newland and twenty of his Patea Rangers rushed the new positions and filled in the pits before returning to safety with no loss of life.

In another redoubt, the Patea Rangers grew low on drinking water. The whole force was running low on rations. Brassey wrote messages requesting relief, and after sealing them in bottles, managed to throw them in the Wanganui River under darkness. One such message was picked up below the Wanganui township and delivered to the Militia Office there. Two Patea Rangers, Sergeant Constable and Private A. Edgecombe, escaped by canoe under darkness, and met the relief expedition under Major Rookes downstream at Hiruharama.

The Forest Rangers, under the command of the recently promoted Major George, were present in the relief force. Von Tempsky was still convalescing in Wanganui. Also present were a company of Wanganui Rangers under Captain Jones and Kepa's 300 strong Native Contingent together with several hundred warriors from the lower Wanganui friendly tribes.

By poling and paddling canoes they reached Pipiriki and relieved Brassey. Not a shot was fired in the relief. On investigation, the Hauhau positions were found to be abandoned. The Hauhau camp at Ohinemutu was burned, the cultivations destroyed, and the niu poles of the Hauhau's Pai Marire faith demolished.

No one was killed in Brassey's force, but about four were wounded. The Hauhau lost about twenty killed and more than twenty wounded.

After a few days, the main body of Major Rookes' force returned to Wanganui leaving Major George and the Forest Rangers in Pipiriki to supplement Brassey's garrison. In August 1865 the Forest Rangers left Pipiriki to return to Wanganui. Only Captain Wilson's No. 8 Company of Taranaki Military Settlers remained. They were soon joined by two companies of the 57th Regiment.

While the Forest Rangers were at Pipiriki, Private John Duggan lost his life on 2 August in an unfortunate incident. Duggan apparently raised his revolver and pointed it in jest at fellow Forest Ranger, Private John Wright. Wright responded by raising his revolver, but this went off unintentionally. Duggan exonerated Wright in a dying statement witnessed by Major George.

CHAPTER 19

Court-martial

Hostilities now shifted to the eastern side of the North Island, where the Reverend Carl Sylvius Volkner had been hanged and beheaded by Hauhau in Opotiki, Bay of Plenty, on 2 March 1865. He had been accused by the Hauhau of forwarding intelligence of Hauhau movements to the colonial authorities. After a few vain attempts to settle the unrest which followed Volkner's death, the authorities planned to send a colonial force to the area in September 1865.

The colonial force was to launch a seaborne attack on Opotiki. The force was to be comprised of the Forest Rangers, Patea Rangers and the Native Contingent under Thomas McDonnell. However, the Forest Rangers refused to join the Opotiki expedition because the Government had changed the terms of their special enlistment in south Taranaki.

Meanwhile von Tempsky, who had returned to Auckland in August 1865 to visit his family, went aboard *Brisk* and sailed on 1 September from Auckland to a rendezvous of ships off Hicks Bay, East Cape. He was expecting the Forest Rangers to come from Wanganui. However, they failed to rendezvous, having refused to sail. So without his company of Forest Rangers, he decided to serve under Major Brassey as a volunteer with the Patea Rangers at Opotiki. A Native Contingent of Kupapa and the Patea Rangers secured Opotiki with supporting fire from *Brisk* off shore. Believing the ragged appearance of their uniforms might be confused with the enemy, von Tempsky hoisted his red Garibaldi shirt on a flagpole within the town to prevent Royal Navy ships from lobbing shells into it.

His Forest Rangers remained in Wanganui. There was an argument about pay rates after the men were asked to take a cut in pay and allowances. They refused to sail for Opotiki because they were offered only three shillings and sixpence per day instead of their usual five shillings per day. Von Tempsky sailed to Wellington from Opotiki to try and settle the pay dispute and by 15 September he seemed to have sorted the matter out. He sent Westrup to Wanganui to explain to his men that with allowances the new pay rate was just over four shillings per day and worth accepting. Westrup and the men came down to Paekakariki and von Tempsky resumed command. But not all men were prepared to go on a proposed expedition to Waiapu, near East Cape, under the new terms. The ones who refused were placed under detention in Wellington.

While in Wellington, von Tempsky was ordered to take his company to the theatre of war at Waiapu and place himself under the orders of Major James Fraser. Both men were majors, but Fraser was junior in appointment having receiving his commission as major at a later date than von Tempsky. This was too much for von Tempsky to cope with! First he refused to accept Fraser's future orders, then he formally resigned. He was called to the suite of the Defence Minister, Sir Harry Atkinson, who solved the seniority problem by ordering von Tempsky to Napier and not Waiapu.

But von Tempsky refused to accept this order, on the grounds that the Forest

Captain Charles Westrup, commander of the Forest Ranger company that served on the East Coast.

From 'Soldiering in New Zealand' by F.J.W. Gascoyne

Rangers were only required to serve in the Auckland province as set out in the terms of enlistment. This was a valid point, as earlier moves by von Tempsky to increase the field of service of the Forest Rangers to cover the whole of the North Island had been unsuccessful. He stamped out of the office in a rage, refusing to accept further orders, and was placed under close arrest.

All the men who refused to go to the East Coast were placed under detention, and they, together with von Tempsky, were to be court-martialled.

A statement of charges against von Tempsky was read on 28 September, and the inquiry opened two days later in the Thorndon Barracks, Wellington. Colonel Haultain presided. The Forest Rangers under detention were also present. In addition to von Tempsky's refusal to go to Waiapu and resignation, an issue about ration money (the sum of £128) being wrongly spent was also brought up. The last matter seems irrelevant to the more serious charges before von Tempsky and were perhaps tabled to discredit him. Von Tempsky stated in his evidence that Westrup took over the task of paymaster on 1 June 1865.

At the close of the hearing the court's findings were passed to Governor Grey for his consideration.

On 16 October, while von Tempsky was still under arrest, the Weld Government changed and Colonel Haultain became the new Minister of Defence. An inquiry was held into von Tempsky's actions and although there was no conclusive result, Governor Grey gave von Tempsky an opportunity to withdraw his resignation. He did this on the understanding that he would not be superseded by Major Fraser. Von Tempsky, and the 30 Forest Rangers still in Wellington, returned to Wanganui on the *Wanganui* on 25 October. On arrival they proceeded to Woodall's Redoubt for duty.

While the dispute progressed in Wellington, Lieutenant Charles Westrup had been promoted to Captain (in the Auckland Militia, attached to the Forest Rangers), dated 23 September 1865, to carry the responsibility of commanding the Forest Ranger No. 2 Company in the absence of von Tempsky and Major George. So Westrup and the Forest Rangers, who were willing to accept the new terms of pay, sailed aboard the *Lord Ashley* for Napier.

George and his company of Waikato Militia, who fought alongside the Forest Rangers in the Wanganui district, formed part of the East Coast Field Force under the command of Willoughby Brassey, for the period 16 August 1865 - 27 March 1866.

Before sailing, Westrup sent Private Lawrence Mitchell to von Tempsky to ask him to come to the wharf and address the men. Von Tempsky refused, on the grounds that his present views would only worsen Westrup's difficulties. Mitchell did not sail with Westrup, remaining in Wellington.

While in Napier Westrup enlisted a group of volunteers before sailing north to Gisborne aboard H.M.S. *Brisk*, along with 60 Colonial Defence Force men. At Gisborne the Colonial Defence Force went ashore. A fatigue party of Forest Rangers also went ashore to assist in the construction of a redoubt. The Forest Rangers re-boarded and sailed on 30 September to Waiapu, near East Cape.

Roll of Westrup's Forest Rangers on East Coast included:

Captain (1): Westrup. *Ensign* (1): Ross. *Sergeants* (3): William Bond, Butter, Watters. *Corporals* (3): McGuirk, James Osborne, Hardy. *Privates* (33): Allen, Babington, Bannister, William Bell, Benson, Phillip Bond, Carter, Clinton, Clotworthy, Crawford, Curran, Elston, Foster, Hennessey, George Hill, Jones, Liebig, McCarthy, McCulloch, McDonnell, McHerron, Maki, Martin, Moylan, Robinson, James Ryan, William Sibley (see note below), Skelly, Shuker, Simmonds, Treadwell, Woods, Wright.

Due to difficulties in finding rolls of Forest Rangers who served on the East Coast, the above roll is possibly incomplete.

William Henry Sibley later (in 1910) claimed compensation from the Defence Department stating that he served during this campaign with the Forest Rangers but received no pay. No verification of this can be found.

A file in National Archives, Wellington, 93/1263, No. 1740/2, contains the names of 11 men. The file is a pay sheet dated 7 August 1866. The file reads:

> Colonial Defence Office, Wellington, 7 August 1866.
> Sir, By direction of the Honourable the Defence Minister, I have the honour to request you will pay the men, named in the margin, who belonged to the Forest Rangers and were employed on the East Coast, pay at the authorised rate from the 9th July last to the date on which they last left Poverty Bay in the S.S. *St Kilda*. (Signed) Captain Percival, Paymaster East Coast District, Wellington.

A postscript mentions "the men are also to receive an additional 1s/6d per diem each in lieu of rations for the above period."

The 11 men named were: Mark Arnold, Bernard Bulow, Lewis Castin (Louis Castaign), Michael Crowe, William Evans, Henry Fisher, John Gardiner, Edward Guning, H.H. Hewson, Patrick O'Connor, John Rose.

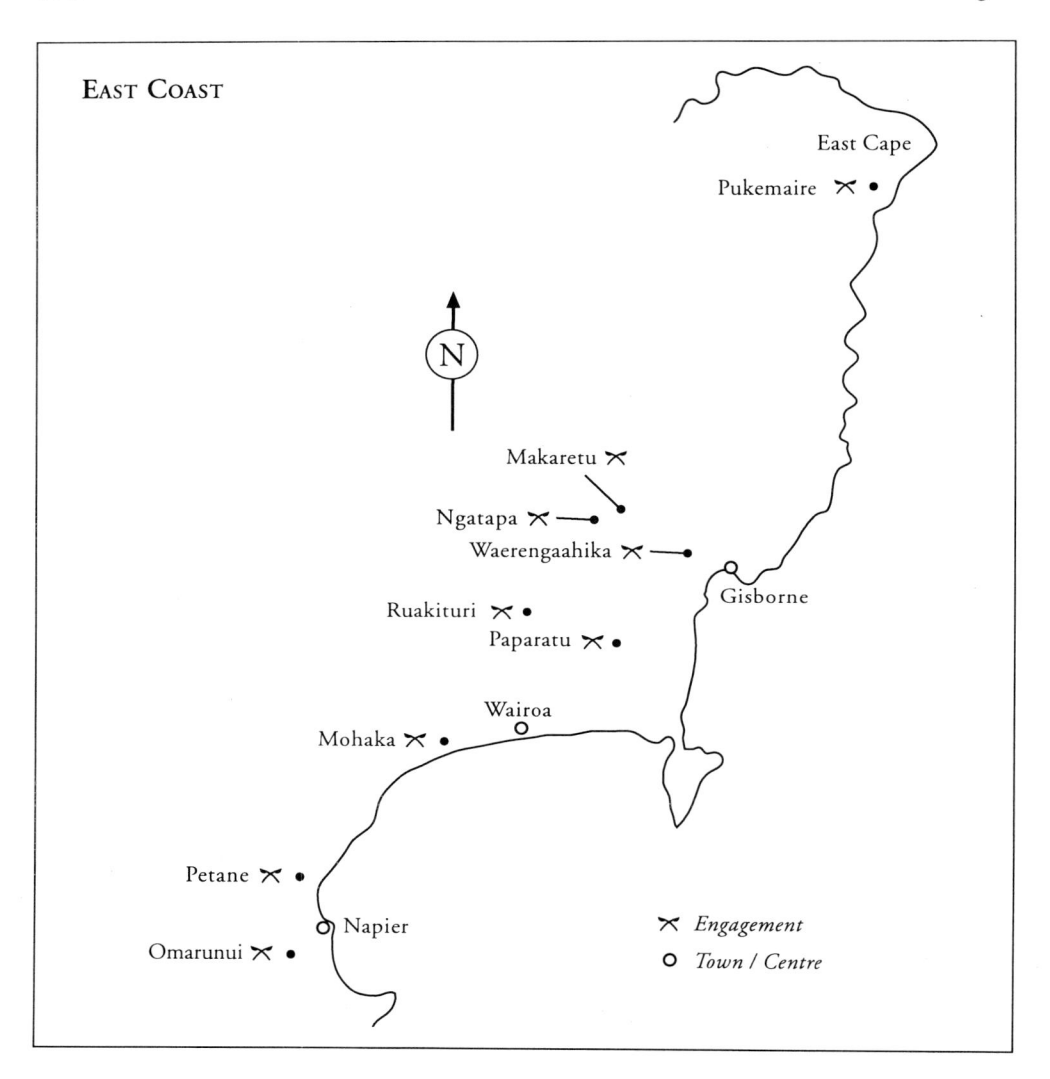

East Coast

- East Cape
- Pukemaire ✗ •
- Makaretu ✗
- Ngatapa ✗ •
- Waerengaahika ✗
- Gisborne
- Ruakituri ✗ •
- Paparatu ✗ •
- Wairoa
- Mohaka ✗ •
- Petane ✗ •
- Napier
- Omarunui ✗ •

✗ *Engagement*
○ *Town / Centre*

CHAPTER 20

Fight in the rain

The company of Forest Rangers (45 men all ranks) landed at Te Awanui, near the mouth of the Waiapu River, close to East Cape, from H.M.S. *Brisk* on 1 October 1865. Under the command of Captain Westrup and Lieutenant Ross they reinforced Major James Fraser's force against the Hauhau at the nearby Pukemaire pa.

Fraser, with his force, had already been involved in skirmishes and engagements in the area since landing there on 5 July. His force consisted of about one hundred Europeans (military settlers and volunteers from Hawke's Bay with Lieutenant R. Biggs, Lieutenant Frederick Gascoyne and Ensign Tuke), local friendly natives of the Ngatiporou, and Ropata with about ninety followers.

The force of about 380 men under Fraser and Ropata marched against Pukemaire on 3 October in pouring rain. They attacked in skirmishing order up the ridge towards the entrenchments and opened a flying sap. Realising the possible frail nature of the palisades, Ropata and twelve of his men attempted to bring down a section of the wall. They got up close to the pa, one man threw a stout branch tied to the end of a rope over the palisade, and they all pulled on the rope, causing a few yards of wall to collapse. Ropata immediately led the assault through the breach but a heavy downpour of rain at this moment frustrated efforts to complete the attack. The men were cold and drenched and many firearms were ineffectual, so Fraser gave the order to withdraw. Nine Hauhau were killed.

The force returned to Te Hapete carrying two of their dead. From Te Hapete the bulk of the force moved to Wai-o-Matatini settlement and awaited better weather to renew their attack.

With improved weather the next assault was planned for 9 October. On the night of 8 October Captain Westrup and his Forest Rangers marched out of Te Hapete and took up a position at the rear of the pa. The next morning the rest of the force marched to the front of the pa to attack, but the pa was found to be deserted. It was later burnt.

Apparently the Hauhau had escaped just prior to the assault and headed north through rugged bush, and eventually fortified themselves upon a hill called Hungahunga-toroa, meaning in Maori "down of the albatross", about twenty miles from Waiapu towards Kawakawa. This stronghold was successfully taken during October, by Ropata and Biggs leading a small force which included a few Forest Rangers including Privates Allen, William Bell, Butter and Hardy. Though the pa was encased by steep cliffs, Biggs and Ropata scaled a dominating height nearby with 20 marksmen. From here they shot into the pa with deadly effect, killing 20 and wounding many. The pa soon surrendered. Obviously this pa was constructed in the days before rifles played an important part in battle.

On 8 November the force left Waiapu in the Government steamer *Sturt* heading to Poverty Bay to protect the settlers there, for the Hauhau in the district had built a strong pa at Waerengaahika. On the following day 250 Ngatiporou, loyal to the colonial government, arrived aboard H.M.S. *Esk*.

CHAPTER 21

Seven day siege at Waerengaahika

Many of the Hauhau who fought against Fraser near Waiapu in August and September had escaped south before the Pukemaire engagement and amassed in Waerengaahika pa and nearby Pukeamionga, about seven miles from Gisborne.

The colonial force that amassed before Waerengaahika pa included: the Hawke's Bay Cavalry or the Colonial Defence Force Cavalry under command of Captain La Serre; Hawke's Bay Military Settlers under Lieutenant Wilson; and the force which served at Pukemaire under Major Fraser and newly promoted Captain Biggs, including the Forest Rangers under command of Captain Westrup and Ensign Ross. The force totalled about 200 Europeans and 300 Maori.

Fraser's force took up positions on three sides of the pa, which was constructed on level ground with its rear facing a swampy lagoon. Construction of the pa consisted of three outer walls: an outer sloping fence about six feet high, a second middle stout fence about 10 feet high, and an inner earthworks about 4 feet 6 inches high. The outer fence of stakes supported by spaced posts had a gap beneath of about one foot allowing Maori behind the middle fence a line of fire just above ground level.

Bishop William William's house was about 300 yards from the front of the pa. Fraser commandeered the Bishop's house as his headquarters and positioned his best snipers in the upstairs room where outer boards had been removed for the task. Men of the Colonial Defence Force and military settlers entrenched themselves behind a hawthorn hedge which commanded two angles of the pa. The Forest Rangers took up their position near the lagoon, to the left and front of the hawthorn hedge and closer to the pa. An orchard that lined the lagoon edge with trees.

The siege was to last seven days with continual rifle fire. Anxious for an early victory, Fraser sent Lieutenant Wilson and 30 of his Hawke's Bay Military Settlers to the north side of the pa where a sap was started. At 5 pm on the evening of 18 November, when the sap was quite close to the pa, Wilson and his men were attacked from behind by a large force of Hauhau who were reinforcing the pa from a nearby village. Wilson ordered his men to charge away from the pa through the Hauhau to the main body. In doing so six of Wilson's men were killed and five wounded. This heady success for the Hauhau threw them into a night of wild celebration. Their tohunga (religious leaders), predicted that the siege would be broken the following day. They perceived colonials to be like church missionaries and their followers, and underestimated the calibre of the Forest Rangers and military settlers. It was to prove a fatal decision.

The next day, 19 November, the religious Hauhau, after some Pai Marire prayers, charged the men holding the hawthorn hedge. It is believed they held up their right hands in the belief that they could stop the bullets. In fifteen minutes 63 Hauhau had been slaughtered. The remainder retreated back to the pa. Fraser's only casualty was one man slightly wounded in the leg.

After seven days' siege Fraser decided to use his only artillery piece on the pa.

Major James Fraser.
From 'Soldiering in New Zealand' by F.J.W. Gascoyne

This was a six-pounder brought ashore from the steamer *Sturt*. They used salmon tins filled with shrapnel as projectiles. Only two rounds were fired into the pa before the garrison hoisted the white flag and surrendered. About 400 Hauhau laid down their arms and gave themselves up. It is believed a number escaped across the lagoon.

At the time of surrender the defenders were low in morale and powder, and with so many casualties the use of artillery proved too much for them. The two shots that entered the pa probably caused no casualties but the effect on morale was overwhelming – especially after a week of siege. Morale was probably further lowered by many of the defenders who were not staunch believers of the Pai Marire faith.

The siege ended on 21 November. Over 100 Maori were killed and about the same number wounded. The Government's losses were 11 killed and 20 wounded. The pa was destroyed. Many of the captives were released but the more troublesome prisoners were sent to the Chatham Islands. One such prisoner was Te Kooti Rikirangi, who was arrested for treason. While he was fighting for the Government troops it was noticed he removed the bullets from his cartridges and fired only the powder. Te Kooti was believed to be in collusion with the Hauhau and in communication with the defenders. He later escaped from the islands, became better known as Te Kooti, and with his new followers exacted a terrible revenge.

Major Fraser gave his version of the action at Waerengaahika in a letter to the Agent for the General Government, Hawke's Bay, dated 21 November 1865:

> I marched as I had previously determined, and halted at Mr Goldsmith's for the night, from whence I proceeded early the next morning to attack the rebel pa built near the Bishop of Waiapu's residence. We were not molested on our march by the enemy until near the paddocks belonging to the Bishop, when we were fired on by the enemy, who had been reconnoitring us from their pa; they thus may be said to have fired the first shots of the war. Captain

Ruins of Waerengaahika pa showing the Bishop of Waiapu's house in the rear. Note the sacred niu pole prostrate in the foreground. Alexander Turnbull Library

WAERENGAAHIKA ENGAGEMENT *15-22 November 1865*

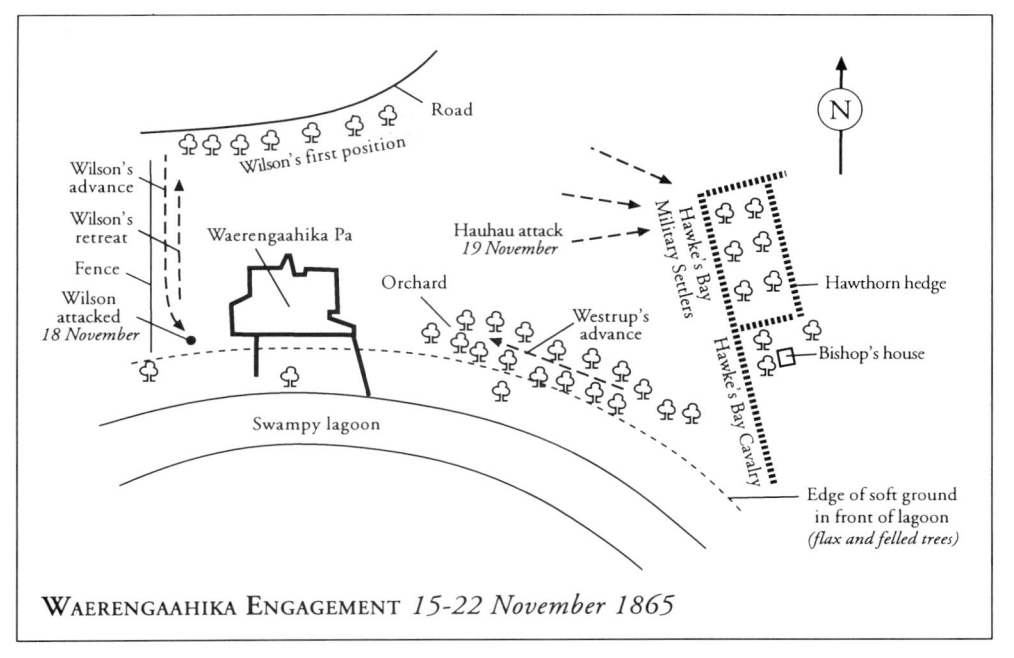

Westrup and his Rangers soon dislodged the enemy's skirmishers, who fell back upon their pa, around which we then took up our several positions under a heavy fire. Before proceeding further, I must mention that all the houses, barns, and other buildings, except the Bishop's house, had been utterly destroyed by the rebels. The Bishop's house had been thoroughly dismantled, the paper being torn off the walls, glass broken and all his valuable books torn and strewn about the floors. It was only our sudden arrival that prevented them from burning it – a most fortunate thing for us, as it is the most favourable position we could have chosen. The firing on both sides continued until evening, when we as far as possible entrenched ourselves, and slept out in the vicinity of the pa. Captain Westrup and his Rangers took up a position to the left of the pa, looking from the Bishop's house. Lieutenant Wilson and Military Settlers, with the Tuparoa under Te Hotina, were on the opposite flank; the Colonial Defence Force, Hawke's Bay Volunteers and the remainder of the Natives, were posted between the flanks and in front of the pa; a swampy lagoon is in rear of the pa, and is impassable, so none of the force was posted there.

I regret to have to state that owing to the heavy fire from the enemy the following casualties took place:

Forest Rangers: Ensign Ross, shot through the head; dangerous, but going on well; Private Ryan, shot through shoulders, severe.

1 Tuparoa Native, 1 Turanga Native killed; 2 Tuparoa Natives severely wounded. From subsequent information I have learnt that five of the enemy were killed; number of wounded not known. Nothing happened further until next day, when an affair occurred, which, had it not been for the courage displayed by

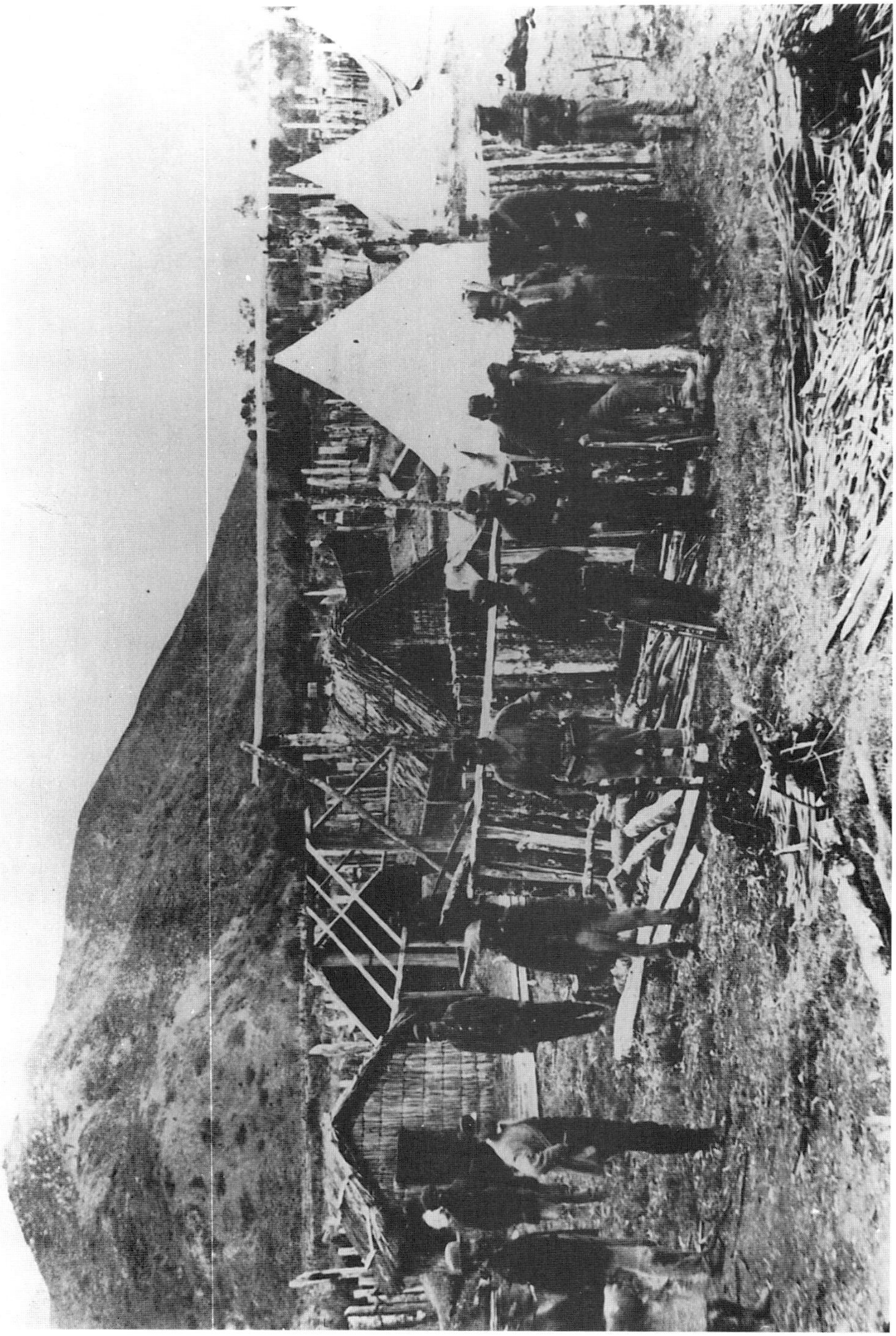

A photograph (opposite) of Westrup's Forest Rangers taken in camp at Poverty Bay after the engagement at Waerengaahika shows clearly the men's clothing. Although it was common for local settlers to pose in such photos, most of those pictured are believed to be Forest Rangers. They are still in possession of their Callisher and Terry breech-loading percussion carbines with leather shoulder straps. There is no sign of bowie knifes, although these could be hidden below coats. Their trousers and tunics or jackets seem to be a mixture of military and civilian with a variety of colours (probably greys and dark blue). Many are in possession of peaked forage caps of dark colour (presumably dark blue, a common colour of the period). A few are wearing round crown hats of the bowler type with narrow curved brims – obviously of civilian origin and probably impractical in the field. Nearly all are wearing heavy leather shoulder straps passing diagonally over the left shoulder, supporting a small pouch on the breast (probably containing percussion caps). Many have one or two leather pouches supported on their waist belts and rugged boots with trousers over the top. The general appearance of the unit is rugged. No two men have the same attire. Judging by the way they pose, one can assume they are fairly campaign hardened and ill-disciplined off the battle field.
The gentleman to the left with hands on hips is possibly Westrup in typical civilian attire. At this camp, sited in a Maori settlement, they are quartered in bell tents. This could well be Kohanga Karearea where the Forest Rangers were doing garrison duty after the battle of Waerengaahika.
In contrast, the Forest Rangers serving on the West Coast were issued with new clothing and equipment prior to Chute's expedition.
_{Alexander Turnbull Library}

the officers and men concerned, must have been attended with very serious consequences. To enable you to understand the whole circumstances of the case, I must inform you, that I have ever since taking the field had to contend with great difficulties on account of the lukewarmness of our Native allies of Turanga, who instead of assisting either by keeping sentry, digging trenches, or taking up positions in conjunction with Europeans when ordered, have been content to remain entirely in the background, and to throw all the work upon the Europeans, Tuparoa and Henare Potae's men. Accordingly the Tuparoa have been obliged as well as we to do double work; and had the other Natives simply done their duty and obeyed orders, what I am about to relate would most probably never have occurred.
On Saturday Captain Westrup, with his usual zeal and perseverance, had pushed his position and entrenched himself within about fifty yards of the pa. Orders were therefore sent to Lieutenant Wilson, on the other flank, to select a place for entrenching himself, and to get as close to the pa as possible on his side. I went round to see his position, accompanied by Captain Biggs, and we both considered that he had got an excellent one. A number of the Natives had early in the day been ordered round to support him, as those who had been with him the previous night had left him. These were supposed to have reached him, and had they done so the advantage subsequently gained by him would have been much greater. As it was, however, a large Native reinforcement came up to join the rebels about 5 pm. Lieutenant Wilson had not finished entrenching, his men were fatigued, the enemy made a sally from the pa, and he was surrounded on all sides. Under these circumstances, where most would have failed them, British pluck carried the day. Our men, though taken aback, and, till fired upon, believing the rebels

to be the Queen's Natives coming up to the support, fought bravely. Lieutenant Wilson ordered them to charge; they burst through the enemy, killing eight and wounding thirteen of their number, the loss on our side being as follows:
Killed: Sergeant Doonan, Privates Borthwick, Martin, Wilkie and Swords.
Wounded: Lieutenant Wilson (slightly), Private Pierson (severely), Private Sheldon (seriously), Private Chibbon (seriously), Private Wellfit (slightly) and Private Kennedy (slightly).
One Turanga Native, Andre Thuruke, was severely wounded. Only three Natives were with Lieutenant Wilson's party at this time.

This incident occurred on 18 November and most of the above named Europeans belonged to the Hawke's Bay Military Settlers. Pierson later died.

The operations elsewhere on this day consisted in our keeping up a hot fire on the enemy's pa, and in entrenching ourselves. I am very sorry to state that I have lost the valuable services of Assistant Surgeon Ormond, who was accidentally severely wounded by a shot coming through a window in the Bishop's house. A ball passed through his fingers, which were in his trousers pocket at the time, entering the left thigh and passed through the right, the injury to the right thigh being very slight. I am able to report most favourably of his condition; no alarm need be felt by his friends. Next day (Sunday) we were attacked about 8 am in the most deceitful manner, by about 200 of the enemy, who advanced armed, in three bodies, close to our main position, under a flag of truce, their intention to take us off our guard, and then fire at us. We however, providentially, did not pay any attention to the flag, as no flag of truce should be respected carried by such a large body of armed men, and I ordered them to be fired on before they could come up to us. This was the signal for them to begin, and we had a fair hand-to-hand fight, with about equal numbers, in an open place, and without the aid of trenches, in which the enemy were totally defeated, with the loss of 34 killed, and at least that number wounded, their men falling in all directions as they attempted to regain their pa, from which, I may add, a hot fire was kept up during the engagement. Our loss consisted of Trooper Hirtzel of the Colonial Defence Force being slightly wounded in the leg.

There was some concern from the Government about the matter of firing on the white flag but after obtaining statements from each officer present the action was approved.

Fraser's force moved to Turanganui, taking the prisoners with them. The least guilty were released soon after and allowed to return to Oweta and other villages. Captain Westrup and the Forest Rangers were sent to garrison the village of Kohanga Karearea, to observe their behaviour. The worst defenders were shipped to the Chatham Islands.

Westrup remained on the East Coast with his Forest Rangers. Many left the district early in 1866, and the remaining men were discharged on or before 8 July 1866. After this date the men who remained in Poverty Bay may have enlisted in local units and have seen further action.

The Forest Rangers who had land grants around Te Awamutu returned to their land during February 1866.

CHAPTER 22

Chute's conquest of Taranaki

On von Tempsky's return to Wanganui from Wellington in mid October 1865, he was instructed to increase the strength of his force and introduce new rates of pay. Under his command he was to have a company of Forest Rangers as well as a native contingent, with a maximum combined strength in excess of 100 men.

The new force was to be comprised of (with daily rates of pay in brackets):

European force of 34 men: 1 major commanding – Von Tempsky, (30s); 1 captain (18s); 1 lieutenant (14s 6d); 1 ensign (12s 6d); 1 staff sergeant (6s); 2 sergeants (4s 6d); 2 corporals (4s); 25 privates (3s 6d). The instruction for a new captain was soon dropped.

Native Contingent of 72 men: 1 lieutenant (14s 6d); 1 ensign (12s 6d); 4 sergeants (4s 6d); 4 corporals (4s); 62 privates (3s 6d).

Von Tempsky argued that he only wanted good men that he could trust and train personally in the art of bushfighting. He did not want the Maori unit. He also said that the Maori available for service were too fractured because they were of different tribes, and impossible to group in time for service over summer because many were out of the district.

In von Tempsky's letter (dated 6 November) to Colonel Haultain, Adjutant General, he proposes:

> If my force of white men could be raised to sixty men, and eight native guides attached to the force (guides at the rate of 6 shlgs per day – their former rate of pay), I could reconnoitre and prepare the way for this summer's campaign.

In a following letter von Tempsky adds:

> ... I can get twenty men here if required – of course I would prefer having some tried men who are in service now – or better still – if I could get Capt. Westrup and his men if their services are no longer required at the East Cape.

Von Tempsky had a persuasive way with words making an offer that was difficult to refuse:

> The local knowledge required for the coming campaign is solely in the hands of half a dozen natives, fugitives from that locality. These men expect to be enrolled as guides with somewhat higher pay than other natives. I have had these men before in my service and they are indispensable.

It is probable that these men were already camped outside the Forest Ranger camp and von Tempsky determined himself to gain their services.

Finally the Colonial Defence Office struck a compromise, allowing von Tempsky to enlist a further 20 European men and 8 Maori scouts. Responsibility of the Native Contingent was passed on to Thomas McDonnell.

The Colonial Defence Office offered the Maori guides less than 6s pay per day.

South Taranaki / Wanganui

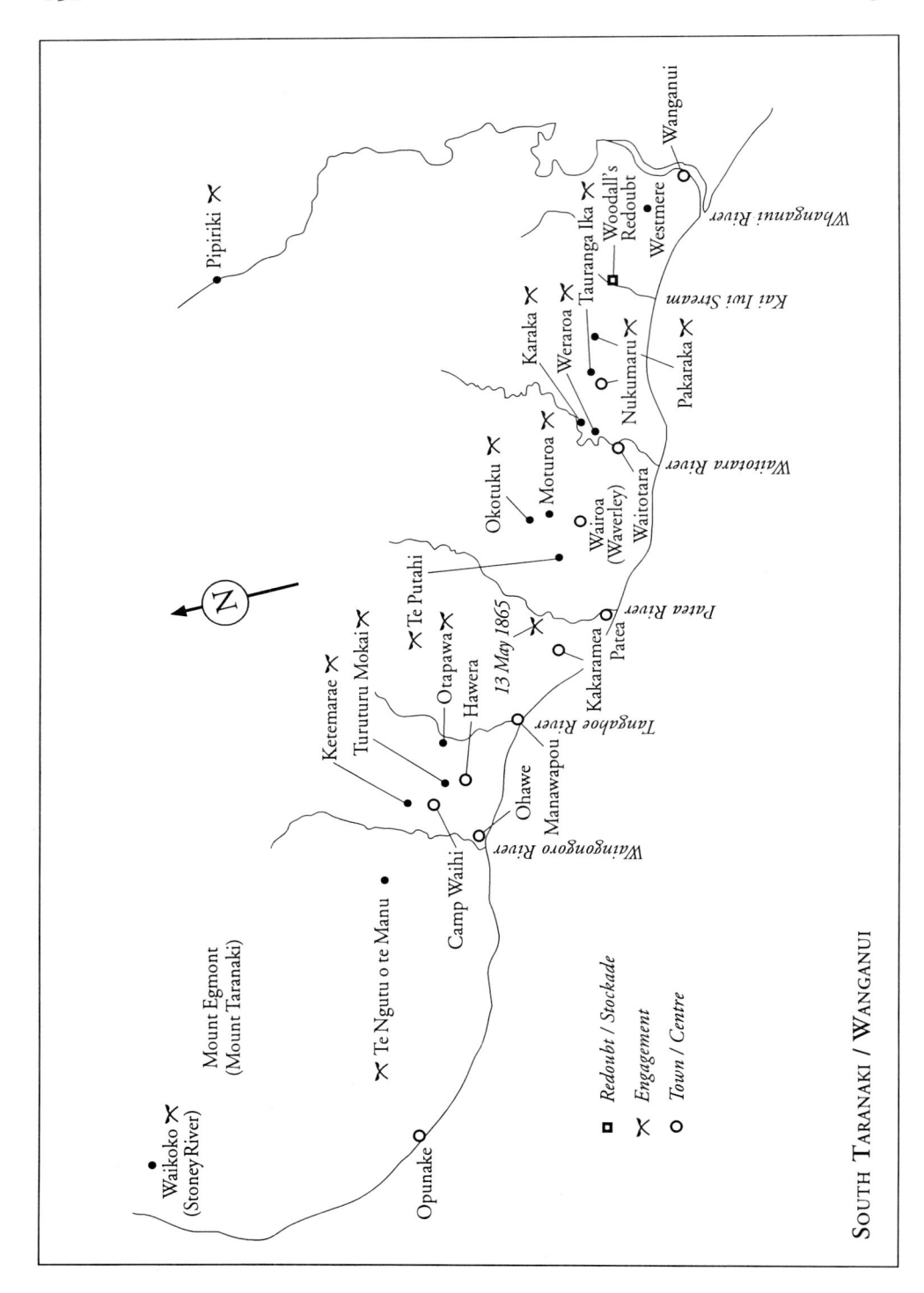

Major-General Trevor Chute commenced his campaign against the West Coast tribes at the end of 1865. In contrast to his predecessor, General Cameron, who hated bush fighting and endeavoured to keep his 6000 or so troops as near to the coast as possible or in open spaces, Chute was prepared to engage the Maori in the bush and storm their bush retreats. He was considered a tough, venturesome and vigorous soldier, eager to prove his worth in the New Zealand campaign.

At this time von Tempsky and the 30 Forest Rangers who did not proceed to the East Coast were at Woodall's Redoubt awaiting developments. While waiting they patrolled the outskirts of the settled districts on the lookout for hostile Maori.

Roll of Forest Rangers at Camp Abraham, November 1865 included:

Major (1): Von Tempsky. *Colour Sergeant* (1): Birchfield. *Sergeants* (2): Lawrence Burns, Lawrence Mitchell. *Corporals* (2): Devlin, Amelius Taylor. *Privates* (33): Anderson, Beetham, Brooking, John Burns, Burley, Allister Campbell, Codling, Cullinan, Drew, Duffy, Dunckley, Erskine, Ferris, Fischer, Gillanders, Hearfield, Henshaw, Hollister, Jeffares, Knight, Lee, Lloyd, McGrath, O'Brien, O'Connell, John Ryan, Colin Smith, Spencer, William Stephenson, Thomas, Varette, Thomas Wallace, Watson.

Von Tempsky had some company changes to contend with over this period. Six men, originally from the Waikato, requested discharge. Substitutes were found: some who had recently joined, and others from outside the unit. The six substitutes carried on the entitlement to land grants around Te Awamutu.

Changes were (with dates of discharge and substitution in brackets); Beetham (10 November) substituted by Duffy (10 November); Cullinan (13 November) substituted by Thomas Wallace (21 October); Hearfield (27 November) substituted by Jeffares (28 November); Liebig (22 September) substituted by Gillanders (24 October); Lloyd (13 November) substituted by John Ryan (23 October); Colin Smith (27 November) substituted by Burley (4 September).

Lloyd was originally substituted by O'Brien, who was accidentally shot by a comrade. He was later replaced by John Ryan.

On 28 November 1865 McDonnell and his Native Contingent arrived back from Opotiki aboard SS *Stormbird*.

In preparation for the forthcoming campaign, von Tempsky asked the authorities for more ammunition for the revolvers held by his unit. Lieutenant-Colonel Edward Gorton, of the Wanganui Military District, in a letter to the Colonial Defence Office, Wellington dated 28 December 1865, relayed the request:

> I regret I am unable to purchase in Wanganui Colt revolver ammunition of the size requested for the 30 Colt revolvers now in possession of Major von Tempsky's men. Seventeen large revolvers have been issued to Major von Tempsky from this office, and it is my intuition to collect as many as I can from the Cavalry Volunteers on their next visit and exchange them with Major von Tempsky for the smaller size. At the same time I trust ammunition for the latter will be able to be purchased at Wellington or elsewhere and sent up here as soon as possible.

The large revolvers referred to are English made 54 gauge revolvers. Gorton left his request too late as the Forest Rangers had already left Wanganui to join Chute.

Von Tempsky would have got ammunition for his English revolvers from Chute's commissariat.

Gorton also mentioned the issuing of nine pairs of boots with wooden soles painted black to the Forest Rangers. Von Tempsky rejected the boots and asked for them to be replaced. Gorton stated in a letter to the suppliers:

> I have the honour to inform you that nine (9) pairs of boots out of the quantity supplied by you at Wellington for the use of Major von Tempsky's force which arrived here in October last have turned out to have wooden soles – two pairs out of the nine were issued and returned, the remaining seven are as received from you.
>
> These boots are painted and to outwards appearance were similar to the other boots wherefore I feel sure you knew nothing about it. But I must request you will as soon as possible send me free of expense nine pairs of boots similar to the remaining portion which have been issued and instruct me where I am to send the nine pairs of condemned boots.

It seems like some boot maker made some quick money out of the New Zealand Government!

On 5 December von Tempsky requested 20 Callisher and Terry carbines and 20 sets of accoutrements for the new enlistments. These were shipped from Wellington to Wanganui aboard SS *Stormbird* on 14 December.

A requisition for 50 waterproof haversacks and 50 greatcoats arrived during December, but Major Atkinson ordered that the men who refused to sail to the East Coast should pay for their replacements, whereas the new enlistments were to receive theirs free. Von Tempsky was not impressed by this, and after a few angry letters managed to get free replacements for all his men.

Another dispute concerned a horse that von Tempsky had borrowed from the Government while he was in the Wanganui district. After having it shod he applied for reimbursement of the cost, which was only a few shillings. Letters were exchanged but the matter was never resolved.

This constant bickering from the Government took its toll on von Tempsky and many of his Forest Rangers, slowly turning them against the colonial service.

Chute left Wanganui on Saturday, 30 December 1865, and after stopping at Weraroa he was joined by the Forest Rangers and Native Contingent. On 3 January, when crossing the Waitotara River, the force consisted of: Forest Rangers (2 officers, 3 sergeants and 41 men – Major von Tempsky commanding) 46 all ranks; Royal Artillery with field guns (1 officer, 2 sergeants, 30 men – Lieutenant Carre commanding) 33 all ranks; 2nd Battalion 14th Regiment (8 officers, 11 sergeants, 4 drummers, 250 men – Lieutenant-Colonel Trevor commanding) 273 all ranks; Native Contingent and other Maori (12 officers, 8 sergeants, 96 men, 150 Kupapa – Major McDonnell commanding) 266 all ranks. The total was 618 all ranks. Also present was the Transport Corps with 45 two horse drays.

The force advanced on Okotuku, a village on the edge of high ground about five miles inland from Wairoa, now Waverley. On 4 January 1866 the Forest Rangers (2 officers and 33 men), two companies of the 14th Regiment (3 officers, 4 sergeants, 1 drummer and 100 men) and a Maori force (3 officers and 200 men) advanced on the village which had been abandoned and burnt by the Native Contingent the previous day. They intended to destroy food sources of potatoes and maize nearby. But when a small advance-guard were within 350 yards of the pa, they were heavily fired on from a breastworks of logs stacked horizontally between thick upright stakes. The Forest Rangers were positioned on the extreme left with the 14th Regiment in the centre and the Native Contingent on either flank and in reserve. The position was stormed at bayonet point killing three enemy Maori. The Forest Rangers and members of the Native Contingent then pursued the enemy through the bush, killing three more. More than 20 enemy Maori are believed to have been killed, but owing to the density of the forest this could not be confirmed. The British losses were one killed and six wounded. The defences of the pa and whare were burnt before the troops returned to camp.

As Chute moved along the coast he expected the local garrisons to supplement his force while it was in that area. Troops of the 2nd Battalion, 18th Regiment and the 50th Regiment garrisoned at Patea, reinforced Chute's column on 6 January before the attack on Te Putahi pa.

On 7 January the force attacked a strong Hauhau pa at Te Putahi, on high ground above the Whenuakura River. The spurs and densely wooded terrain made the position difficult to assault.

In the darkness before dawn a force comprised of Forest Rangers (2 officers, 2 sergeants and 38 men – von Tempsky commanding), 14th Regiment (6 officers, 9 sergeants, 3 drummers and 204 men), 2nd Battalion, 18th Regiment (5 officers, 4 sergeants, 2 drummers and 89 men), 50th Regiment (4 officers, 4 sergeants, 2 drummers and 90 men), Royal Artillery (1 officer, 2 sergeants and 28 men) and the Native Contingent (10 officers and 200 men) carefully climbed to the plateau where the pa stood. On entering the clearing before the pa, the Forest Rangers were opened out in skirmishing order and lay down to cover the following troops as they emerged from the forest into the clearing. The Forest Rangers opened fire from 300 yards interrupting a Hauhau ceremony. But the Maori soon returned an accurate fire, severely wounding Private Allister Henry Campbell of the Forest Rangers in the left thigh. Private John Ryan, under fire, went to the assistance of Campbell, for which action he was personally thanked by von Tempsky after the battle. The force waited for about an hour under fire, then advanced, leaving the Native Contingent to guard the rear. Under heavy fire the troops moved to within 80 yards of the pa and then charged. The 200 enemy Maori defended strongly but the pa was soon overrun with a bayonet charge. Von Tempsky was one of the first into the pa. Just behind him, Private James Robert Malcolm of the Forest Rangers was severely wounded in the right leg. The Maori retreated to the bush beyond, followed by the Native Contingent for a short distance. The pa with its whare were looted, then destroyed and burnt before the force returned to camp. The British force lost 2 imperial soldiers killed and 12 wounded (McDonnell received a bullet wound to his foot), while it is recorded that the Hauhau lost 16 killed – 15 in the pa and one in the retreat. Again, as at Okotuku, many more Hauhau casualties could have been carried off.

In a whare beside the Whenuakura River the Forest Rangers discovered a whale boat carefully concealed. It had been lost from the steamer *Gundagai* some months previously. The Forest Rangers speedily despatched the boat to the Patea River.

Chute mentioned the good service given by von Tempsky in his despatch covering

Von Tempsky watercolour depicting the Forest Ranger camp in front of Te Putahi pa on the Whenuakura River, 7 January 1866. Dr Featherston is shown at centre rear. Te Putahi pa can be seen on high ground across the river. Alexander Turnbull Library

the engagement:
> Where all have behaved so gallantly, it is difficult to select any names for favourable mention; but, of the Colonial Forces, I beg especially to bring to your Excellency's notice Major von Tempsky, commanding Forest Rangers...

Von Tempsky had a premonition of death before Te Putahi. The fear of the unknown prompted him to write and post what he thought was his last letter of endearment to his wife:
> Camp before Te Putahi, Jan 6, '66. My own dearest, Tonight at three o'clock we're going to attack the Hauhau pa Te Putahi. I am to command what I well may term a forlorn hope, and as the position is strong and the enemy numerous, there is every chance of your not seeing me again. Receive therefore my inmost thanks for your unceasing love and devotion, and be assured that my last thoughts in this world will be our love – my last word your dear name. Pray for me as I am not worthy to pray myself. To my dear children give my last adieu and love.

On 8 January the reinforcements of the 2nd Battalion, 18th Regiment and the 50th Regiment under command of Major Rocke returned to Patea. Meanwhile, one non-commissioned officer and 15 gunners, with two six-pounder Armstrong guns joined the force from Patea on 9 January.

Sergeant Lawrence Mitchell, of the Forest Rangers, was reduced to the rank of private for drunkenness and abuse of a superior officer.

In a letter to Captain Holt, Under Secretary to the Defence Office (dated 12 February 1866), von Tempsky explains the dilemma:
> I have the honour to state, in reply to a letter enquiring into the causes of reduction of Sergeant Mitchell, that on the 9th of Jan. 1866, while on the march from Patea to Kakaramea, Sergeant Mitchell was drunk and used abusive language to Lieut. Pilmer.
> Sergeant Mitchell apologised the following morning but as this was the second time I had seen him drunk, and as this was the first time during a period of three years that any one of my officers had been spoken to in such a way, I saw the necessity of making an example.
> Being in the field and on a line of march where no duty day was given, I could not hold a Court Martial, neither could I carry with me a man in the position of prisoner; I therefore reduced Sergeant Mitchell on the spot.

Under the circumstances, Mitchell was lucky the matter did not go any further. He stayed at the rank of private until his discharge.

On 10 January, the bush near Kakaramea was reconnoitred and two deserted villages destroyed. The next day 50 men of the Native Contingent, with the use of 32 horses captured from Hauhau before joining Chute's column at Weraroa, joined the scouts in their activities.

On 12 January Chute's force moved towards the Hauhau position at Otapawa pa, about five miles from present day Hawera. Otapawa pa was on the edge of a plateau high above the west bank of the Tangahoe River. The pa was of strong construction above steep banks in a half circle of the river. On the landward side of the pa were two lines of high palisading, rifle pits and trenches – the flanks of which fell away to the river. At the rear of the pa overlooking the river were two

Von Tempsky watercolour depicting the attack on Otapawa pa, 14 January 1866. Lieutenant-Colonel Jason Hassard of the 57th Regiment is shown in the foreground being carried off mortally wounded. Two Forest Rangers are shown on the right. Spain, the Maori guide attached to the Forest Rangers, who was accidentally killed, is possibly shown on the left. Robert McDougall Art Gallery

**OTAPAWA ENGAGEMENT
14 January 1866**

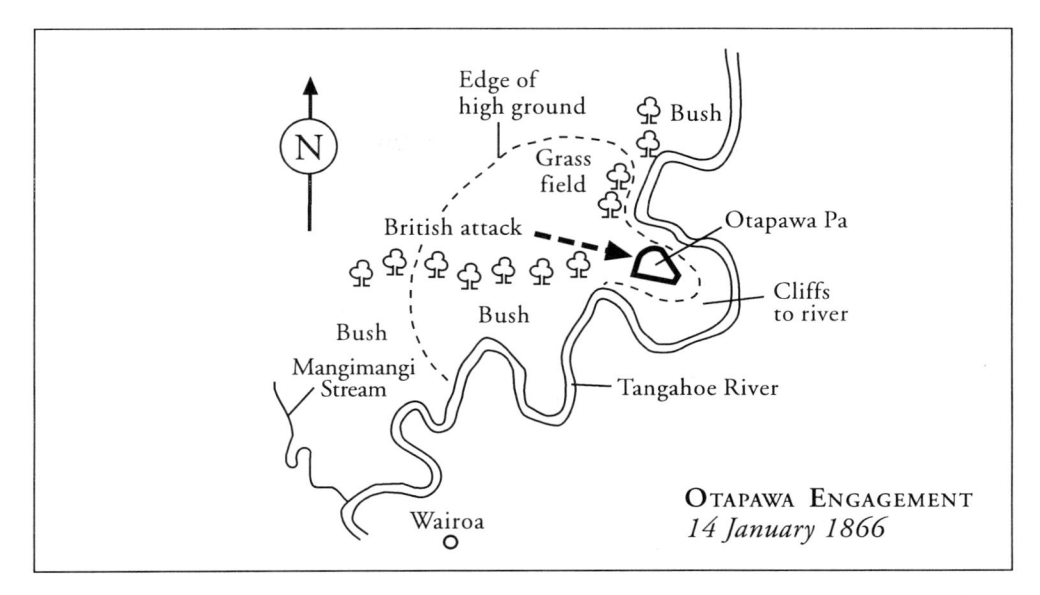

deep ditches and three parapets. Chute based his force on the plain at Tawhiti, within easy striking distance.

Further reinforcements joined the column from posts at Waingongoro and Manawapou on 12 January. These were a detachment of the 57th Regiment (5 officers, 6 non-commissioned officers and 120 men) from Waingongoro, and a further detachment of the same Regiment (4 officers, 6 non-commissioned officers and 120 men) from Manawapou, all under the command of Lieutenant-Colonel Butler.

Ensign William McDonnell (brother of Major McDonnell) and some Native Contingent Maori scouted the enemy position. They were discovered but escaped unscathed. The camp was aroused at 1 am on the morning of 14 January. Following a light meal, the main force marched to attack the position, while 200 men of the Native Contingent under Major McDonnell moved to the rear of the pa to cut off a possible retreat. The main force was comprised of: 37 Forest Rangers under Major von Tempsky's command; 200 2nd Battalion, 14th Regiment under Lieutenant-Colonel Trevor; 130 57th Regiment under Lieutenant-Colonel Butler and three six-pounder Armstrong guns and teams under Lieutenant Carre.

The artillery was positioned on high ground at a range of 1300 yards and commenced to fire rounds into the pa. This gave cover to the advancing troops who gathered in a depression about 150 yards in front of the pa. Assault positions were taken up: the 57th Regiment to the left in skirmishing order with the Forest Rangers in support; the 2nd Battalion 14th Regiment extended to the right; and a detachment of the Native Contingent in reserve. General Chute gave the order, "57th, advance! Rangers, clear the bush!" The 57th and 14th detachments advanced against the landward fortifications. When the main force closed to within 40 yards of the pa, the enemy fired a heavy volley, and a second volley as the soldiers charged with fixed bayonets. After hacking with tomahawks and bayonets at the vine fastenings of the palisades, the soldiers soon breached the pa. The Hauhau escaped to the rear, down the steep banks and across the river, avoiding contact with the Native

Von Tempsky watercolour depicting General Chute's column marching via the east side of Mount Egmont to New Plymouth, January 1866. Dr Featherston and Major-General Chute are shown to the left. Takiora, a woman and guide, is shown on horseback followed by three Forest Rangers (left to right): von Tempsky, Birchfield and Ross. *Alexander Turnbull Library*

Contingent as McDonnell did not have enough time to get into position.

The Forest Rangers, after receiving their order to advance, worked on the left flank of the imperial soldiers where the terrain was steep and densely wooded, falling away to the river. There they made contact with the enemy and cleared the area of some Hauhau who were firing at the assault force. They followed the soldiers into the pa and worked their way to the left rear hoping to catch the Hauhau before they escaped. They caught sight of the enemy, including many women and children, making for the bush and the river. After a brief skirmish the Hauhau disappeared from sight and the recall was sounded.

The British lost eleven killed (including Lieutenant-Colonel Jason Hassard of the 57th Regiment) and twenty wounded. Casualties to the Forest Rangers included: a Maori named Spain, who as a guide attached to the unit, was killed by a musket ball to the chest; and a private who was slightly wounded. The Hauhau lost about thirty killed and many more wounded.

Von Tempsky wrote in a letter to Colonel Gorton dated 31 January:

> ... I regret to say that while entering first the pa I lost my most valuable guide Spain; he was behind me and went into a whare, on scallying, he was shot dead (by mistake) by some soldiers of the 14th [Regiment].

Gudgeon, in *Reminiscences of the War in New Zealand*, gives another opinion of Spain's death which is in direct conflict with von Tempsky's description. He writes that Spain entered the whare to bring out a dead Hauhau, and while so engaged a party of Forest Rangers approached and asked who was in the whare. The reply was "A white man," meaning a friend. Unfortunately the Forest Rangers concluded that this meant the deserter Kimble Bent and immediately fired a volley into the whare, mortally wounding Spain.

Whichever is the correct explanation, the unintentional death of Spain was a tragedy.

Von Tempsky again received a special mention in Chute's despatch:

> ... I take this opportunity of expressing my thanks to Major von Tempsky, commanding Forest Rangers.

With the principal Hauhau stronghold now captured, Chute proceeded to the stockaded village of Ketemarae, about one mile from present day Normanby, just north of Hawera, a well known meeting place for West Coast Maori. The village was attacked by a section of Chute's column including 40 Forest Rangers all ranks, on the morning of 15 January. They killed ten Hauhau with no loss to the column. Neighbouring villages, including Keteonetea and Puketi, were cleared after some sharp skirmishing by the Native Contingent with help from the Forest Rangers.

From Ketemarae, the force advanced on the same day past Waihi, over the Waingongoro River, and captured Mawhitiwhiti village killing seven Hauhau. Several other villages were also destroyed during the day. Most of this work was carried out by the Native Contingent, with Kepa te Rangihiwinui (later Major Kemp) distinguishing himself.

Chute, after successfully destroying the Hauhau strongholds in the Hawera-Patea district, decided to proceed to New Plymouth, not by the more usual coastal route, but by the more direct route via the east side of Mount Egmont. Because this trail was disused and almost overgrown, the task proved very difficult, especially for the

67 packhorses and 24 saddle-horses. Chute wanted to prove to the Maori the commitment and ability of his troops, and also demonstrate to the colonists the ability of the British soldiers to withstand hardship.

Chute's column left from Ketemarae heading north on 17 January. The column consisted of: Forest Rangers (1 field officer – von Tempsky, 1 Captain, 2 sergeants and 57 men), a selected body of the Native Contingent (1 subaltern, 2 sergeants and 67 other ranks), the 2nd Battalion 14th Regiment (1 field officer, 2 captains, 3 subalterns, 10 sergeants, 4 drummers and 236 men) and a detachment of Royal Artillery (1 subaltern, 1 sergeant and 36 men) – a total of 425 all ranks. The only provisions were one day's biscuit rations carried by the men, and three day's provisions on the pack horses.

With delays to cut tracks and build bridges for the horses, it took nine days to cover the open country between Ketemarae and New Plymouth. On the first day out from Ketemarae, the Native Contingent which was in advance, encountered seven Hauhau on the track, and shot three of them. When the column encountered dense bush and the many streams on the lower slopes of Mount Egmont, the Forest Rangers took the lead and did good work cutting a track and bridging creeks and swampy gullies with tree fern trunks for the horses to cross. Rain slowed the column at this stage, making the Forest Rangers' work difficult. Working parties of the 14th Regiment now assisted the Forest Rangers at the front. On the night of 20 January, a small group consisting of a few officers and some Maori pushed forward on a forced march to Mataitawa Stockade in north Taranaki to secure provisions and return to the column. Progress was so slow that on 21 January the column covered only four miles. A horse was butchered that night to supplement the near exhausted provisions. A second horse was killed the next day and on that evening supplies arrived from Mataitawa Stockade carried by a party of the 43rd and 68th Regiments. During three days of rain the column was weary and cold with no fires to warm up by or cook on. Meanwhile, some of the Forest Rangers and Native Contingent hurried on ahead to the open country and waited for the column to rejoin. The complete column arrived exhausted at Mataitawa on 25 January and the next day continued to New Plymouth and a heroes' welcome. The column camped by the Waiwhakaiho River, four miles north of New Plymouth.

That same day Chute, with an Armstrong gun and 100 men of the 43rd Regiment, sailed from New Plymouth north along the coast to make contact with Maori, but returned unsuccessful.

Chute wasted no time starting his return journey from New Plymouth to Wanganui, moving out on 27 January, this time via the west side of Mount Egmont heading for Oakura. The Forest Rangers were in the advance again. At Stoney River, Captain Mace's Mounted Corps and 70 men of the 43rd Regiment joined the column. A company of Taranaki Bush Rangers under Captain Corbett also joined with the prospect of action against the Hauhau in the Warea district.

Before daylight on 1 February General Chute left camp with a strong force and followed a track which had been scouted by a party of Native Contingent the previous day.

The force consisted of: Forest Rangers (von Tempsky, 1 captain, 3 sergeants and 31 men); Taranaki volunteers (captain Corbett and 16 men); Native Contingent (1 subaltern and 60 other ranks); Royal Artillery (1 subaltern, 1 sergeant and 30 men);

2nd Battalion 14th Regiment (1 field officer, 2 captains, 2 subalterns, 6 sergeants, 3 drummers and 180 men); and 43rd Regiment (2 captains, 2 subalterns, 5 sergeants, 1 drummer and 90 men). The force totalled 440 men.

The force advanced through bush and scrub and entered a clearing 500 yards in front of Waikoko pa. In skirmishing order with the 43rd Regiment to the left, the 14th Regiment to the right and the Forest Rangers in the centre, they rushed the pa. The other units followed immediately behind. The Hauhau fought bravely but soon retreated to the rear, leaving four dead in the pa.

As usual the whare and cultivations were destroyed before the force returned to camp. One man of the 14th Regiment was killed, while a sergeant in Corbett's Rangers and two of the Native Contingent were wounded.

Amongst the Forest Rangers, Private Alexander Davidson was severely wounded in the left thigh by a musket ball.

The column reached Opunaki on 2 February, and Waingongoro on 4 February. While at Manawapou on 5 February a detachment, which did not include the Forest Rangers, was sent to destroy Mere Mere pa and neighbouring cultivations. From here the column continued its march without any further contact with Hauhau, and arrived in Patea on 6 February, Waitotara on 7 February, Alexander's Farm on 8 February and finally Wanganui on 9 February 1866.

Roll of Forest Rangers in Wanganui and South Taranaki districts, December 1865 - February 1866 included:

It can not be assumed that all these men served with General Chute's expedition.

Major (1): Von Tempsky. *Lieutenant* (1): Pilmer. *Ensign* (1): McKenna. *Staff Sergeant* (1): Birchfield. *Sergeants* (3): Lawrence Burns, Lawrence Mitchell (demoted to private during expedition on 9 January), Amelius Taylor. *Corporals* (3): Devlin, John Burns (travelled to Waikato 9 January 1866), James Taylor. *Privates* (41): Thomas Anderson, Atkins, Bisland, Burley, Allister Campbell, Codling, Colston, Crommelin, Daley, Alexander Davidson, Donald, Duffy, Erskine, Fischer, C. Fisher, Gillanders, Henshaw, Hollister, Howell, J.H. Jackson, Jeffares, Kiely (discharged 29 January 1866), Lee, McGrath, McKelson, Malcolm, Medex, Morton, Newman, John Ryan, Shaddock, William Stephenson, Sullivan (served 12 – 18 December 1865), Thornton (joined 29 January 1866), George Vart, James Wallace (joined at Oakura 28 January 1866), Thomas Wallace, John Ward (joined at Oakura 28 January 1866), Warden (served 14 – 22 December 1865), Watson, Winmill.

Maori guides (7): Hari Aroreta, Rio Kawiti, Penamina, Te Pene (discharged 13 January 1866), Reihana, Tamati Waka, Horima Watene.

The above names indicate that there were at least seven Maori guides serving at the time, six of them joining at Woodall's Redoubt on 6 December 1865. Reihana joined at Te Putahi on 9 January 1866, replacing Tamati Waka who was discharged on 8 January 1866.

The first task von Tempsky undertook on reaching Wanganui was to write to Colonel Gorton, Commander Wanganui District, requesting new outfits for his men. In a letter dated 9 February, he explained:

> ... the arduous services performed by them through very rough country has left them literally in rags.

Whether his request was met is not known.

CHAPTER 23

Final disbandment

By now the Forest Rangers' uniforms were in a shabby state. They were torn and dilapidated from the recent march through Taranaki. Many treated themselves at personal expense to new clothes on their return. There was no Government compensation. A few of the men lost their firearms during the heat of assault when rushing some of the pa, and the Government demanded that these men make good their lost. Morale was slipping and few had regrets about a possible disbandment of the unit.
All the men who joined the unit in the Wanganui and South Taranaki districts, except Alexander Davidson, were discharged on or about 17 February 1866 in Wanganui. As they did not come under the same terms of enlistment as did the men who joined in south Auckland, they received no grants of land. Alexander Davidson remained on full pay until the end of September 1866 while he recovered from the wound he received at Waikoko.
Colonel Haultain, Defence Minister, wrote on 12 February to his Wanganui Office:

> This corps of Forest Rangers was enrolled to act in conjunction with the Native Contingent. But I think their services are no longer required. A few of them (about 19) have land allotted them in the Waikato and should be sent back there and struck off pay. The remaining 28 can be discharged after a month's notice, and are not entitled to land.

The 28 men did not have to serve their month but received one extra month's pay and immediate discharge.

Lieutenant Pilmer and Ensign McKenna, who remained in Wanganui, served till 31 March 1866. They probably took care of returning the last of the equipment to stores and any remaining clerical duties.

Von Tempsky and the remaining 19 Forest Rangers who had land grants in the Te Awamutu district stayed in camp at Wanganui until they embarked aboard SS *Stormbird* for Onehunga on 17 February 1866. Thomas McDonnell, on sick leave, was also aboard. The men proceeded to the Waikato, reporting to Lieutenant-Colonel Moule, Commanding Officer of the Waikato Militia, on 2 March. Von Tempsky returned to Auckland with McDonnell.

Roll of Forest Rangers who returned from Wanganui to the Te Awamutu district, February 1866:

Major (1): Von Tempsky. *Staff Sergeant* (1): Birchfield. *Sergeants* (2): Lawrence Burns, Amelius Taylor. *Corporals* (4): John Burns (returned early to Waikato leaving south Taranaki 9 January 1866), Devlin, Lee, William Stephenson. *Privates* (13): Thomas Anderson, Burley, Codling, Allister Campbell, Duffy, Fischer, Gillanders, Hollister, Jeffares, McGrath, Lawrence Mitchell, John Ryan, Thomas Wallace.

Final disbandment

Roll of Forest Rangers who remained in the Te Awamutu district, May 1865:

No. 1 Company: *Staff Sergeant* (1): Bertram. *Sergeants* (3): James Cunningham, Holden, Long. *Corporal* (1): Johns. *Privates* (28): Alexander, Argue, Richard Bell, David Bruce, Robert Bruce, William Bruce, Chapman, Costello, Robert Cunningham, Drury, Hannay, Hendry, Humphries, Jolley, McEnaney, Mahoney, Matheson, John Murray, Robert Murray, Preston, Rowden, William Smith, Temple, William Thomson, Vaughan, Vincent, Wells, Thomas Williams.

No. 2 Company: *Staff Sergeant* (1): McMinn. *Sergeants* (2): Southey, Toovey. *Corporals* (2): Clifford, Mulligan. *Privates* (22): Bidgood, Buttle, Cochrane, Conrad, Fraser, Hellkessel, Keena, Lander, Lindsay, Lott, McClymont, Magole, Napier, Neil, Pohlen, Quinn, Rogers, Ruhstein, Stanley, Sturmer, James Taylor, Wilson.

At this time the Government was anxious to cut back on its expenditure, and the high rate of pay for the Forest Rangers was a prime target.

The men of No. 1 Company took possession of their land grants and were struck off pay on 8 March 1866. The men of No. 2 Company took possession of their land grants and were later struck off pay on 31 March 1866.

The delay in locating No. 2 Company was caused by von Tempsky's absence in Auckland and by the loss of the "tracing" or surveyor's map of Harapepe when it was wrongly lent to another surveyor.

The matter of the lost firearms also resurfaced. The dispute between von Tempsky and the Colonial Defence Office over the disappearance of four revolvers also contributed to the delay of placing men on their land. Captain Holt, Under Secretary to the Colonial Defence Office, demanded their return. When the 20 Waikato men left Wanganui on 17 February they took with them 20 revolvers. But the Wanganui quartermaster disputed that another four were unaccounted for.

Both Companies went on fuel allowance, a basic allowance to purchase fuel such as fire wood, of one penny per day. Men who stayed behind at Harapepe instead of travelling to Wanganui in 1865 were placed on their land and struck off pay. They were also put on the same fuel allowance. The Forest Ranger unit was officially disbanded on 30 October 1867 because the Armed Constabulary Act took effect the following day.

Four men remained on full pay for various reasons. These were: the two Company Sergeant-Majors, Bertram of No. 1 Company and McMinn of No. 2 Company, probably in case of an emergency call-out and to organise musters, drill and equipment; Sturmer of No. 2 Company and Daniel McKenzie of No. 1 Company, acting as Company Clerks.

Forest Ranger town land grants were at Kihikihi (No. 1 Company) and Harapepe (No. 2 Company), near Te Awamutu. Their farm lots were positioned as close as possible to their town lots. Farm lots were in the districts of Puniu and Rangiaowhia (which includes Hairini) for those with Kihikihi town lots, and at Pirongia on the foothills of Mount Pirongia down to the Waipa River for those with Harapepe town lots.

The men who decided not to travel to Wanganui and remained in Harapepe received little help from the Government. On 18 May 1865 the men in the various Waikato centres who were not on garrison or river transport duties were struck off pay and given possession of their land. The men continued to receive rations for a further 12 months but were considerably dissatisfied. Few men possessed enough money to buy the equipment necessary to sow crops and many months passed before the more fortunate men could harvest theirs.

An extract from Henry Sewell's diary sums up the land situation:

> We cannot abandon it, we cannot colonise it, we have difficulty in defending it.

There was no local employment and little prospect of finding it elsewhere. Under their terms of enlistment the Forest Rangers, in order to qualify for a farm grant, were required to serve three years. Even after taking up their farms they were required to attend monthly muster parades and forbidden to leave their own district without a pass from their commanding officer. So for many the choice was between obedience with starvation and leaving the district. Large numbers of men deserted the Waikato settlements. To counter this, permits were issued for three months' leave but even this measure did not stem the flow. Searancke, in his Resident Magistrate's letter-book, states, in effect, that by July 1868 half the population of the Waikato had left.

The Forest Rangers and the few Waikato Militiamen who remained at Harapepe worked hard to turn the fern and bush into productive farms. By the end of August 1865 many had fenced sufficient land to run stock. Their great need now was for roads, particularly to Raglan, so that a sea link could be made with Auckland. A route was surveyed from Alexandra (present day Pirongia) through Harapepe and over the saddle between the Kaniwhaniwha and Upper Waitetuna Valleys (present day Aramiro track). An attempt was made at construction by militiamen but the Government, being low on funds, let it lapse when contracts ran out. The Harapepe men signed a petition asking for the recommencement of construction. This was strongly supported by Captain William Tisdall, who commanded the district. He said in a letter to Colonel Moule who commanded the Waikato district:

> For the want of a few culverts it is impossible to reach the settlement which is isolated for want of a road either from Alexandra or Raglan, or a pontoon bridge at Te Rore. There is no possible means of soldiers getting stores, procuring cattle, much less such necessary appliances for an agricultural settlement as drays, ploughs etc., or any other agricultural implement that cannot be carried on a packhorse or floated down the Waipa.

The promised blockhouse for Harapepe still had not been constructed because of lack of funds. The men knew that the Government would take notice of their needs if von Tempsky was still in the district.

At last, in the middle of 1866, construction commenced on a blockhouse. By the beginning of September 1866 a garrison of Waikato Militia was formed. A few days later they left for Tauranga leaving only Sergeant-Major McMinn still on pay and his settler Forest Rangers.

In hindsight the men of No. 2 Company by now must have been having some misgivings about von Tempsky's strong endorsement of the Harapepe option rather than the Tauranga option.

Jackson's No. 1 Company, at Kihikihi did not share the same problems, as no river divided them from Te Awamutu and Hamilton.

Many men did not receive their land grant papers until 1868. This may have

Final disbandment *171*

hampered their plans to sell and leave, causing some to walk off their land.

It is believed that a few Forest Rangers were still on pay right up to, and even after, the formation of the Armed Constabulary.

Roll of Forest Rangers on fuel allowance at Camp Alexandra, 9 June 1866:
Sergeants (2): Southey, Toovey. *Corporals* (3): Mulligan, Clifford, Devlin. *Privates* (30): Anderson (deserted 13 June 1866), Beckwith, Bidgood, Buttle, Allister Campbell, Caughey, Patrick Clinton, Codling, Elvin (on roll his name is crossed out and noted as being on the East Coast), Fisher, Gillanders, Hardy, George Hill, Hollister, Jeffares, Keena, Lynch, McDonald, McGrath, McGuirk, Marsh, Lawrence Mitchell, Pohlen, Quinn, Rogers, Roper, Smith, Stevenson, J.H. Thompson, George Wilson.

Lieutenant Roberts at this time was at Otarapipi.

CHAPTER 24

Joining the Armed Constabulary

With the final disbandment of the Forest Rangers and other forces, and the new era of constabulary beginning, many ex-Forest Rangers chose to continue campaigning.

On 10 October 1867 the Armed Constabulary Act was passed, and a Proclamation on 22 October brought it into being on 1 November. At the same time the 1st, 2nd, 3rd and 4th Regiments of Waikato Militia, the Forest Rangers, and local forces in Taranaki, Hawke's Bay and Wanganui were disbanded. Lieutenant Colonel Moule, in command of the Waikato district, was instructed to raise two divisions of Armed Constabulary, to be designated Nos. 4 and 5 Divisions. Moule himself was to command No. 4 Division with headquarters at Cambridge, and Major von Tempsky was invited to command No. 5 Division with headquarters at Alexandra (now Pirongia). Both men were given the rank of Inspector. Roberts was made von Tempsky's second-in-command.

The No. 5 Division settled down to garrison duties at Alexandra and a few outposts. The Maori caused no trouble, so von Tempsky took advantage of the available time to weld his new men into an efficient and disciplined unit.

The No. 5 Division was raised in the Te Awamutu district and was often referred to as the Alexandra Division. Moule apparently raised the unit, but von Tempsky immediately took command on returning to the district. Many ex-Forest Rangers joined when they heard von Tempsky was in command.

Roll of No. 5 Division Armed Constabulary:

The unit totalled 77 men all ranks.
Inspector (1): Gustavus Ferdinand von Tempsky.
Sub-Inspectors (2): Duncan Michie Brown, John Mackintosh Roberts.
Senior Sergeant (1): 32 Edward Graham McMinn.
Sergeants (3): 36 David Anderson, 45 William Dart Fenton, 46 John Toovey.
Corporals (3): 22 William Jordan, 41 John Burns, 8 William McLean.
Lance-Corporals (6): 38 George Edward Cooper, 51 Peter Curran, Samuel Woodwall Davies, 69 James Kennedy, 67 Samuel Boyd, Jesse Sage.
Constables (61): 59 John Adie, 14 John Baskerville, 29 Richard Bell, 55 William Curtis Birmingham, 4 William Birss, 48 Phillip Bond, 1 Britain (Breton) Collins (not present at Te Ngutu o te Manu, 7 September 1868), 2 James Collins, 33 James Costello, 13 Thomas Mark Woodwall Davies (not present at Te Ngutu o te Manu, 7 September 1868), 20 Israel Davis (killed in action at Te Ngutu o te Manu, 7 September 1868), 49 Michael Dillon, 43 William Henry Downs (killed in action at Te Ngutu o te Manu, 7 September 1868), 28 John Dunne, 34 William James English, 60 Benjamin E. Evans, 56 John Evans, 7 Edward George Farrand (killed in action at Te Ngutu o te Manu, 7 September 1868), 62 Cuthbert Featherstonaugh (not present at Te Ngutu o te Manu, 7 September 1868), 31 Robert Fleming, 65 Robert Gemmell, 63 Joseph Gilgan (killed in action at Te Ngutu o te Manu, 7 September 1868), John Gillanders, 5 John Goodwin, 40 Joseph Gower, 16 John

Hollings Griffiths, Patrick Haggarty, 68 David Harlow, 42 John Andrew Higginson, 24 Edwin Lewis Hope, 11 Joseph Roger Hynes, John James (not present at Te Ngutu o te Manu, 7 September 1868), 58 John Keenan, 50 Robert McGruther, 21 John Mackie (killed in action at Te Ngutu o te Manu, 21 August 1868), 17 Edwin Martin, 9 George Maunder, 25 Donald Munro, 30 Maxwell Newell, 54 James Owen, 44 William Powell (not present at Te Ngutu o te Manu, 7 September 1868), 18 Edwin Robinson, 15 Alfred Rysdale, 26 James Shanaghan, 27 John Sheen, 52 Henry Thomas Sibley, 57 George Smith, 3 Henry Smith, 47 Joseph Smith, 23 Robert Smith (accidentally killed when two colonial detachments fired on each other about two miles from Manutahi, 30 September 1868), 70 Henry Southey, 10 Thomas Stafford, 61 Alexander Stronach (not present at Te Ngutu o te Manu, 7 September 1868), 66 Karl Temm, 35 Douglas Johnstone Urquhart, 64 Patrick Vallily (not present at Te Ngutu o te Manu, 7 September 1868), 37 George Wadman, 6 Richard Walsh (killed in action at Te Ngutu o te Manu, 7 September 1868), 19 Edward Oliver Wasley, 12 Samuel Whiteside, 39 William Yeoman.

Roll of former Forest Rangers in No. 5 Division:
Richard Bell, Phillip Bond, John Burns, Curran, Gillanders, McMinn, Roberts, Sibley, Southey, Toovey, von Tempsky. A total of 11 men.

The other divisions of Armed Constabulary contained ex-Forest Rangers but not to the same extent as No. 5 Division.

The No. 5 Division left Alexandra (Pirongia) on 23 June 1868, arriving in Auckland on 25 June. They waited for the *Sturt* to arrive, boarding her on 28 June. From Onehunga they sailed for Wanganui.

On reaching Wanganui the men were immediately sent on to Patea to continue training. Von Tempsky followed later on horseback, arriving on 8 July. The next day he marched his division as far as Manawapou, continuing on to Waihi Redoubt near Hawera on 10 July. The following morning Von Tempsky sent a large party into neighbouring bush to cut and collect fire wood.

Based at Waihi Redoubt was Thomas McDonnell, recently promoted to Lieutenant-Colonel, and in charge of the mixed-race Patea Field Force in south Taranaki.

On Sunday, 12 July, Titokowaru's men attacked the unfinished redoubt at Turuturu Mokai. McDonnell was absent, leaving von Tempsky in command at Waihi Redoubt. During an early morning parade, von Tempsky was informed of firing coming from Turuturu Mokai. As the redoubt was four miles distant, shots could not be heard, but the muzzle flashes were seen in the morning twilight.

Von Tempsky made a disastrous decision to set off on foot with the No. 5 Division rather than send the handful of cavalry at his disposal and in full readiness under Major William Hunter. Yet again von Tempsky was in pursuit of self-importance, thinking this to be another opportunity to glorify himself. Unfortunately the troopers did not realise that von Tempsky had given Hunter strict orders to remain in camp. Since von Tempsky had already decided to proceed to Turuturu Mokai on foot, Hunter now could not leave with the cavalry for fear that the undermanned Waihi Redoubt could come under attack. Later the Government and general public accused Hunter of cowardice and incompetence.

Von Tempsky's senseless decision was the first of a succession of shortcomings.

J. McDonald painting of Major (Inspector) von Tempsky, commanding officer of the No. 5 Division Armed Constabulary. Museum of New Zealand

Roberts took a detachment to cut off the Hauhau's retreat between the redoubt and the forest, but got no nearer than 800 yards to the Hauhau.

Von Tempsky did not pursue the enemy on arrival at Turuturu Mokai redoubt, but attended to the carnage – ten defenders killed and six wounded.

Much of this carnage would have been averted had the troopers been permitted to rescue the redoubt. Von Tempsky, at a later inquiry, defended his actions on the grounds that it was not usual to deploy mounted men against a fortified position.

He also cleverly shifted the blame onto the defending garrison – the carelessness of the sentries and Captain Ross, the commanding officer, sleeping outside the redoubt.

Turuturu Mokai was only the first in a string of blunders committed by officers over the following months. As well, the colonial forces were up against Titokowaru, possibly New Zealand's greatest battle tactician, European or Maori.

Roberts with 33 men of No. 5 Division were afterwards stationed at Turuturu Mokai to bring the defence of the redoubt up to a full complement.

While escorting a convoy from Patea to Waihi Redoubt during the morning of 29 July, a small party of 12 men from the 5th Division came under attack by Maori about two miles short of the redoubt. Von Tempsky believed that because many of the men present were ex-Forest Rangers, they didn't panic and withheld the attack. He wrote in a letter to McDonnell dated the same day:

> Just returned from a skirmish – the natives attacked a convoy about a mile from here; there were only 12 of my men (No. 5 Divisioners) under Sergeant Toovey as escort and the natives numbered 100 – my men showed a good form – shot two natives – and got one of their own hit (John Evans, badly). I was soon on the spot with 40 men and drove the natives before us; they fled back into the bush as they saw further reinforcements coming. They ought to have killed every man in that convoy – we are so short handed that we cannot send large escorts.

CHAPTER 25

The Bird's Beak

The sudden attack on Turuturu Mokai was Titokowaru's strategy to provoke a premature assault on his stronghold at Te Ngutu o te Manu, "The Bird's Beak", a fortified village in heavy bush north of Hawera. He knew that McDonnell's force was under strength and ill-prepared.

McDonnell took the bait and decided to strike at Titokowaru's stronghold with an attack on 21 August 1868. The plan was for Hunter to lead the frontal attack while the No. 5 Division worked on the left flank.

At daybreak they started out in mist which soon turned to rain. They crossed the Waingongoro River and followed a narrow track in single file. On reaching Te Ngutu o te Manu McDonnell had to wait until his force was in position. A quick action drove the Maori from the village – a tactical withdrawal on Titokowaru's command.

Arms and ammunition were collected and whare burnt. No. 5 Division carried the casualties back to base while Hunter's force, acting as rearguard, fought against the Maori who had rallied a counter-attack. The river by now was in flood and presenting a serious obstacle to the retreating force. By dusk the men arrived at Waihi, tired and wet.

The attack was unsuccessful and there were few Hauhau casualties. Titokowaru defended the position with a reduced force as most of the Hauhau were elsewhere.

There were two officers and 49 men of No. 5 Division present at this engagement.

Shortly after, the Native Contingent of 110 Kupapa under Kepa te Rangihiwinui arrived at Waihi Redoubt.

McDonnell was now pressured by the Government to decisively defeat Titokowaru in order to allay settlers' fears of neglect of their interests. His force was in a state of chaos and dissension. Many of the new recruits were untrained, especially in bush fighting, and were intent on making some quick money and resigning as their short-term contracts lapsed. Unfortunately McDonnell succumbed to the pressure, deciding to attack Titokowaru at Ruaruru, a neighbouring village to Te Ngutu o te Manu. This time Titokowaru was at full force and ready for him.

The force under Colonel McDonnell consisted of three detachments:

First detachment (under von Tempsky): No. 2 Division Armed Constabulary (16); Patea Rifle Volunteers (14) under Captain Palmer; No. 5 Division Armed Constabulary (59) under Sub-Inspectors Brown and Roberts; Wellington Rifles (45) under Lieutenants Hastings and Hunter; Taranaki Rifle Volunteers (26) under Lieutenant Rowan; Waihi Volunteers (2). Total: 162 men excluding commanding officers. Dr. Walker accompanied this detachment as surgeon.

Second detachment (under Major W. Hunter): No. 3 Division Armed Constabulary (32) under Sub-Inspectors Newland and Goring; Wellington Rangers (65) under Captain G. Buck, Lieutenant Fookes and Ensign Hirtzel; Patea Cavalry (dismounted) (11) under Captain O'Halloran. Total: 108 men excluding commanding officers. Dr. Best accompanied this detachment as surgeon.

Third detachment: Maori Contingent of Wanganui Kupapa (110) under Captain

William McDonnell and Kepa te Rangihiwinui and other chiefs.

Takiora, a woman, accompanied the column as a guide, and Father Rolland was also present. Mr Pringle, late of the 18th Regiment, accompanied the expedition as a volunteer.

The force left Waihi after midnight on 7 September 1868. A circuitous route was taken to avoid contact with the Hauhau and because of the extra distance involved, contact was not made until the afternoon. McDonnell realised they were back at Te Ngutu o te Manu and not Ruaruru as planned. The force encircled the village but came under tremendous fire from the Maori who were cleverly concealed in strategic places. About 80 men ran from the battlefield, reporting on arrival at Waihi that the rest were wounded or dead.

McDonnell, seeing that the situation was hopeless, decided to withdraw. This was too much for von Tempsky who at the time was contemplating an attack. He protested to McDonnell and then moved forward to gain a better view of the crisis.

It was then that von Tempsky was killed by a musket ball penetrating his forehead. In the confusion that followed a few men were killed or wounded trying to retrieve von Tempsky's body, but it was left on the battlefield with many others.

The battlefield dispute between McDonnell and von Tempsky seems to be the first rift in their five year friendship.

In the retreat the No. 5 Division, now under command of Roberts, got cut off from the main body and decided to find their own way back to camp. With them were a few Kupapa, some Wellington Rangers, Wellington Rifles and some wounded men.

On nightfall they halted and resumed their trek when the moon rose at 2 am. Using a Maori guide they eventually arrived at Waihi Redoubt at 8 am with no further casualties.

McDonnell at Te Ngutu o te Manu made the same error as Cameron made at Rangiriri and Carey made in the early stages of Orakau: he failed completely to reconnoitre the position with a few scouts to ascertain the impenetrable nature of the stronghold. This should have taken place the day prior to the attack. In advancing on Te Ngutu o te Manu, if McDonnell had sent forward a small experienced vanguard, the dangerous situation would have become apparent, and with the minimum of casualties he would have been able to retreat to fight another day.

The Kupapa had fired at some huts well before arriving at the main position, giving ample warning and time for Titokowaru to position his clever defence. We will never know why McDonnell had not tried to move quietly around these obstacles or upon detection, retreated. These command blunders are easily noted in McDonnell's watered-down report of the engagement.

In reading McDonnell's report one gets the impression that he was fatalistic about the outcome, with plenty of his errors of judgement actually mentioned in his own handwriting. Maybe he had already decided to resign at this early stage of the aftermath of battle. He probably didn't want another inquiry like the one after Turuturu Mokai, and have his name dragged through the newspapers.

There were too many casualties, too many bad decisions. The 5th Division Armed Constabulary was correct in their criticism of McDonnell. If it had not been for Roberts' calm and courageous rearguard action and retreat, the engagement would have been a total disaster.

A painting of the battle of Te Ngutu o te Manu as depicted by J. McDonald. Waikato Museum of Art and History

McDonnell's report is as follows:

> Camp Waihi. 9th September, 1868.
> Sir, I have the honour to state, for the information of the Hon. the Minister for Colonial Defence, that I left here at 4 am on the 7th inst. with a force intending to reach Te Rua-aruru [Ruaruru] through the bush, attack that village and return by Te Ngutu o te Manu. On reaching Mawhiti-ahiti we struck inland on the main track to Te Ngutu o te Manu and to seaward of the track that is supposed to exist and marked out on the map [a fact taken for granted by McDonnell without proper reconnaissance], to Te Rua-aruru. After proceeding for some distance on a very old trail, it ceased altogether; we then headed in the supposed direction of the place named. We got into very rough country, intersected with gullies and streams, and a perfect network of supple-jacks. About 1 pm we ascended a bush ridge, and, on the advice of Honi Papara, our guide, struck for the sea to try and hit a track.

They were obviously lost. The men were weary and in no condition to engage the Maori in pitched battle. Doubts must be cast over the Maori guides, and their confidence and maybe their loyalties were in question. McDonnell should have retired, but he and his men blundered on. Titokowaru, the Napoleon of New Zealand, chose the perfect locality for a stronghold. One wonders if his scouts had already detected McDonnell's cumbersome column and sent a messenger to Ruaruru.

> After struggling in the bush for another hour we heard voices ahead, and I sent a native up a tree to investigate. He could only see smoke. Pushing on in the direction of the voices, we came upon three or four bark huts, which were rushed by the Kupapa, who fired into them, the inmates rushing away, leaving two killed [possibly women or children], and three children, who were taken.

The Kupapa had sabotaged the whole operation by their "whoops" and premature shooting. McDonnell, not knowing anything of the position to his front and with his only advantage of surprise lost, should have immediately called a general retreat. But he and his detachments moved on into Titokowaru's now alerted and prepared trap.

> I then left the Kupapa to bring up the rear, and directed Major von Tempsky to lead on the men under his immediate command, sending Honi Papara and a few friendly natives on in front. We soon got onto a fair track, and, after proceeding about 400 or 500 yards we saw some more huts and a tent to the right of the path, and afterwards, to our surprise, found it was Titokowaru's sleeping place. Of course there was no one inside, the shots that had been fired having warned them. Following sharp on the attack, we crossed a creek [Mangotahi], and on rising the opposite bank we received a sharp fire. As fast as possible I got the men formed up and returned it. In a very few minutes we were fired upon from front, right and rear, but except within the palisading in the clearing in our front, we could see no enemy.

The soldiers had drifted into Titokowaru's lair of hidden rifle pits. Shots were coming from just above ground level from pits strategically placed around the

180 Forest Rangers

The death of von Tempsky as depicted in a colour lithograph by K. Watkins. Waikato Museum of Art and History

The Bird's Beak

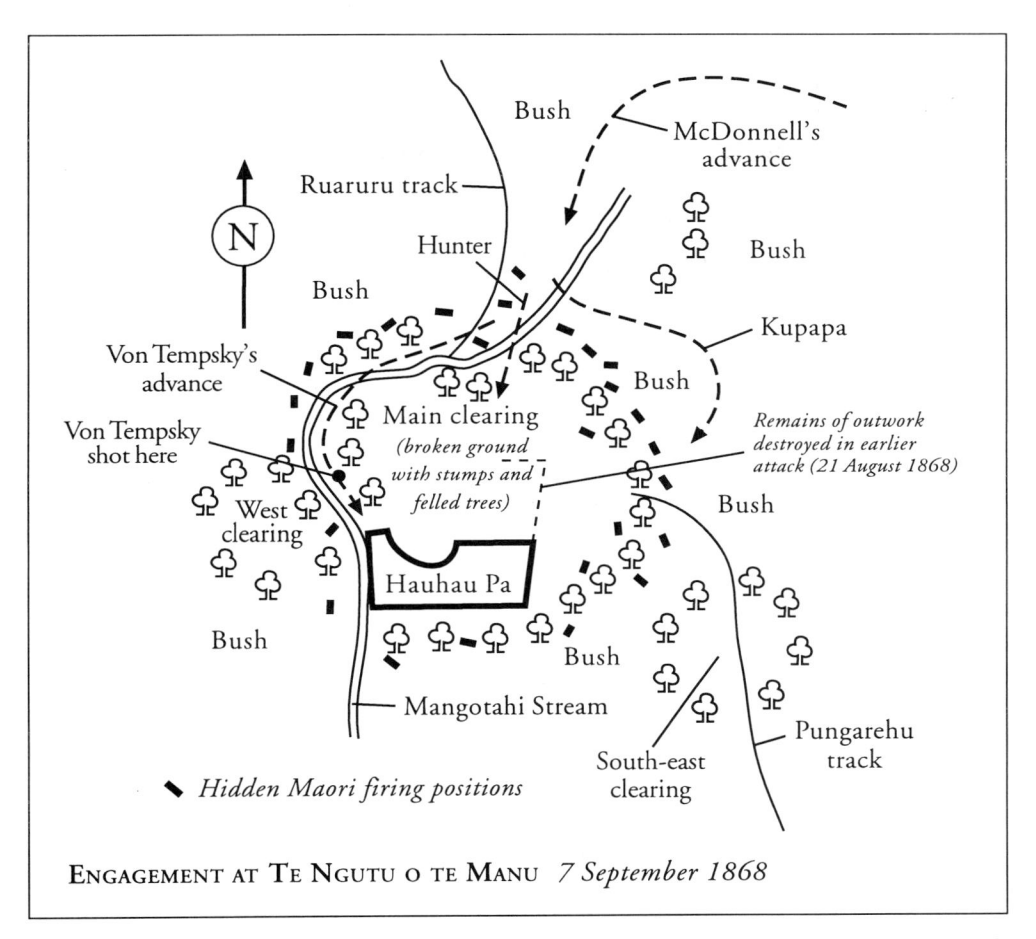

ENGAGEMENT AT TE NGUTU O TE MANU *7 September 1868*

stronghold. The pits were cleverly dug and concealed with undergrowth, with interconnecting slit trenches and covered access routes. The Maori could move freely between the pits without being seen. Titokowaru even had a few of his men hidden in the tops of several large trees, giving signals as to the attackers' positions and enfilading them with rifle fire.

> In examining the place more closely I found we were at the rear of Te Ngutu o te Manu, and not at Te Rua-aruru, and that a new stockade had been erected and the old one rebuilt. As I could see that it would be impossible to rush, and, even if successful, to hold the place, as the enemy were only occupying [the stockade] but [also] around three sides of it, and up in the rata trees, some of which were hollow at the butt and loopholed, I determined to collect the wounded, now seven in number, and endeavour to push to my left, the only point that appeared open. There was no track, and the few natives that were with us not knowing of one, I directed Inspector Hunter to accompany the wounded with Captain Newland, instructing the latter to keep Honi Papara in view, who had promised to strike a way out.

Soon the confusion of the position was to turn to tragedy with the deaths of some fine officers and men. McDonnell had still not taken control of the battle and was only reacting to Titokowaru's pressure. His detachments were already scattered with broken lines of communication.

> I was obliged to trust in his knowledge of the country, he having lived there for some time. I then returned to Major von Tempsky, and sent Kemp to collect as many of his men as he could, and send them to join Captain Newland in front. I then desired Major von Tempsky to collect the rest of the men to form a rearguard and come on at once. I told Captain Cumming to come on with me. During the whole of this time the enemy were firing heavily at us in every direction. Our way had to be cut through supple-jacks and undergrowths, which, with the eight stretchers we now had, was a work of toil and difficulty. We at length reached the creek that runs through Timaru, but still no track.

Titokowaru had done his job well. He placed his position a little further on than was anticipated causing the attack to be out of position and peter out when it came up against his snipers. In addition, an absence of tracks caused the detachments to become disorientated when moving through the undergrowth. Titokowaru's master stroke of placing men in well-concealed rifle-pits and a few up trees meant that colonial soldiers did not know where the firing was coming from and in which direction to find shelter.

McDonnell then received the news of von Tempsky being shot and the confusion this had caused.

> Presently the news was brought to me that Major von Tempsky, Captain Buck, Captain McDonnell [his brother] and Lieutenant Hunter were shot dead; but just then Captain McDonnell came up and stated that Major von Tempsky, Captain Buck and Lieutenant Hunter were killed, and that he had told Lieutenant Hastings that the only chance was to carry out the orders that had been given to Major von Tempsky; at once his reply was that "Captain Buck is senior", and he would consult him. Captain McDonnell then went to see Captain Buck, but found that he was killed, and the enemy by this time in were possession of the place where the bodies of Buck, Major von Tempsky and two men lay. He returned then, and pointed out to Mr Hastings the necessity of retiring. The fire at this time was very heavy from the front, rear, and right, and from the tops of the rata trees. He then followed on my trail, with eight natives and ten Europeans, and reported as above. I had now with me about 80 men, including natives – hardly sufficient to carry our wounded, now increasing in number, and to keep down the fire from our right. Knowing that a large proportion of the force was in the rear, and several good officers, I moved on, feeling sure they were covering our retreat; but I presently found that the enemy had got between us, and it appears from what Sub-Inspector Roberts tells that soon after Captain McDonnell had left, the Hauhau succeeded in completely surrounding the rearguard, and it was only with the greatest difficulty they cut their way through them. The Hauhau then left him (as he struck to the left further

John Mackintosh Roberts.

From 'Soldiering in New Zealand' by F.J.W. Gascoyne

into the bush) and came after us, overtaking us before we struck the main track leading into Te Ngutu o te Manu. Captain McDonnell meanwhile had taken up a position at Te Maru to keep our front open; our wounded had by this time increased to twelve, who had to be carried, beside several who had been hit but could walk.

Some very gallant efforts were made by the officers to control the retreat, to stop the action turning into a rout. Morale was low, with men exhausted and hungry and running short of ammunition. Most conspicuous were the efforts of Roberts and Captain McDonnell to encourage the men.

> The men with our party worked hard, but were so done up as to require every persuasion and advice I and my officers could think of to keep the majority from abandoning the wounded; one man dead I had to leave, and Dr Best was badly hit in going to ascertain his state. The doctor had to be carried off on rifles, having no more stretchers in my party. The natives now swarmed in our rear, and kept up a heavy fire, which I was obliged to return only occasionally, as my ammunition was very short, Captain Cumming and myself loading and firing now and then. I was afraid the enemy might have got round to the crossing of the Waingongoro River before I could reach it. We attained the opening at Ahi Pai pa just at dusk, and here received a parting volley from the enemy.

This was Titokowaru's first mistake. He obviously did not realise that victory would come so easily. Had he been prepared he could have doubled McDonnell's casualties by despatching a flying column to cut off McDonnell's retreat and hold him up till dark.

> They followed on yelling, and commenced a war dance in the open ground out of the bush. I caused my men to cheer and gave them a volley which I should think took effect, as their dance ended rather abruptly, and they did not molest us any more.

The Maori were very wise not to pursue McDonnell into the open as their advantage lay only in the bush. In the open the soldiers' rifle fire would be accurate and deadly.

> I may state that for some time I had not heard any distant firing, and therefore concluded the remainder of the force had got in advance of me. I pushed on across the river and found a few friendly natives holding the crossing. We got the men and wounded safely across and reached camp about 10 pm. A mixed party of natives and Europeans, the latter numbering about 80, had arrived before me, and reported that all the officers were killed or wounded and left behind, myself included. On roll being called, I found that Sub-Inspector Roberts, Captain Palmer, Lieutenant Hastings, and Ensign Hirtzell, with about 80 men and four natives, were still absent. I caused three rockets to be fired, and sent a party to the heights above the river and they sounded bugles, but no response was heard. Being satisfied that I could do nothing till daylight, and the officers and men being exhausted, they were dismissed. I had arranged to start the natives to hunt up the missing men in the morning, and just as they were about to start, a party was seen approaching the camp, which proved to be Sub-Inspector Roberts, Ensign Hirtzell and 62 men, with four natives, who reported Captain Palmer and Lieutenant Hastings had been killed. I enclose the statement of Sub-Inspector Roberts of what took place from the time when he became senior officer of the rearguard. It is, I feel, a most difficult task to do justice to the brave officers I have had the honour to command on this occasion. I simply say they did their duty like Englishmen. Their gallant conduct under the most galling fire; their inspiring and cheerful demeanour to encourage men when weary, exhausted, and almost giving up, saved many lives, and commanded respect and obedience in situations rarely exceeded for difficulty and danger.

McDonnell was right to praise his core of officers. They certainly saved the day and saved McDonnell from total humiliation and disaster. In his report, McDonnell tried to shift the focus away from his own actions, or lack of action:

> And I feel confident that if Major von Tempsky or Captain Buck had lived a few minutes longer, I would not have to regret for ever the loss of so many gallant comrades whose services at this time the colony so much requires. The conduct of the men was excellent, until they found that the enemy was in force on all sides, when some of them became dispirited; but the noble example of many of their number, with the assistance of many of their officers and non-commissioned officers, helped to instil fresh heart, notwithstanding seven hours scrambling through dense forests had almost exhausted them before they reached the enemy.

Many men received special mention in his report. But since much of their good work was done during the retreat, McDonnell was trying to distract the Colonial Defence office from the main events and follies of the engagement and make more of the rearguard action. Very little is mentioned of the main action – their exact positions, orders and progress – and he concentrated much of his report on his only limited success, the fall back to the river.

> Of the conduct of the Kupapa I can speak highly: I never saw them behave better. Kemp, Power, and their small party with us, and the guide Horo Papara, deserve the special thanks of the Government.

McDonnell was still set on making some good from the attack, Papara was probably the main cause of their confusion as he did not know his whereabouts during the action.

> The services of Ngatiapa, under Hunai, Hakiki Pirimona, Peete, Hunta, and others in assisting Europeans through the bush when cut off from us, I consider deserve to be recognised by the Government. The five men who remained with Sub-Inspector Roberts [the true hero of the engagement] when they might have left him and party to their own resources are Kakeru, Tarei, Te Waikuine, and Waikitoa or Pita; the men were so grateful for the conduct of the Kupapa that they subscribed some money and presented it to them.

Thinking that the donation of some small change would be payment for what the Kupapa did seems rather patronising. It is an unnecessary comment to make in an official report.

> Amongst the non-commissioned officers and men whose conduct deserves special notice was Sergeant-Major Scannell (for whom I would be grateful if the Government would do something in the Armed Constabulary); Sergeant Davey, No. 2 Division A.C., who got up a tree and fired at the enemy; Sergeant Bennett, No. 3 Division A.C.; Corporal Cahill, No. 3 Division A.C.; Constables Ready, Kelly, Percy, and Quigley, No. 3 Division A.C.; Corporal Boyd, No. 5 Division A.C.; Sergeant Fleur, Wellington Rangers; and Volunteers Sergeants Livingston, Blake, and Pope. And now, in conclusion, I would beg most strongly to represent to the Hon. the Minister for Colonial Defence the fact that the natives who accompanied me and who, it is known, killed fifteen of the enemy, yet themselves suffered no loss, not even a man wounded; this I trust, will prove that, to fight the natives successfully in bush, every tree and track of which is known to them, requires men who have been long and carefully trained in such difficult work. Instead of my men dispersing and taking cover, they could not be prevented from huddling together in small lots, affording a good target to the enemy. My efforts, and those of my officers, were in most cases without effect in convincing them of the mistake they were making. Though willing and anxious to do their duty, their short training had not been sufficient to teach them how.

These last comments are another attempt to shift the focus away from McDonnell's own shortcomings. He almost lays the failure of the action with the weaknesses of his new recruits.

Von Tempsky set a bad example to his men by standing in the open. He subsequently took a bullet through the forehead. Even the paintings and illustrations of the action (although I doubt their authenticity) show men standing and firing in lines, exposing their full torsos to the enemy. This wasn't Rangiriri or Orakau where the Maori guns were mostly tupara. By now many were armed with Enfield rifles or equivalent arms, many of these stolen, taken in earlier actions or purchased. Also they were more competent in firing them – not using too much powder and not snap-shooting.

> Mr Pringle, late of the 18th Royal Irish, accompanied the expedition as a volunteer. On the way back I desired him to take charge of some men, which he did in such an excellent manner that I promised him, on the field, to recommend him for a commission in the force.
> I beg to enclose a list of my casualties which I deeply deplore are very heavy, but I am satisfied that the enemy's is much heavier. The Kupapa killed fifteen, and the known killed by the Europeans are thirteen, making a total of twenty-eight. This does not include the loss they must have suffered when we were fighting our way out.
> I have the honour to be, Sir, Your most obedient servant, Thos. McDonnell, Lieutenant-Colonel.
> N.B. – I omitted to mention that father Rolland again accompanied the force and shared the same dangers. He also assisted to carry the wounded with my party, and his example was a great incentive to my men to persevere. For fear there might be any mistake, I regret to state that the dead had all to be left behind.

Casualties at Te Ngutu o te Manu, 7 September 1868:
Killed: No. 2 Division Armed Constabulary: Constable R. Darlington. **No. 3 Division Armed Constabulary:** Corporal James Russell, Constables Alexander Elkin, Richard Fennessy, Richard Hart. **No. 5 Division Armed Constabulary:** Major Gustavus Ferdinand von Tempsky, Constables Israel Davis, William Henry Downs, Edward George Farrand, Joseph Gilgan, Richard Walsh. **Wellington Rangers:** Lieutenants Henry Charles Holland Hastings, Henry Hunter, Privates George Henry Dore (reported dead in error. He came into camp two days later, having been wounded in the arm), George Hughes. **Wellington Rifles:** Captain George Buck, Lance-Corporal George Lumsden, Private Thomas Grant. **Taranaki Volunteers:** Private John Hicks Deeks. **Patea Rifles:** Captain Alfred Pickering Palmer.

Wounded: Staff: Assistant-Surgeon W. Best (severely). **No. 2 Division Armed Constabulary:** Constables P. Burke (slight), J. Houston (severely), William O'Brien (slight), John O'Connor (severely). **No. 3 Division Armed Constabulary:** Constables W. Fulton (slight), J. Hogan (severely), T. Walton (severely). **No. 5 Division Armed Constabulary:** Sergeant John Toovey (slight), Constables Robert Gemmell (slight), James Shanaghan (severely). **Wellington Rangers:** Privates W. Caldwell (slight), George Henry Dore (arrived in camp two days later after being reported dead: arm amputated), John Goddard (slight), David Madan Harris (severely), McGennisken (slight), M. McManus (slight). **Wellington Rifles:** Lieutenant W.C. Fookes (severely: accidentally wounded in camp), Lance-Corporal James Walden (severely), Privates

John Griffiths (severely), P.F. Jancey (slight), William Loder (severely). **Taranaki Volunteers:** Lieutenant Frederick Charles Rowan (dangerously), Privates S. Crosby (slight), John Flynn (severely), W.A. Halloway (slight), James Hamblyn (slight), L. Hyland (slight), John Melvin (severely), George Wells (mortally wounded; since dead). **Patea Yeomanry Cavalry:** Private Crawley (slight).

The higher number of casualties among the Wellington Rangers and Wellington Rifles is quite noticeable. These being new recruits, they tended to bunch together for support, giving a better target to the Maori. The veterans skirmished in extended order.

There is no mention in McDonnell's report of the 80 or so men who ran – deserted – from the battle and on reaching Waihi camp spread the wild story that the rest of the force was wiped out. Maybe McDonnell thought he could hide the incident which would be seen as a blot on his ability, or maybe the above report was action-packed enough and he decided to save this information for some later report.

McDonnell had been too eager for revenge so soon after Turuturu Mokai. Also he didn't prepare his green recruits enough for battle and decided they would get their instruction from veterans while in battle at Te Ngutu o te Manu.

The colony reeled at the implications of Te Ngutu o te Manu. A handful of "savages" had routed New Zealand's so-called crack forces. In reality the whole affair was an expertly executed ambush by Titokowaru's skilfully deployed men.

A Patea correspondent reported:

> God help the country if McDonnell is to retain the management of affairs here.

This was followed by an editor's comment:

> What charm can Colonel McDonnell possess which infatuates the Ministry to still keep him in command, not withstanding his unpopularity both with the European and native forces?

The Government, which earlier called for action and revenge, now claimed that the troops were totally unacquainted with bush fighting and disorganised prior to the engagement. McDonnell was saddled with a scratch force, many of whom had never fought in the bush before, and a colonial Government who were determined to force him into premature action. McDonnell could not win either way.

A short time later Lieutenant-Colonel Thomas McDonnell resigned his command and Colonel Whitmore (Commandant of the Armed Constabulary) took charge of the West Coast force. Whitmore acknowledged that McDonnell's problems had not been all of his own making; that he had been forced to build an undersized army in too short a time.

Te Ngutu o te Manu destroyed McDonnell as a commander. He had to live with the stigma till his death. McDonnell made enemies of Whitmore and Haultain who probably prevented him from getting the New Zealand Cross for nearly 20 years.

CHAPTER 26

Disgrace and mutiny

On 8 September 1868, there was trouble in the Waihi camp. The Wellington Rifles were angry at the number of wounded and dead being left behind, including their own officer Captain Buck. The unrest spread to the No. 5 Division, many of whom vowed not to go into the field under McDonnell again as they blamed him for the death of von Tempsky.
A man from their own ranks also died because of McDonnell's reported neglect. Most said they had no confidence in him. A written complaint was submitted by the Division protesting at the lack of proper medical attention for the wounded at Camp Waihi.
Several days later Constable Keenan (No. 5 Division) was locked in the guard room for insubordinate behaviour towards Major Hunter on the parade ground by refusing to extinguish his pipe.
At a following special parade the men requested that the prisoner be released. This was refused, and disregarding an order to ground their arms, the men prepared for a march to Patea. Their ringleader, Maunder, shouted "Boys let us rush the guard room!" and "Let us take our swags and arms to Patea!" He was then isolated and locked in the guard room. That night four No. 5 Division men deserted.

Under the advice of Haultain, who had recently arrived at Waihi (17 September), the men were marched to Patea. This was on the eve of the expected engagement at Taiporohenui, thus consolidating the belief of the men of No. 5 Division that they were "under the imputation of cowardice". At Patea the trial of four "ringleaders" went ahead but Sergeant Fenton refused to name the ringleaders. After the conviction of Maunder and Keenan, Haultain paraded No. 5 Division and asked for the "well disposed" men to step forward and separate themselves from those who would not serve. Only Sergeant Anderson stepped forward. This was the last straw for Haultain who then disbanded the unit, dumping them in Wanganui.

Sergeant D. Anderson wrote a document of evidence at Patea, dated 22 September 1868, in which he discussed events leading to the mutiny and to the degree of commitment by the so called mutineers. He played down the event as just a rush of hot blood and a few bad ringleaders, namely Keenan and Maunder. Anderson stated:

> I was not present when the men made a disturbance in camp the day after the late engagement [at Te Ngutu o te Manu] but am aware that the men of my division [section] did not take part in it. It is probable that one or two individuals may have committed themselves, but I do not know that any did.
> ... after breakfast when I heard one of the men [Maunder] say "let us pack our swags boys and go to Patea", I saw them go to the tents and come out afterwards with their swags and arms. They went to the parade ground and stood about. I went round the tents and spoke to the men, to dissuade them from taking part in what was going on. After a little, the men with swags, some 12 or 14, began to move off. I spoke to Roberts about what was going

on and he reported to Major Hunter who ordered the "assembly" and "double" to be sounded. The camp turned out at once under arms.

This response indicates the low level of commitment to the possible mutiny. Anderson continues:

> The men with swags thereupon returned to the lines, left their swags in the tents and came on parade. When the roll was called all the men were present. Nothing further occurred but next day 4 men [Collins, Robinson, Rysdale and G. Smith, one taking his firearms] were reported absent at roll call who have not since been heard of.

From the officers' point of view it seems to have been a genuine mutiny; there was talk of using the other divisions to fire into them if they didn't return to duty. Whitmore complained that they followed von Tempsky like a clan of highlanders followed their chief, and that the men thought their war was over when "their" von Tempsky was killed – a sad consequence of von Tempsky getting too "close" to his men.

Sergeant William Fenton explained the reasons for the disturbance:

> I was aware that throughout No. 5 Division there was general dissatisfaction among the men after the late engagement arising from an idea that there had been some incapacity shown by Colonel McDonnell.

The same feelings also ran strong among the men of the Wellington Rifles. Fenton then puts the blame on one man:

> The principal man in the insubordination was Maunder. On the parade when they fell in to speak to Major Hunter many were really not aware of what they were fallen in for.

At their request, McMinn wrote on behalf of the men of the No. 5 Division stating their dissatisfaction. This letter was passed on to Major Hunter. After realising he had breached regulations by writing a letter of complaint, he wrote a second letter on behalf of the men stating the first letter had no insubordination intent. Because of these actions McMinn's later application for the New Zealand Medal was rejected.

Whitmore, after seeing the men at Patea, wrote a comprehensive report. He believed No. 5 Division felt they were considered cowards because they were ordered to the rear at Te Ngutu o te Manu by McDonnell. They also felt they were singled out from the whole force to bear the blame of those few who misbehaved in the engagement. Whitmore states:

> ... there are a very large number of really good men who wholly disapprove of them [acts of mutiny] and did keep aloof from those who committed them.
> ... the division with few exceptions appears to me to have become imbued with a very lamentable feeling of hostility to McDonnell, most unjustifiably connecting him in some way with the death of the late Major von Tempsky and the other misfortunes which befell the rearguard.
> ... This feeling sits at the bottom of the whole matter and arises in part from

the wrong notions the men had as regards the independent constitution of their division. They seem to have regarded the loss of Major von Tempsky as leaving them without a leader and like a highland clan that under such circumstances they could or should be allowed to cease to serve if they desire to do so.
... I believe the Division should be disbanded with very few if any exceptions but some men might be kept and others re-enlisted.

No. 5 Division was disbanded for mutinous conduct at Patea (the disbandment was approved by the Governor on 29 September 1868), never to reform. Some men went to other Divisions of the Armed Constabulary. The once proud and experienced unit, von Tempsky's own, the heirs of the Forest Rangers, ceased to exist.

They were a stout-hearted faithful lot who preferred being dumped on the streets of Wanganui and told to make their own way home as best they could rather than serve under McDonnell, whom they considered had brought about von Tempsky's death through his bungling. This is ironical because von Tempsky and McDonnell were bosom friends, beginning letters to each other with such titles as "My dear Von" and "Dear Mac, my dear old boy". It was only just prior to von Tempsky's death that a rift between the two was first apparent.

Whitmore's roll of the No. 5 Division Armed Constabulary after the battle at Te Ngutu o te Manu (giving his comments marked on the roll):
Sub-Inspectors (2): Duncan Michie Brown, John Mackintosh Roberts.
Colour Sergeant (1): E.G. McMinn (Good).
Sergeants (3): D. Anderson (Good), W.D. Fenton (neutral), J. Toovey (bad).
Corporals (3): Jordan, Burns (neutral), McLean (good).
Lance-Corporals (6), Cooper (good), Kennedy (good), Boyd (good), Curran (bad), Davies (neutral), Sage (good).
Constables (48): Adie (Good), Baskerville (bad), Bell (bad), Birmingham (bad), Birss (bad), Bond (absent), Collins (deserted), Costello (very bad), Dillon (bad), Dunne (bad), English (absent), B. Evans (neutral), J. Evans (wounded and absent), Fleming (bad), Gemmell (neutral), Goodwin (notably bad. Ringleader), Gower (neutral), Griffiths (good), Gillanders (good), Haggarty (very bad. Left the division in the field), Harlow (good), Higginson (good), Hope (wounded in the mouth at Te Ngutu o te Manu on 21 August 1868 and absent), Hynes (bad), Keenan (very bad. Court-martialled and imprisoned), McGruther (bad), Martin (good), Maunder (very bad. Court-martialled and imprisoned), Munro (bad), Newell (good), Owen (bad), Robinson (bad. Deserted), Rysdale (bad. Deserted), Shanaghan (wounded), Sheen (very bad), Sibley (good), G. Smith (bad. Deserted), H. Smith (neutral), J. Smith (bad), R. Smith (bad), Southey (good), Stafford (bad), Temm (good), Urquhart (good), Wadman (good), Wasley (neutral), Whiteside (wounded in the abdomen at Te Ngutu o te Manu on 21 August 1868), Yeoman (neutral).

Those who were wounded were not present at the mutiny and were not later implicated with it.

Sergeant Anderson was retained – the only member still on the payroll – and promoted to Staff Sergeant, as he was the only man to step forward when members of the unit were asked by Haultain if they wished to obey orders.

Sub-Inspector Roberts took his former Division from Patea to Wanganui aboard the *Sturt*. He was then sent on to Auckland to enlist a new division of Armed Constabulary.

Keenan and Maunder, accused of being ringleaders, were tried by a Board of Officers on 29 September 1868 and sent to gaol in Wanganui. A later plea by them for a pardon was refused by Haultain.

The rest of the men, on arrival at Wanganui, were told to find their own way home and debarred from any future military enlistment in New Zealand. Many of the men were glad to be out of the Armed Constabulary and free to return to their families and properties in the Waikato.

The No. 5 Division were the scapegoats for greater problems in the Armed Constabulary hierarchy. But they did have their supporters. Local settlers were dismayed at the removal of such a tightknit, experienced and capable fighting unit, and blamed the constables' superiors for the "mutiny".

The disbandment prevented many of these men from receiving the New Zealand Medal as their applications in later years were rejected. They were deemed never to have fought in the field. The Medal Commissioner stated in a memorandum dated 25 November 1873:

> ... after careful perusal of the several documents relating to the mutinous conduct and consequent disbandment of the non-commissioned officers and men of No. 5 Division A.C., and believing as they [the authorities] do that the value of the medal would be greatly diminished in the eyes of other recipients, were it granted to men who had behaved so disgracefully in the field; they [the authorities] are unable to see any just grounds for interfering with the decision of the late commission.

Forest Rangers who had their medal applications rejected because of the mutiny and were likewise ineligible for a pension were: Richard Bell, McMinn and Southey. Southey's application was at first accepted and a medal was issued, but later the Colonial Defence Office demanded its return. Jackson pushed for the issue of the medals but the applications were still rejected.

Meanwhile, as a gesture of respect, Titokowaru spared von Tempsky the final indignity of being consumed at a cannibal feast. According to Kimble Bent who witnessed the feast, von Tempsky's body was placed on a funeral pyre and burnt. This is possibly incorrect as many Hauhau would have delighted in consuming von Tempsky, known to them as Manu-rau, because of the great mana gained by such an act.

Even in death, von Tempsky was deprived of an award for bravery, something he always strived for but never received. The previous year Charles Heaphy was awarded the Victoria Cross for his services at Waiari. Von Tempsky was obviously envious of this award and wrote in a letter dated 29 April 1867 to Featherston:

> It is exceedingly invidious to apply for honours, but the cold shoulder of the present Government forces me into an active part on my own behalf. Heaphy has the Cross, and McDonnell and I want it.

Maybe his vainglorious behaviour at Te Ngutu o te Manu that led to him being shot was caused by his greater desire to win permanent distinction. Or maybe by this stage of his New Zealand campaign von Tempsky really believed he was immortal

Inspector John Mackintosh Roberts and members of No. 6 Division Armed Constabulary. Roberts has a sword in hand in right foreground. Circa 1869.
Taranaki Museum

and that Maori bullets would never strike him.

In a letter to his wife dated 26 July 1868, von Tempsky talked about his premonition of death and having to pay for the "sins" he had committed. These "sins" may have manifested themselves in social circles while von Tempsky was in Wellington. Maybe he was suffering from severe depression brought on by a guilt complex. He stated in his letter:

> ... an honourable death in the field is a godsend compared to the slow death of depravity from the dangers of sin. Often, in contemplating the almost hopeless tendencies in my character, I wish some bullet would end the weary struggle – and yet I know it is cowardly to wish it.

The mystery of this man and his death may never be resolved.

McDonnell later did get his cross, a New Zealand Cross. And if von Tempsky had survived, would he too have received one?

CHAPTER 27

Frontier cavalry volunteers

The year 1871 was a particularly anxious time in the border townships and on the farms in south Waikato. In that year the settlers in the frontier district from Alexandra (Pirongia), Te Awamutu, Kihikihi and Orakau round the edge of the confiscated lands to Cambridge organised a cavalry corps which proved an exceedingly useful mobile defence force.

The original concept came from Sir Donald Maclean, Minister for Native Affairs and Defence, who visited Alexandra on his way to meet the Kingite chiefs across the border on a mission of conciliation. He suggested to Stephen Westney, a leading settler, that the best frontier patrol was a mounted corps which the Government would arm with the most efficient weapons. Cavalry also suited the open fern-covered terrain surrounding Te Awamutu and Cambridge.

So the Waikato Cavalry Volunteers came into being, consisting of two troops, one based at Te Awamutu and the other based at Cambridge. Initially the unit size was about 60 men, but it later increased to over 80. By common consent, Major Jackson commanded the whole force as well as captaining the Te Awamutu troop. He continued to command for many years until a firm peace was established in the middle 1880's. William A. Cowan and Andrew Kay were his Te Awamutu troop lieutenants. Captain James Runciman commanded the Cambridge troop. These troops were the beginning of a very efficient frontier corps. They were well-mounted and armed with Snider carbines, revolvers and swords. The uniform included blue tunic, bedford cord breeches and leggings.

Many ex-Forest Rangers joined the Te Awamutu Cavalry Volunteers including: Robert Alexander, Richard Bell, Amice Bertram, Thomas Bond (Sergeant), William Bond, Robert Bruce (Lieutenant and later Captain), James Cunningham, Thomas Holden, William Jackson (Major), Charles McDonnell, Edward McMinn, Peter Rogers, Henry Sibley, Charles Temple, William Michael Thomson, James Tristram, James Watters and James Weal.

This list may be incomplete as no roll can be found.

More than once the corps was called out for emergencies, though the alarms never developed into fighting. Divided into small detachments, they patrolled the disturbed country by day and night. There was no doubt that the sight of the cavalry and the Armed Constabulary posts along the border prevented any Kingite plans of raiding.

The Waikato Cavalry Volunteers paraded at the presentation of the New Zealand Cross to John Roberts, at Cambridge on Tuesday, 25 July 1876. Present were: 1 Major, 1 Captain, 2 Lieutenants, 3 Sub Lieutenants, 2 Sergeant-Majors, 6 Sergeants, 5 Corporals, 2 Trumpeters, 1 Farrier and 66 Troopers (total of 89).

APPENDICES

Forest Rangers – Biographical notes

Jackson's No. 1 Company was attached to the 2nd Regiment Waikato Militia as the 11th Company, receiving regimental numbers. A few slipped through before the roll was properly organised and those who were transferred from other Waikato Militia Companies kept their original numbers.

Unfortunately von Tempsky's No. 2 Company was not similarly recorded on the 1st Regiment Waikato Militia where only a few of their names appear, without details. So men of this Company had acquittance roll numbers starting from No. 1. If a member was discharged, his replacement or substitute was given the same number.

Records of the Forest Rangers were destroyed by a fire at the Auckland Drill Shed circa 1902 although many were kept with the Colonial Defence Office in Wellington. Because of the fire there are many gaps in records, and details come from many different sources. Some acquittance rolls are missing for service in the 1866-67 period. So, when discharge dates are missing, "last known month of service" is mentioned in the following biographical notes. In addition, the men who returned to their land around Te Awamutu often did not know if they were still on the Forest Rangers' roll as they went from full pay to a fuel allowance. So end of service could be taken as the date that full pay ended or the date that the fuel allowance was discontinued.

There is often confusion over contemporary names and spellings of engagements. Some engagements can have up to three names. An example is Waiari which was also known as Mangapiko and Paterangi.

The same name can be used for separate engagements (sometimes years apart) fought on the same site or a different site. An example is Moturoa, which is also known as Okotuku – two names for the same site. The now generally accepted names are Okotuku (fought 4 January 1866) and Moturoa (fought 7 November 1868). Moturoa has also been known as Papa-tihakehake.

Because of the lack of unit records available to New Zealand Medal applicants at the time of application, dates are often wrong or missing. I have endeavoured to standardise these in square brackets, such as "Waiapu" being followed by [Pukemaire, 3 October 1865].

To make research even more difficult, the applicants and the Medal Commission were often confused about unit names and spellings. An excellent example is the unit "Mauku Forest Rifles" whose medals can be named to Forest Rifles, Mauku Rifles, Mauku Rangers, Mauku Forest Rangers, Mauku Rifle Rangers, Mauku Rifle Volunteers, Mauku Volunteers, Mauku Cavalry Volunteers, Mauku Forest Rifle Volunteers and Mauku Forest Rifles!

The Medal Commission had minimal access to nominal and acquittance rolls and relied upon the unit's commanding officers' testimonials to prove service. Often these men had already died or could not be contacted. Human error caused incorrect naming on hundreds of medals to Colonial units. This should not detract from the value and authenticity of the medal – if anything, it adds a little local character or

New Zealand Medal. Left: Medal showing obverse side. The ribbon is dark blue with a red central stripe. Right: Patrick Madigan's medal showing reverse side and unofficial clasps fitted on ribbon.

parochialism to medal naming and collecting.

A few of the following men made false or highly exaggerated and inaccurate New Zealand Medal claims. Presumably, it was fashionable at the time to claim that one served with the Forest Rangers, the elite colonial unit of the New Zealand Wars.

Many Forest Rangers could not write or were poor spellers, so every effort has been made to decipher cryptic entries on application forms and letters. Those who could not write called upon officers and lawyers to write on their behalf. Contemporary handwriting caused me many headaches. At times I have pored over key words trying to recognise the spelling.

Medals were normally issued on National Archives AD32 (Army Department) files. All applications were first entered on National Archives AD36/3 Register of Applicants files, but not all AD36/3 entries received medals. Medal application details have been found on National Archives AD36/3 and AD1 (pensions and land grants) files, but in much fewer numbers.

Men who enlisted in the Forest Rangers in the Wanganui district and on the East Coast were not assigned to No. 1 or No. 2 Company, which would have placed them under the conditions of service of the Waikato Militia. This is why they did not receive land grants for Forest Ranger service.

New Zealand Medals were issued from 1871 to September 1930. Medal applications were closed in 1880 but only for a short time, and applications were stopped again on 16 June 1900. Only a few medals were issued between 1900 and 1910. The Medal Commission again accepted applications about 1911 and finally stopped about 1919. During this period a large portion of applicants were "friendly natives" (Maori). After 1919, only replacements for lost medals were issued.

A military Pensions Act was passed in 1911, specifying a pension of the same amount as the Old Age Pension for veterans. This was followed by a more comprehensive Military Pensions Act in 1912 which made the pension available to anyone who served the Crown in the New Zealand Wars and who was awarded the New Zealand Medal for active service. A flood of medal applications followed from 1911 onwards.

All imperial-issue medals were named with impressed serif-style capitals. A general issue of medals with impressed naming was instigated for some colonial units. These were 1st, 2nd, 3rd and 4th Regiments of Waikato Militia, Imperial Commissariat Transport Corps, Imperial Commissariat (included both civilians and volunteers from colonial units), and Auckland Militia. These units were employed and paid by the Imperial Government and most medals were dated 1861-66. But all potential recipients still had to claim for their medals, so a large portion were not issued (unclaimed). Inaccurate medal lists printed during the 1870's indicate that all these medals were actually issued. The New Zealand Government only had a limited number of medals available for issue, so as the Medal Commission ran out of blank medals (previously un-named) for issue to colonial applicants after 1900, they started to re-name impressed medals they still held for the few units mentioned above.

All colonial units (other than those mentioned above) had their medals named locally in "engraved" style. From 1871 onwards the medal commission would send out medals (either in singles or in groups – depending on demand) to local jewellers in Wellington for naming. Hence the different naming styles – some styles are large and deep while others are fine and shallow – but all are authentic. These local styles are well regarded by New Zealand collectors, but tend to be disregarded in Britain. Approximately 3000 medals were issued to colonial units.

Some members of the 1st, 2nd, 3rd and 4th Regiments of Waikato Militia, Imperial Commissariat Transport Corps, Imperial Commissariat, and Auckland Militia applied for medals this century and their allocated impressed medal had already been renamed and issued to another recipient. They, in turn, received renamed engraved medals.

All unclaimed impressed medals still with the Defence Department by 1974 were sold with the naming XXX'd over and the word "specimen" added.

The following alphabetical roll contains all three Forest Ranger companies: Original Company, No. 1 Company and No. 2 Company.

Biographical details of Forest Rangers

Thomas ALBIN
8, No. 2 Company: 19 January – 20 August 1864. Private. Substituted by Thomas Anderson. Absent from unit 1-4 June 1864 without pay probably in search of substitute.

Robert ALEXANDER
Original Company: August – 10 November 1863. Private. **1076, No. 1 Company:** 17 November 1863 – November 1867 (last known month of service). Private. Later served Te Awamutu Cavalry Volunteers. Enrolled at Auckland. Age: 29 years. Height: 5' 7". Hair colour: brown. Eye colour: grey. Complexion: fresh. Occupation: labourer. Country: Scotland. Religion: Presbyterian. Sworn in by Captain William Jackson. Born 1824 Renfrew, Paisley, Scotland. Absent (or clerical error) from unit for month of June 1864 but returned 1 July 1864. Received land: town lot No. 70, Kihikihi; farm lot No. 277, Puniu.

Thomas William ALLEN
Served 24 September 1865 – 8 July 1866. Private. Born 1844. Sailed to New Zealand aboard *Nourmahal*, 1859. Present at reunion to commemorate 50 years of battle of Orakau, 1914.
New Zealand Medal named to Forest Rangers. Medal claim dated 28 June 1871. The Medal Application states "**Address:** C/o Mr Brownhill, Wyndham St, Auckland. **Corps:** Forest Rangers under Major Westrup, as Private about ten months. **Field service:** Engaged against the Rebel Natives at Pukemaire pa [3 October 1865], also pursuit and capture of prisoners at Kawakawa [Hungahunga-toroa, East Cape, October 1865] and the Waerengaahika pa [15-21 November 1865], between the 24th September 1865 and 8 July 1866 [observation of Maori at Kohanga Karearea]. **Remarks:** Name of immediate Commanding Officer: Major Fraser, Captain and Major Westrup." A letter written by Westrup accompanies the medal application "I hereby certify that Thomas W. Allen served under me in the Forest Rangers from 24th Sept 1865 to the 8th July 1866 and was present at the storming of Pukemaire pa, also took part in the pursuit and capture of prisoners at Kawakawa, and at the taking of Waerengaahika pa on the East Coast. He bore a good character in the service". Land claim H23, 1894. Medal claim AD32/2085

John R. ANDERSON
No. 2 Company: 20 January – 20 April 1864. Private. Possible medal claim, AD32/1058. On this file there is a form letter only with no service details.

Thomas ANDERSON
8, No. 2 Company: 1 September 1864 – 13 June 1866 (deserted). Private. Substitute for Thomas Albin. Earlier served 2nd Regiment Waikato Militia, No. 615. Later served 2nd Regiment Waikato Militia. Born 1842, Manchester, Lancashire, England. Received land including town lot No. 295, Alexandra East (Pirongia).

Mark ARNOLD
Period of service unknown. Private. Served with Westrup's Company on East Coast.

William APPLEYARD
Original Company: 11-15 August 1863. Private. Born 1827, Conisborough, Yorkshire, England. Later served 2nd Regiment Waikato Militia, joining 24 August 1863, No. 4. Received land including town lot No. 497, Alexandra East (Pirongia). Possibly received impressed **New Zealand Medal** named to the Commissariat Transport Corps for service while with the Waikato Militia.

Biographical notes

George ARGUE
1298, No. 1 Company: 1 September 1864 – November 1866 (last known month of service). Private. Substitute for No. 326, Hugh Babington. Earlier served 2nd Regiment Waikato Militia, No. 1298. Enrolled at Pukerimu, Cambridge. Occupation: sailor. Religion: Episcopalian. Sworn in by Major William Jackson. Born 1832, Kingston, Dublin. Received land: town lot No. 201, Kihikihi; farm lot No. 250, Puniu.

Hari ARORETA
Served 8 December 1865 – February 1866. Private. Enlisted at Woodall's Redoubt. Discharged at Wanganui.

Richard ATKINS
Served 7 December 1865 – disbandment, 30 October 1867. Private. Earlier served Royal Artillery; Colonial Defence Force, Wellington. Later served Wellington Rangers; No. 7 Division Armed Constabulary. Enlisted in Forest Rangers at Wanganui. Medal claim, AD32/2117. This file can not be located. Possibly received impressed **New Zealand Medal** named to the Commissariat Transport Corps.

William Hugh BABINGTON
326, No. 1 Company: 11 March – 31 August 1864. Private. Substituted by No. 1298 George Argue. Earlier served 2nd Regiment Waikato Militia, No. 326. Enrolled 25 August 1864 at Otago. Age: 21 years. Height: 5' 5". Hair colour: light. Eye colour: grey. Complexion: fair. Occupation: labourer. Country: Tasmania, Australia. Religion: Presbyterian. Born 1841, Launceston, Cornwall, England.
New Zealand Medal named to Forest Rangers. At time of application resided at Runanga, near Taupo. Medal claim AD32/2256

William Henry BABINGTON
4, No. 2 Company: (service period unknown). Present with No. 2 Company at Harapepe in mid 1866. Private. Later served Armed Constabulary in mounted section. Born 1 April 1849, Howick, Auckland. Made application for a pension in relation to his service, 12 January 1921. Made on his behalf by the Wagga Wagga Repatriation Committee, New South Wales, Australia. At the time he resided c/o Mrs Lintott, Edward Street, Wagga Wagga. A statement accompanying this application states "I joined the 'A' Troop of the Wellington Colonial Defence Force in July 1863 in Dunedin, was sent by sea to Wellington (50 strong) and after a month's drill at Thorndon Barracks, was sent with the troops by sea to Wanganui and marched from there to the upper Rangitiki River with Commandant Major Edwards, Captain Leatham and afterwards Captain Noake. We were drilled there and patrolled the district for about 18 months, when the force was disbanded. In the following year I joined von Tempsky's [actually Westrup's] Forest Rangers and served throughout the East Coast campaign of 1865 under Major Fraser, afterwards serving in the New South Wales Mounted Police for 18 months. In the early part of 1870 I joined the Armed Constabulary under Commissioner Dranigan, who was displaced by Col. Moule and served four years, for which service have a Certificate of Discharge. I received the **New Zealand War Medal** for active service and afterwards in 1878 served in the Galeka War under General Thesiger and in the same year took part in the Sekukuni War [Zulu and Basuto Wars] in the Transvaal under Colonel Rowlands (13th Regt) receiving the War Medal for that service. I also served a few months in the Boer War [1899-1902] under General Buller in Natal and was present at the battle of Colenso. I lived in New Zealand altogether 17 years, but as my civil occupation was mostly that of gold prospector, I moved from country to country." Received land: town lot No. 57, Harapepe; farm lot No. 203, Pirongia. Medal claim AD32/1640; AD36/3/105

John BALLENDEN

No. 2 Company: 29 November 1863 – 9 May 1864 (when his pay was stopped, indicating he probably died on this date at Pokeno). Born Inverness, Scotland, although von Tempsky claims he was born in Canada (see below). Dangerously wounded by gunshot to his abdomen at Rangiaowhia, 21 February 1864. Von Tempsky had him sent to Queen's Redoubt hospital at Pokeno to ensure the best possible care. Though still not 21 years old, Ballenden, (who was earlier told by a gypsy that he would not live past 21 years) convinced himself of his fate and died. The doctor later stated "despondency killed him, not the Maori slug". Von Tempsky wrote of him after his wounding at Rangiaowhia "one of my men got shot in the hip – a fine young fellow, John Ballenden. He staggered forward and dropped, never more to rise, though he lingered for months in hospital. (Note: A Canadian by birth, by profession a surgeon, he served as a private with me. An excellent shot, and brave to a fault. I had known him first at Mauku. His comrades have erected a handsome marble slab over his grave at Queen's Redoubt.)" The *Daily Southern Cross* reported him as being in a critical condition on 28 February 1864.

John BANNISTER

Period of service unknown. Private. Present on East Coast with Westrup. Earlier served with the 1st Foot Regiment.

John BARRON

Original Company: 11-25 August 1863. Private.

William BECKHAM

Original Company: 11-25 August 1863. Private. Sailed to New Zealand aboard *Prince of Wales*, July 1847.

Henry BECKWITH (BECKWORTH)

10, No. 2 Company: 22 July 1865 – December 1867 (last known month of service). Private. Received land: town lot No. 37, Harapepe; farm lot No. 207, Pirongia.

Francis Wellesley BEETHAM

1350, No. 1 Company: 10 January – 10 November 1865. Private. Substitute for No. 39 William Evans. Substituted by Duffy. Earlier served 1st Regiment Waikato Militia, No. 253 (joining 9 September 1863 at Melbourne, Australia); Colonial Defence Force, Auckland. Later served Wanganui Yeomanry Cavalry. Enrolled at Auckland. Age: 21 years. Height: 5' 10". Hair colour: light. Eye colour: blue. Complexion: fair. Occupation: settler. Country: England. Religion: Episcopalian. Sworn in by Major William Jackson. Born 1844, Stoke Warrington, Middlesex, England. Sailed to New Zealand aboard *Caduseus*, 1863.
New Zealand Medal named to Colonial Defence Force Cavalry. Medal claim dated 22 December 1870. Medal issued 6 December 1873 at Sydney. The Medal Application states **"Address:** Glen Innes, New South Wales. **Corps:** Colonial Defence Force, Private, 6th January 1864 to 7th Nov 1864. Major von Tempsky's Forest Rangers, Private, from Nov 1864 to 10th November 1865. Wanganui Yeomanry Cavalry, Private No. 78 from 10th Feb 1866 to 27th October 1866. Waikato campaign 1864. Wanganui campaign 1865: Kakaramea 13th May 1865, Weraroa pa 21st July 1865, relief of Pipiriki [July 1865]. East Coast expeditions from 10th Feb 1866 to June 27th 1866. West Coast from July to 27th October 1866. I was also in the 1st Waikato Regiment, No. 9 Company, and was enrolled in 1863 at Victoria [Australia] and got a transfer to the Colonial Defence Force at Papakura 6th January 1864." In a testimonial von Tempsky states "Camp Abraham, Wanganui, 10 November 1865. Private Francis Beetham has been this day discharged from the Forest Rangers at his request." Possibly a medal already named to the Imperial Commissariat Corps on the 2nd Regiment Waikato Militia roll, was issued as this was his initial

unit. Consequently this medal was issued rather than one named to the Forest Rangers. Medal claim, AD32/2182; AD36/3/138

John BELL
No. 1 Company: 1 April 1866 – August 1867 (last known month of service). Private. Born 1847, O'Connell Street, Auckland. Died Paterangi, 1923. Received land: town lot No. 357, Kihikihi; farm lot No. 357, Puniu. Farm lot Nos. 318 and 319, Puniu, were cancelled.

Richard BELL
1322, Original Company: 11 August – 10 November 1863. Private. **No. 1 Company:** 1 December 1864 – October 1867 (last known month of service). Private. Substitute for No. 1087, Thomas Holden. Earlier served Wairoa Rifles. Later served No. 5 Division, Armed Constabulary, No. 29; Te Awamutu Cavalry Volunteers. Enrolled at Wairoa, south Auckland. Age: 23 years. Height: 5' 9". Hair colour: black. Eye colour: brown. Complexion: dark. Occupation: farmer. Country: England. Religion: Episcopalian. Sworn in by Major William Jackson. Born 1841, Preston, Lancashire. Sailed to New Zealand aboard *Duchess of Argyle*, 1842. Died 15 April 1916 and buried Wiri cemetery.
Three medal applications were made, all of them rejected because of Bell's involvement in the No. 5 Division Armed Constabulary mutiny. Medal claim dated 22 May 1872. The Medal Application states "**Address:** Rangiaowhia, Waikato. **Corps:** Forest Rangers from August to Nov 1863. Private. Constable, No. 5 Division Armed Constabulary. Regt No. 29 from March to Oct 1868. **Field service:** Lusk's Farm, Mauku [8 September 1863]. Patea: Relief of Turuturu Mokai [12 July 1868]. Te Ngutu o te Manu [21 August and 7 September 1868]. Escort between Waihi and Hawera [29 July 1868]. Canadian Redoubt. Medal claim AD32/752. Medal claim dated 14 September 1872. The Medal Application states: **Address:** Te Awamutu. **Corps:** No. 1 Company, Forest Rangers. No. 5 Armed Constabulary, Regimental No. 29. **Field service:** Joined Forest Rangers 11 August 1863. Under fire Lusk's farm, Mauku. Relief of Turuturu Mokai, Patea. Te Ngutu o te Manu. Escort on road between Waihi and Canadian Redoubt, Hawera." Written across the application "Rejected for mutinous conduct in the field on 29 September 1868". Medal claim AD32/228; AD36/3/75. Medal claim dated 28 July 1913. The Medal Application states "**Address:** Wiri, Papatoetoe. **Corps:** Served as Private in Flying Column and Forest Rangers under Col Nixon and Major Jackson. In Wairoa Rifles under Capt. Steele [6 months] and later I was about 7 years in the Te Awamutu Cavalry. I was also in No. 5 Division [Armed Constabulary] under Major von Tempsky. **Field service:** At Hunua where Chas Cooper was shot. On banks of Waikato River near Tuakau where Lieutenants Norman and Percival were shot [23 October 1863]. In No. 5 Division at Turuturu Mokai and also Te Ngutu o te Manu where Major von Tempsky met his death." Received land: town lot No. 358, Kihikihi; farm lot No. 320, Puniu. Medal claim AD32/752

William BELL
19, No. 2 Company: September 1865 – October 1866 (last known month of service). Private. Later served Armed Constabulary.
New Zealand Medal named to Forest Rangers. Medal claim dated 4 September 1871. Medal issued 30 December 1871. The Medal Application states "**Address:** Camp Ormond, Poverty Bay. **Corps:** Forest Rangers. Private. Under Capt. C. Westrup Sept 1865 to Jun 1866. **Field service:** Pukemaire [3rd] October 1865. Kawakawa [Hungahunga-toroa] Oct 1865. Waerengaahika [15-21] Nov 1865." Received land: town lot No. 87, Harapepe; farm lot No. 194, Pirongia. Medal claim AD32/2188; AD36/3/188

William BENSON
1077, No. 1 Company: 20 December 1863 – October 1866 (last known month of service). Private. Enrolled at Papakura. Born 1842, York, England. Age: 20 years. Height: 5' 11$^{1}/_{2}$". Hair

colour: sandy. Eye colour: blue. Complexion: fair. Occupation: groom/farmer. Country: England. Religion: Presbyterian. Sailed to New Zealand aboard *Ganges*, October 1863. Sworn in by Ensign Charles Westrup. Received land: town lot No. 43, Kihikihi; farm lot No. 296, Puniu. Died 1911, Ormond, Poverty Bay.

Amice John BERTRAM

1078, No. 1 Company: 22 November 1863 – November 1867 (last known month of service). Staff Sergeant. Earlier served Papakura Valley Rifle Volunteers (renamed Wairoa Rifles later). Later served Armed Constabulary; Te Awamutu Cavalry Volunteers. Enrolled at Papakura. Height: 5' 5½". Hair colour: black. Eye colour: grey. Complexion: dark. Occupation: farmer. Country: Jersey Islands. Religion: Episcopalian. Sworn in by Captain William Jackson. Born 1839, Grouville, Jersey. Died 1927, Mount Eden, Auckland.
New Zealand Medal named to Forest Rangers. Medal claim dated 10 September 1873. The Medal Application states "**Address:** Sergeant Major, Te Awamutu [Cavalry Volunteers] Troop, Waikato. **Corps:** Forest Rangers (No. 1 Coy) from formation to disbandment. **Field service:** Whole term: actively engaged during 1863 and 1864. Rangiaowhia [21 February 1864], Orakau [31 March-2 April 1864], Waiari [11 February 1864], etc." Present at reunion to commemorate 50 years of battle of Orakau, 1914. Received land: town lot No. 205, Kihikihi; farm lot Nos. 180 and 181, Puniu. Medal claim AD32/2200; AD36/3/256

Francis Eldred BEST

1262, No. 1 Company: 20 June 1864 – 14 May 1865 (died of wounds). Private. Enrolled 19 June 1864 at Kihikihi. Age: 20 years, 9 months. Height: 5' 10". Hair colour: brown. Eye colour: brown. Complexion: sallow. Occupation: farmer. Country: England. Religion: Episcopalian. Born 1843, Flyford Flavell, Worcestershire, England. Died of wounds at Kakaramea, Patea (date of action 13 May 1865). His body was found a few days after the engagement in the bush by a search party led by Lieutenant Westrup. It was established that he died of wounds on 14 May 1865.

John BIDGOOD

9, No. 2 Company: 4 January 1864 – November 1867 (last known month of service). Private. Earlier served 1st Regiment Waikato Militia. Later served Poverty Bay Cavalry Volunteers; Armed Constabulary.
New Zealand Medal named to Forest Rangers. Medal claim dated 9 October 1871. The Medal Application states "**Address:** Ormond, Poverty Bay. **Corps:** No. 2 Company Forest Rangers. Private. No. 9. Service 3 years. **Field service:** One and a half years service in the field. Mangapiko [Waiari, 11 February 1864], Rangiaowhia 2 days [and Hairini, 21-22 February 1864], Orakau 3 days [31 March-2 April 1864], Te Karato, Poverty Bay." Received land: town lot No. 65, Harapepe; farm lot No. 131, Pirongia. Medal claim AD32/2204; AD36/3/189

Henry W. BINDON

330, No. 1 Company: 11 March – 31 August 1864. Private. Substituted by No. 1297 Charles Treadwell. Earlier served 2nd Regiment Waikato Militia, No. 330. Enrolled 25 August 1863 at Otago. Height: 5' 8¾". Hair colour: auburn. Eye colour: grey. Complexion: ruddy. Occupation: miner. Country: Sydney, Australia. Religion: Episcopalian. Born 1838, Sydney, New South Wales. Possibly received impressed **New Zealand Medal** named to the Commissariat Transport Corps for service while with the Waikato Militia.

William J. BIRCHFIELD (BURCHFIELD)

11, No. 2 Company: 22 August 1864 – disbandment, 30 October 1867. Private. Promoted to Corporal. Promoted to Colour Sergeant. Substitute for William Burry. Earlier served 65th Regiment, No. 3669; 99th Regiment, No. 2493; 1st Regiment Waikato Militia, No. 4 (joining 1

September 1863 at Melbourne, Australia). Later served 1st Regiment Waikato Regiment, rejoining 14 November 1866. Occupation: labourer. Born 1833, Ballyclough, Cork, Ireland. Sailed to New Zealand aboard *Southern Cross* February 1856. Received land: town lot No. 1, Harapepe and No. 121, Opotiki; farm lot No. 184, Pirongia. Possibly received impressed **New Zealand Medal** named to the Commissariat Transport Corps for service while with the Waikato Militia.

W. BISLAND
Served 5 December 1865 – disbandment, 30 October 1867. Private. Earlier served Colonial Defence Force, Hawke's Bay. Enlisted in Forest Rangers at Wanganui.

Hugh BLACK
No. 1 Company: 14 December 1863 – 20 March 1864. Private. Earlier served 2nd Regiment Waikato Militia, No. 338. Later served 2nd Regiment Waikato Militia, No. 1416; Armed Constabulary. Born 1831, Carlingford, Antrim, Ireland.
New Zealand Medal named to Waikato Militia. The Medal Application states: "**Address:** Napier, Hawke's Bay. **Corps:** Waikato Militia. Jackson's Forest Rangers. **Period of Service:** 2 years, 3 months. **Field Service:** At Orakau 31 March to 2 April 1864. At Rangiaowhia 21 and 22 February 1864 [Hairini, 22 February]." Received land including town lot No. 260, Alexandra West (Pirongia). Medal claim AD32/2220

Joseph BLACKEY
Served (enlistment date unknown) – 1865. Private. Earlier served Colonial Defence Force, Wellington. Land claim H30B, 1892. Medal claim AD32/553

Ernest Louis BOCHOW (BUCHOLZ)
No. 2 Company: 28 December 1863 – 16 May 1864. Private. Earlier served 1st Regiment Waikato Militia, No. 208. Later served as Ensign, Auckland Militia. Occupation: labourer. Born 1841, Gotha, Germany. Sailed to New Zealand aboard *Star of India* 1863. Died 19 June 1876. Buried Symonds Street, Auckland.

James BOND
No. 1 Company: 5 August 1864 – September 1867 (last known month of service). Private. Substitute for James McEnany. Enrolled at Kihikihi, Te Awamutu. Later served No. 6 Division Armed Constabulary. Residence: Auckland. Aged: 19 years. Occupation: miner. Sworn in by Major William Jackson. Born 1846, Adelaide, Australia. Sailed to New Zealand aboard *Auckland*, 1864. Received land: town lot No. 38, Kihikihi; farm lot No. 265, Puniu.

Philip BOND
332, No. 1 Company: 11 March 1864 – August 1867 (last known month of service). Private. Earlier served 2nd Regiment Waikato Militia (enrolled 25 August 1863 at Otago), No. 332. Later served No. 5 Division Armed Constabulary, No. 48. Age: 19 years. Height: 5' 6". Hair colour: fair. Eye colour: grey. Complexion: fair. Occupation: miner. Country: South Australia. Religion: Episcopalian. Born 1844, Adelaide, Australia. Died 17 June 1887.
New Zealand Medal named to Forest Rangers. Medal claim dated 19 March 1870. The Medal Application states "**Address:** Te Rahu, Te Awamutu, Waikato. **Corps:** No. 1 Comp. Forest Rangers. Private from August 1863 to 1866 [includes service in Waikato Militia]. **Field service:** 3 years. Orakau [31 March] 1st and 2nd April 1864. Kakaramea 13th May 1865, Pukemaire 3rd October 1865, Waerengaahika Nov 17, 18, 19, 20, 21, 1865, Te Ngutu o te Manu 20th August 1868." Received land: town lot No. 41, Kihikihi; farm lot Nos. 251A and 256, Puniu. Medal claim AD32/2244; AD36/3/102

Thomas BOND

No. 1 Company: 19 May 1866 – December 1867 (last known month of service). Private. Substitute for Henry Jackson. Later served Te Awamutu Cavalry Volunteers (Sergeant). Enrolled Kihikihi, Te Awamutu. Age: 23 years. Height: 5' 6". Hair colour: fair. Complexion: fair. Occupation: settler. Country: Adelaide, Australia. Religion: Church of England. Born 1843, Adelaide, Australia. Died 18 October 1887. Received land: town lot No. 235, Kihikihi; farm lot Nos. 241, 251, 258 and 260, Puniu.

William BOND

333, No. 1 Company: 11 March 1864 – September 1867 (last known month of service). Private. Promoted to Corporal 8 April 1864. Promoted to Sergeant 1 April 1865. Earlier served 2nd Regiment Waikato Militia, No. 333 (enrolled 25 August 1863 at Otago). Later served No. 4 Division Armed Constabulary; Te Awamutu Cavalry Volunteers. Age: 25 years. Height: 5' 7½". Hair colour: tan. Eye colour: grey. Complexion: fair. Occupation: miner. Country: South Australia. Religion: Episcopalian. Born 1839, Adelaide, Australia.
New Zealand Medal named to Forest Rangers. Medal claim dated 15 August 1870. The Medal Application states "**Address:** Constable Armed Constabulary Force. **Corps:** No. 1 Co. Forest Rangers. Sergeant. Period of service 3 years. **Field service:** 3 years. Orakau, [31 March] 1st and 2nd April 1864; Gentle Annie, Kakaramea, West Coast, 13th May 1865; Pukemaire, East Coast, 3rd Oct 1865; Waerengaahika, 17, 18, 19, 20, 21 Nov 1865." Received land: town lot No. 67, Kihikihi; farm lot Nos. 175, 232 and 232A, Puniu. Medal claim AD32/2245; AD36/3/131

Joseph BOURKE

Original Company: 11 August – 11 November 1863. Sergeant.

William BOURKE

10, No. 2 Company: 16 June 1864 – January 1865 (deserted). Private. Substituted by No. 10 James Taylor.

James BOYD

Original Company: 11 August – 10 November 1863. Sergeant.

George BRAYLEY

Claimed to have served with "von Tempsky's Forest Rangers" but no confirmation. Born 1838, St Philip, Bristol, England. Earlier served Taranaki Military Settlers (from 20 January 1864). Later served No. 1 Division Armed Constabulary (4 November 1868 – 10 October 1869). Sailed to New Zealand aboard *Brilliant* from Melbourne, Australia.

BRASSEY

Period of service unknown but present with the unit late 1863. Aide-de-camp. Jackson used the services of Brassey, because of his knowledge of Maori habits and trails. After deserting from the British Army, for 15 years Brassey lived amongst various tribes. He married a Maori and had children who were later taken from him at the outbreak of hostilities in south Auckland. Brassey set out on a course of vengeance and joined up with the Forest Rangers. Being a deserter, he never officially enlisted, but just remained "attached" to the unit for fear of retribution. Jackson made Brassey an aide-de-camp but soon found him unmanageable when under the effects of alcohol. Von Tempsky took over responsibility of Brassey and after a little "roughing-up" made a good man out of him. There is doubt about his real name being Brassey, as von Tempsky writes of him in his manuscript *Memoranda of the New Zealand Campaign*. If Brassey was still alive the document would surely have incriminated him.

Henry BRERTON (BRETON)
Original Company: 11 August – 10 November 1863. Private. Sailed to New Zealand aboard *Joshua Fletcher* August 1859.

Henry Lowry Stewart Corry BROOKING
Served 1 November 1865 – 15 March 1866. Private. Earlier served United States Army, possibly in American Civil War; Wellington Rifle Volunteers. Later served Poverty Bay Military Settlers; No. 1 Division Armed Constabulary. Born 1840, Monaghan, Ireland. Sailed to New Zealand aboard *John Taylor* 1851.
New Zealand Medal named to Armed Constabulary (possibly named to Forest Rangers). In a letter accompanying his application for a grant (presumably a pension), dated 26 June 1910, Brooking states "I have made an application for a grant on account of Military Services during the New Zealand War, but find that a copy of my discharge is required before my application can be accepted. I served in von Tempsky's Rangers, Wellington Rifle Volunteers, No. 1 Division A.C. [Armed Constabulary], Ormond Military Settlers, between the years of 1862 and 1870. I was engaged in both the East and West Coast campaigns and was present at 8 of the engagements but did not receive a discharge from any of the Corps in which I served." His service was described by the Council of Defence office (dated 28 July 1910) as "Forest Rangers, enrolled 1/11/1865 and served till 15/3/1866. Wellington Rifles. Poverty Bay Mil. Settlers, no rolls in possession of Department. A.C. Force, Constable enrolled 22/11/1868, discharged 1/10/1869." Medal claim AD32/2018; AD36/3/248

Alexander BRUCE
1314, No. 1 Company: 3 November 1864 – 5 December 1866. Private. Substitute for No. 1264, Frederick Lysaught. Occupation: labourer. Born 1842, Wick, Caithness, Scotland. Received land: town lot No. 355, Kihikihi; farm lot No. 330, Puniu.

David BRUCE Junior
1313, No. 1 Company: 3 November 1864 – August 1866 (last known month of service). Private. Substitute for No. 1265, George Lysaught. Occupation: labourer. Born 1841, Wick, Caithness, Scotland. Sailed to New Zealand aboard *Romulus* 1862. Died 22 January 1893. Buried Symonds Street, Auckland. Received land: town lot No. 74, Kihikihi; farm lot No. 254, Puniu.

David BRUCE Senior
No. 1 Company: 31 October 1865 – November 1866 (last known month of service). Private. Substitute for John Hannay. Enrolled at Kihikihi, Te Awamutu. Residence: Te Rahu. Age: 40 years. Height: 5' 10". Hair colour: grey. Complexion: fair. Occupation: farmer. Country: Scotland. Religion: Presbyterian. Sworn in by Major William Jackson. Born 1824, Thurso, Caithness, Scotland. Sailed to New Zealand aboard *Romulus* 1862. Received land including town lot No. 346, Kihikihi.

George BRUCE
No. 1 Company: 1 June – November 1866 (last known month of service). Private. Enrolled Kihikihi, Te Awamutu. Age: 29 years. Occupation: settler. Born 1837, Watten, Caithness, Scotland. Died 1 November 1905, Ormond, Poverty Bay. Received land: town lot No. 227, Kihikihi; farm lot No. 224, Puniu.

Robert BRUCE
1080, No. 1 Company: 8 December 1863 – October 1867 (last known month of service). Private. Later served Te Awamutu Cavalry Volunteers (Lieutenant and later Captain). Enrolled at Auckland. Age: 21 years. Height: 5' 5½". Hair colour: light. Eye colour: blue. Complexion: fair.

Occupation: labourer. Country: Scotland. Religion: Presbyterian. Sworn in by Captain William Jackson. Born 1842 Watten, Caithness, Scotland. Died 16 April 1884. Buried Symonds Street, Auckland. Received land: town lot No. 9, Kihikihi; farm lot No. 257, Puniu.

William BRUCE Junior

1079, No. 1 Company: 8 December 1863 – September 1867 (last known month of service). Private. Enrolled at Auckland. Age: 22 years. Height: 5' 7½". Hair colour: brown. Eye colour: grey. Complexion: pale. Occupation: labourer. Country: Scotland. Religion: Presbyterian. Sworn in by Captain William Jackson. Born 1841, Caithness, Scotland. Received land: town lot No. 353, Kihikihi; farm lot No. 225, Puniu.

William BRUCE Senior

No. 1 Company: 1 June 1866 – (discharge date unknown). Private. Enrolled at Kihikihi, Te Awamutu. Age: 38 years. Occupation: settler. Country: Scotland. Born Caithness, Scotland. Received land: town lot No. 32, Kihikihi; farm lot No. 226, Puniu.

John BUCHANAN

No. 2 Company: Private. Earlier served 3rd Regiment Waikato Militia; Auckland Militia. Born 1840, United States of America. Occupation: lawyer. There is doubt that this man served with unit, as he does not appear on pay sheets.

Bernard BULOW

Period of service unknown. Private. Served with Westrup's Company on East Coast. Earlier served Colonial Defence Force, Wellington.

Peter BURLEY (BURLEIGH)

Served 4 September 1865 – March 1866 (last known month of service). Private. Substitute for Colin Smith. Earlier served Colonial Defence Force, Wellington. Later served Wanganui Bush Rangers.

John BURNS

16, No. 1 Company: 29 February – 30 November 1864. Private. Promoted to Corporal. Earlier served 2nd Regiment Waikato Militia, No. 16 (enrolled 25 September 1863 at Sydney). Age: 20 years. Height: 5' 4". Hair colour: light. Eye colour: blue. Complexion: fair. Occupation: seaman. Country: Scotland. Religion: Presbyterian. Born 1843, Lanark, Strathclyde, Scotland. Sailed to New Zealand aboard *James Patterson* 1863.

John BURNS

24, No. 2 Company: 7 March 1865 – (discharge date unknown). Private. Substitute for Edgar Mitchell. Earlier served 2/14 Regiment, No. 53; 2nd Regiment Waikato Militia, No. 1151. Later served No. 5 Division Armed Constabulary, No. 41. Occupation: soldier. Born 1835, Histon, Cambridge, England. Sailed to New Zealand aboard *Boonerges* 1860. Left von Tempsky in the South Taranaki and travelled to the Waikato 9 January 1866. Received land including town lot No. 269, Alexandra East (Pirongia).

Lawrence Bumford BURNS

1081, No. 1 Company: 17 November 1863 – March 1866 (last known month of service). Private. Promoted to Sergeant 21 October 1865. Later served Wanganui Bush Rangers. Enrolled at Auckland. Age: 33 years. Height: 6'. Hair colour: light. Eye colour: blue. Complexion: fresh. Occupation: millwright. Country: Ireland. Religion: Roman Catholic. Sworn in by Captain William Jackson. Signed his enlistment with a mark. Served on West Coast. Born 1830, Longford, Leinster, Ireland.

William BURNS
Original Company: 11-25 August 1863. Private.

William BURRY
11, No. 2 Company: 23 December 1863 – 21 August 1864. Private. Substituted by William Birchfield. Earlier served Auckland Militia; 1st Regiment Waikato Militia, No. 262. Occupation: farmer. Born 1824, Dundee, Scotland.

Alexander BUTTER
12, No. 2 Company: 16 January 1864 – October 1866 (last known month of service). Private. Promoted to Sergeant. Earlier served 3rd Regiment Waikato Militia. Later served as Ensign, Poverty Bay Militia; Armed Constabulary.
New Zealand Medal named to Forest Rangers. Medal claim dated 10 February 1870. In 1872 Butter requested that his medal be forwarded to the Armed Constabulary Station, Opepe, near Taupo. The Medal Application states "**Address:** Armed Constabulary Office, Wellington. **Corps:** No. 2 Co. Forest Rangers. Sergeant. Dec/63 – July/66. Poverty Bay Militia, Ensign, July/68 to November 1869. **Field service:** 4 years or thereabouts in field service. Waiari [11 February 1864], Rangiaowhia [21 February 1864] and Orakau [31 March-2 April 1864] in the Waikato. Kakaramea [13 May 1865], Weraroa [21 July 1865] and Pipiriki [July 1865] on the West Coast. Pukemaire at Waiapu [3 October 1865], Kawakawa [Hungahunga-toroa, October 1865] at Waiapu. Waerengaahika [15-21 November 1865], Paparatu [20 July 1868], Makaretu [3 December 1868] and Ngatapa [1-5 January 1869] in Poverty Bay district. **Remarks:** The dates of the above I am unable to give in consequence of my swag, in which all my papers were, being stolen in transit on shifting from one district to another." In a testimonial dated 9 July 1866 at Auckland, von Tempsky stated "His character has been excellent; his conduct in the field, for coolness, readiness and courage has been of the highest order." Received land: town lot No. 92 Harapepe; farm lot Nos. 122 and 123, Pirongia. Medal claim AD32/2359; AD36/3/91

Thomas BUTTLE
Original Company: 11 August – 10 November 1863. Private. **13, No. 2 Company:** 25 November 1863 – October 1867 (last known month of service). Private. Sailed to New Zealand aboard *Joseph Williams*. Received land: town lot No. 97 Harapepe; farm lot No. 156, Pirongia.

Hans BYGUM
No. 2 Company: 28 November 1863 – 20 April 1864. Private. Later served Wanganui Bush Rangers. Born Aaldorg, Denmark. Sailed to New Zealand aboard *Sea Shell* 1862. Died August 1889, Auckland.
New Zealand Medal named to Forest Rangers. Medal claim dated 21 March 1871. The Medal Application states "**Address:** Victoria Street East, Auckland. **Corps:** Private. Von Tempsky's Forest Rangers. **Field service:** Orakau March 31st, April 1st and April 2nd 1864. **Remarks:** Name of immediate commanding officer: Captain von Tempsky (now killed)." Medal claim, AD32/2361; AD36/3/89

Owen CAIN (CANE)
64, No. 2 Company: August – December 1867 (last known month of service). Private. Earlier served 65th Regiment, No. 3133. Born St Thomas, Dublin. Received land: town lot No. 104 Harapepe; farm lot No. 180, Pirongia.

Allister Henry CAMPBELL
31, No. 2 Company: 17 September 1865 – August 1866 (last known month of service). Private. Wounded in the left thigh at Te Putahi 7 January 1866, while a member of General Chute's

Taranaki expedition. Received land: town lot No. 6 Harapepe; farm lot No. 132, Pirongia.

John CAMPBELL

1272, No. 1 Company: 23 July 1864 – April 1865 (last known month of service). Private. Enrolled at Pukerimu, Cambridge. Residence: Auckland. Age: 19 years. Height: 5' 7³/₄". Hair colour: brown. Eye colour: grey. Complexion: fair. Occupation: horse breaker. Country: Tasmania, Australia. Religion: Roman Catholic. Sworn in by Major William Jackson. Discharged in the Wanganui district but failed to return his arms and accoutrements, which were sought by the Colonial Defence Office. Campbell wrote to them in December 1865 stating they had been stolen. Born 1844, Hobart, Tasmania.

Henry CARRAN

Original Company: 26 August – 10 November 1863. Private. **18, No. 2 Company:** 30 November 1863 – 26 April 1864. Private. Promoted to Sergeant. Born 1837, Rushen, Isle of Man. Sailed to New Zealand aboard *Clydersee* January 1840.
New Zealand Medal named to Forest Rangers. Medal claim dated 20 March 1872. The Medal Application states "**Address:** Thames Goldfield, Punga Flat. **Corps:** Von Tempsky's Forest Rangers. Sergeant 9 months. **Field service:** 9 months. Feb 1864 Rangiaowhia [and Hairini] 21st & 22nd. Orakau [31 March-2 April 1864] 2nd, 3rd and 4th April 1864. **Remarks:** Engaged on several minor occasions, dates forgotten." The Defence Office did make enquiries to ascertain if Carran served in the No. 5 Division Armed Constabulary and if involved in the mutiny. Medal claim AD32/2417; AD36/3/413

John CARROL

Original Company: 11 August – 10 November 1863.

John CARTER

Original Company: 11 August – 10 November 1863. Private. **1082, No. 1 Company:** 17 November 1863 – January 1867 (last known month of service). Private. Enrolled at Auckland. Age: 22 years. Height: 5' 7". Hair colour: brown. Eye colour: grey. Complexion: light. Occupation: labourer. Country: England. Religion: Episcopalian. Sworn in by Captain William Jackson. Born 1841, Bromley, Middlesex, England. Sent 18 March 1864 to Maketu by Captain Jackson from Pukerimu Redoubt, Cambridge in support of the Arawa Friendly Natives. Rejoined Forest Rangers 3 November 1864. Received no pay while absent, possibly because he was placed on McDonnell's Arawa acquittance roll. Served on both East Coast and West Coast. Received land: town lot No. 68, Kihikihi; farm lot No. 270, Puniu.

Lewis (Louis) CASTIN (CASTAIGN)

Period of service unknown. Private. Served with Westrup's Company on East Coast.

David CAUGHEY

39, No. 2 Company: June 1866 – November 1867 (last known month of service). Private. Received land: town lot No. 69, Harapepe; farm lot No. 134, Pirongia.

Edward CHAPMAN

1263, No. 1 Company: 31 May 1864 – June 1865 (last known month of service). Private. Enrolled at Auckland. Age: 27 years. Height: 6'. Hair colour: light. Eye colour: blue. Complexion: fair. Occupation: gentleman. Country: Ireland. Religion: Episcopalian. Born 1836, Cork, County Cork, Ireland.

Charles CLAYFORTH

No. 1 Company: 13 June 1865 – November 1866 (last known month of service). Private.

Substitute for George Cole. Enrolled at Kihikihi, Te Awamutu. Residence: Auckland. Single. Age: 23 years. Height: 5' 11". Hair colour: fair. Eye colour: blue. Complexion: fresh. Occupation: farmer. Country: Sherburn, Yorkshire, England. Sworn in by Major William Jackson. Religion: Episcopalian. Born 1843, Sherburn, Yorkshire, England. Sailed to New Zealand aboard *Ganges* 1863. Received land: town lot No. 10, Kihikihi; farm lot No. 313, Puniu.

Henry George CLIFFORD

14, No. 2 Company: 6 January 1864 – November 1867 (last known month of service). Private. Promoted to Corporal. Earlier served 1st Regiment Waikato Militia, No. 1309. Sailed to New Zealand aboard *City of Manchester*.
New Zealand Medal named to Forest Rangers. Medal claim dated 28 November 1871. Medal issued 28 November 1873. The Medal Application states "**Address:** Sussex Hotel, Dunedin. **Corps:** Von Tempsky's Company of Forest Rangers. Corporal. **Field service:** 3 years. Paterangi pa [attempted night attack. Probably Waiari, 11 February 1864], Te Awamutu. Kihikihi [skirmish], Rangiaowhia [21 February 1864] and other places – names and dates of which I forget. **Remarks:** Served under Lieut. Roberts, Ensign Sherret – under General Cameron." Received land: town lot No. 101, Harapepe; farm lot No. 159, Pirongia. Medal claim AD32/2467; AD36/3/416

Patrick John CLINTON

15, No. 2 Company: 3 May 1864 – September 1867 (last known month of service). Private. Substitute for William Race. Earlier served 1st Regiment Waikato Militia, No. 310 (joined 1 September 1863 at Melbourne, Australia). Occupation: labourer. Born 1840, Killala, Mayo, Ireland. Sailed to New Zealand aboard *Star of India*, 1863.
New Zealand Medal named to Forest Rangers. Medal claim dated 2 April 1870. The Medal Application states "**Address:** Harapepe, Waikato. **Corps:** 2nd Company Forest Rangers. Private 1st Sept 63 [including service with Waikato Militia] to 4th June 1866. Regimental No. 15. **Field service:** 19th Oct 63 to 4 June 1866. Kakaramea 13th May 1865. Pukemaire 3rd Oct 1865. Waerengaahika 17th, 18th, 19th, 20th, 21st and 22nd November 1865. **Remarks:** Major von Tempsky commanded at Kakaramea. Capt. Westrup commanded company at Pukemaire and Waerengaahika. Major Fraser in command." Clinton's medal was first sent to Hamilton but because Clinton had in the meantime left the district, the medal was returned to Wellington. Received land: town lot No. 80, Harapepe; farm lot No. 165, Pirongia. Medal claim AD32/2471; AD36/3/2622

George CLOTWORTHY

1341, No. 1 Company: 28 December 1864 – February 1867 (last known month of service). Private. Substitute for No. 1102 John Smith. Later served Wanganui Bush Rangers on East Coast; Armed Constabulary. Enrolled at Kihikihi, Te Awamutu. Residence: Auckland. Age: 27 years. Height: 5' 10". Hair colour: black. Eye colour: brown. Complexion: dark. Occupation: farmer. Country: Killead, Antrim, Ireland. Religion: Presbyterian. Born 1837, Killead, Antrim, Ireland. Sworn in by Major William Jackson.
New Zealand Medal named to Forest Rangers. Medal claim dated 7 March 1870. The Medal Application states "**Address:** [None]. **Corps:** Forest Rangers. Private, period of service eighteen months. **Field service:** One year and two months under fire at Kakaramea in [13th] May 1865 – Poverty Bay in November same year [Waerengaahika, 15-21 November 1865]. **Remarks:** The exact dates are forgotten." Received land: town lot No. 44, Kihikihi; farm lot No. 242, Puniu. Medal in private collection. Medal claim AD32/2474; AD36/3/315

William COCHRANE

16, No. 2 Company: 21 January 1864 – May 1866 (deserted). Private.

Elijah CODLING

26, No. 2 Company: 15 April 1865 – October 1866 (last known month of service). Private. Earlier served 2nd Regiment Waikato Militia, No. 233. Born 1839, Auckland. Joined in Wanganui.
New Zealand Medal named to Forest Rangers. Medal claim dated 19 November 1872. Medal issued 14 December 1876. The Medal Application states "**Address:** Upper Barrack Street, Auckland. **Corps:** Forest Rangers, Private. **Field service:** From 15th April 1865 to April 18th 1866 and was present at the actions: Okotuku [4 January 1866], Te Putahi [7 January 1866], Otapawa [14 January 1866], Ketemarae [15 January 1866]." In a testimonial von Tempsky states "Harapepe April 18 1866. Private Elijah Codling has served with me from the 15th April 1865 till this day. He was present at the actions of Okotuku, Te Putahi, Otapawa and Ketemarae. His character as a man and a soldier is good." Received land: town lot No. 32, Harapepe; farm lot No. 178, Pirongia. Medal claim AD32/2481; AD36/3/450

Charles (Steve) COGHLAN

432, No. 1 Company: 10 December 1863 – 2 April 1864. Corporal. Earlier served 2nd Regiment Waikato Militia, No. 432. Died from a bullet wound to the abdomen received when carelessly placing a gabion above the sap at Orakau on 1 April 1864. First Forest Ranger to be killed. Sailed to New Zealand aboard *Deborah*, 1841. Possibly next of kin received impressed **New Zealand Medal** named to the Commissariat Transport Corps for service while with the Waikato Militia.

George Lewis COLE

Original Company: 11 August – 27 October 1863. Sergeant/Guide. **1083, No. 1 Company:** 17 December 1863 – 15 June 1865. Private. Later served No. 6 Division Armed Constabulary. Died of wounds 18 November 1868 at Wanganui and buried Wanganui cemetery. Enrolled at Papakura. Age: 18 years. Height: 5' 11". Hair colour: light. Eye colour: blue. Complexion: fair. Occupation: saddler. Country: New Zealand. Religion: Wesleyan. Sworn in by Ensign Charles Westrup. Born 1845 in Auckland.
New Zealand Medal named to Forest Rangers. Medal claim dated 21 November 1872. The Medal Application states "**Address:** George Loverson Cole, father, Papakura. **Corps:** Forest Rangers – Colonial Defence Force and Armed Constabulary. Private, Trooper and Constable. **Field service:** Rangiaowhia [21 February 1864], Orakau [31 March-2 April 1864], and all through the Waikato campaign in the years 1863 & 1864, Okotuku [Moturoa] Nov 7 1868 when he was wounded and subsequently dying from the effects thereof in the Wanganui hospital Nov 18th 1868. **Remarks:** On account of my son George Lewis Cole deceased." Medal claim (next-of-kin) AD32/2485; AD36/3/451

Henry COLLINS

No. 2 Company: 6 January – 9 May 1864. Private. Earlier served 70th Regiment, No. 3196. Possible medal claim, AD32/1147, but more likely received medal for imperial service.

George COLSTON

Served 6 December 1865 – disbandment, 30 October 1867. Private. Enlisted at Wanganui. Possibly the same man as below re-enlisting.

George William COLTON

58, No. 2 Company: 5 January – 3 May 1865. Private. Substitute for James Walker. Earlier served Taranaki Military Settlers, No. 160. Possibly the same man as above with split service with the Forest Rangers.

Louis CONRAD

17, No. 2 Company: 1 April 1864 – February 1866 (last known month of service) Private.

Biographical notes

William CORBOY
No. 1 Company: 2 June 1866 – July 1867 (last known month of service). Private. Substitute for Laurence Burns. Enrolled at Kihikihi, Te Awamutu. Born 1840. Sailed to New Zealand aboard *Liverpool*, 1866. Corboy, with Andrew Ross and Mr Sloan (nominated Europeans), visited the Maori, south of the Puniu River, to improve relations. Was the original owner of the Alpha Hotel at Kihikihi. Died 2 December 1882 aged 42 years. Buried Hairini Roman Catholic cemetery. His brother Patrick served in the Waikato Militia. Received land: town lot No. 2, Kihikihi; farm lot No. 333, Puniu.

Clement A. CORNES
Original Company: 11 August – 10 November 1863. Private. Made land claim.

John COSTELLO
429, No. 1 Company: 10 December 1863 – October 1867 (last known month of service). Private. Earlier served 2nd Regiment Waikato Militia, No. 429. Enrolled 7 September 1863 at Auckland. Age: 23 years, 7 months. Height: 5' 9". Hair colour: black. Eye colour: blue. Complexion: dark. Occupation: labourer. Country: Ireland. Religion: Roman Catholic. Born 1839, New Hall, Clare, Ireland. Sailed to New Zealand aboard *Queen of the North*, 1862. Received land: town lot No. 4, Kihikihi; farm lot No. 297, Puniu.

James CRAWFORD
1324, No. 1 Company: 1 December 1864 – 25 January 1865. Private. Substitute for No. 1085 Robert Gibb. Earlier served Papakura Valley Rifle Volunteers (renamed Wairoa Rifles later). Later served 3rd Regiment Waikato Militia, commissioned Ensign 23 September 1865. Enrolled at Wairoa, south Auckland. Age: 20 years. Height: 5' 9$^{1}/_{2}$". Hair colour: fair. Eye colour: blue. Complexion: ruddy. Occupation: labourer. Country: Scotland. Religion: Presbyterian. Born 1844, Isle of Bute, Scotland. Died 25 July 1896 at Clevedon, near Papakura. Sworn in by Major William Jackson. Received land including town lot No. 333, Cambridge West. There is a medal claim for a James Crawford (AD/32/1570), but no proof that this is the same man.

J. CROMMELIN
Served 2 December 1865 – disbandment, 30 October 1867. Private. Enlisted at Wanganui.

Michael CROWE
Served 9 August 1865 – (discharge date unknown). Private. Served with Westrup's Company on East Coast.

William CRYMBLE
61, No. 2 Company: July 1866 – November 1867 (last known month of service). Private. Earlier served 3rd Regiment Waikato Militia, No. 877. Born 1830. Sailed to New Zealand aboard *Alpha*. Received land: town lot No. 61, Harapepe; farm lot No. 170, Pirongia.

Ralph CULLINAN
1358, No. 1 Company: 1 February – 13 November 1865. Private. Substitute for Laurence Laurensen. Substituted by Wallace. Later served Wanganui Bush Rangers; No. 2 Division Armed Constabulary. Enrolled at Kihikihi, Te Awamutu. Single. Age: 23 years. Hair colour: dark. Eye colour: brown. Complexion: dark. Occupation: surgeon. Country: Ireland. Religion: Episcopalian. Born 1842, Drumcliff, Clare, Ireland. Received land, No. 173, Kakaramea.

James CUNNINGHAM
101, No. 1 Company: 29 February 1864 – July 1867 (last known month of service), broken service. Corporal. Promoted to Sergeant 21 March 1864. Earlier served 2nd Regiment Waikato

Militia, No. 101. Later served Wanganui Bush Rangers, joining as Private 10 February 1866; Wanganui Veteran Volunteers; East Coast Force as Ensign (from 16 December 1865); Te Awamutu Cavalry Volunteers. Enrolled 4 September 1863 at Otago. Age: 25 years. Height: 6'. Hair colour: light. Eye colour: grey. Complexion: sallow. Occupation: gentleman/miner. Country: Scotland. Religion: Presbyterian. Born 1839, Renwick, Kirkcudbright, Galloway, Scotland. Sailed to New Zealand aboard *Glimpse*. Later resided in Hokitika.
New Zealand Medal named to Forest Rangers. Medal claim dated 30 May 1871. The Medal Application states "**Address:** Rangiaowhia, Waikato. **Corps:** No. 1 Company Forest Rangers. Rank: Sergeant. Period of service 1 year 8 months. **Field service:** Period of service in the field 1 year 8 months. Under fire at Orakau April 2nd & 3rd 1864 [actually 31 March-2 April]. **Remarks:** Held rank of Sergeant at above dates. Since promoted to Lieutenant [Ensign]." Received land: town lot No. 200, Kihikihi; farm lot Nos. 189, 190, 191, 284 and 337, Puniu. Medal claim AD32/2588; AD36/3/381

Robert CUNNINGHAM

25, **No. 1 Company:** 29 February 1864 – July 1867 (last known month of service). Private. Earlier served 2nd Regiment Waikato Militia. Enrolled 4 September 1863 at Otago. Age: 23 years. Height: 6' 3". Hair colour: light. Eye colour: grey. Complexion: fair. Occupation: gentleman. Country: Scotland. Religion: Presbyterian. Born 1841, Renwick, Kirkcudbright, Galloway, Scotland.
New Zealand Medal named to Forest Rangers. Medal claim dated 3 August 1872. The Medal Application states "**Address:** Rangiaowhia. **Corps:** Forest Rangers. Private – Feb 1864 till 1865. **Field service:** Orakau [31 March] 1st & 2nd April 1864." Received land: town lot No. 42, Kihikihi; farm lot Nos. 288 and 336, Puniu. Medal claim AD32/2591; AD36/3/441

Peter CURRAN

18, **No. 2 Company:** 1 August 1864 – October 1867 (last known month of service). Private. Later served as Lance-Corporal, No. 5 Division Armed Constabulary, No. 51. Born 1836, Carlow, Carlow, Ireland. Sailed to New Zealand aboard *White Star*, 1862. Received land: town lot No. 94, Harapepe; farm lot No. 291, Pirongia.

C. DALEY

Served 5 December 1865 – disbandment, 30 October 1867. Private. Enlisted at Wanganui.

James DARROW

No. 1 Company: 13 October 1865 – September 1866 (last known month of service). Private. Substitute. Enrolled at Te Awamutu. Age: 24 years. Occupation: carter. Sworn in by Major William Jackson. Born 1841. Died 20 September 1908 at Thames. Received land: town lot No. 345, Kihikihi; farm lot No. 323, Puniu.

Alexander DAVIDSON

Served 3 December 1865 – 30 September 1866. Private. Remained on full pay while recovering from wound, while other men who enlisted in Wanganui were discharged in February 1866. Enlisted and discharged at Wanganui. Occupation: seaman. Severely wounded in the left thigh by a musket ball at Waikoko, 1 February 1866, while with General Chute's campaign.
New Zealand Medal named to Forest Rangers. Medal claim dated 19 January 1870. The Medal Application states "**Address:** Wanganui. **Corps:** Forest Rangers. Private. Dec 1865 to Feb 1866. **Field service:** From December 1865 to 1st Feb 1866. Otapawa [14 January 1866], Te Putahi [7 January 1866]. Wounded at Waikoko [1 February 1866]." Medal claim, AD32/2607; AD36/3/499

Biographical notes

George DAVIDSON (VART)
Served 3 December 1865 – disbandment, 30 October 1867. Private. *See details under George VART.*

Edward DAVIS
1251, No. 1 Company: 1 April 1864 – 4 January 1865. Private. Substituted by No. 1348 Henry Lloyd. Enrolled at Auckland. Age: 37 years. Height: 5' 11". Hair colour: brown. Eye colour: blue. Complexion: ruddy. Occupation: seaman. Country: England. Born 1827.

John R. DEARLOVE
1257, No. 1 Company: 4 April – 16 June 1864. Private. Sailed to New Zealand aboard *Golden City*, 1864. Died of disease in hospital at Paparimu, 16 June 1864.

W. Henry DEVLIN
55, No. 2 Company: 17 September 1865 – October 1866 (last known month of service). Private. Promoted to Corporal 21 October 1865. Earlier served Colonial Defence Force, Hawke's Bay. Served on West Coast. Received land: town lot No. 48, Harapepe; farm lot No. 294, Pirongia.

Matthew DONALD
6 December 1865 – disbandment, 30 October 1867. Private. Possibly earlier served with Wanganui Yeomanry Cavalry. Later served Poverty Bay Militia. Born 8 April 1844, Barony, Glasgow, Scotland.
New Zealand Medal named to Forest Rangers. Medal claim dated 13 November 1912. Medal issued 19 December 1913. The medal was officially renamed, erasing the name of Private Edward Frost, 2nd Waikato Regiment of Militia. The dates "1861-66" on the reverse were deleted and polished. The Medal Application states "**Address:** 114 Childers Road, Gisborne. **Corps:** Rank: Private. No. 2 Company, Forest Rangers under Major von Tempsky. **Field service:** One year. Otapawa [14 January 1866], Stony Creek [River], Ketemarae [15 January 1866]. Hangaroa on the West Coast and Makaretu on the East Coast. **Remarks:** Also engaged in outpost duty at Wanganui and marched under the command of General Chute from Wanganui to Taranaki." The following descriptions are compiled from Donald's medal application file. Donald was present at Kakaramea 13 May 1865 (possibly with Wanganui Yeomanry Cavalry) and with General Chute on his Taranaki campaign 1866 under von Tempsky. Actions included: Okotuku 4 January 1866; Te Putahi 7 January 1866; Otapawa 14 January 1866; Ketemarae 15 January 1866; the march that left Ketemarae on 17 January 1866 and Waikoko 1 February 1866. Donald was then in the Poverty Bay Militia under Major Richardson for 2 years while occupying land at Waerengaahika 1868-70. While here he saw action at Paparatu 20 July 1868 and Makaretu 3 December 1868 – where Te Kooti attacked the escort in charge of Sergeant Butter, Donald being one of 3 rearguards covering the retreat. On the East Coast Donald served under Biggs, Westrup, Pitt, Gudgeon and Porter. He was sworn in by Major Biggs in 1868. Donald in his medal application states "I claim as a militiaman. I first joined von Tempsky's corps which served in General Chute's campaign. I served for about 3 to 4 months with the corps. I then joined the militia in Poverty Bay in 1868. I was on the commissariat escort to Makaretu [3 December 1868] during Te Kooti's war. I was under fire at this place. I served in the Militia until our arms were called in." Donald has signed his medal application with a mark. Medal claim, AD32/394; AD36/3/3392

James DONOVAN
No. 2 Company: 28 December 1863 – 31 July 1864. Private.

John DREW
Served 21 October 1865 – (discharge date unknown). Private. A John Drew received a New Zealand Medal (Medal claim AD32/2682) named to 3rd Waikato Regiment of Militia or

Commissariat Transport Corps, at Wellington on 28 September 1872.
Vallancy DRURY
1285, No. 1 Company: 6 September 1864 – October 1866 (last known month of service). Private. Substitute for William Ryan who enlisted but did not serve. Enrolled at Alexandra Camp, Te Awamutu. Age: 28 years. Height: 5' 10½". Hair colour: brown. Eye colour: blue. Complexion: ruddy. Occupation: clerk. Country: Ireland. Religion: Episcopalian. Born 1836, Killybegs, Donegal, Ireland. Died 17 June 1867. Sworn in by Major William Jackson. Sailed to New Zealand aboard *Bosphorus*, 1864. Received land: town lot No. 215, Kihikihi; farm lot No. 252, Puniu.

Henry DUESBURY
19, No. 2 Company: 8 June – 15 December 1864. Private. Substituted by John Wright. Earlier served 1st Regiment Waikato Militia, No. 364. Occupation: miner. Christian name has also been recorded as Herbert.

Patrick DUFFY (DUFFEY)
No. 1 Company: 10 November 1865 – June 1866 (last known month of service). Private. Substitute for Beetham. Enrolled at Wanganui. Age: 32 years. Height: 5' 8". Hair colour: ruddy. Complexion: fair. Occupation: labourer. Country: Dublin, Ireland. Religion: Roman Catholic. Born 1836, Dublin, Ireland. Served on West Coast. Received land: town lot No. 354, Kihikihi; farm lot No. 282, Puniu.

John DUGGAN
31, No. 1 Company: 29 February 1864 – 2 August 1865. Private. Earlier served 2nd Regiment Waikato Militia. Enrolled 20 September 1863 at Auckland. Age: 24 years. Height: 5' 7". Hair colour: black. Eye colour: brown. Complexion: sallow. Occupation: seaman/bushman. Country: England. Religion: Roman Catholic. Born 1839, Maryport, Cumberland, England. Shot dead as result of accident at Pipiriki, 2 August 1865, by John Wright. *See entry for John Wright.*

John William DUNCKLEY
Served 23 October 1865 – 15 February 1866. Private. Later served Wellington Rangers; No. 1 Division Armed Constabulary. Born 1844, Houghton Conquest, Bedfordshire, England.
New Zealand Medal named to Forest Rangers. Medal claim dated 5 August 1871. Medal issued 3 April 1876. The Medal Application states "**Address:** Masonic Hotel, Wanganui. **Corps:** Forest Rangers, Private from October 26th 1865 till Feb 15th 1866. **Field service:** In General Chute's Campaign of 6 weeks – was present at the actions of Okotuku [4 January 1866], Te Putahi [7 January 1866], Ketemarae [15 January 1866], Otapawa [14 January 1866] and Waikoko [1 February 1866] and the burning of several villages. **Remarks:** Served also in the Wellington Rangers [Corporal] from June 1868 till Sept 68 and the 1st Division A.C. [Armed Constabulary] from Oct 68 till Jan 1869. Present at Te Ngutu o te Manu (Ruaruru) [21 August and 7 September 1868], Moturoa [7 November 1868], and the fall of Ngatapa [1-5 January 1869]." Medal claim AD32/2693; AD36/3/541

James DUNN
Original Company: 11 August – 26 September 1863 (deserted). Sergeant. Marked on acquisition roll for September 1863 "Pay for 27, 28, 29 & 30 stopped for being absent without leave." Previously 58th Regiment. Sailed to New Zealand aboard *Sir Robert Sale* August 1847.

Henry ELSTON
30, No. 2 Company: 5 January 1865 – (date of discharge unknown). Private. Substitute for Edward Husband.
New Zealand Medal named to Forest Rangers. Medal claim dated 28 January 1912 and received

26 February 1912. Medal issued 20 February 1913. The medal was officially renamed, erasing the name of Private John Broadbent, Auckland Militia. Dates "1861-66" were also deleted and polished. The Medal Application states "**Address:** Palmerston South. **Corps:** I have the honour to say I joined No. 2 Company Forest Rangers in the year 1865 at Cambridge, Waikato. Major von Tempsky was my commanding officer for about 6 months. **Field service:** I was first under fire at Patea, Wanganui [Kakaramea, 13 May 1865]. I was then sent on to Waiapu, East Coast, under Major Fraser and Captain Westrup [Pukemaire, 3 October 1865.] I was then sent to Poverty Bay in October 1865. Was under fire at Waerengaahika [15-21 November 1865]. Continual firing for eight days and nights – 192 hours less one hour to bury the dead. Te Kooti and his followers were taken prisoner. Was at Poverty Bay when Te Kooti escaped from the Chatham Islands. Was under fire near Gisborne for nine hours under Major Westrup. Was under fire again for 4 days within 21 miles of Gisborne. Was at Poverty Bay at time of the Poverty Bay Massacre [10 November 1868]. 51 killed – 32 whites and 19 Maori. My homestead and store were burnt. I lost every penny and never got any compensation. I believe the Government should have given me a grant of good land in compensation for the massacre." In a declaration in support of Elston's medal application, James McGuirk states "I fought with Henry Elston now of Palmerston South and was under fire with him at Kakaramea near Patea, Wanganui 13 May 1865 and also at Waerengaahika, Gisborne [15-21 November 1865] in August or September 1865. At Waiapu near East Cape [Pukemaire, 3 October 1865] and at Weraroa [21 July 1865], Wanganui District and went to the relief of Pipiriki [19-30 July 1865]." After the campaign on the East Coast he settled in the area. Received land: town lot No. 56, Harapepe; farm lot No. 142, Pirongia. Medal claim AD32/50; AD36/3/3179

Robert ELVIN

24, No. 2 Company: 8 July 1866 – October 1867 (last known month of service). Private. Earlier served 40th Regiment, No. 2411. Received land: town lot No. 3, Harapepe; farm lot No. 153, Pirongia.

Robert ERSKINE

Served 14 November 1865 – 15 March 1866. Private. Later served No. 3 Division Armed Constabulary; Wanganui Veteran Volunteers. Enlisted in Forest Rangers at Wanganui. **New Zealand Medal** named to Armed Constabulary. Medal claim dated 27 May 1884. The Medal Application states "**Address:** Patea. **Corps:** Von Tempsky's Rangers and A.C. [Armed Constabulary] Force. Private. From 1865 to 1870. **Field service:** About 5 years. Te Ngutu o te Manu [21 August and 7 September 1868], Waitotara [probably referring to Okotuku, 4 January 1866], Otapawa [14 January 1866 while with Chute's expedition]." There was obviously confusion over which unit Erskine served in. A letter in support of his claim for a grant of land (dated 2 June 1892) states "Erskine states as follows – 'I enlisted at Wanganui, I think about two months before Major General Chute started on the expedition from Wanganui. I was sworn in before Major von Tempsky and Captain [Lieutenant] Pilmer and received my arms and accoutrements from the militia office at Wanganui, then in charge of Colonel Gorton'. ... that my name is in the books I am positive, because I was given the **New Zealand Medal** for my services in the Armed Constabulary." A letter from the Acting Under Secretary for Defence (dated 7 June 1892 from Westport) states "... a further search was made through the rolls of the various corps then serving on the West Coast when his name was discovered on the pay rolls of a company of 'Wanganui Rangers' under Capt. [Lieutenant] Pilmer, from the 14th November 1865 to the 15th March 1866, this accounts therefore for his name not appearing on the pay rolls of the original corps of Forest Rangers (von Tempsky's) the members of which corps all received a grant of land on the expiration of their term of service." This is a typical example of the confusion that occurred when Forest Rangers were confused with other Ranger units. Erskine, while at Westport, did however apply for and receive a duplicate medal during 1901 at the cost of 7s. 6d. Medal claim

AD36/3/2801; AD1/1892/781 (on land claim file)
William EVANS
39, No. 1 Company: 29 January 1864 – 9 January 1865. Private. Substituted by No. 1350 Francis Beetham. Earlier served 2nd Regiment Waikato Militia. Enrolled 25 August 1863 at Auckland. Age: 38 years. Height: 5' 7". Hair colour: brown. Eye colour: blue. Complexion: ruddy. Occupation: miner. Country: England. Religion: Episcopalian. Born 1825, Tower Hamlets, Middlesex, England.

William EVANS
Served 9 August 1865 – (date of discharge unknown). Private. Later served No. 8 Division Armed Constabulary. Served with Westrup's Company on East Coast.

John FAHEY
Original Company: 11 August – 10 November 1863. Private. Farmer. Probably son of a couple killed at Bombay by Maori.

Joseph FALLON
5, No. 2 Company: 23 December 1863 – 21 November 1864. Private. Promoted to Corporal 5 August 1864. Substituted by John Hearfield. Earlier served 1st Regiment Waikato Militia, No. 465 (joined 1 September 1863 at Melbourne, Australia). Occupation: butcher. Born 1833, Shropshire, England.
New Zealand Medal named to Forest Rangers. Medal claim dated 1 February 1870. The Medal Application states "**Address:** Grahamstown, Thames. **Corps:** Major von Tempsky's Forest Rangers. Corporal – 2 years. No Regt number. **Field service:** Continually in the field. At Rangiaowhia [and Hairini] on the 21st and 22nd March [actually February] 1864. Under fire and at Orakau [31 March-] April 1st and 2nd. **Remarks:** Received from Major Jackson, Forest Rangers, a gold watch [Taylor's] for rescuing Sergeant Taylor from under the [Orakau] pa when shot, at the time under fire." Medal claim AD32/2761; AD36/3/653

James B. FERRIS
Served 21 November – December 1865 (last known month of service). Private. Earlier served Colonial Defence Force, Hawke's Bay.

Robert Daniel FINDLAY
346, No. 1 Company: 11 March – 22 July 1864. Private. Substituted by No. 1272 John Campbell. Earlier served 2nd Regiment Waikato Militia. Enrolled 27 August 1863 at Dunedin. Age: 20 years. Height: 5' 10". Hair colour: black. Eye colour: brown. Complexion: dark. Occupation: clerk. Country: Scotland. Religion: Presbyterian. Born 1844.

James FINLAY
Original Company: 11 August – 10 November 1863. Private. Later served Armed Constabulary. Sailed to New Zealand aboard *James Booth* April 1861.
New Zealand Medal named to Forest Rangers. Medal claim dated 1871. Medal issued 30 October 1873. The Medal Application states "**Corps:** Jackson's Forest Rangers. Private. Seven months. **Field service:** Wellwood, Mauku [Lusk's Clearing, 8 September 1863]." Found guilty of two offences February 1874 while with the Armed Constabulary, Auckland: 15 February 1874 – drunk when on picket and using obscene language to Lieutenant Eyre. Received 7 days drill/ 7 days confined to camp. Found out of camp on 16 February when confined thereto by order of Captain Howell. Reprimanded. Made a military pension claim in 1914. Medal claim AD32/1524; AD36/3/693

Carl Fred Theodore FISCHER

21, No. 2 Company: 1 August 1864 – August 1867 (last known month of service). Private. Earlier served 2nd Regiment Waikato Militia, No. 142. Later served 3rd Regiment Waikato Militia, No. 1539; No. 7 Division Armed Constabulary; New Zealand Militia. Occupation: miner. Born 1838, Brunswick, Germany. Died 16 November 1914, Pihama, Taranaki. Received land: town lot No. 2, Harapepe; farm lot No. 257, Pirongia.

Henry FISHER

Served 9 August 1865 – (date of discharge unknown). Private. Served with Westrup's Company on East Coast.

Richard FITZGERALD

1084, No. 1 Company: 1 December 1863 – 18 March 1864. Private. Enrolled in Otago on 10 November and sailed to Auckland and joining the corps 1 December (receiving pay from 10 November). Age: 35 years. Height: 5' 9^3/$_4$". Hair colour: brown. Eye colour: blue. Complexion: light. Occupation: miner. Country: Ireland. Religion: Roman Catholic. Born 1828. Sent 18 March 1864 to Maketu from Pukerimu Redoubt, Cambridge, by Captain Jackson in support of the Arawa Friendly Natives. Did not rejoin Forest Rangers. Possibly he was placed on McDonnell's Arawa acquittance roll while at Maketu.

Edward FLANAGAN

This man probably never served with the Forest Rangers, but served with Captain George's Waikato Militia Company, which for a period of time fought alongside the Forest Rangers. Either Flanagan was confused, or he fabricated his service with the Forest Rangers.

Flanagan mentions as serving April – 31 August 1865. Private. Earlier probably served 3rd Regiment Waikato Militia (Captain George's Company). Later served 1st Regiment Waikato Militia, No. 139; No. 3 Division Armed Constabulary. Born 1841, Donagher Kings, Ireland. Sailed to New Zealand aboard *Starting Fawn* 1862. Received land including town lot No. 295 Te Papa, near Tauranga; No. 310 Cambridge East.

Received **New Zealand Medal.** Two medal applications. His earlier Medal Application (dated 2 March 1870) states "**Address:** Quartermaster's Office, Spit, Napier. **Corps:** 3rd Waikato Regt. Afterwards joined Major von Tempsky's bushrangers on the West Coast." Fuller details of service are presented in his second application (dated 26 April 1871) which states "**Address:** Armed Constabulary Force, Tarawera Station, Taupo District. **Corps:** service in 3rd Regiment Waikato Militia (1863-66) as Private and Armed Constabulary (October 1868 to date of application, 26 April 1871). **Field service:** 12 months from May 1865 to May 1866. Gentle Annie under von Tempsky [Kakaramea, 13 May 1865], Weraroa [21] July 1865 under von Tempsky, Opotiki 1 September 1865 [with Waikato Militia] under Major Brassey, Kiorekino 15 October 1865 under Major Brassey, Waimana November 1865 under Colonel Lyons, Ngatapa 1-5 January 1869 under Colonel Whitmore." Medal claim AD32/2797; AD36/3/654 and 676

Frederick Alfred Chamber FOSTER

21, No. 2 Company: 6 April 1864 – February 1867 (last known month of service). Private. Von Tempsky's batman. Earlier served 1st Regiment Waikato Militia, No. 420. Later served Armed Constabulary. Born 1831, Dublin, Ireland. Sailed to New Zealand aboard *Star of India* 1863. **New Zealand Medal** named to Frederick W. Foster (not Frederick A.C. Foster), Forest Rangers. Medal claim dated 1871. The Medal Application states "**Address:** Ormond, Poverty Bay. **Corps:** Forest Rangers. 11 months [probably refers to period under fire]. **Field service:** Waiapu [Pukemaire 3rd October 1865], Waerengaahika [15-21 November 1865]." Received land: town lot No. 64 Harapepe; farm lot No. 129, Pirongia. Medal claim AD32/2824; AD36/3/683

William FRASER
22, No. 2 Company: 1 April 1864 – 16 June 1865. Private.

John FREEMAN
18, No. 2 Company: 8 January – 14 September 1864. Private. Substituted by Edward McGrath. Later served Patea Rangers. Sailed to New Zealand aboard *Shalimar* 1859.

Robert FROST
41, No. 1 Company: 29 February – 15 July 1864. Private. Substituted by No. 1269 John McCulloch. Earlier served 2nd Regiment Waikato Militia. Occupation: grocer. Born 1835.

Philip GALLIE
1253, No. 1 Company: 28 December 1863 – 23 June 1864. Private. Substituted by No. 1265 George Lysaught. Earlier served 2nd Regiment Waikato Militia. Born 13 March 1827, St Savior, Croizere, Jersey. Sailed to New Zealand aboard *Queen of Beauty* 1863. Died 11 October 1910, Matakohe.

John GARDINER (GARDNER)
Served 7 August 1865 – (discharge date unknown). Private. Earlier served No. 57 Regiment, No. 3254. Later served Armed Constabulary. Born 1839, Belfast, Ireland. Sailed to New Zealand aboard *Star Queen* 1861. Served with Westrup's Company on East Coast.

Richard E. GARVEY
Original Company: 11-25 August 1863. Private. Sailed to New Zealand aboard *Nimrod* April 1863.

Robert GIBB
1085, No. 1 Company: 30 November 1863 – 30 November 1864. Private. Enrolled at Papakura. Age: 19 years. Height: 5' 8". Hair colour: dark. Eye colour: grey. Complexion: fresh. Occupation: blacksmith. Country: Scotland. Religion: Presbyterian. Sworn in by Ensign Charles Westrup. Born 1843, Cupar, Fife, Scotland. Sailed to New Zealand aboard *Shooting Star* 1859.

John GILLANDERS
34, No. 2 Company: 24 October 1865 – September 1866 (last known month of service). Private. Substitute for Liebig. Von Tempsky's batman. Earlier served 1st Regiment Waikato Militia, No. 478. Later served Wellington Rifle Volunteers; No. 5 Division Armed Constabulary. Born 1845, Halifax, Nova Scotia, Canada. Sailed to New Zealand aboard *Gertrude* December 1856.

New Zealand Medal named to Forest Rangers. No medal application form can be found, probably because Gillanders applied before they were printed. A letter of application dated 3 December 1869 from Auckland states "Application for the Medal. Sir. I served as Private in Major von Tempsky's Company of Forest Rangers for five months. I've been in all the engagements that [are] mentioned in my character [reference]. Major von Tempsky was in command of the Forest Rangers at each of those fights and General Chute was commander in chief." A notation on the letter verifies that Gillanders' signature matches those on acquittance rolls. Gillanders does not mention his Armed Constabulary service. In a testimonial, von Tempsky stated "Harapepe April 13, 1866. Private John Gillanders has served with me from the 24th October 1865 to this date. He was present at the actions of Okotuku [4 January 1866], Te Putahi [7 January 1866], Otapawa [14 January 1866], Ketemarae [15 January 1866] and Waikoko [1 February 1866]. His character as a man and a soldier is excellent." Received land: town lot No. 59 Harapepe; farm lot No. 120, Pirongia. Present at reunion to commemorate 50 years of battle of Orakau, 1914. Medal claim AD32/2882; AD36/3/718

Robert GOLDSMITH
Period of service unknown. At time of service the distinction between No. 1 and No. 2 Companies had been dropped.
New Zealand Medal named to Hawke's Bay Colonial Defence Force (an error as this unit disbanded in 1864). Medal claim dated 13 November 1911 and received 21 October 1912. Medal issued 2 April 1913. The medal was officially renamed erasing that of Sergeant A. Jennings, Auckland Militia. Dates "1861-66" were also deleted and polished. The Medal Application states "**Address:** Waerengaahika, Poverty Bay. **Corps:** Forest Rangers. Poverty Bay Mounted Rifle Volunteers. 1 year in Forest Rangers. 5 years in Poverty Bay Mounted Rifle Volunteers. **Field service:** 3 years. Under fire at Waerengaahika [15-21 November 1865]; Paparatu (where I was severely wounded) [20 July 1868]; Makaretu [3 December 1868]; Ngatapa [1-5 January 1869]; and several skirmishes. Also scouting duty and carrying despatches. **Remarks:** When taking bullocks to Makaretu [in the Scouts under Captain Gascoyne, November/December 1868] we were ambuscaded, and several occasions we had to fight our way out when scouting." Goldsmith stated in his application "I served in the Forest Rangers in the year 1865. I also served in the Poverty Bay Mounted Rifle Volunteers from about 1867 to 1871 and was engaged in scouting duty whilst attached to that corps. I was under fire at Waerengaahika [15-21 November] in the year 1865 for seven days. I was under fire at Paparatu [20 July] in 1868 where I was severely wounded. I was also under fire at Makaretu [3 December] in 1868. Also at Ngatapa [1-5 January 1869] in the same year. I was ambuscaded when taking bullocks for the commissariat at Ngatapa and had a very narrow escape and also under fire at Pukepuke [20 November 1869] when scouting." Medal claim AD32/483; AD36/3/3205

Joseph J. GRIGG
1086, No. 1 Company: 17 November 1863 – 4 February 1865. Private. Substituted by William Smith. Enrolled at Auckland. Age: 20 years. Height: 5' 5^1/$_2$". Hair colour: light. Eye colour: blue. Complexion: fair. Occupation: seaman. Country: England. Religion: Episcopalian. Sworn in by Captain William Jackson. Born 1843, Antrim, County Antrim, Ireland. Sailed to New Zealand aboard *Shooting Star* 1859.

Edward GUNING (GUNNING)
Served 7 August 1865 – (discharge date unknown). Later served Armed Constabulary. Served with Westrup's Company on East Coast.

Alfred W. HAINES
No. 1 Company: 10 December 1863 – 20 March 1864. Private. Sailed to New Zealand aboard *Tyburnia* 1863.

William HANNAH
No. 1 Company: 28 December 1863 – 20 March 1864. Private. Earlier served 1st Regiment Waikato Militia, No. 95. Sailed to New Zealand aboard *Queen of Beauty*, August 1863.

John HANNAY
357, No. 1 Company: 14 December 1863 – 31 October 1864. Private. Earlier served 2nd Regiment Waikato Militia. Enrolled 25 August 1863 at Otahuhu. Age: 20 years. Height: 5' 8". Hair colour: sandy. Eye colour: blue. Complexion: ruddy. Occupation: grocer. Country: Ireland. Religion: Presbyterian. Born 1843, Shanklin, Isle of Wight.
New Zealand Medal named to Forest Rangers. No. and date of Gazette: No. 31, 31 May 1871, Roll A. Medal issued 10 April 1872. The Medal Application states "**Address:** Auckland. **Corps:** Private. Forest Rangers. **Field service:** Waikato 1864." Medal claim AD36/3/820

Adolphus Frederick HARDY

56, No. 2 Company: 29 November 1864 – 31 July 1866. Private. Promoted to Corporal. Substitute for No. 56 James Taylor. Later served as Commanding Officer for 8 years of the first volunteer corps in Gisborne, of which he was a member for 10 years.

New Zealand Medal named to Forest Rangers. Medal claim dated 15 May 1876. Medal issued 12 September 1911 at Patutahi, Gisborne. First applied for a New Zealand Medal in 1871. Received the medal shortly after. In a duplicate medal application letter dated 16 June 1911, Hardy states "... Corporal A.F. Hardy No. 2 Company Forest Rangers – the more important engagements in which I took part were: Orakau [31 March-2 April 1864], Kakaramea [13 May 1865], Weraroa [21 July 1865], Pipiriki [July 1864], Pukemaire [3 October 1865], Kawakawa [Hungahungatoroa, October 1865] and Waerengaahika [15-21 November 1865]." In a later letter dated 21 July 1911 Hardy states "In the year 1899 my home and contents including the medal referred to above were accidentally destroyed by fire." The cost for the duplicate medal was 7s. 6d. Received land: town lot No. 81 Harapepe; farm lot No. 284, Pirongia. Medal claim AD32/187; AD36/3/877

Robert HARKIN

24, No. 2 Company: 1 August – 21 November 1864. Private. Substituted by Edgar Mitchell. Earlier served 1st Regiment Waikato Militia, No. 1308.

John HARRIS

No. 2 Company: 12 January – 31 July 1864. Private. Earlier served 3rd Regiment Waikato Militia, No. 321. Land claim LS69/38-2283. A John Harris received a New Zealand Medal (Medal claim AD32/2997) on 11 March 1873 named to 3rd Waikato Regiment of Militia, but not sure if he is the same person.

William HARTLAND

26, No. 2 Company: 23 December 1863 – 13 April 1865 (deserted in Wanganui district). Private. Earlier served 1st Regiment Waikato Militia, No. 1192. Born 1839, Gournal, Staffordshire, England. Sailed to New Zealand aboard *Caduseus* 1863.

Thomas HARVEY

25, No. 2 Company: 5 August – 15 December 1864. Private. Substituted by Amelius Taylor.

William McGregor HAY

Original Company: 11 August – 10 November 1863. Ensign. Born 1844 in Wellington. At time of service he was a law student. He later became a barrister and solicitor, practising in Hamilton for many years. In October 1863 the Flying Column was divided into two detachments, to extend its effectiveness. Likewise the Forest Rangers were split into two detachments with Hay in command of the west detachment at Mauku. Died at Brighton Road, Parnell, Auckland, 29 September 1893 and buried Papakura Cemetery. Von Tempsky wrote of him in *Memoranda of the New Zealand Campaign* "This officer, though very young and in his first campaign, seemed to me to possess great abilities for his temporary profession. His courage and coolness combined with great judgement had been often admired by me, and I was sorry to learn afterwards that during a pause in Forest Ranging, he had been recalled to his legal studies by the wish of his father."

New Zealand Medal named to Forest Rangers. Medal claim dated 12 October 1870. The Medal Application states "**Address:** Solicitor, Auckland. **Corps:** Forest Rangers. Ensign. Three months. **Field service:** Four months. Lusk's Farm, Mauku, September 8th 1863. Afterwards at Pokeno Hill with Col Nixon. **Remarks:** Name of immediate commanding officer: Major Jackson. Name of officer in general command: Col. Nixon." A land claim in 1887 was rejected. Medal claim AD32/3303; AD36/3/886

Robert HEALAS
No. 2 Company: 11 January – 23 May 1864. Private. Earlier served 3rd Regiment Waikato Militia, No. 1101, joining in Otago, 18 December 1863. Born 1829, Selby, Yorkshire, England.

John Gunson HEARFIELD
5, No. 2 Company: 22 November 1864 – 27 November 1865. Private. Substitute for Joseph Fallon. Substituted by Jeffares. Earlier served Colonial Defence Force, Hawke's Bay. Later served Patea Field Force. Born 1840, Hull, Yorkshire, England. Name recorded in some places as Harefield.
New Zealand Medal named to Forest Rangers. Medal claim dated 15 May 1876. The Medal Application states "**Address:** Taranaki Street, Wellington. **Corps:** Defence Force under Major Whitmore. Private – 12 months. Forest Rangers under Major von Tempsky. Corporal – 15 months. **Field service:** Two and a quarter years. Kakaramea [13 May 1865], Nukumaru [skirmishes in the area], Pipiriki [July 1865], Te Ngutu o te Manu [Patea Field Force] August 21 1868." Medal claim AD32/2989

Maurice HEFFERNAN
Original Company: 11-28 August 1863. Private. Born 1831 Killarney, Ireland. Previously No. 140, 65th Regiment. Occupation: labourer. Also 1st Regiment Waikato Militia and No. 4 Division, Armed Constabulary.

Philipp HELLKESSEL (Helkessell or Hellkepel)
27, No. 2 Company: 23 December 1863 – July 1865 (last known month of service). Private. Earlier served 1st Regiment Waikato Militia, No. 1193 (joined 11 September 1863 at Melbourne, Australia). Later served 1st Regiment Waikato Militia, No. 1365. Occupation: engineer. Born 1839, Cologne, Germany. Sailed to New Zealand aboard *Caduseus* 1863. Received land including town lot No. 242 Opotiki.

Charles Frederick Henry HENDRY
Original Company: 11 August – 10 November 1863. Private. **1088, No. 1 Company:** 17 November 1863 – September 1867 (last known month of service). Private. Later served Armed Constabulary. Enrolled at Auckland. Residence: Wairoa, south Auckland. Age: 21 years. Height: 5' 9". Hair colour: light. Eye colour: blue. Complexion: fair. Occupation: bushman. Country: Denmark. Religion: Episcopalian. Sworn in by Captain William Jackson. Born 1842, Schleshing, Denmark. Died 3 October 1927 and buried Hillsboro cemetery, Auckland. Received land: town lot No. 351 Kihikihi; farm lot No. 246, Puniu. Medal claim AD36/3/833

Martin HENNESSEY
4, No. 2 Company: 22 November 1864 – August 1865 (last known month of service). Private. Substitute for Henry Wakeford.

Thomas Joseph HENSHAW
Served 27 October – December 1865 (last known month of service). Private. Earlier served Rifle Brigade; Colonial Defence Force, Wellington. Later served Wanganui Bush Rangers. Enlisted in Forest Rangers at Wanganui. Born 1841. Died 1888 at Onehunga. Made land claim 1892.

H.H. HEWSON
Served 7 August 1865 – (date of discharge unknown). Private. Served with Westrup's Company on East Coast.

Frederick HIGGINS
28, No. 2 Company: 11 January – 23 November 1864. Private. Substituted by Andrew Moylan.

Earlier served 3rd Regiment Waikato Militia, No. 1102. Drowned in Waikato River.

Alexander HILL

Original Company: 11 August – 10 November 1863. Private. Earlier served Auckland Militia.
New Zealand Medal named to Forest Rangers. The Medal Application (dated 19 March 1914) states "**Address:** 88 Derby Street, Westport. **Corps:** Forest Rangers – Private 6 months. Flying Column – Guide 6 months. **Field service:** Ring's Redoubt, Wairoa Road. Patumahoe. Paparata – Hunua Valley." In a letter accompanying his application (dated 30 March 1914), Hill states "I was a mine manager until the last 2 or 3 years. I do nothing now – am too old to work. I shall be 70 on 25 June next. I served in the Forest Rangers. I joined in 1863 in the winter. We were then quartered in Papakura. The officers were Capt. Jackson, Lieut. von Tempsky and Ensign Hay. I was with them until they disbanded. We went from Papakura round the Hunua Ranges, thence to Patumahoe. We had a skirmish with the Natives there. I was under fire there. The Natives ambushed us and fired on us when we were looking out for them. One of our men got a slight wound on top of the shoulder. I was under Sergeant Roberts. He is Colonel Roberts now. He was present at that skirmish at Patumahoe. Thomas Pollock of Tuakau was in the same squad as myself. We went from Patumahoe to the Queen's Redoubt at Mercer. Then we went to Papakura and Hunua. We had an engagement with the Natives at Paparata. I was under fire then. [Hill was present as a guide.] Several Natives killed and wounded. Dan Mutton and I took their flags [from other accounts this is probably untrue]. ... Before the Forest Rangers were formed I volunteered and went with W. Jackson to Ring's Redoubt near Papakura on the Wairoa Road. I was under fire there at Ring's Redoubt." *See Daniel Mutton's entry for further information.* Made land claim. Medal Claim AD32/372; AD36/3/3445

George Rowland (Rowley) HILL

29, No. 2 Company: 8 June 1864 – July 1866 (last known month of service). Private. Earlier served Royal Navy; 2nd Regiment Waikato Militia. Later served No. 1 Company Military Settlers, Hawke's Bay; No. 1 Division Armed Constabulary until disbanded in 1886; Submarine Mining Section, New Zealand Militia. **New Zealand Medal** named to Hawke's Bay Military Settlers (probably wrongly named to Napier Militia).
Received the New Zealand Cross. Details of issue are: Recommended by: Colonel Whitmore. Service: "On the 10th April, 1869, Constable (now Sergeant) George Hill, of No. 1 Division, Armed Constabulary, accompanied the Wairoa Natives who, under Ihaka Whanga, proceeded to relieve Mohaka, then being attacked by Te Kooti. A party volunteered to run the gauntlet of the enemy's fire, and to dash into the Jerusalem pa, then sorely pressed. This was a dangerous service, and it was in a great measure due to the example set by Constable Hill, who led that party, that it was successfully carried out. During the subsequent portion of the siege Constable Hill animated the defenders by his exertions, and contributed greatly to the repulse of Te Kooti; and his conduct is spoken of with admiration by the Natives themselves." New Zealand Gazette entry: No. 34, 26 June 1869.
Born 9 September 1837, Ringsash, Devon, England. Joined the Royal Navy in 1851 at 14 years of age and served in the Baltic and Crimea. At the outbreak of the Indian Mutiny he was serving aboard H.M.S. *Shannon* and joined Captain Peel's Naval Brigade. Wounded at Lucknow and Cawnpore. While serving in the Mediterranean in 1862 he deserted ship and joined Garibaldi's Army of Liberation. He saw action at Palerm, Capua and in the straights of Messina, again being wounded. In due course he was taken by a naval picket and returned to his Royal Navy ship. But it appears that his desertion was overlooked since British sympathy for Garibaldi ran high. Leaving the Navy, Hill came to New Zealand in 1864 aboard the troopship *Empress*. While the troopship was anchored in Waitemata Harbour he jumped overboard and swam ashore. He served in 17 engagements against the Maori. Was awarded two medals by the Royal Humane Society for saving

life, one in 1860 and the other in 1896. Tried unsuccessfully to enlist for the South African War 1899-1902 at the age of 63. Retired to Takapuna, Auckland, and died in Auckland on 15 February 1930 aged 93. Occupation: seaman. Religion: Baptist. Received land: town lot No. 60, Harapepe; farm lot No. 200, Pirongia. Medal claim AD32/1784; AD36/3/869

Edwin HINCHCLIFFE

Period of service unknown. Later served 4th Regiment Waikato Militia, No. 208. Although he claimed Forest Ranger service in his application, there is no record of him on any Forest Ranger acquittance roll. He was in Captain George's Company of Waikato Militia. This company fought alongside the Forest Rangers for a period, so if Hinchcliffe did not serve with the Forest Rangers, he was either confused or fabricated his medal application. Born 1845, West Maitland, New South Wales. Sailed to New Zealand aboard *Kate*, 1864.

New Zealand Medal named to Forest Rangers. Medal claim dated 11 May 1883. The Medal Application states "**Address:** Postmaster, Millfield, New South Wales. **Corps:** Major von Tempsky's Forest Rangers. Private. 3 years service with time allowance. **Field service:** Twelve months near Kakaramea [13 May 1865], Weraroa pa [21 July 1865]. Pipiriki [July 1865] and Opotiki [September 1865], winter of 1865. Volunteer from 4th Company, 4th Regiment [Waikato Militia]." In a letter accompanying his application, Hinchcliffe states "I served under Major von Tempsky in the Patea district and was present in an engagement near Kakaramea [13 May 1865] when Ensign Whitfield and two privates were killed. I was also present at the taking of the Nukumaru pa, at the relief of Pipiriki [July 1865], and in a skirmish at Opotiki [8 or 9 September 1865] under Lt George [Waikato Militia] and afterwards servant to yourself [Colonel Lyons] at Opotiki." Received land including town lot No. 167, Hamilton East, with the 4th Regiment Waikato Militia. Medal claim AD1/1883/1227; AD32/3379; AD36/3/2787

Thomas HOLDEN

Original Company: 11 August – 10 November 1863. Private. **1087, No. 1 Company:** 17 November 1863 – 18 March 1864. Sergeant. Enrolled at Papakura. Age: 24 years. Height: 5'9". Hair colour: brown. Eye colour: grey. Complexion: light. Occupation: settler/farmer. Country: England. Religion: Episcopalian. Sworn in by Captain William Jackson. Born April 1838, Spilsby, Lancashire, England. **1327, No. 1 Company:** (re-enlisted) 11 December 1864 – October 1867 (last known month of service). Private. Promoted to Sergeant. Substitute for No. 51 James Jennings. Enrolled 1864 at Auckland. Age: 25 years. Sworn in by Major William Jackson. Sent 18 March 1864 to Maketu by Captain Jackson from Pukerimu Redoubt, Cambridge in support of the Arawa Friendly Natives. Rejoined Forest Rangers 3 November 1864. Received no pay while absent, possibly because he was placed on McDonnell's Arawa acquittance roll. Later served Te Awamutu Cavalry Volunteers. Present at reunion to commemorate 50 years of battle of Orakau, 1914. Died 26 January 1920 and buried Hairini cemetery, Te Awamutu.

New Zealand Medal named to Forest Rangers. Medal claim dated 6 October 1874. Medal issued 6 March 1875. The Medal Application states "**Address:** Te Awamutu, Waikato, Auckland. **Corps:** No. 1 Coy Jackson's Rangers. Sergeant. Three years. **Field service:** Two years. Waiari [11th] Feb 1864. Rangiaowhia [21st] Feb 1864. Maketu [21-26] April 1864." Received land: town lot No. 76 Kihikihi; farm lot Nos. 187 and 243A, Puniu. Medal claim AD32/3110; AD36/3/1131

Robert Patterson HOLLISTER

28, No. 2 Company: 4 September 1865 – 13 April 1866. Private. Earlier served Colonial Defence Force, Hawke's Bay. Later served Wanganui Yeomanry Cavalry; No. 1 Division Armed Constabulary. Born 25 October 1840, Winterbourne, St Michael, Dorset. Died 4 April 1868 at Whakatane.

New Zealand Medal named to Colonial Defence Force. Medal claim dated April 1872. Made by his mother, Helen Edmonds. The Medal Application states "**Address:** Helen Edmonds, as mother of Robert Hollister. Little Taranaki Street, Wellington. **Corps:** Hawke's Bay Defence Force, Trooper. Major von Tempsky's Rangers, Private and Major Fraser's Force. **Field service:** Commenced service in June 1863 – in Colonial Defence Force and served in various Col. Corps until time of death. Okotuku [4 January 1866], Kaiteriria [Captain Mair's camp at Rotokakahi], etc. **Remarks:** Died April 4 – 1868 in camp, Whakatane, while serving under Lt Col. Fraser." Von Tempsky wrote a testimonial for Hollister on request. The document is badly damaged with some details illegible "Harapepe. April 13, 1866. Private Robert Hollister has served with me from the 4th September 1865 till this date. He was present at the actions of Okotuku [4 January 1866], Te Putahi [7 January 1866], Otapawa [14 January 1866], Ketemarae [15 January 1866] and Waikoko [1 February 1866]. His conduct as a soldier was of the highest order. Major von Tempsky." Received land: town lot No. 31 Harapepe; farm lot No. 234, Pirongia. Medal claim AD32/3115; AD36/3/1076.

William Joseph HOWELL

Served 5 December 1865 – 20 February 1866. Private. Earlier served 58th Regiment, No. 2685; Taranaki Militia. Later served Wanganui Bush Rangers; Carlisle Rifle Volunteers. Enlisted in Forest Rangers at Wanganui. Born 1834, Woolwich, Kent, England.
New Zealand Medal claim made 18 October 1913 in a letter from Suva, Fiji, where he travelled to in 1869. The letter states "I herewith apply for the New Zealand War Medal. I enclose my discharge from the Forest Rangers. I afterwards served in the Wanganui Rangers and lived on my farm allotment near Kakaramea for 12 months. I afterwards served in the Carlisle Rifles at Patea. I had previously served in the Taranaki Militia at Bell Block under Captain Hirst." A copy of his discharge accompanied his application. It states "Wanganui, 20 February 1866. Private W. Howell has served in the Forest Rangers for three months, was in General Chute's Campaign and at the actions of Okotuku [4 January 1866], Te Putahi [7 January 1866], Otapawa [14 January 1866], Ketemarae [15 January 1866] and Waikoko [1 February 1866], also at the burning of 14 fortified villages, and the march through the bush around Mt Egmont; he has always been a pleasure to his officers from his good conduct both in camp and action, and I part from him with regret. [Signed] Alexander Anthony Pilmer, Captain, Forest Rangers." Medal claim AD32/905; AD36/3/3365

Arthur HUDDLESTON

Original Company: 28 August – 10 November 1863. Private.

William HUMPHRIES

49, No. 1 Company: 15 January – July 1865 (deserted). Private. Earlier served 2nd Regiment Waikato Militia, joining in Auckland 15 September 1863. Occupation: labourer. Religion: Episcopalian. Born 1832, Stepney, Middlesex, England.
The Lands and Survey District Office in Auckland requested (24 October 1893) information from the Defence Department about Humphries' service as he had made a claim for the return of land earlier granted to him. The land in question was one town acre at Kihikihi and 50 acres at Rangiaowhia. The Defence Department's reply was: ... "with reference to service of William Humphries in the Forest Rangers and Waikato Militia, I beg to inform you that the above Company was attached to the 2nd Regiment Waikato Militia stationed at Kihikihi, and he first appeared in the pay rolls as having joined on 15 January 1865 and returned on the monthly pay rolls from that date down to July of same year; but on the rolls for months of Aug, Sept, Oct and Nov he is marked as 'absent without leave' and as having deserted. On our non-effective lists he is returned as having deserted at Kihikihi, during October 1865, and in the descriptive book of the Waikato Militia is described as having deserted on 1 November 1865." This information is on file AD32/4658.

Edward HUSBAND
30, No. 2 Company: 29 April 1864 – 4 January 1865. Private. Substituted by Henry Elston. Earlier served 1st Regiment Waikato Militia.

Henry Bower JACKSON
Original Company: 11 August – 10 November 1863. Private. **1089, No. 1 Company:** 17 November 1863 – 18 March 1864. Private. Enrolled at Auckland. Age: 24 years. Height: 5' 7½". Hair colour: brown. Eye colour: blue. Complexion: light. Occupation: miner. Country: England. Religion: Episcopalian. Sworn in by Captain William Jackson. Born 25 December 1841, Riccal, Yorkshire, England. Sent 18 March 1864 to Maketu by Captain Jackson from Pukerimu Redoubt, Cambridge in support of the Arawa Friendly Natives. Did not rejoin Forest Rangers. He may have been placed on McDonnell's Arawa acquittance roll while at Maketu.

J. Howard JACKSON
Served 3 December 1865 – January 1867. Private. Enlisted at Wanganui. Later served Auckland Engineer Volunteers. Sailed to New Zealand aboard *Excelsior* 1859.
New Zealand Medal named to Auckland Volunteer Engineers. The medal claim (date 18 February 1870) states: **Address:** Grahamstown, Thames. **Corps:** Auckland Volunteer Engineers. Private. Joined January 1867. There is no mention of earlier service with Forest Rangers. Medal claim AD32/3193; AD36/3/1182

William JACKSON *(pictured)*
Original Company: Lieutenant, Commanding Officer. **No. 1 Company:** 9 November 1863 – disbandment, 30 October 1867. Promoted Captain 9 November 1863 and Commanding Officer of both Companies of Forest Rangers. Promoted Major 3 April 1864. Earlier served Papakura Valley Rifle Volunteers (later called Wairoa Rifle) as Sergeant, enlisting in 1862. Later commanded Te Awamutu Troop (Te Awamutu Cavalry Volunteers), Waikato Cavalry Volunteers, in the 1870's. Born 1832, Green Hammerton, near York, North Yorkshire, England. Emigrated to New Zealand in the early 1850's, secured land in the Papakura area and commenced farming. In 1862 he volunteered in the Papakura Valley Rifle Volunteers and as a sergeant showed excellent leadership. He particularly drew attention to himself with some distinguished leadership in repelling an attack on Ring's Redoubt. He started to developed guerrilla warfare techniques later used effectively with the Forest Rangers. After hostilities ended, Jackson entered politics in 1872 as a Member of the House of Representatives (MHR) for Waikato in the Stafford Government, New Zealand's fifth parliament. In 1875 he returned to farming at Hairini. Twelve years later in 1887 he was back in parliament representing Waipa and survived two years of the eventful tenth parliament of the Atkinson Ministry. He was Government whip for three sessions. Jackson devoted much energy while in Parliament to securing for the Forest Rangers and Colonial Defence Force the privileges granted to others who served in the war. Of special interest were land claims by men who served in the original company of Forest Rangers. Jackson received 200 acres and remission certificates of £100 in his claim dated 9 June 1890. But Jackson was never to receive his entitlement – he was

believed to be lost overboard from the Union Steamship *Rotorua* en route to Onehunga on the night of 29 September 1889, when he was returning home from Parliament. At 10 pm he had been seen asleep in his cabin by the steward. In the morning an officer went to arouse him for breakfast but found his cabin empty. It was surmised that he had become seasick and had gone to the side of the steamer. The sea was rough, and a sudden roll of the ship probably sent Jackson overboard in the darkness with none to see or hear him. His watch with chain was found under his pillow in his cabin (now in the family collection), along with his purse, and pocket-book. Possibly Jackson committed suicide as he was in some financial difficulties. Some ex-Forest Rangers reported seeing and speaking to Jackson later than 1889 in the goldfields of California, indicating Jackson may have slipped out of New Zealand unnoticed.

Jackson was considered a skilful farmer, giving a helping hand to many ex-Forest Rangers who settled near his property on Picket Hill (Hairini). He was always regarded as their chief and leader. Later he went to live on his acre section in Kihikihi. Jackson gained the respect of Maori, and while residing in Kihikihi, Maori often crossed the confiscation line to talk with Jackson about their problems on his house porch. He was survived by his wife, Bridget, who later died 15 May 1913 and was buried in the Roman Catholic Cemetery, Hairini. After William's death, Bridget purchased land at Kihikihi in 1892, lots 35, 36 and 37. William was an Anglican and Bridget a Roman Catholic, and it was common knowledge at the time that religion was the cause of much strife between them. They had no family. A rather battered foolscap account book, labelled on the back "Troop Accounts Te Awamutu Volunteer Cavalry, 1878" is believed to have been his. This book contains Conditions of Enlistment of Volunteer Militia Settlers; a form of oath; names of men enlisted in the Forest Rangers (incomplete) with personal details; and accounts of the Te Awamutu cavalry unit. The book is now held in the Te Awamutu District Museum.

James Cowan remembers "Some of the Rangers were our neighbours at Kihikihi, and Major Jackson's house on Kenny's Hill seemed to command the scene of the soldier settlement as he had commanded the men in the field in the years of the Waikato conquest. The Major was sturdy and square and blocky of figure, with a habitual air of determination and resolution. He was one of the few clean-shaven men in that era of luxuriant whiskers. The most he permitted himself to wear in the way of face adornment was his closely trimmed sideburns."

A *New Zealand Herald* obituary, dated 30 September 1889, states "Jackson was as vigorous a politician as he had been a soldier. He made his presence felt among the Atkinson Ministry, in which he was whip for three sessions, and he not infrequently proved a thorn in the side of the administration by his assiduous championing [often considered to be hot-headed], in season and out, of the rights of the men who had fought in the Maori wars and who, at the end of hostilities, found themselves with neither possessions nor prospects. Captain Jackson was more a guerrilla than a trained soldier, and everything he achieved in the field was the result of unorthodoxy of a kind that irked, and sometimes incensed, the hard core of regular soldiers who commanded most of the colonial detachments. Thus he had much in common with von Tempsky."

New Zealand Medal named to Forest Rangers. Medal claim dated 22 March 1870. The Medal Application states "**Address:** Rangiaowhia, Waikato. **Corps:** No. 1 Forest Rangers. Major. Three years service. **Field service:** Three years. Orakau [31 March-2 April 1864]." Jackson's medal was first sent to Hamilton but was returned to Wellington as Jackson was attending the General Assembly there. Received land: town lot No. 80, Kihikihi; farm lot Nos. 271, 272, 272A, 273 and 278, Puniu. Medal claim, AD32/3194; AD36/3/1165

Samuel JACOB

Original Company: 11-25 August 1863. Private. Sailed to New Zealand aboard *John Scott*, March 1859.

Henry JEFFARES

5, No. 2 Company: 18 May 1865 – December 1866 (last known month of service). Private. Substitute for Hearfield. Left unit for a period (granted passage to Auckland) and re-enlisted (28 November 1865) at Patea. Received land: town lot No. 24 Harapepe; farm lot No. 196, Pirongia.

James JENNINGS

51, No. 1 Company: 29 February – 10 November 1864. Private. Earlier served 2nd Regiment Waikato Militia, No. 51, (joined 24 August 1863 at Sydney). Later served Hawke's Bay Military Settlers, No. 145. Age: 30 years. Height: 5' 8". Hair colour: brown. Eye colour: blue. Complexion: reddish. Occupation: farmer. Country: Ireland. Religion: Roman Catholic. Born 1834, Charlestown, Galway, Ireland. Sailed to New Zealand aboard *Lord Ashley*.
New Zealand Medal named to Forest Rangers. Medal claim dated 17 October 1870. The Medal Application states "**Address:** Clifton, Greymouth, Westland. **Corps:** Forest Rangers – 10 months. Col Fraser's Co. of Military Settlers 18 months. Private. Regt number for latter Co. 145. **Field service:** Two years. Engaged at the following places: Orakau, 1st & 2nd April 1864. [The following actions are with the Hawke's Bay Military Settlers.] At Pukemaire, Waiapu [3rd] October 1865. Also near East Cape, same month. Also at Waerengaahika at Poverty Bay, near Bishop Williams' House, [15-21] November 1865. Te Wairoa [Omaru-hakeke, near Wairoa], 25th December 1865. **Remarks:** The only officer, now alive, who can certify to the above is Major Westrup. From memory, I have given dates and places to the best of my ability. I have also been under fire in many minor affairs." Medal claim AD32/3206; AD36/3/1187

William JOHNS

1090, No. 1 Company: 17 November 1863 – November 1867 (last known month of service). Private. Promoted to Corporal 11 January 1865. Enrolled at Auckland. Age: 22 years. Height: 5' 9". Hair colour: brown. Eye colour: blue. Complexion: fair. Occupation: sailor. Country: Wales. Religion: Episcopalian. Sworn in by Captain William Jackson. Born 1841, Dungarvon, Cardigan, Wales. Received land: town lot No. 8 Kihikihi; farm lot Nos. 214, 215 and 281, Puniu. Present at reunion to commemorate 50 years of battle of Orakau, 1914. Medal claim AD32/213; AD36/3/1224

Alfred JOLLEY (JOLLY)

368, No. 1 Company: 15 January 1865 – (discharge date unknown). Private. Earlier served 2nd Regiment Waikato Militia, No. 368. Enrolled at Kihikihi, Te Awamutu. Age: 35 years. Occupation: miner. Religion: Episcopalian. Sworn in by Major William Jackson. Born 1830, Edmonton, Middlesex, England. Received land: town lot No. 356, Kihikihi; farm lot No. 316, Puniu.

William JONES

No. 2 Company: 11 January – (month unknown) 1865. Private. Served on both West Coast and East Coast.

Hamiora KAIWHAKATAKA

No. 2 Company: Period of service unknown. Private.
New Zealand Medal named to Native Contingent. Medal claim dated 12 October 1912 and received 5 December 1912. The medal was officially renamed, erasing the name of Private Thomas Jones, 3rd Regiment Waikato Militia. Dates "1861-66" were also deleted and polished. The Medal Application states "**Address:** Te Arai, Manutuke. **Corps:** Forest Rangers in 1865. Native Contingent. In Forest Rangers 6 months and in Native Contingent about 2 years. **Field service:** About 9 months. Actually under fire at Waerengaahika [15-21 November 1865]; Paparatu [20 July 1868]; Pukepuke [20 November 1868]; Makaretu [3 December 1868] and Ngatapa [1-5

January 1869]." John Brooking, once a member of the Poverty Bay Mounted Rifle Volunteers, stated in a declaration with Kaiwhakataka's medal application "I was present at the fight against Te Kooti and his followers in that year [1868] at Paparatu after their landing at Whareongaonga [after their escape from the Chatham Islands]. We had only 30 rounds of ammunition per man when the fight began. We were greatly outnumbered – and our arms were defective. When our ammunition was expanded and we were forced to retire under a heavy fire from the enemy, a considerable number of Maori arrived – but the only ones among them that came to our assistance were Hamiora Kaiwhakataka (the applicant), Paora Kate, Wi Maki and Wi Rangiwhaitiri who was killed as soon as he reached us. When we were retiring I saw Hamiora Kaiwhakataka with us, and heard him encouraging the men telling them not to get demoralised – but to retire gradually and keep our front to the enemy." Kaiwhakataka signed his medal application form with a mark. Medal claim AD32/522

Rio KAWITI

Served 6 December 1865 – February 1866. Private. Enlisted at Woodall's Redoubt. Discharged at Wanganui.

Thomas KEENA

Original Company: 11 August – 10 November 1863. Private. **32, No. 2 Company:** 24 November 1863 – December 1867 (last known month of service). Private. Born Wales. Received land: town lot No. 63 Harapepe; farm lot No. 155, Pirongia.

David KENEALY (KINEALY)

Service in Forest Rangers doubtful: no record of period of service, no record of his name on any Forest Ranger roll or pay sheet. Believed to be a bogus Forest Ranger. Earlier served 58th Regiment, No. 2550; Remuera Rifle Volunteers. Born Cork, Ireland. Sailed to New Zealand aboard *True Britton*, 1853.
Never received the New Zealand Medal. Made three known applications for New Zealand Medal with a few letters in support, each time fabricating his service with the Forest Rangers. His details progressively get more unbelievable with each application! His earliest letter states "I served under Major Jackson in the Forest Rangers. I do not know when I joined . I served for 3 or 4 years. I never applied for land – I stayed with the Company until it was struck off pay." His applications dated (1) 26 October 1896, (2) 7 September 1900, and (3) 20 September 1910 variously state "**Address:** Hauraki Road, Remuera, Auckland. **Corps:** (1) Capt. Jackson's Forest Rangers as Private, three years, 1863-64-65. (2) I purchased my discharge from H.M. 58th Regiment of Foot on 30 October 1858 to settle in the colony of New Zealand. I joined the City Rifles 6 months afterwards and in 1864, I volunteered for active service to Jackson's Forest Rangers. **Field service:** (1) Three years, in several skirmishes with Natives in the Hunua-Wairoa valley, ranges and elsewhere. (2) 3 months, 14 days. Engaged in the action at Kirikiri Ranges, Hunua Block, between Wairoa and Papakura. With the imperial forces. I was disabled by running a piece of supplejack through my boot into my foot. After my foot was alright I was appointed Sergt and Drill Instructor to Remuera Rifle Volunteers with Capt. David Graham. (3) 3 months, 14 days. Wounded in the foot. Do not remember dates. Seven years service all together. Was drill instructor to the volunteers. Was in the first company formed." In a letter dated 16 December 1896 Kenealy states "I ran a piece of supplejack, which had been cut on a survey track, in to the instep of my foot and was so injured by it that I was not able to march. I had the privilege of going to Hospital or to my own home. Being a married man I preferred to go home and was attended by Doctor Goldsborough. I was several weeks laid up and it was months before I was properly well. I was then appointed drill instructor to the Remuera Volunteers in which I remained for over 7 years." Land claim rejected 1887. Medal claim AD32/222

James KIELY
Served 5 December 1865 – 29 January 1866. Private. Earlier served Taranaki Military Settlers, No. 449. Later served No. 4 Division Armed Constabulary. Enlisted in Forest Rangers at Wanganui. Born 1831, Manchester, England.

Reuben Charles KNIGHT
Served 12 November – January 1866 (last known month of service). Private. Earlier served 2nd Regiment Waikato Militia, No. 158 (joined 21 August 1863 at Sydney, Australia. Occupation: blacksmith). Present at Otapawa, 14 January 1866. Born 1828, Gloucestershire, England. Sailed to New Zealand aboard *William Denny* 1856. Medal claim AD32/133; AD36/3/1298

John KNOWLES
Original Company: 11 August – 10 November 1863. Private. Sailed to New Zealand aboard *Royal Charlie* July 1862.

Angus A. LANDER
33, No. 2 Company: 2 April 1864 – 10 July 1866. Private. Sailed to New Zealand aboard *William Denny*, 1856.

Laurence LAURENSEN
1326, No. 1 Company: 11 December 1864 – 30 January 1865. Private. Substitute for No. 1094 John Morgan. Enrolled at Auckland. Age: 31 years. Height: 5' 5½". Hair colour: light. Eye colour: blue. Complexion: ruddy. Occupation: seaman. Country: Scotland. Religion: Presbyterian. Sworn in by Major William Jackson. Born 1833, North Nesting Bay, Shetlands.

William LEE
1267, No. 1 Company: 1 July 1864 – January 1867 (last known month of service). Private. Earlier served Auckland Militia; 3rd Regiment Waikato Militia, No. 488. Enrolled at Pukerimu, Cambridge. Residence: Auckland. Age: 28 years. Height: 5' 7½". Hair colour: brown. Eye colour: blue. Complexion: sallow. Occupation: seaman. Country: Ireland. Religion: Roman Catholic. Sworn in by Major William Jackson. Signed enlistment with a mark. Absent without pay for one day 28 September 1864. Born 1834, Arklow, Wicklow. Sailed to New Zealand aboard *Alice Cameron* September 1862. Served on West Coast. Received land: town lot No. 72 Kihikihi; farm lot No. 178, Puniu. Possibly received impressed **New Zealand Medal** named to the Commissariat Transport Corps for service with the Waikato Militia.

Carl LIEBIG
34, No. 2 Company: 16 January 1864 – 22 September 1865. Private. Substituted by Gillanders. Earlier served 2nd Regiment Waikato Militia, No. 1031. Discharged in Wanganui district. Occupation: miller. Born 1830, Prussia. Naturalised in New Zealand, 1863.
New Zealand Medal named to Forest Rangers. Medal claim dated 11 July 1871. The Medal Application states "**Address:** Coromandel. **Corps:** [includes] … six months service in the 2nd Waikato [Militia] No. 10 Company under Capt. Davidson. … transferred to Major von Tempsky's Forest Rangers No. 2 Company on the 15th January 1864 and served to my discharge from Major von Tempsky and Lieutenant Westrup on the 22nd September 1865. **Field service:** I joined General Cameron's forces at Whatawhata, it then being in the field on the 15th Feb 64 and continued in the field to 22 Sept 65. I was at a general engagement at Paterangi [Waiari, 11 February] in 64 being the same engagement where Major Heaphy won his Victoria Cross. Also two engagements at Rangiaowhia [also Hairini, 21-22 February 1864] when Colonel Nixon was deadly wounded. One engagement at Orakau [31 March-2 April 1864]. Also at Wanganui at the battle of Kakaramea [13 May] in 65. … At the battle of Kakaramea as Major George can testify I

almost without any assistance had to cut a new track through the bush for a distance of two miles in order to carry our wounded men through as we could not get back again over the Gentle Annie with our wounded. I am a Prussian Hussar and only fought for Queen Victoria for honour in New Zealand." In a letter accompanying his application to the Defence Minister, Liebig states "I joined the 2nd Waikato's No. 10 Company, Commanded by Captain Davidson in 1863 – but seeing that there was no chance of any immediate engagement with the enemy I forthwith got myself transferred to Major von Tempsky's Rangers. I was first under fire in a general engagement at Paterangi; 2nd engagement at Rangiaowhia which lasted for two days; 3rd at Orakau. On the 6th April 1865 I volunteered to Wanganui where I was under fire at the battle of Kakaramea under Major von Tempsky. Afterwards under fire at Patea. In conclusion I may inform you that I am a Prussian by birth and served my time as a soldier in the Hussars and that I only fought in New Zealand for the honour and if any honour is to be conferred on any one, I consider that I am fairly entitled to my share." Medal claim AD32/3381; AD36/3/1362

James LINDSAY

35, No. 2 Company: 21 January 1864 – July 1865 (last known month of service). Private.
New Zealand Medal named to Forest Rangers. Medal claim dated 6 March 1899 and received 13 April 1899. Medal issued 11 November 1899. The medal was officially renamed erasing an already named/unclaimed medal. The Medal Application states "**Address:** Palmerston, Port Darwin, Northern Territory, Australia. **Corps:** Rank: Private. Forest Rangers. Served for 3 years. **Field service:** Served three years on the Waikato and Waipa. Present at Rangiaowhia [21 February 1864] and Hairini [22 February 1864] and Orakau [31 March-2 April 1864]. With General Chute [Taranaki campaign 1866]. **Remarks:** Officers: Major von Tempsky, Lieutenant Roberts, Ensign Sherret, and Non-Commissioned Officer McMinn." Died at Darwin, Australia. Medal claim AD32/4565; AD36/3/3058

Henry H. LLOYD

1348, No. 1 Company: 5 January 1864 – 13 November 1865. Private. Substitute for No. 1251 Edward Davis. Substituted by John Ryan. Earlier served 1st Regiment Waikato Militia; Colonial Defence Force, Auckland. Later served with Wanganui Bush Rangers on East Coast. Enrolled at Auckland. Age: 22 years. Height: 5' 9". Hair colour: dark. Eye colour: blue. Complexion: dark. Occupation: settler/farmer. Country: Ireland. Religion: Episcopalian. Sworn in by Major William Jackson. Served on West Coast. Born 1843, Rathkeale, Limerick, Ireland. Sailed to New Zealand aboard *Caduseus*, 1863. Possibly received impressed **New Zealand Medal** named to the Commissariat Transport Corps for service with the Colonial Defence Force.

Henry LONG

Original Company: 11 August – 10 November 1863. Private. **1096, No. 1 Company:** 17 November 1863 – November 1867 (last known month of service). Private. Promoted to Corporal 1 March 1864. Promoted to Sergeant. Enrolled at Papakura. Age: 24 years. Height: 5' 8" Hair colour: brown. Eye colour: grey. Complexion: fair. Occupation: farmer/labourer. Country: Ireland. Religion: Episcopalian. Sworn in by Captain William Jackson. Born 1838, Monaghan, Ireland. Sailed to New Zealand aboard *African* August 1862. Died 15 January 1905 and buried Hairini cemetery, Te Awamutu.
New Zealand Medal named to Forest Rangers. Medal claim dated 6 October 1874. The Medal Application states "**Address:** Te Awamutu, Waikato, Auckland. **Corps:** Jackson's Forest Rangers. Sergeant. Two years. **Field service:** Two years. Tuakau [skirmishing in the area] 1863. Paparata [13 December] 1863." Received land: town lot No. 77, Kihikihi; farm lot Nos. 176, 177 and 177A, Puniu. Medal claim AD32/4074; AD36/3/1392

James Richardson LOTT

36, No. 2 Company: 26 April 1864 – March 1866 (last known month of service). Private. Earlier served 1st Regiment Waikato Militia. Later served 1st Regiment Waikato Militia; No. 1 Division Armed Constabulary. Born 1841, Scarborough, Yorkshire, England. Sailed to New Zealand aboard *Queen of Beauty*, 1863. Received land including town lot No. 306, Opotiki.

John LYNCH

52, No. 2 Company: June – September 1866 (last known month of service). Private. Earlier served Royal Cavalry Volunteers, Howick Troop.
Made grant claim (AD32/2002) which is undated but believed to be post 1900. Uncertain whether a New Zealand Medal was issued. The grant claim states "**Address:** Rout Lane, off High Street, Auckland. **Corps:** Private in the Howick Cavalry Troop joining in 1863. **Field service:** Mostly despatch work." There is no mention of Forest Ranger service on the application. Received land: town lot No. 34, Harapepe; farm lot No. 263, Pirongia.

Frederick LYSAUGHT

1264, No. 1 Company: 17 June – 2 November 1864. Private. Substitute for Martin Nolan. Enrolled at Auckland. Age: 24 years. Height: 6' 1". Hair colour: dark. Eye colour: grey. Complexion: pale. Occupation: gentleman. Country: England. Religion: Roman Catholic. Born 1840, Cheltenham, Gloucestershire, England. Sailed to New Zealand aboard *Broadwater*, 1861.

George LYSAUGHT

1265, No. 1 Company: 24 June – 2 November 1864. Private. Substitute for 1253 Philip Gallie. Substituted by No. 1313 David Bruce. Enrolled at Auckland. Age: 25 years. Height: 6' 3$^{1}/_{2}$". Hair colour: dark. Eye colour: grey. Complexion: fair. Occupation: gentleman. Country: England. Religion: Roman Catholic. Born 1839, Cheltenham, Gloucestershire, England.

John N. McBAIN (MacBean)

963, No. 1 Company: 25 January – 13 May 1865. Private. Earlier served 2nd Regiment Waikato Militia, No. 963. Occupation: miner. Received bullet wound to head at Kakaramea near Patea, 13 May 1865, and died during the return to base. He was buried there temporarily, and conveyed to camp on the following day. Born 1835, Strath Spey, Inverness, Scotland. His wife received land including town lot No. 348, Kihikihi. **New Zealand Medal** issued to next of kin 12 October 1871.

Patrick McCARTHY

40, No. 2 Company: 16 June 1864 – April 1867 (last known month of service). Private. Earlier served Mauku Rifle Volunteers.
New Zealand Medal named to Forest Rangers. Medal claim dated 12 March 1870. The Medal Application states "**Address:** P.O. Shortland [Grahamstown]. **Corps:** Mauku Volunteer Rifles [10 October 1863 – 13 February 1864]. No. 2 Company Forest Rangers. Private. Served from July 1863 to about May 1865 [includes service in Mauku Rifle Volunteers]. **Field service:** From July 1863 to May 1865. Engagements at Titi near Mauku on 24 [actually 23rd] October 1863 under Captain Lusk [with Mauku Rifle Volunteers]. Engaged at Kakaramea near Wanganui [13 May 1865]. Pukemaire near Waiapu [3 October 1865]. Poverty Bay [Waerengaahika, 15-21 November 1865]. Weraroa pa, Wanganui [21 July 1865]. **Remarks:** Never before any officer for misconduct." Received land: town lot No. 15, Harapepe; farm lot No. 101, Pirongia. Medal claim AD32/3618; AD36/3/1601

Andrew Galbraith McCLYMONT

41, No. 2 Company: 11 January 1864 – July 1865 (last known month of service). Private. Earlier served 3rd Regiment Waikato Militia, No. 1094. Died at Ardmore.

New Zealand Medal named to Forest Rangers. Medal claim dated 11 April 1871. The Medal Application states "**Address:** Papakura. **Corps:** No. 2 Company, Forest Rangers. Private – 18 months. **Field service:** Mangapiko [Waiari, 11 February 1864], Rangiaowhia [21 February 1864], Orakau [31 March-2 April 1864]." Medal claim AD32/3628; AD36/3/1649

John McCULLOCH (McCULLOUGH)

1269, No. 1 Company: 16 July 1864 – October 1866 (last known month of service). Private. Enrolled at Pukerimu, Cambridge. Age: 21 years. Height: 5' 10". Hair colour: light. Eye colour: grey. Complexion: fair. Occupation: clerk. Country: Ireland. Religion: Presbyterian. Sworn in by Major William Jackson. Served on both West Coast and East Coast. Born 1842, Dromore, Armagh, Ireland. Received land: town lot No. 34, Kihikihi; farm lot No. 227, Puniu.

Hugh McDONALD

1093, No. 1 Company: 1 December 1863 – 18 March 1864. Private. Earlier served 2nd Regiment Waikato Militia. Enrolled in Otago on 10 November and sailed to Auckland and joining the corps 1 December (receiving pay from 10 November). Sent 18 March 1864 to Maketu by Captain Jackson from Pukerimu Redoubt, Cambridge in support of the Arawa Friendly Natives. Did not rejoin Forest Rangers. Possibly he was placed on McDonnell's Arawa acquittance roll while at Maketu. May have served later in Patea Field Force in 1868.

Moses McDONALD

962, No. 1 Company: 14 April 1864 – November 1865 (deserted). Private. Earlier served 2nd Regiment Waikato Militia, No. 962. Enrolled at Otago. Age: 23 years. Complexion: fair. Occupation: miner. Country: Scotland. Religion: Episcopalian. Born 1840, Staffordshire, England.

Charles McDONNELL

58, No. 2 Company: 1 November 1865 – December 1866 (last known month of service). Private. Later served 1st Regiment Waikato Militia, No. 1321; Te Awamutu Cavalry Volunteers. Received land: town lot No. 68, Harapepe; farm lot No. 119, Pirongia.

James McENANEY (McENANY)

70, No. 1 Company: 29 February 1864 – 31 July 1865. Private. Earlier served 2nd Regiment Waikato Militia, No. 70 (joined 25 September 1863 at Sydney, Australia. Occupation: confectioner); Baker in Imperial Commissariat. Later served 1st Regiment Waikato Militia, No. 1393. Age: 20 years. Height: 5' 8". Hair colour: brown. Eye colour: brown. Complexion: sallow. Occupation: baker. Country: Ireland. Religion: Roman Catholic. Born 1833, Monaghan, Ireland. Sailed to New Zealand aboard *Lord Ashley* 1863. Received land including town lot No. 294, Opotiki.

Edward McGRATH

23, No. 2 Company: 15 September 1864 – January 1867 (last known month of service). Private. Promoted to Corporal. Substitute for John Freeman. Earlier served 40th Regiment, No. 2843. Later served No. 2 Division Armed Constabulary. Served on West Coast. Broken service with discharge mid 1865. Granted passage to Auckland. Re-enlisted 20 November 1865 in Wanganui district. Received land: town lot No. 99, Harapepe; farm lot No. 126, Pirongia.

James McGREGOR

Original Company: 11 August – 10 November 1863. Private. Promoted to Sergeant 26 September to replace Dunn who deserted. Earlier served 58th Regiment, No. 1398. Sailed to New Zealand aboard *Indian Empire*, October 1862.

James McGUIRK

42, No. 2 Company: 6 April 1864 – December 1867 (last known month of service). Private. Promoted to Corporal, 1 April 1865. Earlier served 1st Regiment Waikato Militia, No. 740 (joined 1 September 1863 at Ballarat, Australia). Occupation: miner. Born 1830, Rathdrum, Wicklow, Ireland. Sailed to New Zealand aboard *Star of India*, 1863. Died 20 May 1922 and buried Harapepe cemetery.

New Zealand Medal named to Forest Rangers. Medal claim dated 28 March 1870. The Medal Application states "**Address:** Harapepe, Waikato. **Corps:** 2nd Company Forest Rangers. Corporal from 19th September 63 [includes service in Waikato Militia] to 4th June 66 [still received pay after this date while at Harapepe]. Regimental No. 42. **Field service:** 19th October 63 to 4th June 1866. Kakaramea 13th May 65, Major von Tempsky in command. Pukemaire 3rd October 65, Major Fraser in command. Waerengaahika 17th, 18th, 19th, 20th, 21st & 22nd November 65, Major Fraser in command. Captain Westrup commanding company." In a declaration for Elston's medal application McGuirk states "... at Weraroa [21 July 1865], Wanganui District and went to the relief of Pipiriki [19-30 July 1865]." Present at reunion to commemorate 50 years of battle of Orakau, 1914. Received land: town lot No. 100, Harapepe; farm lot Nos. 121 and 199A, Pirongia. Medal claim AD32/3666; AD36/3/1620. Medal and cap badge held in the Te Awamutu District Museum.

John Richard McHERRON

55, No. 2 Company: 1 December 1864 – August 1865 (last known month of service). Private. Earlier served on Her Majesty's Colonial Sloop of War *Victoria* during 1860-61 as a Petty Officer. Claimed land H13, 1898. Later resided at Nine Mile Beach, Charleston.

In an attempt to claim land, McHerron stated in a letter dated 29 May 1894 "I have served in the Forest Rangers under Major von Tempsky for three years [an exaggeration] during the Maori war, thereby becoming entitled to fifty acres of land and a town allotment. I got my discharge papers but left the North Island without taking up the land or otherwise. I had served as captain of the foretop on the steamer *Victoria* during its cruise about Australia and through the Gulf of Carpentaria in search of Burke and Wells. ... I got my discharge from the *Victoria* and had it with the other discharge papers in a box which was consumed by a fire that occurred in my dwelling." This information is on file AD32/4595.

Peter McKELSON

Served 2 December 1865 – disbandment, 30 October 1867. Private. Enlisted at Wanganui.

Edward McKENNA VC

Served 14 December 1865 – 31 March 1866. Ensign. Colour Sergeant McKenna of the 65th Regiment was awarded the Victoria Cross (*London Gazette* 16 January 1864) for bravery in an engagement near Camerontown on 7 September 1863. He was promoted to Ensign on 8 September 1863. After his discharge in New Zealand he joined the Forest Rangers as Ensign and served throughout the Chute expedition. Born Leeds, Yorkshire, England. Died 1908, Wanganui. McKenna's Victoria Cross citation reads "For gallant conduct at the engagement near Cameron Town on 7 September 1863 after both his officers, Captain Smith and Lieutenant Butler, had been shot, in charging through the position of an enemy heavily outnumbering him, and drawing off his small force, consisting of two sergeants, one bugler and 35 men through a broken and rugged country with the loss of one man killed and another missing. Lieut-General Cameron C.B. commanding Her Majesty's Forces in that Colony, reports that in Colour-Sergeant McKenna the detachment found a commander whose coolness, intrepidity and judgement justified the confidence placed in him by the soldiers brought so suddenly under his command."

Daniel McKENZIE

953, No. 1 Company: 15 April 1864 – February 1867 (last known month of service). Private. Earlier served 2nd Regiment Waikato Militia, No. 9 Company. Later served No. 1 Division Armed Constabulary. Date of transfer 15 April 1864. Enrolled 12 August 1863 at Otago. Age: 31 years. Height: 5' 9". Hair colour: light. Eye colour: grey. Complexion: fair. Occupation: miner. Country: Scotland. Religion: Presbyterian. Born Kilmarnoch, Scotland. Received land: town lot No. 202, Kihikihi; farm lot No. 237, Puniu. Medal claim AD36/3/1602

William McKENZIE

Original Company: 11 August – 10 November 1863. Colour Sergeant.

Edward Graham McMINN

Original Company: 26 August – 11 November 1863. Private. **37, No. 2 Company:** 30 November 1863 – December 1867 (last known month of service). Private. Promoted to Corporal 1 December 1863. Promoted to Staff Sergeant 10 March 1864. Later served No. 5 Division Armed Constabulary, No. 32 (joining 14 March 1868; aged 24; 5' 11" in height); Te Awamutu Cavalry Volunteers. Born 1844, Dundonald Down, Scotland. Sailed to New Zealand aboard *Mermaid* October 1859. Became Member of Parliament for Waipa. Died 28 March 1883 and buried Pirongia cemetery, near Te Awamutu.
Made two medal claims, dated 12 March 1870 and 21 October 1872. Both applications were rejected because of McMinn's involvement in the No. 5 Division Armed Constabulary mutiny. **Was refused the New Zealand Medal.** The Medal Applications state "**Address:** Harapepe, Waikato. **Corps:** 2nd Company, Forest Rangers. Staff Sergeant. 26 August 1863 to 7 October 1868 [first application]; 30 November 1863 to 1 November 1866 and No. 32 Senior Sergeant No. 5 Div. A.C. 14 March 1868 to 9 October 1868 [second application]. **Field service:** Numerous actions listed with dates: Mangapiko [Waiari], 11 February 1864; Rangiaowhia, 21 and 22 February 1864; Orakau, 31 March, 1 and 2 April 1864, Te Ngutu o te Manu, 21 August 1868; Te Ruaruru [final battle at Te Ngutu o te Manu] 7 September 1868. **Remarks:** Captain von Tempsky commanding Company at Mangapiko, Rangiaowhia and Orakau. Lieutenant-General Cameron in command. Major von Tempsky commanding Division at Te Ngutu o te Manu and Te Ruaruru. Colonel McDonnell in command." Written across the application "Rejected for mutinous conduct in the field." Received land: town lot No. 11, Harapepe; farm lot Nos. 159A, 160A, 163 and 164, Pirongia. Medal claim: AD36/3/1619

Alexander Fortescue McNAMARA

Original Company: 11 August – 11 November 1863. Private. **No. 1 Company:** 17 November – 9 December 1863. Private. **No. 2 Company:** 10 December 1863 – 20 April 1864. McNamara was transferred to No. 2 Company and promoted to Corporal dated 10 December 1863. Demoted from Corporal to Private 22 February 1864 for drunkenness. Discharged for drunkenness. Occupation: miner. Sworn in by Captain William Jackson.
New Zealand Medal named to Forest Rangers. Medal claim dated 29 September 1911 and received the medal 29 May 1912. Because of the late issue, medal was officially renamed erasing the naming of T. Acheson, Auckland Militia and dates "1861-66" on the reverse were deleted and polished. The Medal Application states "**Address:** Murchison. **Corps:** First in Major Jackson's corps of Forest Rangers and afterwards in Major von Tempsky's corps of Forest Rangers. **Field service:** 1863-64. Under fire several times but cannot remember the Maori names of the places."
In a letter accompanying the application (dated 13 September 1911) McNamara states "I was a private in Major Jackson's Forest Rangers. Col. Roberts was a Sergeant. I was transferred into von Tempsky's corps as a Corporal. I was wounded in action. I had my cap and some hair shot off while on sentry duty. I think at Waiuku [1863]. I was in many skirmishes. I was about 2 years in

the Forest Rangers [he was discharged for drunkenness after serving less than one year]. I never got a medal. I got £25 about 15 years ago in lieu of grant of land. I was discharged because I was incapacitated from active service. Never did anything unworthy of a soldier." Applied for a war pension in 1908. Received land H36C, 1892. Medal claim AD32/262; AD36/3/3151

Patrick MADIGAN (Patsy)

1091, No. 1 Company: 27 November 1863 – 1 July 1864. Private. Enrolled at Papakura. Born in Ireland 1843. Emigrated to New Zealand arriving 1849. Age: 20 years. Height: 5' 6$^{1}/_{2}$". Hair colour: black. Eye colour: grey. Complexion: dark. Occupation: farmer/labourer. Country: Ireland. Religion: Roman Catholic. Sworn in by Captain William Jackson. Sailed to New Zealand aboard *Caduseus*, 1863. Madigan was absent (received no pay) from unit 31 April to 18 May 1864. He was probably searching for a substitute for himself and received permission to leave the unit to do so.

New Zealand Medal named to Forest Rangers. Medal claim dated 13 January 1870. Medal issued 31 October 1879. The Medal Application states "**Address:** Auckland. **Corps:** No. 1 Company, Forest Rangers. **Field service:** 13th December 1863, engaged against the natives at Paparata. Officer commanding Captain William Jackson. 11 February 1864, engaged against the natives before Paterangi [Waiari on the Mangapiko Stream, 11 February 1864], Waikato. Officer commanding Captain William Jackson." The early hand-written medal application is signed by "William Jackson, Major". Became Sergeant, No. 5 Company, 3rd Battalion Auckland Militia. He was sworn in by Colonel Balneavis in February 1860 aged 16, and served until 1863. Joined No. 1 Company Forest Rangers at Papakura as a Private 27 November 1863. Appears on Forest Rangers pay rolls up to 30 June 1864. Madigan was present at Kirikiri 22 July 1863, two miles from Papakura on the Clevedon Road, near Ring's Redoubt. After settlers were attacked by 40-50 Maori, a band of 16 volunteers, including Madigan, under Captain Clare rushed to the scene from Papakura and were soon joined by regulars. Together they pushed the Maori up the slope, suffering two dead and four wounded. Was also present at Paparata 13 December 1863, Waiari 11 February 1864, Rangiaowhia 21 February 1864, Hairini 22 February 1864 and Orakau 31 March-2 April 1864. Madigan states in a pension claim (dated 2 July 1910) that he served in the Forest Rangers until 1866, total active service of 6 years, 39 months of this time engaged against the "Queen's enemies". Resided at 50 Pollen Street, Grey Lynn and later at Wynyard Road, Mount Eden, Auckland. Worked as a gaoler at Mount Eden Prison, Auckland. Had five unofficial clasps made and fitted onto the ribbon of his New Zealand Medal. Engraved on these were "Kirikiri", "Paparata", "Waiari", "Rangiaowhia" and "Orakau". Present at reunion to commemorate 50 years of battle of Orakau, 1914. Medal in private collection. Medal claim AD32/3458; AD36/3/1458

Philip MAGILL (McGILL)

37, No. 2 Company: 11 January 1864 – July 1865 (last known month of service). Private. Earlier served 3rd Regiment Waikato Militia, No. 1119. Von Tempsky misspelled Magill's name as Mogol and Magole in his writings.

Stephen MAHONEY

Original Company: 11 August – 11 November 1863. Private. **1092, No. 1 Company:** 17 November 1863 – May 1866 (last known month of service). Private. Later served 1st Regiment Waikato Militia from 25 May 1866. Enrolled at Papakura. Residence: Auckland. Age: 25 years. Height: 5' 6". Hair colour: brown. Eye colour: grey. Complexion: dark. Occupation: bushman. Country: Ireland. Religion: Roman Catholic. Sworn in by Captain William Jackson. Signed enlistment with a mark. Born 1838, Cork, County Cork, Ireland. Sailed to New Zealand aboard *Jura* January 1860.

New Zealand Medal named to Forest Rangers. Medal claim dated 28 April 1871. The Medal

Application states "**Address:** Te Teko, Matata, East Coast. **Corps:** Forest Rangers No. 2 Compy under Major Jackson. Private. 3 years and 3 months. **Field service:** At Orakau [31 March-2nd] April 1864 under General Cameron." The medal application was made on a beautifully handwritten form (not printed Government form) written by another person as Mahoney could not write. Received land including town lot No. 21, Opotiki. Medal claim AD32/3466; AD36/3/1505

Rawiri MAKI (Ra Mackay or Maki Rawiri)

No. 2 Company: Private. Joined during 1865. Dates of service unknown but served about 12 months. Probably a guide.
New Zealand Medal named to Forest Rangers. Medal claim dated 15 June 1914 and issued 21 September 1914. The medal was officially renamed, erasing the name of Private William Ball, 1st Regiment Waikato Militia. Dates "1861-66" on the reverse were deleted and polished. The Medal Application states "**Address:** Made claim c/o George Hill (New Zealand Cross holder), Melrose, Devonport, Auckland. **Corps:** No. 2 Company, von Tempsky's Forest Rangers. Served for 12 months in this unit. **Field service:** Under fire at Waerengaahika [15-21 November 1865], Poverty Bay, November 1865, under the command of Captain Westrup." In a declaration in support of Maki's medal application George Hill states "I George Hill NZC certify that Ra Mackay was in my company of No. 2 Forest Rangers during the attack on the Waerengaahika pa at Poverty Bay and was under fire for nearly a week at that place. He was also under the late Major Biggs at Paparatu [20 July 1868] and subsequently at Ruakituri [8 August 1868] under Colonel Whitmore and is quite entitled to the New Zealand Medal". Medal held in Auckland Institute and Museum collection. Medal claim AD32/1238; AD36/3/3613

James Robert MALCOLM

Served 3 December 1865 – 7 January 1866. Private. Enlisted at Wanganui. Served in initial stages of Chute's expedition, being severely wounded in right leg on entering Te Putahi pa, 7 January 1866. Born 1839, Dundee, County Angus, Scotland. Name appears on Wanganui War Memorial.

David MANNING

Original Company: 11 August – 10 November 1863. Private. Sailed to New Zealand aboard *City of Poonah* August 1848.

Nicholas MARSH

22, No. 2 Company: 17 June 1865 – September 1867 (last known month of service). Private. Earlier served 2nd Regiment Waikato Militia, No. 1357, from 1 February-13 June 1865. Later served Armed Constabulary. Born 1843, Ravensthorpe, Northampton, England. Sailed to New Zealand aboard *Eagle Speed*, 1864.
New Zealand Medal application refused because Marsh was not under fire in any engagement with the enemy. Medal claim dated 2 March 1914. The Medal Application states "**Address:** Aln Street, Oamaru. **Corps:** 2nd Waikato Regiment for 10 months as a Private. No. 2 Forest Rangers for 12 months as a Private. Thames Volunteers (Tararu Rifles) as Corporal for about 5 months. Served for about 9 years with the Armed Constabulary." Marsh states in a letter accompanying his medal application, dated 11 March 1914 "First joined No. 1 Company, 2nd Waikato Regiment. In 1865 joined von Tempsky's Forest Rangers. Got land at Harapepe [near Te Awamutu] and remained there till Thames goldrush broke out and went to Thames November 1867. About 1869 the Government sent to Thames asking for volunteers to go to Alexandra [Pirongia], Waikato as Alexandra was in danger of being attacked by Te Kooti. Captain Finerty raised a company and I went with him as a non-commissioned officer. Remained there four or five months and built a small blockhouse. Danger being over we returned to Thames and were thanked by the Government for services. Te Kooti did not attack Alexandra. Joined the Armed

Constabulary in January 1870. Went to Taupo from Wellington. Met at Napier by Captain Swindley. After 5 days march reached Opepe [outside Taupo]. Two days after arrival an expedition was organised to go after Te Kooti. I went with them but did not meet him [Te Kooti]. About twelve months later went out again with Captain Gudgeon to try and check Te Kooti from getting into King Country but again he gave us the slip. We were out two or three months. In 1872 transferred from Taupo to Opotiki where remained for about five years serving under Major Goring and Major (now Colonel) Roberts. In 1878 sent to Cambridge, Waikato and after being there about six months applied for and received discharge from Colonel Lyons." Received land: town lot No. 28, Harapepe; farm lot No. 157, Pirongia. Medal claim AD32/1230

James William MARTIN

1353, No. 1 Company: 26 January 1865 – January 1867 (last known month of service). Private. Substitute for No. 1324 James Crawford. Enrolled at Kihikihi, Te Awamutu. Residence: Auckland. Single. Age: 34 years. Hair colour: light. Eye colour: hazel. Complexion: fresh. Occupation: seaman. Country: Surrey, England. Religion: Episcopalian. Saviour and cross on left arm. Sworn in by Major William Jackson. Born 1831, Rotherhythe, Surrey, England.
New Zealand Medal named to Forest Rangers. Medal received 29 November 1882. Transcript medal application states "**Address:** None given. **Corps:** Private. Forest Rangers. **Field service:** Waiapu [Pukemaire 3 October 1865]." Received land: town lot No. 199, Kihikihi; farm lot No. 236, Puniu. Medal claim AD36/3/2776

Robert Alexander MATHESON

1288, No. 1 Company: 17 August 1864 – September 1865 (last known month of service). Private. Substitute for No. 1110, George Ward. Enrolled at Pukerimu, Cambridge. Residence: Auckland. Age: 30 years. Height: 5' 9½". Hair colour: dark. Eye colour: grey. Complexion: fair. Occupation: miner. Country: Scotland. Religion: Presbyterian. Sworn in by Major William Jackson. Born 1833, Kilmore, Inverness, Scotland.

James MEDEX

Served 14 December 1865 – disbandment, 30 October 1867. Private. Enlisted at Wanganui.

Edward MELLON

No. 1 Company: (period of service unknown). Private. Earlier served Colonial Defence Force in Auckland. He was the last man to be enlisted on Jackson's roll of the No. 1 Company, Forest Rangers, but no dates are mentioned. Born 1842.
An application dated 24 February 1919 for a Military Pension on behalf of Mellon states "... enlisted as a trooper in the Colonial Defence Force at Otahuhu in July 1863 and was discharged at his own request, his period of service having expired. He also states he served in the Waikato Campaign in 1863 and 1864 and the Tauranga Campaign in 1864." There is no mention of service with the Forest Rangers. In answer the Commissioner of Pensions denied that Mellon received a medal which is incorrect. **New Zealand Medal** named to Auckland Cavalry Volunteers. Received land: town lot No. 213, Kihikihi; farm lot No. 245, Puniu. Medal claim AD32/1605; AD36/3/1412

William METHVEN

Original Company: 11 August – 10 November 1863. Private. Later served 1st Regiment Waikato Militia, No. 1424. Born 1832, Fife, Scotland. Made land claim for Forest Ranger service; received land including town lot No. 295 Opotiki for service in the Waikato Militia.

Edgar M. MITCHELL

24, No. 2 Company: 22 November 1864 – 6 March 1865. Private. Substitute for Robert Harkin.

Substituted by No. 24 John Burns. Earlier and later served 1st Regiment Waikato Militia. Also later served Armed Constabulary. Born 1841, Fianna, Antrim, Ireland. Sailed to New Zealand aboard *Star of India*, 1863. Possibly received impressed **New Zealand Medal** named to the Commissariat Transport Corps for service with the Waikato Militia.

Lawrence Bumford MITCHELL

38, No. 2 Company: 1 April 1864 – August 1866 (last known month of service). Private. Promoted to Sergeant in Wanganui district. Later served Patea Bush Rangers. Reduced to the rank of private for drunkenness and abuse of Lieutenant Pilmer. In a letter dated 12 February 1866 to Captain Holt, Under Secretary to the Defence Office, von Tempsky explains the unusual situation "… on the 9th of Jan. 1866, while on the march from Patea to Kakaramea, Sergeant Mitchell was drunk and used abusive language to Lieut. Pilmer. Sergeant Mitchell apologised the following morning but as this was the second time I had seen him drunk, and as this was the first time during a period of three years that any one of my officers had been spoken to in such a way, I saw the necessity of making an example. Being in the field and on a line of march where no duty day was given, I could not hold a Court Martial, neither could I carry with me a man in the position of prisoner; I therefore reduced Sergeant Mitchell on the spot." Von Tempsky went on to say that "Mitchell had done his duty over the last two years in an exemplary way". Received land: town lot No. 26, Harapepe; farm lot Nos. 192 and 199, Pirongia.

John MOHR

39, No. 2 Company: 29 November 1863 – 15 December 1864. Private. Substituted by No. 39 Colin Smith. Discharged at Pukerimu, Cambridge. Private. Earlier served Mauku Forest Rifles. Later served 2nd Regiment Waikato Militia. Born 1841, Fleisen, Germany.
New Zealand Medal named to Forest Rangers. Medal claim dated 9 June 1880. The Medal Application states "**Address:** Madras Street, Sydenham, Sydenham Bakery. **Corps:** Forest Rangers under Maj. von Tempsky. Private. 18 months service. No regimental number. **Field service:** 18 months. Mauku [Titi Hill, 23 October 1863, before joining Forest Rangers], Paterangi [Waiari, 11 February 1864], Rangiaowhia [21 February 1864], Orakau [31 March-2 April 1864]. **Remarks:** Was sworn in under Commissioner Naughton as special Constable. Was in the engagement when Lieut. Percival was killed [Titi Hill, 23 October 1863]." Medal claim AD1/1880/1000; AD36/3/2762

John MORGAN

Original Company: 26 August – 10 November 1863. Private. **1094, No. 1 Company:** 17 November 1863 – 10 December 1864. Private. Promoted to Corporal 17 March 1864. Earlier served Papakura Valley Rifle Volunteers (renamed later to Wairoa Rifles). Enrolled at Auckland. Residence: Wairoa, south Auckland. Age: 22 years. Height: 5' 7¹/₂". Hair colour: brown. Eye colour: blue. Complexion: sallow. Occupation: bushman. Country: England. Religion: Episcopalian. Sworn in by Captain William Jackson. Born 1842, St Philip, Gloucester, England.

James A. MORTON

Served 6 December 1865 – disbandment, 30 October 1867. Private. Earlier served Colonial Defence Force, Wellington. Later served 4th Regiment Waikato Militia. Enlisted in Forest Rangers at Wanganui. Born 1841, Swansea, Wales. Received land including town lot No. 267, Hamilton East.

Andrew MOYLAN

28, No. 2 Company: 16 December 1864 – August 1865 (last known month of service). Private. Substitute for Frederick Higgins. Earlier served 2nd Battalion, 14th Regiment, No. 1039; Colonial

Defence Force, Hawke's Bay. Land claim H23N, 1894. Has empty file at National Archives: AD32/4614.

Joseph MULLIGAN (MILLINGHAM)

6, No. 2 Company: 11 January 1864 – July 1866 (last known month of service). Private. Promoted to Corporal 16 May 1864. Earlier served 3rd Regiment Waikato Militia, No. 726. Born 1837. Received land: town lot No. 91, Harapepe; farm lot No. 181, Pirongia.

Colin MUNROE

No. 1 Company: 16 April 1866 – September 1867 (last known month of service). Private. Enrolled 16 April 1866 at Rangiaowhia, Te Awamutu. Residence: Te Rahu. Age: 42 years. Height: 5' 10". Hair colour: grey. Complexion: fair. Occupation: farmer. Country: Scotland. Religion: Presbyterian. Sworn in by Major William Jackson. Born 1825, Caithness, Scotland. Died 8 February 1908, Waipawa. Received land: town lot No. 207, Kihikihi; farm lot No. 331, Puniu.

John MURRAY

388, No. 1 Company: 14 December 1863 – 4 September 1864, when he deserted. Private. Earlier served 2nd Regiment Waikato Militia, No. 4 Company. Enrolled 15 August 1863 at Otago. Age: 30 years. Height: 5' 6½". Hair colour: dark. Eye colour: brown. Complexion: dark. Occupation: miner. Country: Scotland. Religion: Presbyterian. Born 1832, Cumnock, Scotland. Received no pay for the month of September 1864. Land claim H36C, 1892.

Robert W. MURRAY

1287, No. 1 Company: 17 August 1864 – September 1865 (last known month of service). Private. Substitute for No. 1112, William Williams. Enrolled at Pukerimu, Cambridge. Residence: Auckland. Age: 32 years. Height: 5' 7½". Hair colour: light. Eye colour: blue. Complexion: fresh. Occupation: engineer. Country: England. Religion: Episcopalian. Sworn in by Major William Jackson. Born 1832, St Lawrence, Kent, England.

John H. MUSKETT

Original Company: 11 August – 10 November 1863. Private. Sailed to New Zealand aboard *Egmont* July 1960.

Daniel Jenkins MUTTON

Original Company: 11 August – 10 November 1863. Private/Guide. Born 1834, St John's Thanet, Kent, England.
In an application for a pension, a reference from Alexander Hill states "... served with him during the Maori War in the Forest Rangers under Major Jackson and Captain von Tempsky and that through the war he was steady and brave, complimented by his officers, and beloved by the men. ... My father and mother, who lived at Hunua were in extreme danger during one period of the war, being in the centre of the disturbed district, that Daniel Mutton volunteered to go with me to rescue them, when even the soldiers held back, that he went through many risks and dangers with me, and I may say that mainly through his help and assistance at that time my father and mother were rescued, that during the time that I served with him, no one in the force bore a better character, for bravery, discipline and sobriety." This information on file AD32/312. Made land claim.

Robert NAPIER

43, No. 2 Company: 6 April 1864 – August 1865. Private. Earlier served 1st Regiment Waikato Militia, No. 804 (joined 1 September 1863 at Melbourne, Australia. Occupation: ironmonger). Born 1830, Dundee, Scotland. Sailed to New Zealand aboard *Star of India*. Died August 1865.

Henry William NAPPER
Original Company: 11-25 August 1863. Private. Born 1836, Kew, Surrey, England. Sailed to New Zealand aboard *Nourmahal* December 1859.

Robert NEIL
44, No. 2 Company: 11 January 1864 – September 1867 (last known month of service). Private. Earlier served 3rd Regiment Waikato Militia, No. 1144.
New Zealand Medal named to Forest Rangers. Medal claim dated 10 June 1871. The Medal Application states "**Address:** Papakura. **Corps:** 2nd Company Forest Rangers. Private. One year and seven months. **Field service:** Twelve months – 21st and 22nd Feb 1864 at Rangiaowhia [and Hairini] and at Orakau on 31st March and 1st [and 2nd] April 1864. **Remarks:** Belonged to Major von Tempsky's Company. At Rangiaowhia under Lieut. General Cameron and at Orakau under the same General." Died 19 February 1908, Pirongia. Received land: town lot No. 38, Harapepe; farm lot No. 258, Pirongia. Medal claim AD32/3720; AD36/3/1713

James NEWCASTLE
Original Company: 11 August – 11 November 1863. Private. Later served 3rd Regiment Waikato Militia. Builder. Born 1838, St Andrews, Bishop Auckland, Durham, England. Sailed to New Zealand aboard *Susanne* June 1863. Made land claim.

William Joseph NEWMAN
Served 2 December 1865 – January 1866 (last known month of service). Private. Enlisted at Wanganui.
New Zealand Medal named to Forest Rangers. Medal claim dated 22 January 1876. Medal issued 22 September 1876 at Newcastle, Australia. The Medal Application states "**Address:** Town and Country Journal Office, Sydney, New South Wales. **Corps:** Forest Rangers. Private. Five months. **Field service:** Four months. Okotuku [January 4 1866]. Te Putahi [7 January 1866]. Otapawa [14 January 1866]. Ketemarae [15 January 1866]. And several skirmishes at which a general or imperial officer was not present. March to Taranaki and return to Wanganui. Invalided in camp before Waikoko [1 February 1866]. I was the first man to enter the pa at Ketemarae, as, I think, Dr Featherston can testify to. **Remarks:** Having only received a discharge on paper when the Company was disbanded, and it having worn out since, this form is only filled from memory, but the books in the office will no doubt bear out the truth." A second Medal Application dated 22 February 1876 states "**Address:** Town and Country Journal Office. **Corps:** Private. Forest Rangers. **Field service:** Okotuku [Moturoa] 7 November 1868." There was some confusion as to which Rangers Newman belonged. Westrup, when approached by the Medal Commission, stated that Newman did not belong to the Forest Rangers believing he was with another company of rangers under Thomas McDonnell. Westrup's statement is probably incorrect. Westrup was on the East Coast at the time. Medal claim AD32/3732; AD36/3/1733

James E. NEWTON
Original Company: August – 10 November 1863. Private. Later served 3rd Regiment Waikato Militia. Born 1826, Norwich, England. Sailed to New Zealand aboard *Shalimar* December 1862.

John Charles NOLAN
1098, No. 1 Company: 28 November 1863 – 28 June 1864. Private. Enrolled 28 November 1863 at Papakura. Age: 22 years. Occupation: farmer. Religion: Roman Catholic. Sworn in by Captain William Jackson. Born 1841. Sailed to New Zealand aboard *Will o the Wisp*, 1852. Applied for an "Old Soldiers" grant in 1910. Grant information on file AD32/1813. Medal claim AD36/3/1707

Martin NOLAN

1097, No. 1 Company: 5 December 1863 – 15 June 1864. Private. Later served Armed Constabulary. Enrolled at Papakura. Age: 19 years. Occupation: labourer. Religion: Roman Catholic. Sworn in by Captain William Jackson. Born 1844. Sailed to New Zealand aboard *Invincible*, 1853.

First **New Zealand Medal** claim and issue 1871. Named to Forest Rangers. This medal was later lost. Duplicate New Zealand Medal also named to Forest Rangers. Medal renamed erasing the name of "J. Dingle" and dates "1861-66" on the reverse deleted and polished. Duplicate medal claim dated 13 September 1910. Medal issued 21 April 1913 at the cost of 7s. 6d. The duplicate Medal Application states "**Address:** C/o of H. Corles, 42 Cobden Street, Newton, Auckland, with actual address Parua Bay (engaged as a gumdigger). **Corps:** Forest Rangers." In a letter accompanying the second application, Nolan states "I served in Major Jackson's Forest Rangers. Engagements at Hunua Ranges at Paparata [13 December 1863], Paterangi [Waiari, 11 February 1864] and Rangiaowhia [21 February 1864] in the Waikato." Land claim H23, 1894. Medal claim AD32/548; AD36/3/1706

James O'BRIEN

Served 27 October – 11 December 1865. Private. Became substitute for Lloyd who was discharged on 13 November 1865. A short time later O'Brien was accidentally shot by a comrade, so he was substituted by John Ryan upon his own discharge. Earlier served Taranaki Military Settlers. Later served Taranaki Bush Rangers; No. 3 Division Armed Constabulary. Born 1845, Dublin, Ireland.

Patrick O'CONNELL

Served 23 October – 9 November 1865. Private. Enlisted at Wanganui.

Patrick O'CONNOR

Served 9 August 1865 – (dated of discharge unknown). Private. Served with Westrup's Company on East Coast.

James OSBORNE

392, No. 1 Company: 14 December 1863 – October 1866 (last known month of service). Private. Promoted to Corporal, 1 April 1865. Earlier served 2nd Regiment Waikato Militia, No. 4 Company. Enrolled 12 August 1863 at Auckland. Age: 20 years. Height: 5' 4". Hair colour: black. Eye colour: blue. Complexion: sallow. Occupation: seaman. Country: England. Religion: Presbyterian.

New Zealand Medal named to the Forest Rangers. Osborne made an early medal application, probably before forms were printed. In a letter of application dated 24 November 1869, Osborne states "I was a Corporal in No. 1 Compy Forest Rangers, and was in the engagement of Rangiaowhia, Waikato Feb [21st] 22nd, 1864. Lieut. Gen. Sir D. Cameron commanding and Capt. von Tempsky my immediate commanding officer. I was also present at the capture of Orakau, Waikato [31 March and] 1st and 2nd April 1864. Gen. Carey commanding and Capt. Jackson my immediate commanding officer. Also present at an engagement on the banks of the Patea River, near Kakaramea May 13th 1865. Major von Tempsky commanding and Lieut. C. Westrup my immediate commanding officer. I was also present at the capture of the Weraroa pa, Wanganui [21 July] August 1865. His Excellency Sir George Grey commanding and Lieut. Westrup my immediate commanding officer. I was present at an attack on the Pukemaire pa, Waiapu, East Cape, Oct 3rd 1865. Major Fraser commanding and Capt. Westrup my immediate commanding officer. I was present at the siege and capture of Waerengaahika pa, Poverty Bay and engaged from the [15th] 17th till 22nd November 1965. Major Fraser commanding and Capt. Westrup my immediate commanding officer. I completed the term of three years in the Forest

Rangers for which I have obtained a grant of 60 acres of land." Received land: town lot No. 40, Kihikihi; farm lot No. 267, Puniu. Medal claim AD32/3789; AD36/3/1737

William OSBORNE

No. 2 Company: Joined 1866 – (date of discharge unknown). Private. Substitute for Amelius Taylor. Earlier served 65th Regiment, No. 2988. Later served No. 7 Division Armed Constabulary. Born 1832, Peterborough, Cambridgeshire, England. Sailed to New Zealand aboard *Euphrates*, 1849. Received land: town lot No. 90, Harapepe; farm lot Nos. 193 and 195, Pirongia.

John OWENS

45, No. 2 Company: 26 March 1864 – 31 May 1865. Private. Earlier served 70th Regiment, No. 3403. Later served Wanganui Bush Rangers on East Coast. Discharged in the Wanganui district and granted a passage to Auckland. Sailed to New Zealand aboard *Daniel Rankin*, 1861.
Made an application for a land grant, dated 4 November 1890. Address given as Enfield Road, Napier. The application states "... All the officers under whose command I served being dead. I beg to request, you will be kind enough, to send me proof of my service – I joined the Forest Rangers in Feby 1864 and left in 1866 [31 May 1865]." This information is on file AD32/4577.

Daniel PARR

Original Company: 11 August – 11 November 1863. Private. Sailed to New Zealand aboard *Constance*, November 1861.

John Dawson PARSONS

Period of service unknown. Private. Later served Armed Constabulary. Born 28 August 1849 which makes him very young for Forest Ranger service. His claim to Forest Ranger service (mentioned below) may be fabricated. Brother of William (below). Died 16 May 1914 at Gisborne.
A letter written by the Commissioner of Pensions to New Zealand Military Forces, Wellington, dated 9 February 1914, states "Military Pension Claim 1451 – John Dawson Parsons. Would you be good enough to inform me whether there is any record of the issue of a New Zealand War Medal to the above-named applicant, particulars of whose service are as follows: **Corp:** Von Tempsky's Rifles and Forest Rangers. Rank: Guide. **Period of service:** 3 years. **Localities of actions:** Wanganui, Patea, Omarunui, Wairoa and Meanee. The applicant states that a medal was issued to him in the year 1878, and was subsequently lost in a flood at Meanee." The applicant's address is given as 52 Herbert Road, Gisborne. Parsons wrote to the Minister of Defence requesting a duplicate medal. He states "... in the year 1878 at Meanee, Hawke's Bay, I lost the whole of my personal effects (including the medal) by reason of a flood and as I am now an applicant for the military pension, I cannot produce the medal as evidence that I am entitled to the pension. [Signed], late von Tempsky's Forest Rangers." This information is on file AD32/1088. There is no reference to any medal being issued.

William D. PARSONS

Original Company: 11 October – 11 November 1863. Private. **No. 2 Company:** 27 November 1863 – 4 August 1864. Private. Promoted to Corporal 22 February 1864. Sailed to New Zealand aboard *Ida Zeigler* August 1861. Brother of John (above).
New Zealand Medal named to Forest Rangers. Medal claim dated 5 November 1912 and medal issued 2 April 1913. The medal was officially renamed erasing the name of Private Charles Smith, 2nd Regiment Waikato Militia. Dates "1861-66" on the reverse were deleted and polished. The Medal Application states "**Address:** Komata Reefs, Upper Thames. **Corps:** Major Jackson's and von Tempsky's Forest Rangers. **Field service:** Present at Mauku (Lusk's Clearing) [8 September 1863]; Paterangi, Waikato [Waiari 11 February 1864]; Rangiaowhia, Waikato [21 February

1864]; Orakau, Waikato [31 March-2 April 1864]." Parsons joined the Mauku Forest Rifle Volunteers in 1859, discharged and joined the Jackson's Forest Rangers in 1863. Parsons writes in a note accompanying his medal application "I first joined Forest Rangers in 1863 under Major Jackson. I was under fire at Mauku. I was camped with my company at Papakura and we were sent on an expedition against the Maori at Mauku. The engagement lasted the greater part of the day. I joined von Tempsky's 2nd Company of Forest Rangers and we were sent to the Queen's Redoubt near Mercer. Then we went to Te Rore in the Waikato. I was engaged in repelling an attack made on the 12th [actually 40th] Regiment by the Maori at a place called Paterangi [engagement at Waiari on the Mangapiko Stream 11 February 1864]. From there we went to Rangiaowhia. There I was under fire in two engagements [Rangiaowhia and Hairini]. Each engagement lasted a day. We came back to Te Awamutu and from there were sent to attack the pa at Orakau. We were three days under arms, fighting all the time. The Orakau pa expedition was the last affair in which I was engaged". Parsons was also under fire on several other occasions. Parsons discharged himself from the Forest Rangers because of a knee injury incurred at Ohaupo late 1864. He states with his medal application that he lost everything in a house fire later in life. Medal claim AD32/13; AD36/3/3231

PENAMINA
Served 6 December 1865 – February 1866. Private. Enlisted at Woodall's Redoubt. Discharged at Wanganui.

TE PENE
Served 6 December 1865 – 13 January 1866. Private. Enlisted at Woodall's Redoubt.

James PETERS
1099, No. 1 Company: 1 December 1863 – 18 March 1864. Private. Enrolled in Otago on 10 November and sailed to Auckland. Joined the corps 1 December, receiving pay from 10 November. Age: 30 years. Height: 6'. Hair colour: brown. Eye colour: blue. Complexion: light. Occupation: miner. Country: Ireland. Religion: Roman Catholic. Sent 18 March 1864 to Maketu by Captain Jackson from Pukerimu Redoubt, Cambridge in support of the Arawa Friendly Natives. Did not rejoin Forest Rangers. He was possibly placed on McDonnell's Arawa acquittance roll while at Maketu.

Octavus PIERCE (PEARCE or PIERSE)
Period of service believed to be 14 months. Present with unit during October and November 1865. Born 1825. Earlier served Colonial Defence Force in Wellington; Hawke's Bay Military Settlers. Later served Wanganui Cavalry Volunteers; No. 1 Division Armed Constabulary.
Received two **New Zealand Medals** from two separate and quite different medal applications using different names. The first application is named Octavus Pierse while the second is named Octavius Pierce. But both signatures are from the same hand! The two commanding officers are different men. One New Zealand Medal is named to the Forest Rangers and the other to the "Wanganui Cavalry Volunteers". The earlier Medal Application (dated 21 February 1870) states **"Address:** Octavus Pierse, Armed Constabulary, Crown Hotel, Eastern Spit, Napier, Hawke's Bay, New Zealand. **Corps:** Wanganui Cavalry Volunteers. Trooper. Five months. **Field service:** Five months. Kakaramea [13 May 1865] near Patea, Province of Taranaki, March 1865. Attached to military train. Also engaged Pukemaire [3 October 1865] and at Waerengaahika [November 1865] on East Coast. **Remarks:** Been seven years in the Colonial forces: Defence Force [no record], Wanganui Rangers, Forest Rangers, Hawke's Bay Military Settlers, Mounted Troop, Armed Constabulary." Medal claim AD36/3/1787. The later Medal Application (dated 24 April 1871) states **"Address:** Octavus Pierce, I.I.M. Hamilton Esq., Latimer Square, Canterbury, New Zealand. **Corps:** Forest Rangers. Private. 14 Months. **Field service:** Pukemaire pa [3 October

1865], Waerengaahika [November 1865], Ruakituri [River, 8 August 1868]." Medal claim AD32/3868; AD36/3/1813. The above two applications were an obvious ploy to obtain two medals, perhaps he received two pensions!

Alexander Anthony Gordon PILMER
Served 23 October 1865 – 31 March 1866. Lieutenant. Earlier served as Captain in the Wellington Rifle Volunteers. Commissioned as Lieutenant in New Zealand Militia 23 October 1865 but resigned this commission next day on joining the Forest Rangers at Wanganui. Died in Queensland 24 March 1885. Mrs Rosa Pilmer of Kilbirnie, his wife, claimed for a military grant in 1910 in respect of services rendered.
A letter attached to the AD32/1817 file states "Appointed Lieutenant under Militia Act 1858 in N.Z. Militia dated 23/10/1865. Resigned Commission as Lieutenant 24/10/1865 on joining von Tempsky's Corps at Wanganui. Forest Rangers. Served from 23/10/1865 till 31/3/1866." Medal claim AD32/1817; AD36/3/1782

Wilhelm Heinrich (Henry) POHLEN
46, No. 2 Company: 21 December 1863 – December 1867 (last known month of service). Private. Earlier served 2nd Regiment Waikato Militia, No. 394. Occupation: miner. Born 1825. In 1881 Pohlen attacked McMinn at Harapepe with a fern-hook, severely wounding him. At the resulting court case Pohlen was fined £5, but as he could not pay the fine he was sent to Mt Eden Prison. In 1883 Pohlen threw lime in John Henry Thompson's face after poison had killed Pohlen's dog. The poison had been laid to kill stray dogs that worried Thompson's sheep. Reciprocal prosecutions resulted with both claiming assault and abusive language.
New Zealand Medal named to Forest Rangers. Medal claim dated 28 March 1870. The Medal Application states "**Address:** Harapepe, Waikato. **Corps:** 2nd Company Forest Rangers. Private 22nd August 63 to 31st July 1865. Regimental No. 46. **Field service:** 19th September 63 to 31st July 1865. Mangapiko [Waiari] 11th February 1864, Rangiaowhia [and Hairini] 21st and 22nd February 1864. Orakau 31st March 1st & 2nd April 1864. **Remarks:** Capt. von Tempsky commanding company at Mangapiko, Rangiaowhia & Orakau. Lt General Cameron in command." Received land: town lot No. 66, Harapepe; farm lot No. 169, Pirongia. Medal claim AD32/3877; AD36/3/1800

Thomas MacDonald POLLOCK
Original Company: 3 September – 10 November 1863. Private. Later served Colonial Defence Force, 1st Auckland Troop. Born 13 September 1840 at Whangarei. Reputed to be the first European child to be born at Whangarei. Married Mary Jane Nixon on 12 May 1863 at Hunua. Died 22 May 1923 at Pukekohe.
New Zealand Medal named to Forest Rangers. Medal claim dated 5 April 1911 and received 13 April 1899. Medal issued 24 May 1911. The medal was officially renamed erasing the name of Sergeant Thomas Hany, 3rd Regiment Waikato Militia. The dates "1861-66" were also deleted and polished. The Medal Application states "**Address:** Pukekohe. **Corps:** Private. Forest Rangers. Served for 3 months. **Field service:** Hill's Big Clearing, Mauku, about September 1863 [Lusk's Clearing, 8 September 1863]. **Remarks:** I served with my company from the time they were raised till disbanded in November 1863. The officers of my company – Captain Jackson, Mr W. McG. Hay and Mr von Tempsky – are now all dead." Pollock stated in his medal application that he was very anxious to obtain the medal as he considered it would be an heirloom in his family. Received land 1890, although men of the Original Company, Forest Rangers, and Colonial Defence Force did not get land grants. Medal claim AD32/629; AD36/3/3109

George PRESTON
1266, No. 1 Company: 5 July 1864 – November 1867 (last known month of service). Private. Enrolled at Pukerimu, Cambridge. Residence: Auckland. Age: 28 years. Height: 5' 8". Hair colour: brown. Eye colour: blue. Complexion: ruddy. Occupation: sawyer. Country: England. Religion: Roman Catholic. Sworn in by Major William Jackson. Born 1834, Birmingham, England. Received land: town lot No. 39, Kihikihi; farm lot No. 221, Puniu.

John QUINLAN
Original Company: 11 August – 30 October 1863. Sergeant.

James QUINN
47, No. 2 Company: 1 April 1864 – July 1866 (last known month of service). Private. Earlier served 58th Regiment, No. 1758. Received land: town lot No. 85, Harapepe; farm lot No. 99, Pirongia.

William RACE
No. 2 Company: 24 December 1863 – 2 May 1864. Private. Substituted by Patrick John Clinton. Earlier served 1st Regiment Waikato Militia, No. 914 (joined 1 September 1863 at Melbourne, Australia). Occupation: surgeon. Born 1838, Northampton, England. Sailed to New Zealand aboard *Star of India*, 1863. Wrote a manuscript about service in the Forest Rangers, *Under the Flag,* circa 1900.

Andrew RAMSAY
No. 1 Company: 13 June 1865 – November 1866 (last known month of service). Private. Substitute for Edward Chapman. Enrolled at Kihikihi, Te Awamutu. Residence: Rangiaowhia. Single. Age: 22 years. Height: 5' 7". Hair colour: fair. Eye colour: blue. Complexion: fresh. Occupation: farmer. Country: Donegal, Ireland. Religion: Presbyterian. Sworn in by Major William Jackson. Born 1843, Donnylemore, Donegal, Ireland. Died 27 September 1931 and buried at Hautapu, Cambridge. Received land: town lot No. 211, Kihikihi; farm lot No. 275, Puniu.

George RAMSAY
No. 1 Company: 1 October 1865 – July 1867 (last known month of service). Private. Substitute for Robert Murray. Enrolled 1 November 1865 Te Awamutu. Residence: Rangiaowhia. Age: 18 years. Occupation: farmer. Sworn in by Major William Jackson. Signed enlistment with a mark. Born 1847. Received land: town lot No. 335, Kihikihi; farm lot No. 269, Puniu.

Robert RAMSAY
No. 1 Company: Joined 1866 – October 1867 (last known month of service). Private. Earlier served Colonial Defence Force in Auckland. Died 19 January 1870 at Auckland. Received land: town lot No. 5, Kihikihi; farm lot Nos. 244, 264, Puniu.

William James RAVEN
Original Company: 11 August – 10 November 1863. Private. Earlier served Auckland Rifle Volunteers. Later served Auckland Militia; Christchurch Artillery Volunteers; Lyttelton Naval Volunteers; "D" Battery; Blenheim Rifle Volunteers. Received Long Service Medal. Born 1843, St Leonards, Sussex, England. Sailed to New Zealand aboard *William Miles* November 1862. Watchmaker. Died 5 December 1901 and buried Wellington cemetery.
New Zealand Medal named to Forest Rangers. Medal claim dated 19 August 1871. The Medal Application states **"Address:** Christchurch. **Corps:** Forest Rangers Volunteers. **Field service:** Three months. Lusk's Farm, Mauku, September 8th 1863." Land claim rejected 1887. Medal claim AD32/3928; AD36/3/1975

Thomas RAY
Original Company: 11 August – 11 November 1863. Private. Sailed to New Zealand aboard *Breadalbane* March 1862 or *Constance* December 1862.

REIHANA
Served 9 January – February 1866. Private. Replacement for Tamati Waka. Enlisted at Te Putahi. Discharged at Wanganui.

William REYNOLDS
Original Company: 11 August – 10 November 1863. Private. Sailed to New Zealand aboard *Egmont* July 1860.

William RICHARDS
Original Company: 11 August – 11 November 1863. Private. Sailed to New Zealand aboard *Lord Worsley* April 1860.

Henry ROBERTS
Original Company: 11-28 August 1863. Private. Later served 3rd Regiment Waikato Militia. Possibly received impressed **New Zealand Medal** named to the Commissariat Transport Corps for service with the Waikato Militia.

John Mackintosh ROBERTS
Original Company: 11 August – 10 November 1863. Sergeant. **No. 2 Company:** 23 November 1863 – disbandment, 30 October 1867. Ensign. Promoted to Lieutenant 10 March 1864. Later served 3rd Regiment Waikato Militia, Private, No. 1751; No. 5 & 6 Divisions Armed Constabulary; Hawke's Bay Militia. Commissioned in Auckland Militia, attached to Forest Rangers, dated 23 November 1863.
New Zealand Medal named to Armed Constabulary (Inspector).
Received the New Zealand Cross. Details of issue are: **Recommended by:** Colonel Whitmore.
Service: "For the gallant and conspicuous example shown by him (when Sub-Inspector) at Moturoa on the 7th November, 1868, to his young and newly raised division while covering the retreat from the pa, although outnumbered, and at one time almost surrounded. To Inspector Roberts' fortitude and officer-like qualities it was due chiefly that these young soldiers, who had only joined the force one day, not only maintained their ranks and discipline in a dense bush in spite of the repeated efforts of the enemy to close with them, but were enabled so efficiently to perform the dangerous duty entrusted to them that the force, encumbered with many wounded, was able to draw off in good order. It must also be remembered, to the honour of Inspector Roberts, that it was mainly owing to his fortitude and resolute bearing that the great bulk of the force left behind at Te Ngutu o te Manu were rallied and safely brought off to Waihi, reaching that post the day after the rest of the force had arrived and given them up for lost." **New Zealand Gazette entry:** No. 27, 11 May 1876. The New Zealand Cross was presented to John Roberts at Cambridge on Tuesday, 25 July 1876, with the Waikato Cavalry Volunteers (89 men) and Armed Constabulary (60 men) present.
Born in Bombay, India, 31 December 1840 and educated in Scotland before emigrating to New Zealand in 1855 aboard the *Carnatic* with his parents who took up land at Hunua. He worked in his uncle's timber business at Hunua until he travelled to Otago and the Gabriel's Gully goldfield. He soon returned to Hunua and when the settlement was burned by raiding Maori he joined the Forest Rangers. Served with the Forest Rangers. Later Inspector, Armed Constabulary. In 1869 he commanded the Urewera expedition column. From 1870 to 1878 he commanded the Taupo and Tauranga districts, and from 1879 to 1881 he commanded in Taranaki being in command at Parihaka. Was first Officer Commanding the Permanent Militia, with the rank of Lieutenant-

Colonel, when that body was formed in 1886 after the disbandment of the Armed Constabulary. He relinquished his military duties in 1888 and served as a magistrate in the Wairarapa, Tauranga and Opotiki, finally retiring in 1909. Died at Wanganui on 12 October 1928 and buried Wanganui cemetery. Received land: town lot No. 17, Harapepe, and No. 11, Cambridge East; farm lot Nos. 187, 188, 189 and 191, Pirongia. His sword is in the Principal's office, St Kentigen's College, Pakuranga, Auckland. Medal claim AD32/1746

Thomas W. ROBINSON

45, No. 2 Company: Joined 1865 – January 1867 (last known month of service). Private. Later served Armed Constabulary. Served on East Coast. Born 1824, Clare, Ireland. Sailed to New Zealand aboard *Euphrates*, 1854. Received land: town lot No. 102, Harapepe; farm lot No. 213, Pirongia.

Peter ROGERS

48, No. 2 Company: 27 August 1864 – June 1866 (last known month of service). Private. Earlier served 1st Regiment Waikato Militia, No. 877 (attached to the Commissariat Transport Corps). Later served Te Awamutu Cavalry Volunteers. Born 1838, Monagh, Tipperary, Ireland. Occupation: filesmith. Sailed to New Zealand aboard *Rainbow*. Received land: town lot No. 62, Harapepe; farm lot No. 133, Pirongia. Possibly received impressed **New Zealand Medal** named to the Commissariat Transport Corps for service with the Waikato Militia.

Thomas ROPER

27, No. 2 Company: 20 April 1866 – January 1867 (last known month of service). Private. Earlier served 3rd Regiment Waikato Militia (attached to the Commissariat Transport Corps). Born 1835. Died 20 April 1910 at Ngaruawahia. Received land: town lot No. 21, Harapepe; farm lot No. 104, Pirongia. Possibly received impressed **New Zealand Medal** named to the Commissariat Transport Corps for service with the Waikato Militia.

John ROSE

Served 7 August 1865 – (date of discharge unknown). Private. Served with Westrup's Company on East Coast.

Edward Ogilvie ROSS

No. 2 Company: 23 December 1863 – (date of discharge unknown). Private. Promoted to Corporal 26 April 1864. Promoted to Ensign 25 June 1865. Earlier served 1st Regiment Waikato Militia, No. 913 (joined 1 September 1863 at Melbourne, Australia). Later served No. 4 Division Armed Constabulary. Occupation: miner. Born 1837, Inverness, Scotland. Dangerously wounded at Waerengaahika, 17 November 1865, being shot in the head. Died 1904 at Opotiki. Received land: town lot No. 18, Harapepe; farm lot Nos. 117, 160, 161, and 162, Pirongia.

John ROWDEN

Original Company: 26 August – 10 November 1863. Private. **1100, No. 1 Company:** 17 November 1863 – November 1866 (last known month of service). Private. Enrolled at Auckland. Residence: Wairoa, south Auckland. Age: 21 years. Height: 5' 8" Hair colour: brown. Eye colour: blue. Complexion: pale. Occupation: bushman. Country: England. Religion: Roman Catholic. Sworn in by Captain William Jackson. Signed his enlistment with a mark. Born 1842, Jersey. **New Zealand Medal** named to Forest Rangers. Medal claim dated 23 February 1912 and received 7 June 1912. Medal issued 2 April 1913. The medal was officially renamed erasing the name of Private Robert Myles, Auckland Militia. The dates "1861-66" were deleted and polished. The Medal Application states "**Address:** Waerengaokuri, Gisborne. **Corps:** Private, Forest Rangers. Captain Jackson was in command. **Period of service:** From formation to disbandment of corps. **Field service:** About 3 years. Under fire at Paparata [13 December 1863] where we captured a flag with AOTEAROA inscribed on it. Also at taking of Paterangi pa [Waiari on the Mangapiko Stream, 11 February 1864]. Also under fire for 3 days at Orakau [31 March-2 April 1864]. **Remarks:** Was given 50 acres at Rangiaowhia near Te Awamutu soon after disbandment. Sold it to Mr Ramsey at about the same time." In a declaration by Ezra Smith it is stated "Rowden was also present at a fight at Lusk's Clearing, [8 September] Waikato between the Forest Rangers and the natives." Medal held in Auckland Institute and Museum collection. Received land: town lot No. 349, Kihikihi; farm lot No. 283, Puniu. Medal claim AD32/59; AD36/3/3239. Also seen spelt RODEN or RODON.

Henry ROWLAND
Original Company: Original Company 11 August – 10 November 1863. Private. **1101, No. 1 Company:** 17 November 1863 – 18 March 1864. Private. Enrolled at Auckland. Age: 21 years. Height: 5' 6" Hair colour: brown. Eye colour: grey. Complexion: light. Occupation: bushman. Country: England. Religion: Episcopalian. Sworn in by Captain William Jackson. Sent 18 March 1864 to Maketu by Captain Jackson from Pukerimu Redoubt, Cambridge in support of the Arawa Friendly Natives. Did not rejoin Forest Rangers. Possibly he was placed on McDonnell's Arawa acquittance roll while at Maketu. Born 1842, St Ann's, Soho, London.

Frederick RUHSTEIN
51, No. 2 Company: 16 February 1865 – July 1866 (last known month of service). Private. Substitute for Carl Schacht. Earlier served 2nd (No. 195) and 3rd (No. 1451) Regiment Waikato Militia. Occupation: gardener. Born 1836, Hanover, Germany. Received land: town lot No. 5, Harapepe; farm lot No. 206, Pirongia.

Charles Alfred RUSH
49, No. 2 Company: 31 March 1864 – 4 January 1865. Private. Substituted by William Stephenson.

Frederick N. RUSSELL
Original Company: 11 August – 11 November 1863. Private.
New Zealand Medal named to Forest Rangers. Medal claim dated 3 September 1872. Medal issued 7 August 1874. The Medal Application states "**Address:** Native Office, Wellington. **Corps:** Forest Rangers. Private. Three months. **Field service:** Three months. Lusk's Farm, Mauku, September 8th 1863. Afterwards at Pokeno Hill with Colonel Nixon. **Remarks:** Immediate commanding officers: Major Jackson, Colonel Nixon." Medal claim AD32/4034; AD36/3/1994

James RYAN
No. 1 Company: June 1865 – July 1867. Private. Later served No. 1 & 3 Divisions Armed Constabulary, receiving a bad conduct discharge. Born 1837, Endermine, Wexford, Ireland. Sailed to New Zealand aboard *Mary Ann*, 1864. Died April 1869. Included in Major Fraser's despatch for the battle of Waerengaahika, November 1865, where he states that Private Ryan of the Forest Rangers was severely wounded on 17 November, being shot through the shoulders.
New Zealand Medal named to Forest Rangers. Medal claim dated 11 September 1871. The Medal Application states "**Address:** Patea, Taranaki, NZ. **Corps:** Von Tempsky's Forest Rangers. Private 2 years from June 1865 to July 1867. **Field service:** 12 months – Waiapu [Pukemaire, 3 October 1865], East Coast. Waerengaahika [15-21 November] 1865. **Remarks:** The claimant has also served in the Armed Constabulary about 18 months and was under fire at Okotuku [Moturoa, 7 November 1868], Karaka Flat [3 February 1869], Tauranga-Ika [2 February 1869], Otautu [13 March 1869]. Certified correct by Noake, Major, Commanding District, Patea, 13 September 1871." Application endorsed by Charles Westrup, Major, of Poverty Bay. Written on the application form is "A previous application was forwarded by the claimant but has apparently

miscarried – his name not appearing on either Rolls A or B." Received land: town lot No. 219, Kihikihi; farm lot No. 325, Puniu. Medal claim AD32/4039; AD36/3/1984

John McDonald RYAN

No. 1 Company: 23 October 1865 – 27 March 1866. Private. Substitute for Lloyd. Later served No. 4 Division Armed Constabulary. Enrolled 1865 at Wellington. Age: 19 years. Height: 5' 10". Hair colour: fair. Complexion: fair. Occupation: labourer. Country: Sydney, New South Wales, Australia. Religion: Roman Catholic. Born 1847, Orange, New South Wales. Sailed to New Zealand aboard *John Knox*, 1861.

Duplicate New Zealand Medal named to Forest Rangers. His original medal was named to the Armed Constabulary. Medal claim (for a duplicate medal) dated 25 July 1908 and received 9 September 1908. The Medal Application states **"Address:** Post Office, Rookwood, Sydney, N.S.W. **Corps:** Forest Rangers. Private. 2 years (1865 and 1866). **Field service:** Waitotara campaign [Chute's campaign]. Engagements at Otapawa [14 January 1866], Ketemarae, Waingongoro [15 January 1866]. **Remarks:** And General Chute's march at the back of Mount Egmont. Thanked by Major von Tempsky for going to the assistance of Private [Allister] Henry Campbell while in the firing line who was dangerously wounded at the storming of Te Putahi." This medal was a duplicate issue to replace the original medal that was "in a bush fire in Western Queensland". In a earlier letter to the Minister of Defence, dated 23 June 1908, Ryan claims he was "... under the late Major von Tempsky while attached to the Field Force commanded by General Chute in his campaign round the back of Mount Egmont, Taranaki, and all the engagements on the West Coast. Also served in Armed Constabulary on the East and West Coast under the late Colonel Whitmore." Medal claim AD32/1860; AD36/3/2015

William RYAN

No. 1 Company: 5 September 1864. Private. Was substituted by Vallancy Drury immediately without any service, indicating he may not have left the 2nd Regiment Waikato Militia in which he earlier served. Later served Armed Constabulary. Born 1838, Tipperary, Ireland. Sailed to New Zealand aboard *Kate*, 1863.

John SCALLY

50, No. 2 Company: 12 January 1864 – August 1866 (last known month of service). Private. Earlier served 2nd Regiment Waikato Militia, No. 1210. Later served Wanganui Bush Rangers, East Coast Field Force, August 1865. Born 1848. Sailed to New Zealand aboard *Oriental Queen*, 1849. Received land: town lot No. 84, Harapepe; farm lot No. 130, Pirongia.

Thomas SCANLAN

In his medal application, claims to have served in Forest Rangers at Paparata, Waiari, Rangiaowhia and Orakau. There is no record of his name in any unit. Medal claim AD32/601

Carl L.A. SCHACHT (SCHLACT)

51, No. 2 Company: 21 March 1864 – 15 February 1865. Private. Substituted by Frederick Ruhstein. Sailed to New Zealand aboard *Scimitar*.

Adolphus SCHUMACHER

Original Company: 11 August – 11 November 1863. Private.

New Zealand Medal named to Forest Rangers. Medal claim dated 23 September 1910 and issued 23 May 1911. The medal was officially renamed erasing the name of Private Robert McCormick, 2nd Regiment Waikato Militia. The dates "1861-66" were deleted and polished. The medal was altered officially following an instruction dated 8 May 1911 stating: Erase letters "A.S." and insert the name "A. Schumacher". It seems the original name included just his initials. The Medal

Application states "**Address:** Eden Street, Newton, Auckland. [Prior to this Schumacher resided in Te Aroha]. **Corps:** Forest Rangers from 11 August 1863 to 11 November 1863. Private. Six months [total service]. Waikato War 1863-64. **Field service:** Relief of East Pukekohe Church [14 September 1863]; at Bald Hill, Mauku [Titi Hill, near Pukekohe 23 October 1863] with Mauku Rifles – 10 casualties including Lieutenants Norman and Percival. Also at Camerontown; Purapura; Koheroa; Meremere; Rangiriri and Hunua Ranges. After Rangiriri was attached to the Flying Column under Colonel Nixon (Defence Force) and Captain Rutherford (70th Regiment) to keep communication open between the front and Auckland. If there was any hard work or fighting to be done – it was always Jackson's Forest Rangers by General Cameron's orders. **Remarks:** Major Skinner, Ellerslie, formerly Auckland Rifles and Bugler, Jackson's F. Rangers. Thomas Pollock, Pukekohe. James Finleysen [Finlay], Mauku. Privates, Jackson's F. Rangers. The above old comrades are alive as far as I know and will testify my claim." Medal claim AD32/655; AD36/3/3092

T. SHADDOCK

Served 3 December 1865 – March 1866. Private. Enlisted at Wanganui.

Alexander Stephen SHERRET

Original Company: 11 August – 10 November 1863. Sergeant. **No. 2 Company:** 26 November 1863 – 9 March 1864. Staff Sergeant. Promoted to Ensign, commission dated 10 March 1864. **New Zealand Medal** named to Forest Rangers. Medal claim dated 13 August 1870. The Medal Application states "**Address:** Harapepe, Waikato. **Corps:** Auckland Militia. 1st [Original] and 2nd Corps Forest Rangers. Lieutenant. Served from 22nd July 1863 until July 1865. **Field service:** Two years in the field. Kirikiri, Papakura on or about 22nd July 1863; Mauku [Lusk's Clearing] in [8th] September 1863; Rangiaowhia [and Hairini], February 21st and 22nd 1864. **Remarks:** Part of the time under Major Jackson and part under Major von Tempsky." Received land: town lot No. 12, Harapepe; farm lot Nos. 116, 118, 185, 186, and 190, Pirongia. Medal claim AD32/4116; AD36/3/2086

James SHERRET

64, **No. 2 Company:** 11 July 1866 – disbandment, 30 October 1867. Private. Promoted Staff Sergeant. Received land: town lot No. 27, Harapepe; farm lot Nos. 197 and 199, Pirongia.

Jeremiah SHINE

No. 2 Company: 23 December 1863 – 31 July 1864. Private. Earlier served 1st Regiment Waikato Militia, No. 985 (joined 11 September 1863 at Castlemain, Australia). Later served 2nd Regiment Waikato Militia, No. 1304; 4th Regiment Waikato Militia, No. 511. Occupation: miner. Born 1837, Cork, Ireland. Sailed to New Zealand aboard *Caduseus*, 1863. Received land including town lot No. 286, Hamilton East.

William SHUKER

1320, **No. 1 Company:** 20 November 1864 – July 1866 (last known month of service). Private. Substitute for No. 410, David Torpey. Later served Armed Constabulary. Enrolled at Kihikihi, Te Awamutu. Residence: Auckland. Age: 20 years. Height: 5' 9". Hair colour: Fair. Eye colour: Blue. Complexion: Light. Occupation: storekeeper. Country: England. Religion: Episcopalian. Sworn in by Major William Jackson. Born 1843, Sheffield, Yorkshire, England. After the East Coast campaign he settled in the area.
New Zealand Medal named to Forest Rangers. Medal claim dated 1 July 1871 and issued 13 November 1873. The Medal Application states "**Address:** Gisborne, Poverty Bay. **Corps:** No. 1 and 2 Comp. Forest Rangers from Oct 1864 to June 1866. **Field service:** Kakaramea [13 May] 1865; Weraroa [21 July] 1865; Pipiriki [July] 1865; Pukemaire [3rd] October 1865;

Waerengaahika [15-21] November 1865; Expedition to Te Reinga January 1866; Expedition to Waikaremoana April 1870; Expedition to Tolaga Bay in pursuit of Te Kooti August 1870; Expedition to Ruatahuna January 1871; Expedition in search of Te Kooti May 1871; The four later expeditions were under Major Ropata." It is interesting to note the receipt of the medal "Napier Gaol, 13th November 1873. Sir, I have the honour to acknowledge the receipt of a medal forwarded to me for Wm Shuker a prisoner in my charge. I have the honour to be, Sir, Your Most Obedient Servant, C. Moloney, for Wm Miller, Gaoler." Being in gaol does not seem a fitting end to such a notable military career. Received land: town lot No. 347, Kihikihi; farm lot No. 261, Puniu. Medal claim AD32/4121; AD/36/3/2123

Henry Thomas SIBLEY

No. 1 Company: January 1867 – disbandment, 30 October 1867. Earlier served 70th Regiment. Later served No. 5 Division Armed Constabulary, No. 52; Te Awamutu Cavalry Volunteers. Born 1838, Woolwich, Kent, England. Sailed to New Zealand aboard *Louisa*, 1861. Could be late replacement in Forest Rangers. No record of this man on pay sheets. No record of land grant.
New Zealand Medal named to Armed Constabulary. Medal claim dated 26 July 1871. The Medal Application states "**Address:** Te Awamutu. **Corps:** Armed Constabulary Force, Constable – six months. **Field service:** Three months. Relief of Turuturu Mokai, July 12, 1868. Te Ngutu o te Manu, 21 August 1868. Ruaruru, 7 September 1868. Carried Private Hope from under fire wounded." No mention of Forest Ranger service. Land claim H23, 1894. Medal claim AD32/4122; AD36/3/2141

Joseph SIBLEY

No. 2 Company: 29 November 1863 – 15 May 1864. Corporal. Sailed to New Zealand aboard *Telegraph*, 1863.

William Henry SIBLEY

Joined 1865 – 8 July 1866. Private.
Sibley states that he served in the Forest Rangers on the East Coast in 1865/66. A letter from the Under Secretary of the Department of Lands to the Chief of General Staff, Defence Department (dated 20 September 1910), gives details of his service "Mr William Henry Sibley is making application for compensation on account of military services. He states that he enrolled under Captain Westrup in the Forest Rangers at Napier and was ordered to Waiapu at the time when the Hauhau drove out the Bishop of Waiapu. He was discharged at Poverty Bay on the 8th July, 1866. He states he never received any scrip, land or money for his services."
New Zealand Medal named to Forest Rangers. Medal awarded 12 October 1871. Medal claim AD32/1894. AD36/3/2122

James K. SIMMONS

52, **No. 2 Company:** 11 January 1864 – August 1865 (last known month of service). Private. Earlier served 3rd Regiment Waikato Militia, No. 1130.

William Henry SKINNER

Original Company: 26 August – 11 November 1863. Private/Bugler. Sailed to New Zealand aboard *Harwood* November 1858 or *Joshua Fletcher* August 1859.
New Zealand Medal named to Forest Rangers. Medal claim dated 9 June 1871. The Medal Application states "**Address:** Parnell, Auckland. **Corps:** Forest Rangers. **Field service:** About three months. Wellwood Clearing, Lusk's Farm, [Lusk's Clearing] Mauku 8 Sept 1863. **Remarks:** Name of the immediate commanding officer: Lieutenant Jackson." Made land claim, 1894. Medal claim AD32/4130; AD36/3/2108

Colin Brydges SMITH
39, No. 2 Company: 16 December 1864 – 27 November 1865. Private. Substituted by Burley. Sailed to New Zealand aboard *Surat*, 1864.

Ezra SMITH *(pictured)*
Original Company: 11 August – 10 November 1863. Private. Earlier served Wairoa Rifle Volunteers. Born 19 July 1843, Auckland.
New Zealand Medal named to Forest Rangers. Medal claim dated 16 May 1873. The Medal Application states "**Address:** Post Office, Auckland. **Corps:** Captain Jackson's Forest Rangers, 3 months. **Field service:** 3 months in the field through the Hunua Ranges about October 1863. Under fire at Lusk's Farm, Mauku [Lusk's Clearing, 8 September 1863]. **Remarks:** Names of immediate commanding officers: Major Jackson, Major von Tempsky, Ensign Hay." Medal claim AD32/4147; AD36/3/2191

James SMITH
No. 1 Company: Private. Enrolled 21 November 1863 at Auckland. Age: 32 years. Occupation: digger. Had his enrolment cancelled.

James Hendry SMITH
1103, No. 1 Company: 1 December 1863 – November 1866 (last known month of service). Private. Promoted to Corporal 19 March 1864. Enrolled in Otago on 10 November and sailed to Auckland. Joining the corps 1 December, receiving pay from 10 November. Age: 22 years. Height: 5' 10". Hair colour: black. Eye colour: grey. Complexion: dark. Occupation: miner. Country: Ireland. Religion: Roman Catholic. Received land: town lot No. 198, Kihikihi; farm lot No. 315, Puniu.

John Henry SMITH
1102, No. 1 Company: 5 December 1863 – 27 December 1864. Private. Promoted to Corporal 1 January 1864. Promoted to Sergeant 18 February 1864. Known amongst his friends in the Forest Rangers as Wairoa Smith. Enrolled at Auckland. Residence: Wairoa, south Auckland. Age: 23 years. Height: 5' 10¹/₂". Hair colour: brown. Eye colour: blue. Complexion: fresh. Occupation: labourer. Country: England. Religion: Episcopalian. Sworn in by Captain William Jackson. Born 1840, Preston, Lancashire, England. Arrested on 24 May 1864 and held prisoner without pay awaiting court-martial. Returned to unit 12 July 1864 and was absent for one day on 14 August 1864 presumably for the court-martial. Smith was probably not found guilty at the court-martial,

Biographical notes 253

as he received all pay he lost. In a receipt dated 29 September 1864, Smith stated "Received from Major W. Jackson, Forest Rangers, the sum of eighteen pounds Stg [Sterling] being the amount of pay stopped by court-martial from 25th May till 11th July 1864 ... J. Smith [signed]." Land claim H23, 1894.
New Zealand Medal named to Forest Rangers. Medal claim dated 23 December 1873 and received 20 July 1875. The Medal Application states "**Address:** Cook Street, Auckland. **Corps:** Major Jackson and Forest Rangers. Sergeant. One year and six months. **Field service:** About 18 months, Paparata, Wairoa district, 13th December 1863. At Mangapiko, Waiari [11 February 1864], Rangiaowhia [21 February 1864]. At the assault of Orakau 31st March-1st and 2nd April 1864. **Remarks:** Immediate commanding officers: Major Jackson and von Tempsky and Generals Carey and Cameron." The medal application processing was delayed because the Defence Office was concerned that Smith was ineligible because of the mutiny in the ranks of No. 5 Division Armed Constabulary. The Medal Commission wrote to Major Tisdall (dated 23 March 1874) "Will you be good enough to state whether this man was in No. 5 Division Armed Constabulary on the West Coast with Major von Tempsky in 1868 – or can you obtain any information whether he was or was not?" The answer was (dated 30 March 1874) "Not having access to the Division roll, I cannot say. Colonel Haultain informs me that he had rolls of these 'disobedient' men of No. 5 Division A.C. filed carefully in Defence Office for reference. So you can there ascertain above point definitely." Later a similar letter was send to Major Jackson but no reference of his reply can be found. One assumes Jackson spoke in favour of Smith or thought it more appropriate to remain silent. Whatever the Medal Commission discovered, Smith eventually got his medal. Medal claim AD32/4158; AD36/3/2200

Peter John Lewin SMITH

Original Company: 11 August – 10 November 1863. Private/Guide. Born 21 May 1841 at sea.
New Zealand Medal named to Forest Rangers. Medal claim dated 18 June 1873. The Medal Application states "**Address:** Auckland. **Corps:** Forest Rangers. Three months. Guide. **Field service:** Three months. Mauku, October 1863 [actually Lusk's Clearing, 8 September 1863 and others]. **Remarks:** Commanding officers: Captain Jackson, von Tempsky and Ensign Hay." Medal claim AD32/4160; AD36/3/2189

Philip SMITH

17, No. 2 Company: June – July 1866 (last known month of service). Private. Born 1824. Sailed to New Zealand aboard *Alfred*, 1864. Died 22 June 1876 at Thames. Received land: town lot No. 52, Harapepe; farm lot No. 102, Pirongia.

Thomas J.L. SMITH

1057, No. 1 Company: 28 December 1863 – 10 April 1864. Private. Earlier served 2nd Regiment Waikato Militia. Born 1835. Land claim H51, 1890.

William SMITH

Original Company: 11-25 August 1863. Private. May be the William Smith below.

William SMITH

1359, No. 1 Company: 5 February 1865 – November 1866 (last known month of service). Private. Substitute for No. 1086 Joseph Grigg. Enrolled at Kihikihi, Te Awamutu. Residence: Auckland. Single. Age: 23 years. Height: 5' 7". Hair colour: light. Eye colour: blue. Complexion: fair. Occupation: telegraphist. Country: Scotland. Sworn in by Major William Jackson. Religion: Presbyterian. Born 1841, Abbey Paisley, Renfrew, Scotland. Received land: town lot No. 71 Kihikihi; farm lot No. 239, Puniu.

Henry SOUTHEY (SOUTHEE)

Original Company: 11 August – 10 November 1863. Sergeant. **2, No. 2 Company:** 24 November 1863 – October 1867 (last known month of service). Sergeant and Scout. Later served No. 5 Division Armed Constabulary, No. 70. Born 1839, Wanganui. A half-caste Maori. A favourite of von Tempsky, who once described him as "… our guide Sergeant Southey, a brave and intelligent half-caste." Occupation: seaman. Also seen recorded as "Southee" but his signature was always "Southey".

Southey made many different **medal applications**, each being turned down because of his involvement in the No. 5 Division Armed Constabulary mutiny. In fact he made applications dated on: 26 March 1870, 4 November 1872, 31 August 1892, 3 October 1892 and lastly 4 February 1913. Later applications did not mention No. 5 Division (mentioned only in his first application of which details are shown below), and Southey had made a sworn statement before a Stipendiary Magistrate that he never previously applied for a medal! A medal was issued, and Southey received it on 3 April 1913. Apparently the Medal Commission then realised their mistake, and in a letter addressed to Southey at Sunny Farm, Waiorongomai, Te Aroha (were he earlier worked as a miner) said "… regret to state that the medal forwarded to you on 29th ultimo [March] must be returned to this office immediately." This medal was renamed over "R. Stewart, 3rd Waikato Regiment" with the dates "1861-66" on the reverse deleted and polished. Below is the best example of Southey's medal applications, being his first application dated 26 March 1870 (which mentions all units and dates) "**Address:** Harapepe, Waikato. **Corps:** 2nd Company Forest Rangers. Sergeant 24th Nov 1863 to 30th June 1865. Regimental No. 2. No. 5 Division A.C. [Armed Constabulary], Constable. Div. No. 70. 24th May 1868 to 30th Sept 1868. **Field service:** 24th Nov 1863 to 30th June 1865. 1st July 1868 to 30th Sept 1868. Mangapiko [Waiari, 11th] 10th February 1864. Rangiaowhia [and Hairini] 21st and 22nd February 1864. Orakau 31st March, 1st and 2nd April 1864. Te Ngutu o te Manu 21st August 1868. Waihi Road about 14th August 1868. Te Ruaruru [second battle at Te Ngutu o te Manu] 7th September 1868. Kakaramea [skirmish] 30th September 1868. Capt. von Tempsky commanding Company at Mangapiko, Rangiaowhia and Orakau. Lieut. Gen. Cameron commanding. Major von Tempsky commanding Division at Te Ngutu o te Manu and Te Ruaruru. Sergt Toovey commanding escort Waihi Road. Capt. Smith commanding Company at Kakaramea. Col McDonnell commanding." In his last claim Southey states "For my services in the Forest Rangers I received the usual Military Grant of land (80 acres)." Present at reunion to commemorate 50 years of battle of Orakau, 1914. Received land: town lot No. 96, Harapepe; farm lot No. 125, Pirongia. Medal claim AD32/359; AD36/3/2072 (file numbers for other applications may exist)

SPAIN

Not on any Forest Ranger roll, but attached to the unit. A Maori guide who was highly regarded by von Tempsky. Killed in action at Otapawa pa, 14 January 1866.

According to von Tempsky, was accidentally shot, with a musket ball to the chest, by soldiers of the 14th Regiment mistaking him for one of the enemy, while he was searching inside a whare. Another version of Spain's death recorded in Gudgeon's *Reminiscences of the War in New Zealand*, is in direct conflict with von Tempsky's description. Spain entered the whare to bring out a dead Hauhau, and while so engaged a party of Forest Rangers approached and asked who was in the whare. The reply was "A white man," meaning a friend. Unfortunately the Forest Rangers concluded that this meant the deserter Kimble Bent and immediately fired a volley into the whare, mortally wounding Spain.

George SPENCER

Served 27 October – 20 December 1865. Private. May be the George Spencer who earlier served with the Colonial Defence Force at Auckland and with the Native Contingent.

Biographical notes 255

New Zealand Medal named to Colonial Defence Force. Medal claim dated 22 January 1877. The Medal Application states "**Address** 'Parawai', Thames. **Corps:** Colonial Defence Force, Trooper, No. 48. **Field service:** Twelve months. Rangiaowhia [21 February 1864], Te Ranga, Tauranga [21 June 1864]. Native Contingent, Maketu, Matata." No mention of Forest Ranger service. Medal claim AD32/4178; AD36/3/2221

William STANLEY

No. 2 Company: 23 December 1863 – July 1865 (last known month of service). Private. Earlier served 1st Regiment Waikato Militia, No. 943. Occupation: miner. Born 1837, York, North Yorkshire, England. Joined Waikato Militia at Melbourne, Australia, 17 September 1863. Sailed to New Zealand aboard *Caduseus*.
Applied for New Zealand Medal. First medal claim dated 20 June 1900. The Medal Application states "**Address:** Devonport, Auckland. **Corps:** First Waikato No. 3 Company. **Field service:** Twelve months. Kirikiri near Papakura [22] July 1863 and Meremere [probably Commissariat service], some months after the above." No mention of Forest Ranger service. No medal was issued.
Stanley's second application for a medal was in a letter dated 20 April 1910 "I have the honour to apply for the New Zealand Medal for service while in Pitt's Militia and the 1st Waikato Regt. I was under fire near Drury under command of Capt. Stack in 1863 and also at Meremere on the Waikato River." This application is endorsed by W.E. Gudgeon who states "I have every reason to believe that this application is bona fide. Stanley served under me in the A.C. Force and was a man of excellent character." No medal was issued.
Stanley's third application for a medal, dated 12 May 1913, states "**Address:** Devonport. **Corps:** Militia Volunteers. First 400 under Major Pitt. Also served in the A.C.F. [Armed Constabulary Force]. **Field service:** Between Papakura and Drury and Meremere under General Cameron."
On 17 April 1917 Stanley of 85 Wakefield St, Auckland, stated in a declaration that "On 1 March 1917 – I was driving along custom St West and jumped out of the trap to catch a horse that had bolted – after which I found my medal missing. I advertised for same, and offered a reward, but I have not heard of anything since. The medal was given for services in the 1st Waikatos, No. 3 Company, during the Maori War 1863-4."
A very confusing sequence of medal applications. His earlier applications were possibly turned down because the Government closed correspondence on medals at about 1900. Also, Stanley was not under fire while in the Armed Constabulary. He did not distinguish his service with the Forest Rangers (probably from memory lapse) and only mentioned being under fire around Papakura in 1863. He may have received a medal in 1913 and then lost it in 1917, or never received a medal and fabricated the "lost medal" story thinking that the Defence Department would not know any better. Medal claim AD32/635; AD36/3/3332

William STEENSON

Original Company: 11 August – 10 November 1863. Private. Born 1839, Ireland. Died 7 July 1900 and buried Mauku cemetery. Made land claim.

John STEPHENSON

No. 1 Company: 28 December 1863 – 30 April 1864. Private.

William Frederick STEPHENSON

49, No. 2 Company: 5 January 1865 – August 1866 (last known month of service). Private. Substitute for Charles Rush. Later served Kai Iwi Cavalry; Armed Constabulary. Born 1836, Burslem, Staffordshire, England.
New Zealand Medal named to the Forest Rangers. Medal claim dated 14 September 1874 and issued 6 February 1875. The Medal Application states "**Address:** Matawhero, Poverty Bay. **Corps:** No. 2 Company Forest Rangers. Served 3 years. Regimental No. – none at time of service. **Field**

service: At Kakaramea [13 May 1865], Okotuku [4 January 1866], Te Putahi [7 January 1866], Otapawa [14 January 1866], Waikoko [1 February 1866], Nukumaru and Kai Iwi Cavalry [25 November 1868 where the Kai Iwi Cavalry brutally slaughtered a group of Maori boys out eeling]. 1867 A.C. [Armed Constabulary]." Received land: town lot No. 8, Harapepe; farm lot No. 166, Pirongia. Medal claim AD32/4199; AD36/3/2210

Joseph STRONG

Original Company: 11 August – 11 November 1863. Private. Sailed to New Zealand aboard *Phoenix* February 1860. Made land claim.

Edward STURMER

54, No. 2 Company: 18 January 1864 – December 1867 (last known month of service). Private. Later served No. 4 Division Armed Constabulary. Occupation: seaman. Religion: Episcopalian. Born 1843, Essen, Germany. Sailed to New Zealand aboard *William*.
New Zealand Medal named to Forest Rangers. Medal claim dated 15 August 1870. The Medal Application states "**Address:** Constable, Armed Constabulary, Alexandra [Pirongia], Waikato. **Corps:** No. 2 Co. Forest Rangers and No. 4 Division Armed Constabulary. 3 years service. Regt. No. 54. **Field service:** 12 months. Engaged with Maori at Rangiaowhia 20th [21st] February 1864. Orakau 1st, 2nd and 3rd April 1864 [31 March-2 April 1864]. Under fire of Hauhau ambuscade, between Ahi-Kereru and Tatahoata [Orangikawa], Urewera country, 7 May 1869. Engaged with Hauhau about 2 miles from Tatahoata pa, Ruatahuna Valley, Urewera country, 10 May 1869." Medal later damaged, but not lost, in house fire. Received land: town lot No. 83, Harapepe; farm lot No. 150, Pirongia. Medal claim AD32/4228; AD36/3/2085

John SULLIVAN

Served 12-18 December 1865. Private. Enlisted at Wanganui. Earlier served Wanganui Bush Rangers. Later served No. 2 Division Armed Constabulary.

William SULLIVAN

Served June 1866 – November 1867. Private. Later served Armed Constabulary. Claimed to have served with Forest Rangers, but probably confused service with the Opotiki Rangers. This claim to service with the Forest Rangers is on his Armed Constabulary record only. Born 1844, Queenstown, Cork, Ireland. Sailed to New Zealand aboard *Dauntless*, 1865.

Charles SUMSION

55, No. 2 Company: 23 December 1863 – 8 December 1864. Private. Earlier served 1st Regiment Waikato Militia, No. 939 (joined 4 September 1863 at Melbourne, Australia). Occupation: miner. Born 1837, Bradford, Wiltshire, England. Sailed to New Zealand aboard *Caduseus*, 1863.
New Zealand Medal named to Forest Rangers. Medal claim dated 20 July 1881. The Medal Application states "**Address:** Kumara [Hokitika]. **Corps:** Joined 1st Waikato Regiment 3rd Sept 1863. I was under fire with them under Lieut. Percival in [23rd] Oct 1863 [Titi Hill]. I volunteered to the 2nd Forest Rifles, was engaged with them under Major von Tempsky at Paterangi pa [Waiari, 11 February 1864], known as the bathing party. The next engagement under same command was at Ngaruawahia [Rangiaowhia] about 22 [21st] Feb 1864 – again at Orakau 30-31 March and 1st April [31 March-2 April] 1864. I provided a substitute and left the service on Dec 8th 1864." In a testimonial von Tempsky states "Camp Cambridge, December 8th 1864. I hereby take much pleasure in testifying to the good character of Charles Sumsion, who was this day discharged from No. 2 Co. Forest Rangers on account of substitute. In action I have found him to be invariably brave and his conduct on ordinary occasions has been most exemplary." Medal claim AD32/944; AD36/3/2764

Amelius TAYLOR

25, No. 2 Company: 16 December 1864 – 13 April 1866. Private. Promoted to Corporal and later to Sergeant. Substitute for Thomas Harvey. Substituted by William Osborne. Later served in the Armed Constabulary. Born 1841, Cork, Ireland. Left von Tempsky in South Taranaki and travelled to the Waikato 9 January 1866. On von Tempsky's return to Harapepe, he wrote a testimonial for Taylor (dated 13 April 1866) "Sergeant Amelius Taylor has served with me from the 16th December 1864 to this date; he was present at the engagements of Kakaramea, Okotuku, Putahi, Otapawa, Ketemarae and Waikoko. His gentlemanly and soldierly bearing throughout his service time with me has been a source of constant pleasure to me. In all the actions referred to, his bravery has been conspicuous." This testimonial was later used to authenticate service details in Taylor's medal application.
New Zealand Medal named to Forest Rangers. Medal claim dated 21 December 1871. The Medal Application states "**Address:** Wellington. **Corps:** 2 Company, Forest Rangers. Sergeant. No. 25. **Field service:** 16 months. Present at: Kakaramea [13 May 1865], Okotuku [4 January 1866], Putahi [7 January 1866], Otapawa [14 January 1866], Ketemarae [15 January 1866] and Waikoko [1 February 1866]." Some time elapsed before the medal was issued due to a backlog of applications. Meanwhile Taylor sailed to London giving a London address to forward his to: 50 Warwick Gardens, Kensington. On arrival in England he enquired about the issue of his medal, giving his new address as: 18 Coningham Road, Shepherds Bush, London. Medal claim AD32/4264; AD36/3/2296

James TAYLOR

56, No. 2 Company: 11 January – 28 November 1864. Private. Substituted by No. 56 Adolphus Hardy. Was slightly wounded at Hairini, 22 February 1864, with a gunshot wound to his finger – being the only Forest Ranger casualty during the engagement. Could be same man as below.

James TAYLOR

10, No. 2 Company: 8 February – 21 July 1865. Private. Substitute for William Bourke. Could be the same man as above returning to the unit, but there is no evidence to support this.

William TAYLOR

Original Company: 11 August – 10 November 1863. Sergeant. **1104, No. 1 Company:** 17 November 1863 – 2 April 1864. Corporal. Promoted to Sergeant 19 March 1864. Enrolled at Auckland. Age: 33 years. Occupation: bushman. Country: England. Religion: Episcopalian. Sworn in by Captain William Jackson. Earlier served 70th Regiment, No. 3180. Sailed to New Zealand aboard *Louisa* May 1861. Killed in action at Orakau on 2 April 1864 by bullet to upper chest and throat.
New Zealand Medal named to Forest Rangers. Issued to next of kin, 1871.

Charles TEMPLE

1105, No. 1 Company: 17 November 1863 – disbandment, 30 October 1867. Private. Later served Te Awamutu Cavalry Volunteers. Enrolled at Auckland. Age: 33 years. Height: 5' 6" Hair colour: black. Eye colour: blue. Complexion: pale. Occupation: bushman. Country: England. Religion: Episcopalian. Sworn in by Captain William Jackson. Born 1830, Stockport, Lancashire, England. Died October 1885 at Kihikihi.
New Zealand Medal named to Forest Rangers. Medal claim dated 13 February 1870. The Medal Application states "**Address:** Kihikihi. **Corps:** Forest Rangers – the whole period of enrolment. **Field service:** Waikato Campaign, Paparata [13 December 1863], Waiari [11 February 1864], Orakau [31 March-2 April 1864], and Rangiaowhia [21 February 1864]." Received land: town lot No. 214, Kihikihi; farm lot No. 233, Puniu. Medal claim AD32/4281; AD36/3/2230. Medal and leather pouch (believed to have been Temple's), held in the Te Awamutu District Museum.

Arthur THIRD

Served No. 1 Company. Private. Earlier served 2nd Regiment Waikato Militia, No. 407. Later served No. 6 Division Armed Constabulary. Born 1837, Aberdeen, Scotland. Sailed to New Zealand aboard *Corio*. This claim to service with the Forest Rangers is on his Armed Constabulary record only. Possibly received impressed **New Zealand Medal** named to the Commissariat Transport Corps for service while with the Waikato Militia. Received land including town lot 299 Kihikihi.

Benjamin (*or* Blanchard) THOMAS

Served 27 October – 9 November 1865. Private. There is confusion over his exact identity.
If he was Benjamin Thomas, then he earlier served with the 4th Regiment Waikato Militia. Later served No. 2 Division Armed Constabulary. Born 1834, Stepney, England. Medal claim AD32/4292; AD36/3/2301
If he was Blanchard Thomas, then he earlier served with the Colonial Defence Force, Wellington.

John Henry THOMPSOM

36, No. 2 Company: Private. Served for period in 1866. Was one of the last substitutes in the Forest Rangers.
New Zealand Medal believed to be named to the Imperial Commissariat. In a letter to D. Borkett dated 10 November 1872, Thompson (residing at Harapepe, Waikato) states "Not having received the N.Z. Medal although a long while has elapsed since. I forwarded my address to the Officer Commanding Militia and Volunteers as directed to do. Will you kindly use your influence to find out the cause of my non receipt of the medal. There is a slight mistake in the initials of the name in the list [New Zealand Gazette]. It should be J.H., not A.H., but as I was the only one of the name attached to the Staff Corps, I do not think that it is the cause of the delay." Thompson said he served under fire at Meremere while in the Imperial Commissariat. Received land: town lot No. 53, Harapepe; farm lot No. 173, Pirongia. Medal claim AD32/1220 or 4303

William Michael THOMSON

1106, No. 1 Company: 17 November 1863 – November 1866 (last known month of service). Private. Later served Te Awamutu Cavalry Volunteers; Armed Constabulary; New Zealand Militia in the 1880's. Enrolled 17 November 1863 at Auckland. Age: 23 years. Height: 5' 8" Hair colour: light. Eye colour: blue. Complexion: fair. Occupation: farmer/settler. Country: England. Religion: Episcopalian. Sworn in by Captain William Jackson. Born 1840, Islington, Middlesex, England. **New Zealand Medal** named to Forest Rangers. Medal claim dated 7 November 1910 and received 5 April 1911. Medal issued 25 April 1911. The medal was officially renamed erasing the name of Y. Frazer, 1st Regiment Waikato Militia. The dates "1861-66" were deleted and polished. The Medal Application states "**Address:** Kihikihi, Te Awamutu. **Corps:** 2nd Regiment Waikato Militia. Major Jackson's Forest Rangers. Private. Joined 17 November 1863. Served all through Waikato War. Regimental No. 1106. **Field service:** At Waiari [11 February] and Rangiaowhia in [21] February 1864 and Orakau [31 March-2 April 1864] in April working in the sap and elsewhere. **Remarks:** Signature is in the original enrolment book at Te Awamutu. Enlisted 2nd Regiment Waikato Militia before transferring to the Forest Rangers 17 November 1863." Thomson declares in his medal application "... I was under fire at the battles of Rangiaowhia, Waiari and Orakau during the Maori war and that I have never received a war medal." Received land: town lot No. 78, Kihikihi; farm lot No. 179, Puniu. Present at reunion to commemorate 50 years of battle of Orakau, 1914. Medal in private collection. Medal claim AD32/674 and/or AD32/1648; AD/36/3/3112

Biographical notes

William THOMSON
No. 2 Company: 8 January – 20 May 1864. Private.

Henry THORNTON
Served 29 January – February 1866. Discharged at Wanganui. Private. Earlier served Taranaki Military Settlers. Joined at Warea while unit was with General Chute. Born 1844, Wapping, London, England. Sailed to New Zealand aboard *Otago*.

John THORPE
No. 1 Company: 5 January 1864 – February 1867. Employed as Guide/Interpreter (National Archives file CD63/1717). Received land: town lot 204, Kihikihi; farm lot No. 247, Puniu.

F. William THURSTON
1106, No. 1 Company: 17 November 1863 – 31 March 1864. Private. Enrolled at Auckland. Occupation: mariner. Sworn in by Captain William Jackson. Signed his enlistment with a mark. Discharged, unfit for service.

John TOOVEY
3, No. 2 Company: 23 December 1863 – disbandment, 30 October 1867. Private. Promoted to Corporal 10 March 1864. Promoted to Sergeant 26 April 1864. Earlier served 1st Regiment Waikato Militia, No. 100 (joined 11 September 1863 at Melbourne, Australia). Later served No. 5 Division Armed Constabulary, No. 46, Sergeant. Occupation: seaman. Slightly wounded at Te Ngutu o te Manu, 7 September 1868. Born 1833, Wickham, Hampshire. Sailed to New Zealand aboard *Caduseus*, 1863. Received land: town lot No. 95, Harapepe; farm lot Nos. 151 and 152, Pirongia.

David TORPEY
No. 1 Company: 1 January – 19 November 1864. Private. Substituted by William Shuker. Earlier served 2nd Regiment Waikato Militia, No. 410. Enrolled 27 August 1863 at Otago. Age: 27 years. Height: 5' 10". Hair colour: brown. Eye colour: blue. Complexion: fair. Occupation: miner. Country: Ireland. Religion: Roman Catholic. Born 1837, Tuam, Galway, Ireland. Land claim H13, 1898.

Charles Henry TREADWELL
1297, No. 1 Company: 1 September 1864 – January 1867 (last known month of service). Private. Promoted to Corporal 10 March 1864. Substitute for No. 330 Henry W. Bindon. Later served Wanganui Bush Rangers; Armed Constabulary. Enrolled at Pukerimu, Cambridge. Residence: Auckland. Age: 21 years. Height: 6'. Hair colour: light. Eye colour: blue. Complexion: fair. Occupation: farmer. Country: England. Religion: Episcopalian. Sworn in by Major William Jackson. Born 1843, Yorkshire, England. Served in the Colonial Forces from 1864-69. Retired to Marokopa, south of Kawhia. In 1910 Treadwell applied for an old age pension and admission to the Veteran House at Onehunga. To prove his entitlement he applied to the Defence Department for copies of his discharges. This application information is on file AD32/1855. Received land: town lot No. 216, Kihikihi; farm lot No. 332, Puniu.

Thomas TRELAWNEY
Period of service unknown. Also served Taranaki Cavalry Volunteers (perhaps Taranaki Bush Rangers); No. 7 Division Armed Constabulary. Born 1843, Denby, England. Sailed to New Zealand aboard *City of Hobart*, 1862. This claim to service with the Forest Rangers is on his Armed Constabulary record only.

James Quick TRISTRAM
62, No. 2 Company: July 1866 – disbandment, 30 October 1867. Private. Earlier served 40th Regiment, No. 1962. Later served Te Awamutu Cavalry Volunteers. Born Ashbrittle, Somerset, England. Received land: town lot No. 72, Harapepe, and No. 350, Kihikihi; farm lot No. 246, Pirongia.

James TUBBY
No. 2 Company: 13 January – 31 July 1864. Private. Sailed to New Zealand aboard *Nourmahal*, 1859.

Selby TUCKER
No. 1 Company: 29 February – 4 July 1864. Private. Earlier served 2nd Regiment Waikato Militia, No. 91, No. 1 Company. Enrolled 27 August 1863 at Otago. Age: 31 years. Height: 5' 8^1/$_2$". Hair colour: dark. Eye colour: grey. Complexion: sallow. Occupation: miner. Country: England. Religion: Episcopalian. Born 1833.

William TURNER
Original Company: 26 August – 10 November 1863. Private.

Luke TYRELL (TYRREL *or* TYRRELL)
Original Company: 11 August – 11 November 1863. Private. Born 1837, Wethersfield, Essex, England.

John USHER
57, No. 2 Company: 1 August 1864 – 18 April 1865. Private. Paid off at Waikato Heads just prior to Wanganui detachment leaving for Wanganui (possibly substituted by Codling). Possibly received impressed **New Zealand Medal** named to the Commissariat Transport Corps for service as a boatman on the Waikato River.

Eugene VARETTE
Served 14 November – December 1865 (last known month of service). Private. Later served Wanganui Bush Rangers. Enlisted in Forest Rangers at Wanganui.

George VART (DAVIDSON)
Served 3 December 1865 – disbandment, 30 October 1867. Private. Possibly deserted. Occupation: seaman. Born 1843, Whitby, Yorkshire, England.
Vart's medal application (dated 10 October 1913) states "**Address:** c/o John Bland, 133 Grey Street, Auckland. **Corps:** Forest Rangers raised by Major von Tempsky at Wanganui in December 1865. Private served for 6 or 7 months. Forest Rangers in the expeditionary force under General Chute. **Field service:** Capture of pas by General Chute's force at Okotuku [4 January 1866], Te Putahi [7 January 1866], Otapawa [14 January 1866], Warea and Waikoko [1 February 1866] in Taranaki taking part in capture with the Forest Rangers in the early part of 1866." The application is signed "George Vart". In a letter accompanying his application, Vart states "I was under the name of Davidson in the Forest Rangers. ... A man by name of Alexander Davidson [friend] was wounded [Waikoko, 1 February 1866] ... and I was sent back to Taranaki Hospital as an escort. As soon as he recovered from his wound I was sent to Wanganui to rejoin the Company. It wasn't there at time. I took part in no further engagements and left the Company soon after. There was no number of the Company to my knowledge. Just Forest Rangers. Under Major von Tempsky. There were 45 to 50 in the Company. All the men in charge of Major von Tempsky. Sergeant Birchfield and Sergeant [Lawrence] Burns. ... We were acting as an advance to General Chute's army. I was enrolled at Aramoho, Wanganui. I was a sailor and got discharged from ship. Met Alexander Davidson and we decided to join von Tempsky, which we did. I enlisted under name of Davidson."

John Gillanders made a statement substantiating Vart's application. He says "In view, however, of his admission that he joined under the name of Davidson in order that he might the more easier clear out if he got tired of the service and of the fact that he left the Company before disbandment and went inland to work on a farm under his own name [Vart]." A comment written on his application says "Unable to recommend his application until he proves that he got his discharge. There seems to be a considerable probability that he deserted." There is no proof on the file that a medal was issued. Medal claim AD32/634

Matthew VAUGHAN

1108, No. 1 Company: 8 December 1863 – November 1866 (last known month of service). Private. Enrolled at Auckland. Age: 21 years. Height: 5' 7". Hair colour: light. Eye colour: blue. Complexion: fair. Occupation: farmer. Country: England. Religion: Episcopalian. Sworn in by Captain William Jackson. Born 1842, Dudley, Worcestershire, England. Sailed to New Zealand aboard *Ganges*, 1863. Absent from unit 17-30 June 1864 without pay.
New Zealand Medal named to Forest Rangers. Medal claim dated 16 September 1878. The Medal Application states "**Address:** Queens Street, Grahamstown, Thames. **Corps:** Forest Rangers. Private. 3 years service. No number. **Field service:** 18 months active service. At the storming of Orakau 1st April [31 March-2 April] 1864. Vaughan states in a letter accompanying his application that he was "... in the Forest Rangers as a private during the Waikato War and being engaged with the enemy on many occasions during my term of service." Received land: town lot No. 203, Kihikihi; farm lot No. 259, Puniu. Medal claim AD32/4365; AD36/3/2685

William VINCENT

No. 1 Company: 29 February 1864 – November 1866 (last known month of service). Private. Earlier served 2nd Regiment Waikato Militia, No. 94, No. 1 Company. Age: 26 years. Height: 5' 6". Hair colour: brown. Eye colour: brown. Complexion: fresh. Occupation: platelayer. Country: England. Religion: Episcopalian. Born 1835, Dorset, England. Comment on roll "Want of two teeth in front".
New Zealand Medal named to Forest Rangers. Medal claim dated 6 February 1914 and received 1 April 1914. Medal issued 1 May 1914. The medal was officially renamed erasing the name of Private James Russell, 3rd Waikato Regiment of Militia. The dates "1861-66" were deleted and polished. The Medal Application states "**Address:** Kaihu, Dargaville. **Corps:** No. 1 Company, Forest Rangers under Captain (afterwards Major) Jackson. Rank: Private. Period of service: 3 years (almost). **Field service:** Orakau [31 March-] April 2nd 1864. Rangiaowhia (about six months previously) [actually 21 February 1864]. Various other skirmishes in and around Te Awamutu and Pukerimu [near Cambridge]. Vincent joined the Coromandel Rifle Rangers under Captain Blackenberry 1 September 1863 and transferred to the Forest Rangers 29 February 1864. Also served in Wairoa South (Coromandel District). Under fire in taking of Orakau pa 31 March-2 April 1864." Vincent particularly wanted the medal to wear at the 50 year commemoration of the battle of Orakau in 1914 at which he was present. Received land: town lot No. 11, Kihikihi; farm lot No. 339, Puniu. Medal claim AD32/572; AD36/3/3589

Gustavus Ferdinand VON TEMPSKY *(pictured)*

Original Company: 26 August – 10 November 1863. Ensign. **No. 2 Company:** 10 November 1863 (pay backdated to this date) – disbandment, 30 October 1867. Promoted Captain on 10 November 1863 and later Major on 4 April 1864. Born in Liegnitz, Prussia (then part of Prussia, but now in Poland) in 1828. The son of a senior officer in the Prussian Army, von Tempsky trained at the Berlin Military School and at Potsdam received a commission in the 3rd Fusiliers of Prussia at the age of 16. After four years in the army, von Tempsky travelled to Central America, then to California and the gold fields. After a spell of gold mining he made a remarkable overland return journey to the Mosquito Coast, married Emilia, daughter of the British resident James Stanislaus Bell, and returned with them to Scotland. While in Scotland he wrote of his adventures in his book *Milta*, before travelling to Victoria, Australia in 1856 to take up land for farming. He tried unsuccessfully to join what became the disastrous Burke and Wills expedition – it is said that the Victorian authorities did not like his Prussian manner. But the lure of adventure made him sell up and sail to New Zealand, without his family, aboard *Benjamin Heape*, arriving Auckland, 10 March 1862. Immediately he joined the gold rush at Coromandel. His family arrived aboard the *Kate* during March 1863. When the first shots of the Waikato War were fired, von Tempsky tried unsuccessfully to raise a fighting unit in the gold fields, but could not get his captaincy to command the unit (he had to have New Zealand citizenship to hold a commission). So he became a war correspondent for the Auckland newspaper *Daily Southern Cross*. After rubbing shoulders with Lieutenant Jackson at the Forest Ranger headquarters, the Travellers' Rest inn on the Papakura-Wairoa road, von Tempsky was invited to accompany Jackson on an expedition into the Wairoa Ranges. Because of his military ability, von Tempsky was soon offered a commission as Ensign and military advisor in the Forest Rangers. After the Corps was disbanded 10 November 1863, he was promoted to Captain and invited to raise a second company of Forest Rangers under his direct command. Von Tempsky was later appointed Major in the 1st Regiment Waikato Militia 4 April 1864, immediately after the battle of Orakau. After leading the Forest Rangers into battle near Kakaramea 13 May 1865, von Tempsky was placed under arrest for refusing to serve under Major Fraser, junior in promotion to von Tempsky. But he was reinstated following the withdrawal of his resignation when a new Defence Minister was appointed. Von Tempsky then served in Opotiki without his Forest Rangers. Early in 1866, von Tempsky and the Forest Rangers accompanied

General Chute on his Taranaki march. On 21 February 1866 von Tempsky arrived in Auckland with his Forest Rangers. They proceeded to the Waikato, reporting to Lieutenant-Colonial Moule, Commanding Officer of the Waikato Militia, on 2 March 1866. Von Tempsky returned to Auckland. Because of some disagreement over the return of arms and accoutrements from his unit, von Tempsky's land grants were not received until 29 August 1866, when he received one acre in the town of Harapepe and the next day received 400 acres in the parish of Pirongia. But he returned to the gold mines of Coromandel, then to Auckland. Major von Tempsky was invited to command No. 5 Division of the newly formed Armed Constabulary with headquarters at Alexandra (Pirongia). He was given the rank of Inspector dated from 7 January 1868. The Alexandra Division was back again in Wanganui, and took part in the controversial relief of Turuturu Mokai on 12 July 1868 and in the first engagement at Te Ngutu o te Manu on 21 August 1868. However, he was killed at Te Ngutu o te Manu 7 September 1868 where he received a bullet in the forehead while standing waving his sabre. His body was not recovered by the Armed Constabulary. It was reported that his body was cremated on a funeral pyre. (It is possible that he was consumed by Maori because of the great mana his body possessed.) He was widely admired for his courage, energy and military ability, but deprecated by many for his Prussian arrogance and vainglory. At the time, Prussians were not popular in New Zealand. He is remembered today for his attractive watercolours held in many New Zealand collections. They present a romantic and detailed view of military life, engagements and the Maori during the 1860's. Received land: town lot No. 93, Harapepe; farm lot Nos. 91-98 (8 50 acre lots totalling 400 acres), Pirongia. His family received his **New Zealand Medal** named to the New Zealand Militia, issued 1871. Medal claim AD32/79

Tamati WAKA (WAKAU)
Served 8 December 1865 – 8 January 1866. Private. Enlisted at Woodall's Redoubt. File AD32/1205 under name of Tamati Wakau holds no papers.

Henry John WAKEFORD
Original Company: 26 August – 10 November 1863. Private. **4, No. 2 Company:** 24 November 1863 – 21 November 1864. Sergeant. Substituted by Martin Hennessey. Born 1841, Surrey, England. Sailed to New Zealand aboard *Tornado* September 1859.
New Zealand Medal named to Forest Rangers. Medal claim dated 12 June 1890. The Medal Application states **"Address:** Village Settlement, Pahiatua. **Corps:** First Corps of Rangers as Private under the late Major Jackson and in No. 2 Compy as Sergeant under Major von Tempsky. **Field service:** About two years. Under fire at Paterangi [Waiari, 11 February 1864], Rangiaowhia [21 February 1864], Orakau [31 March-2 April 1864], etc." Land claim H36B, 1892. Medal claim AD1/1890/1279; AD32/269; AD36/3/2935

James WALKER
58, No. 2 Company: 8 June 1864 – 4 January 1865. Private.

James WALLACE
Served 28 January – February 1866. Private. Joined at Oakura while unit was with General Chute. Discharged in Wanganui.

Thomas W. WALLACE
No. 1 Company: 21 October 1865 – 31 March 1866. Private. Substitute for Cullinan. Earlier served 70th Regiment; Colonial Defence Force, Wellington. Later served in No. 4 Division Armed Constabulary. Enrolled at Wellington. Age: 29 years. Height: 5' 9". Hair colour: fair. Complexion: fair. Occupation: soldier. Country: Scotland. Religion: Presbyterian. Born 1838, Kildonan Bute, Arran, Scotland. Sailed to New Zealand aboard *Louisa* May 1861. Died 17 January 1912, Shortland, Thames.

John WALSH
Period of service unknown. Earlier served Royal Navy. Later served Armed Constabulary. Born Newtown, Cork, Ireland. This claim to service with the Forest Rangers is on his Armed Constabulary record only.

Joseph WARBEY
Original Company: 11-25 August 1863. Private. Later served 2nd Regiment Waikato Militia, No. 879. Born 1830, Epping, Essex, England. Received land including town lot No. 466, Alexandra East (Pirongia).

George WARD
Original Company: 11 August – 11 November 1863. Private. **1110, No. 1 Company:** 17 November 1863 – 16 August 1864. Private. Enrolled at Auckland. Residence: Waikato. Age: 25 years. Height: 5' 8". Hair colour: black. Eye colour: black. Complexion: black (Negro). Occupation: bushman. Country: United States of America. Religion: Episcopalian. Sworn in by Captain William Jackson. Signed his enlistment with a mark. Born 1837, Port Penn, Delaware, United States of America.
New Zealand Medal named to Forest Rangers. Medal claim dated 4 October 1870. The Medal Application states "**Address:** Puriri [south of Thames]. **Corps:** Captain Jackson's Forest Rangers. Private. 63/64/65. **Field service:** One year. Waikato. Paparata [13th] December 1863. Orakau, March 31, April 1 & 2, 1864." Medal claim AD32/4404; AD36/3/2403

John Patrick WARD
Served 28 January – February 1866. Discharged at Wanganui. Private. Joined at Oakura while unit was with General Chute. Earlier served Taranaki Military Settlers, No. 367. Later served No. 6 Division Armed Constabulary. Born 1847, Sydney, New South Wales. Sailed to New Zealand aboard *Claude Hamilton*, March 1864. Joined unit in Wanganui district. Ward probably served with another unit at engagements in early 1866.
New Zealand Medal named to the Forest Rangers. In a letter serving as a medal application, dated 7 June 1912 at Owhango, Ward states "Fought under von Tempsky throughout General Chute's West Coast campaign of 1865/66 and was promised a grant of land, which I never got. In this campaign I was present at the battles of Okotuku [4 January 1866], Te Putahi [7 January 1866] – skirmish near Kakaramea. Battles of Otapawa [14 January 1866] and Waikoko [1 February 1866]. I was slightly wounded in this last fight [did not report his injury]. We had to eat our pack horses in the campaign before we cut our way through the bush to Mataitawa. In 1868 I left the Thames goldfield on hearing of the terrible defeat at 'The Beak of the Bird' [Te Ngutu o te Manu] where my gallant old leader von Tempsky was killed and left behind. I at once joined No. 6 Division Armed Constabulary and in it was present at skirmish near Wairoa [Wanganui district]. Battle next day of Papa-tihakehake [Moturoa, 7 November 1868]. My division lost 22 killed, wounded and missing in this action out of 68 all told. Skirmish at Woodall Redoubt. And in the Poverty Bay campaign: Skirmish at Patutahi [20 November 1868]. Action at the 'Crows Nest' – siege and capture of Ngatapa [1-5 January 1869]. In last Taranaki campaign, action at McKenzie's Farm, siege and capture of Tauranga-Ika [2 February 1869], battle of Karaka Flat [3 February 1869], battle of Otauta [13 March 1869], siege and capture of Te Naere. In the Urewera campaign [numerous engagements between 6 May-9 May, including Te Harema, Whataponga, Manawa-hiwi, Te Paripari, Hukanui, Tahora, Orangikawa, Orona and Te Wai-iti]. I took my discharge as Sergeant [in 1884]." If there is no exaggeration in Ward's statement, he saw a lot of action! Pension claim D639/5 (Patea Museum). Medal claim AD32/1761

M. (possibly John) WARDEN
14-22 December 1865. Private. One of the shortest periods of service with the Forest Rangers.

WARFORD
There is reference of this man on the 1st Regiment Waikato Militia's register as being transferred to the No. 2 Company Forest Rangers prior to 14 November 1864. No other reference can be found of service with the Forest Rangers. Possibly he never completed the transfer, was rejected or he fell ill, as he died 6 April 1867.

Horima WATENE
Served 8 December 1865 – February 1866. Private. Enlisted at Woodall's Redoubt. Discharged at Wanganui.

William Frank WATSON (Nicknamed "Duck")
Served 12 November – 22 December 1865. Private. Earlier served Taranaki Military Settlers; Patea Rifle Volunteers; Patea Field Force. Later served Native Contingent. Enlisted in Forest Rangers in Wanganui district. Born 1844, Kingston on Thames, Surrey, England. Land claim H13, 1898. Medal claim AD32/4419

James WATTERS
Original Company: 11 August – 11 November 1863. Private. **1109, No. 1 Company:** 17 November 1863 – August 1867 (last known month of service). Private. Promoted to Sergeant. Later served Te Awamutu Cavalry Volunteers. Enrolled at Auckland. Age: 25 years. Height: 5' 7". Hair colour: black. Eye colour: black. Complexion: black (Negro). Occupation: labourer. Country: United States of America. Religion: Presbyterian. Sworn in by Captain William Jackson. Born 1838, Philadelphia, United States of America. Sent 18 March 1864 to Maketu by Captain Jackson from Pukerimu Redoubt, Cambridge in support of the Arawa Friendly Natives. Rejoined Forest Rangers 3 November 1864. Received no pay while absent, possibly because he was placed on McDonnell's Arawa acquittance roll.
New Zealand Medal named to the Forest Rangers. Medal Application, dated 8 February 1870, states "**Address:** James Watters, Te Rahu, Waikato. **Corps:** No. 1 Company, Forest Rangers. Sergeant. Enrolled August 10th 1863. **Field service:** Mauku [8 September 1863], Paparata [13 December 1863], Waiari [11 February 1864], Rangiaowhia [21 February 1864], Maketu and Matata [April 1864], Kakaramea [13 May 1865], Waiapu, Poverty Bay [Pukemaire, 3 October 1865]. **Remarks:** Been seven years in the Colonial forces: Defence Force, Forest Rangers, Hawke's Bay Military Settlers, Mounted Troop, Armed Constabulary." Received land: town lot No. 73, Kihikihi; farm lot No. 293, Puniu. Medal claim AD32/4423; AD36/3/2369

John Ross WATTS
Served with No. 1 Company for an unknown period of service. Ensign. Earlier served Madras Horse Artillery. Later served No. 4 Division Armed Constabulary, Sub-Inspector. Died 27 March 1877 and buried Symonds Street, Auckland. Received land including town lot No. 120 Kihikihi.
New Zealand Medal named to the Armed Constabulary. Medal Application, dated 26 August 1870, states "**Address:** 2nd Class Sub Inspector, Armed Constabulary, Alexandra [Pirongia]. **Corps:** No. 4 Division Armed Constabulary. Acting Sub Inspector. **Field service:** From 1 Feby 1869 to 31 July 1869. Ambuscade by Hauhau between Ahi-Kereru and Tatahoata, Ruatahuna, Urewera Country, 7 May 1869. Engaged with Hauhau about two miles from Tatahoata, Ruatahuna, 10 May 1869." Medal claim AD36/3/2362

James WEAL
No. 1 Company: 1 June 1866 – August 1867 (last known month of service). Private. Earlier served

40th Regiment, No. 2580. Later served Te Awamutu Cavalry Volunteers. Enrolled 1 June 1866 at Kihikihi, Te Awamutu. Age: 38 years. Born 1828. Sailed to New Zealand aboard *Queen of the South*, 1863. Died 20 October 1909, and buried at Hairini. Received land: town lot No. 1, Kihikihi; farm lot No. 234, Puniu.
New Zealand Medal named to the 40th Regiment.

William WELLS
Original Company: August – 10 November 1863. Private. **1111, No. 1 Company:** 17 November 1863 – October 1866 (last known month of service). Private. Enrolled at Auckland. Age: 25 years. Height: 5' 7". Hair colour: brown. Eye colour: blue. Complexion: leery. Occupation: labourer. Country: England. Religion: Episcopalian. Sworn in by Captain William Jackson. Born 1838, Ripponden, Yorkshire, England. Received land: town lot No. 6, Kihikihi; farm lot No. 253, Puniu.

Charles WESTRUP
Original Company: August – 10 November 1863. Private. **No. 1 Company:** 18 November 1863 – (end of service date unknown). Ensign. Commission in Auckland Militia, attached to Forest Rangers, dated 26 November 1863. Promoted to Lieutenant (Auckland Militia) dated 11 February 1864, the same day of the action at Waiari. Promoted to Captain (Auckland Militia) dated 23 September 1865. Promoted to Major (New Zealand Militia) dated 27 November 1868. Later served Poverty Bay Cavalry Volunteers; New Zealand Militia. Enrolled at Thames. Aged: 23 years. Occupation: farmer. Sworn in by Captain William Jackson. Born 1840, Queenhithe, London, England. Sailed to New Zealand aboard *Northern Bride* October 1860. Later farmed 11,000 acres at Te Arai, Poverty Bay.
New Zealand Medal named to the Forest Rangers. Medal Application (dated 21 August 1872) states "**Address:** Charles Westrup, Major, Poverty Bay. **Corps:** No. 1 Forest Rangers. **Field service:** Orakau, April 1st and 2nd 1864." Approved by Major William Jackson (signed). Received land: town lot No. 69, Kihikihi; farm lot Nos. 192, 193, 195, 196, 197 and 198, Puniu. Medal claim AD32/571; AD36/3/2493

Thomas WHEELER
No. 2 Company: 16 December 1863 – 31 July 1864. Private.

Robert WHITFIELD
No. 1 Company: 14 December 1863 – 13 May 1865. Sergeant. Commissioned as Ensign dated 18 February 1864. Killed in action. Earlier served No. 4 Company, 2nd Regiment Waikato Militia, as Sergeant. Von Tempsky speaks very highly of Whitfield in his account of Orakau "… [he] got his commission for his behaviour at Mangapiko [Waiari]. At Orakau his services were quite as prominent, and should have been recognised more than they were." Mortally wounded at Kakaramea, 13 May 1865. Whitfield was hit by two shots, one breaking his arm and one entering his side. He later died at Patea, 11.30 pm, 13 May 1865. Von Tempsky again spoke highly of Whitfield's bravery at Kakaramea.
New Zealand Medal named to Forest Rangers. Medal claim dated 19 August 1871. The Medal Application states "**Address:** Agnes Whitfield, mother, Te Awamutu. **Corps:** Forest Rangers. Ensign. Nov 10th 1863 [incorrect date probably because application being made by mother] till 13th May 1865. **Field service:** Orakau 31st March, 1st & 2nd April 1864. Rangiaowhia 20th [21st] Feb 1864. Kihikihi [Hairini] 22nd February. Paterangi [Waiari, 11 February 1864]. Kakaramea 15th [13th] May 1865. **Remarks:** Killed in action at Kakaramea, May 15th [13th] May 1865." His wife received land: town lot No. 79, Kihikihi; farm lot Nos. 183, 184, 185 and 186, Puniu. Medal claim AD32/1788; AD36/3/2472

James P. WILLIAMS
No. 1 Company: 10 December 1863 – 20 March 1864. Sergeant. Occupation: seaman. Born Port Elley, Caenarvon, Wales. Died 16 October 1913 at Thames. Land claim H36B, 1892.
New Zealand Medal named to the Forest Rangers. Medal issued 18 September 1873. Transcript of medal application (dated 18 September 1872) states "**Address:** Auckland. **Corps:** Sergeant. No. 1 Forest Rangers. **Field service:** Paparata [13 December 1863], Mangapiko [Waiari, 11 February 1864], and two others." Medal in private collection. Medal claim AD32/3668; AD36/3/2407

Thomas Wetherall WILLIAMS
1323, No. 1 Company: 1 December 1864 – November 1866 (last known month of service). Private. Substitute. Enrolled at Wairoa, south Auckland. Age: 28 years. Height: 5' 9^1/$_2$". Hair colour: light. Eye colour: grey. Complexion: fresh. Occupation: butcher. Country: England. Religion: Episcopalian. Sworn in by Major William Jackson. Born 1836, Newport, Yorkshire. Received land: town lot No. 75, Kihikihi; farm lot No. 182, Puniu.

William WILLIAMS
1112, No. 1 Company: 11 December 1863 – 16 August 1864. Private. Enrolled at Papakura. Age: 34 years. Height: 5' 8". Hair colour: black. Complexion: dark. Occupation: seaman. Country: Wales. Religion: Episcopalian. Sworn in by Captain William Jackson. Signed enlistment with a mark. Born 1829, Port Elley, Caenarvon, Wales.

George WILSON
59, No. 2 Company: 6 April 1864 – October 1867 (last known month of service). Private. Earlier served 1st Regiment Waikato Militia, No. 1015 (joined 11 September 1863 at Ballarat, Australia). Occupation: miner. Born 1836, Banff, Scotland. Sailed to New Zealand aboard *Caduseus*, 1863. Received land: town lot No. 16, Harapepe; farm lot No. 204, Pirongia. Possibly received impressed **New Zealand Medal** named to the Commissariat Transport Corps in 1899 for service while with the Waikato Militia.

Charles George WINMILL
Served 28 December 1865 – February 1866. Private. Earlier served Colonial Defence Force, Wellington. Born 1831, Spitalfields, Stepney, London, England. Enlisted in Forest Rangers in Wanganui district. Discharged in Wanganui.

William S. WOODS
60, No. 2 Company: 11 January 1864 – February 1867 (last known month of service). Private. Sailed to New Zealand aboard *Harwood*, 1861. Received land: town lot No. 14, Harapepe; farm lot No. 154, Pirongia.

John Henry A. WRIGHT (Later Harrie John WRIGHT-ST. CLAIR)
19, No. 2 Company: 16 December 1864 – April 1865 (last known month of service). Private. Substitute for Henry Duesbury. Later served Wanganui Bush Rangers; Armed Constabulary. Born 26 January 1847, Gravesend, Kent, England. Died 13 March 1914 at Ngaruawahia.
New Zealand Medal named to Forest Rangers. Medal claim dated 13 February 1913 and received 17 February 1913. Medal issued 21 July 1913. The medal was officially renamed erasing the name of Private J. Pull, 2nd Regiment Waikato Militia. The dates "1861-66" were deleted and polished. The Medal Application states "**Address:** Ngaruawahia. **Corps:** No. 2 Forest Rangers. G.F. von Tempsky's Company. Rank: Ranger. Period of service: 2 years or more. No regimental number. **Field service:** Gentle Annie, Patea [near Kakaramea 15 May 1865]. Cannot remember date." Wright-St. Clair stated in his medal application "I had run away from a vessel previously to joining the Rangers and I was rather glad for my real name not to be known and that is why I allowed

myself to be enrolled as John Henry Wright. A shipmate of mine who was also in the Rangers used to call me Wright and that is how I first got the name. I was acting as 4th Officer on the ship and he was a passenger. I was more often called Wright on shipboard than St. Clair – my name is Wright-St. Clair (with a hyphen). I and W. Stephenson VC [doubtful] were always the first to 'step out' when volunteers were called for anything special. I was enrolled end of 1863 or 1864 and resigned about 1865 or 1866. I was close on two years on active service. I was in the skirmish at Gentle Annie [near Kakaramea 15 May 1865] with Myles [Private Edmond Myles, No. 9 Company, 2nd Regiment Waikato Militia] and at other skirmishes. Three killed I think. I was actually under fire for many times. I was taken prisoner by the Maori near Kakaramea but escaped about a quarter of an hour later. We were after cattle at the time. Never been guilty of conduct unworthy of a soldier. Accidentally shot a man [John Duggan, a Forest Ranger, on 2 August 1865] with a revolver at Pipiriki during the relief of that place. At the inquest the jury found that it was a pure accident. He [Duggan] raised his revolver and pointed it at me and I raised mine and it went off without my intending it. Major George [Captain Nelson George, 3rd Regiment Waikato Militia] of Wapiti can support my statements. He was present when the man made a dying statement which helped to exonerate me. I was under fire two days prior to the Gentle Annie under von Tempsky's 100 men at Kakaramea."

A grandson writes of Wright "He was born in Gravesend, Kent, on 26 January 1847 as John Henry Wright, son of Edward Sinclair Wright, tailor, and Emma Wright, nee Gaud. On his marriage certificate of 1884 his name was given as Harrie John Wright-St Clair. ... H.J. Wright-St Clair was in the Armed Constabulary, based at Kihikihi and in Alexandra (Pirongia). He was a fluent Maori speaker. When he lived in Ngaruawahia he served as an interpreter for the Maori Land Court in the town. He died at the home of his second daughter, in Ngaruawahia on 13 March 1914." Medal claim AD32/508; AD36/3/3316

Engagements

Engagements involving Forest Rangers and ex-Forest Rangers

1863
Kirikiri, near Papakura .... 22 July 1863
Lusk's (Hill's) Clearing, Mauku, near Pukekohe .... 8 September 1863
Pukekohe East Church, near Pukekohe .... 14 September 1863
Titi Hill (Bald Hill), Mauku, near Pukekohe .... 23 October 1863
Rangiriri, north Waikato .... 20 November 1863
Paparata, Hunua Ranges .... 13 December 1863

1864
Waiari, Mangapiko Stream, near Te Awamutu .... 11 February 1864
Rangiaowhia, near Te Awamutu .... 21 February 1864
Hairini, near Te Awamutu .... 22 February 1864
Orakau, near Te Awamutu .... 31 March-2 April 1864
Maketu, Bay of Plenty .... 21-26 April 1864

1865
Kakaramea, South Taranaki/Wanganui .... 13 May 1865
Gentle Annie, South Taranaki/Wanganui .... 15 May 1865
Weraroa, South Taranaki/Wanganui .... 21 July 1865
Pipiriki (siege of), Wanganui River .... 19-30 July 1865
Pukemaire, East Coast .... 3 October 1865
Waerengaahika, Poverty Bay .... 15-21 November 1865

1866
Okotuku, South Taranaki/Wanganui .... 4 January 1866
Te Putahi, West Coast .... 7 January 1866
Otapawa, South Taranaki .... 14 January 1866
Ketemarae, South Taranaki .... 15 January 1866
Waikoko (Stoney River), Taranaki .... 1 February 1866
Pungarehu, Taranaki .... 2 October 1866

1867 (no engagements)

1868
Turuturu Mokai, South Taranaki .... 12 July 1868
Paparatu, south of Poverty Bay .... 20 July 1868
Ruakituri, inland from Wairoa, Hawke's Bay .... 8 August 1868
Te Ngutu o te Manu, South Taranaki .... 21 August 1868
Te Ngutu o te Manu, South Taranaki .... 7 September 1868
Moturoa, South Taranaki/Wanganui .... 7 November 1868
Poverty Bay Massacre/Matawhero .... 10 November 1868
Pukepuke, inland from Poverty Bay .... 20 November 1868
Makaretu, inland from Poverty Bay .... 3 December 1868
Ngatapa, inland from Poverty Bay .... 5 December 1868

1869
Ngatapa (siege of), inland from Poverty Bay .... 1-5 January 1869

Weapons, uniform and equipment

All three companies – the Original Company, and the No. 1 and No. 2 Companies – were similarly equipped except for the use of the bowie knife (bush knife), which was used almost exclusively by von Tempsky's No. 2 Company. The following descriptions are generally accepted as being at the time the unit was formed, late 1863.

There is evidence (quartermaster records just prior to Chute's campaign in South Taranaki, 1865-66) that a reasonable standard of uniform was maintained. Probably the Forest Rangers who enlisted on the East Coast were the worst dressed, as stores were not readily available in that area.

After long periods in the field, especially in bush country, uniforms quickly disintegrated. When Chute's expedition ended in early 1866, the men's uniforms were in poor condition. By the time the unit was disbanded, there was probably little of the original uniform and equipment remaining.

Revolver

Revolvers were a general issue to the Forest Rangers. These were percussion 5 shot 54 gauge English manufactured revolvers. They were issued first to the original company and later re-issued to both No. 1 and 2 Companies.

With the 24 carbines obtained from the Colonial Defence Force Cavalry, Auckland, on 8 August 1863, came 24 revolvers of mixed type and quality. Of these only 5 revolvers were serviceable, the others being of obsolete type or ammunition, or in un-serviceable condition.

Jackson made a request to the Colonial Defence Office for 57 further revolvers in a letter dated 5 September 1863, wanting a total of 62 serviceable revolvers with the unit.

A Government storekeeper in Auckland noted that only 68 revolvers were in stock: 21 Tranters, 40 Adams and 7 Kerrs, all of 54 gauge. All 57 requested revolvers were despatched on 8 September, Jackson receiving them on 11 September. The 21 Tranters and 36 Adams revolvers were sent. Jackson was informed about the remaining revolvers should he require them.

Later, Jackson was asked what ammunition he required for his unit's revolvers. In a later letter dated 4 December 1863 at Papakura, to the Deputy Adjutant General Militia and Volunteers (Lieutenant-Colonel Balneavis), Jackson replied:

> Sir, In acknowledging the receipt of your letter No. 2428 dated Dec 3rd 1863; I have the honour to inform you, that all revolvers under my charge are of 54 gauge.

The file containing the letter also refers to the revolvers being 54 gauge. Gauge (American term) and bore (English term) were loosely used to describe the same thing – the number of cast balls made to fit a certain size barrel on a firearm out of one pound of lead. For comparison 54 gauge (bore) equates with .44 calibre or 11.2 mm.

The main revolver of 54 gauge (bore) in general issue in New Zealand at the time of the formation of the Forest Rangers was the Beaumont Adams five shot

Jackson's personal revolver, a Tranter Third Model, Double Trigger 54 gauge revolver.

double action revolver, which embodied a modification to the earlier Deane Adams self cocking revolver. This 1855 modification allowed either thumb cocking (i.e. cocking by the use of a hammer spur such as on the Colt single action revolvers) or self cocking by pulling the trigger (such as on the Deane Adams revolvers). In each case the cylinder turned to the next available firing position. Also used by the Forest Rangers were 54 gauge double trigger Tranter revolvers and probably a number of the Deane Adams self cocking revolvers of the same calibre.

The Deane Adams were the first true solid frame design, since the barrel and frame were a single forging. It was a much stronger design than the Colt (in two pieces with the cylinder being unprotected on the top). Being self cocking (a pull of the trigger turned the cylinder, cocked and released the hammer), the Deane Adams lent itself to rapid firing but not to accuracy. The more advanced Beaumont Adams was double action as described above.

The double trigger Tranter contained the equivalent features of both the above models. It had a solid frame as the Adams varieties, and the lower trigger was actually a "cocking lever". This allowed the revolver to be cocked and held ready for aiming for as long as was necessary. The use of the upper trigger meant only a light touch was necessary to fire the weapon. Should rapid fire be required, both triggers could be used together, giving a very fast rate of fire for its vintage. It is on record that this feature was not entirely satisfactory in the hands of a novice, as reports show men in the heat of action at close quarters were known to tug vainly on the lower trigger only, which did not fire the revolver.

Revolvers were carried in British military pattern leather holsters that buttoned down and were worn on the belt. Similar holsters were made in the United States of America.

Beaumont Adams 54 gauge revolver. Shown alongside is a contemporary British pattern holster as issued to the Forest Rangers.

Officers probably made private firearm purchases. Jackson's personal revolver (Tranter Third Model, Double Trigger 54 gauge), used throughout his service, is now held by the Te Awamutu District Museum. This revolver, serial number 15,329T and marked above the barrel by the retailer "HENRY CHALLENER 61 KING ST WEST SYDNEY NSW", may have been from the original batch of 21 Tranters transferred to the Forest Rangers from Government stores. All 21 Tranters may be stamped by the same retailer. A similar revolver (with consecutive serial number 15,328T), also retailed by Challener, is held in a New Zealand collection after being purchased within New Zealand.

It was common practice amongst colonial forces (especially officers) to modify revolver grips with a pierced hole to hold a lanyard. This was to avoid losing revolvers when in the bush or in battle.

If other types of revolvers were used then these were by personal choice and purchase. Von Tempsky was believed to have issued about thirty 1851 .36 calibre Colt Navy revolvers (Government issue) to his No. 2 Company in December 1863, because he favoured this weapon over the British types. This is confirmed by William Race who, in his manuscript, claims to have carried a Colt revolver. Von Tempsky owned two Colt Navy revolvers which he brought from overseas.

Choice also depended on what was available at the time and at what price. The 1851 .36 calibre Navy Colt revolver was favoured for its accuracy and lightness and maybe because von Tempsky had seen its usefulness in California. Colts being single action (the pulling of the hammer is done by the thumb and the trigger only releases the hammer in a single action), were accurate, as they could be held steady throughout firing. The 1860 .44 calibre Army Colt revolver was not readily available in New Zealand because of the demand placed on it by the American Civil War.

Von Tempsky's request for ammunition for the forthcoming Chute's expedition in late 1865 is further evidence that his company used Colts. Lieutenant-Colonel Edward Gorton, in a letter to the Colonial Defence Office, Wellington dated 28 December 1865, wrote:

> I regret I am unable to purchase in Wanganui Colt revolver ammunition of the size requested for the 30 Colt revolvers now in possession of Major von Tempsky's men. Seventeen large revolvers have been issued to Major von Tempsky from this office [Wanganui Military District], and it is my intuition to collect as many as I can from the Cavalry Volunteers on their next visit and exchange them with Major von Tempsky for the smaller size. At the same time I trust ammunition for the latter will be able to be purchased at Wellington or elsewhere and sent up here as soon as possible.

The large revolvers referred to are probably English 54 gauge revolvers.

Carbine

Issued long arms consisted of the Callisher and Terry capping breechloading percussion carbine and the Enfield muzzle-loading rifle. The Enfield only had limited use until replaced by Callisher and Terry carbines as they became available.

The Callisher and Terry carbine, often called the Terry, was imported in limited numbers, the Forest Rangers being one unit that was completely issued with the firearm. The Terry was one of several breechloaders submitted for trial to the War Department in Britain in the 1850's when the British Army was seeking a suitable carbine for the cavalry. Pattern 1 was approved in 1858, Pattern 2 on 13 November 1860, and Pattern 3 on 9 March 1861. The last two patterns differed in minor details only and were the types issued in New Zealand.

Some mounted units, including the Colonial Defence Force Cavalry of Auckland, received the carbine in 1863. Many were earlier issued to the mounted branch of the Constabulary in 1861-62. Other units to receive the carbine were the Taranaki Bush Rangers, Wanganui Cavalry Volunteers and Opotiki Rangers. Units which were known to use the carbine but not necessarily have it as general issue were the Patea Rangers, Wellington Rangers, Wanganui Rangers, Colonial Defence Force Cavalry, Taranaki Mounted Volunteers and Poverty Bay Cavalry. Many were still in service up until 1872. By the time the Forest Rangers were disbanded, other makes of carbines and rifles were used, including the very first Snider firearms to see service in New Zealand.

Of .539 calibre (13.69 mm or 30 bore) the carbine was rifled with five lanes with a twist of one turn in 36 inches, and was sighted to 900 yards (823 metres). The barrel measured 21 inches from nipple to muzzle and the overall length was three feet, two and a half inches. It weighed six and a half pounds. Sling swivels were fitted instead of side rib and ring. Many swivels became loose during bush operations

Callisher and Terry capping breach-loader percussion carbine.

and skilful field repairs can be seen on examples today. The lock plate was marked "CALLISHER & TERRY LONDON". Some carbines had this written in one line, others in two. The barrel was marked over the breech "TERRY'S PATENT 30 BORE" and "CALLISHER & TERRY MAKERS TO H.M. WAR DEPARTMENT" along the top.

The Terry was an exceedingly handy weapon – it shot well – but like most transitional arms it had its share of faults. The paper cartridges were not completely waterproofed and became useless when damp, especially after long periods in the bush. Combustible un-burnt residue clogged up the breech after prolonged firing, and leakage of gas to the rear became severe as wear in the breech mechanism progressed.

In the carbine's favour, the nitrated combustible paper cartridge had a rear sealing wad of greased felt which was left in the breech after firing. When a second cartridge was fired, the first wad pushed through the barrel cleaning and lubricating the bore.

The Terry could not carry a bayonet, as it was originally designed for cavalry use only.

A large order was placed with Messrs Callisher and Terry Ltd by the New Zealand Agent General in London, Mr J. Morrison, during August 1863. The order was for 1000 carbines and 500 Beaumont Adams revolvers (apparently made under licence with probably a "C" suffix serial number). Further smaller monthly orders followed this initial order. The first carbines probably did not reach Auckland until early 1864.

The first 24 carbines came to Jackson from the Colonial Defence Force Cavalry, Auckland, on 8 August 1863.

They probably came from Australia or an earlier order from England or both. The New Zealand Government probably placed an order for Callisher and Terry carbines during 1861-62. The *Birmingham and Midland Hardware Trade Directory* mentions an order during this period for use by mounted police (Constabulary) in New Zealand.

A considerable number of carbines were ordered by the New South Wales Government. These were probably marked "N.S.W." on the trigger guard and

Weapons, uniform and equipment

Von Tempsky watercolour depicting a Forest Ranger fully decked out in his issued uniform. Note the revolver in holster, bowie knife and blanket. No silver badge is worn on the cap.
Waikato Museum of Art and History

butt and were principally issued to police and cadets. In 1863 a shipment of (about 200) carbines came to New Zealand from Australia at the request of the New Zealand Government because of the imminent war in the south Auckland district.

New Zealand issue numbers were stamped on the butt cap tang starting from No. 1. The lower the number the earlier the issue. Examples with numbers over 1500 exist in collections today. A manufacturer's serial number is stamped on all major parts. The butt plate was fitted with a small trap in which were kept a cleaning brush and a short section of the cleaning rod, the larger part being fitted beneath the barrel.

Captain Holt, Under Secretary to the Colonial Defence Office, in February 1866 demanded the whereabouts of two carbines probably lost during Chute's expedition. He quoted their issue numbers: No. 1401 and No. 1394, stating they came out of quartermaster stores in Wanganui. This indicates that high serial numbered carbines were in general issue as early as 1866.

A Callisher and Terry in poor condition is held in the Auckland Institute and

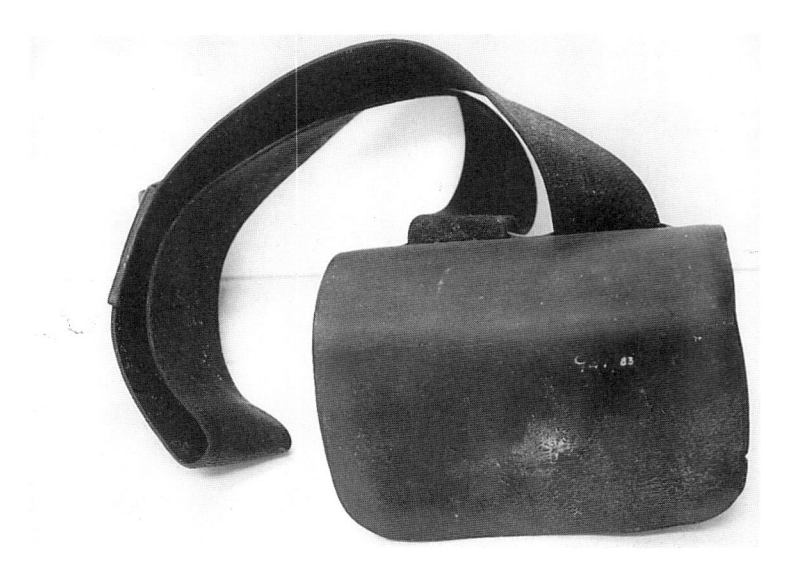

Leather pouch with strap attributed to Charles Temple of the Forest Rangers.
Te Awamutu District Museum

Museum collection. On the butt tang is engraved: A/F 567 (the "A" is at 90° to the "F", read from the rear of the gun) and engraved on the trigger guard is: N.S.W (the dots between the letters are at half letter height). Does the "A" indicate that the carbine was issued from Auckland and the "F" indicate Forest Rangers? This may be possible but there is no evidence verifying this claim.

Another example held by the Te Awamutu District Museum, is attributed to the Forest Rangers. The butt tang is engraved with: N.Z. 1584. Higher serial number examples may have joined the unit in the Wanganui district.

With only 24 carbines with the Forest Rangers at the start of service, they had to use Enfield rifles on early expeditions. Jackson put in a request to the Colonial Defence Office for a further 39 carbines on 28 August. These arrived shortly after. Not including one un-serviceable carbine the final total of carbines used by the original company of Forest rangers was 62. The Forest Rangers discontinued the use of Enfield rifles immediately.

Forage cap (often called the pill-box cap) of navy blue serge was fitted with a thin leather chin strap. This cap was of plain manufacture for non-commissioned officers and other ranks. The officers had a band of black oak leaf patterned lace around the forage cap, and possibly a cloth covered button centred on top.

Silver badge. It is recorded that the "FR" (Forest Rangers) silver incised badge was worn on the front of the cap. This was possible at time of issue, but in practice the Forest Rangers did not like a shimmering silver badge showing on their foreheads while creeping through undergrowth; also they tended to remove their caps while in the bush, as they were easily brushed off. The badges were more likely to be worn on leather ammunition or despatch pouches or stored in their kit. Only a few were manufactured, with probably the officers and non-commissioned officers wearing them and a few men who joined the unit first. The badge, being incised or "hand-chiselled", meant that the cost of mass production was prohibitive, even in the 1860's, further supporting the argument that only a few were made.

Weapons, uniform and equipment 277

Captains William Jackson (left) and Gustavus Ferdinand von Tempsky (right) as they might have appeared in 1864. Both officers wear the usual "pill" box cap, navy blue trousers with red welt down the outer seam, together with standard blue serge jumper of a lighter blue. Their footwear consists of top boots of the type called "Napoleon" boots. Both men are armed with swords and revolvers and carry telescopes and/or water bottles.

Rear view (centre) of an officer showing the leather covered glass water bottle suspended from a brown leather strap, telescope contained in leather case suspended by a shoulder strap and bowie knife attached to waist belt.

Drawings by Tim Ryan

Non-Commissioned Officer and Private in full marching order. The N.C.O. (left) carries his swag (blanket roll) suspended from pack straps on his back. The Private (right) wears his swag tied across his chest. Both men's blanket rolls would be enclosed in a waterproof oilskin sheet, which would double as a ground sheet at night. Canvas haversacks and brown or black leather shoulder straps suspending black ammunition pouches at the rear are worn on either shoulder. The ammunition cross belts have percussion cap pockets fixed to the front of them. Both men are armed with revolvers and Callisher and Terry carbines. The Sergeant wears a bowie knife on his belt. The small pouch on the waist belt would be for revolver ammunition.

Weapons, uniform and equipment

Private (left) in haversack order minus his swag.

Rear view (right) of a Private showing his water bottle, haversack strap and ammunition belt suspending a black leather 20 round pouch. He also carries a tomahawk thrust into his waist belt.

William Race wrote of having a forage cap bearing a "FR" German silver badge in front at his time of enlistment – 24 December 1863. But there is doubt as to whether he or other men of the unit actually wore a badge.

A fine example of this extremely rare badge is held by the Te Awamutu District Museum. *See photograph on title page.*

Shirt of navy blue serge.

Jumper of navy blue serge. This was the main upper garment and was of heavy woollen manufacture like a modern bush shirt. The jumper was of lighter blue colour than the trousers. Possibly two jumpers were issued.

Trousers of navy blue serge with a quarter inch wide red stripe down the outer seams. Possibly two pairs were issued.

Haletights. Thought to be long combination natural wool underwear similar to long johns.

Leggings of black leather which reached to just below the knees. These leggings were worn by non-commissioned officers and other ranks and were fastened by three buttons in the manner of the shorter gaiters worn by the imperial troops.

Ankle boots of black leather were worn by non-commissioned officers and other ranks. These were of the square toe British Military type which were known during the American Civil War as "Brogans" and in Britain as "Blucher Boots". Remains of these boots have been discovered during archaeological excavations at Te Awamutu. They show the boots to be hobnailed and often with horseshoe shaped plates on the heels. Possibly two pairs were issued.

Officer knee boots of black leather. These were of the type called "Hessian" or "Wellington Boots" and reached to just below the knee.

Blue blanket. These army blankets had fastenings attached so they could be used as bivouack shelters. There were two blankets for every four men. In bush camps a simple pole was laid between trees and the two blankets joined over the pole gave shelter for four men against rain. Most likely they carried the blanket as a swag.

Swag. These consisted of the rolled up blue blanket and/or greatcoat, also containing spare clothing and other necessities enclosed in a "waterproof" (oilskin). The swag could be worn either on the back supported by shoulder straps or rolled and tied across the chest (over either shoulder).

Navy blue greatcoat, often not carried because of its bulk and weight.

Water bottle. Typically of the "torpedo" shaped "soda pop" glass bottle type, which was encased with leather and supported on a leather strap across the chest. Often containing the rum ration rather than water. Two good tots were allowed each day. According to William Johns:

> It was the rum that kept us alive. We had so much wet, hard work, swimming and fording rivers and creeks, and camping without fires. When we camped in the bush on the enemy's trail it was often unsafe to light a fire for cooking and warmth, because we never knew when we might have a volley poured

into us. So we just lay down as we were, wet and cold, and we'd have been dead but for the rum.

Haversack of un-bleached heavy linen was slung over either the right or left shoulder, and contained rations and other necessities. Rations were usually three days' ration of meat (cooked or raw) and half a bottle of rum. The haversack could be of either the single or double buttoned British Army style. No. 2 Company's light coloured haversacks were replaced by black waterproof haversacks after von Tempsky's request dated 26 May 1864. He said that the canvas model got wet and was too conspicuous.

Cartridge box of black leather suspended from the **waist belt** of the same colour. This piece of equipment was probably of British Army issue. Lined on the inside with a metal box that contained 20 rounds of ammunition. Could also be suspended from the wide cross-belt of the same colour.

Percussion cap pocket (pouch) of black leather suspended in a horizontal position at chest height on the wide cross-belt. The wide cross-belt could be worn over either shoulder.

Officers and non-commissioned officers of both companies tended to dress differently to the men, wearing personal boots, shirts, trousers etc.

The above uniform descriptions are supported by references in the writings of John Featon, William Race and von Tempsky. The paintings of von Tempsky also give valuable detail on uniforms and equipment.

In his book *With the Lost Legion in New Zealand* Hamilton-Browne describes clothing and equipment carried by Forest Rangers at about the time of General Chute's Taranaki expedition in January 1866. Although Hamilton-Browne never served in Chute's expedition, he gives a vivid account of the appearance of the Forest Rangers. This description was probably drawn from the reminiscences of veterans who were present on the march around Mount Egmont:

> The Rangers were, at this time, armed with a breechloading carbine of the most primitive pattern. It was loaded with a cartridge the powder of which was contained in a thin skin bag at the base of the bullet, and when loading in a hurry it was quite on the cards you burst the skin and spilt the powder. Then you had to fit on a cap, and after you had the weapon loaded you were more likely to miss a church two hundred yards distant than hit it. Heavy muzzle-loading revolvers, tomahawks and sheath knives completed our outfit of lethal weapons, and every man had to carry one hundred carbine cartridges [believed to be nearer half this amount] and thirty revolver ones. Besides this, a man had to hump his swag, the amount and weight of each swag depending entirely on the strength and ability of the humper and the country over which it had to be humped. We had no transport of any kind nor knapsacks, so whatever we carried was wrapped up in our blankets, which were rolled, drum-shape, and suspended up and down our backs by straps over the shoulders, but not worn across the chest, this method giving free play to the arms; but it required a man to be square-shouldered and not shaped like a soda-water bottle.

> It must not be imagined there was any hard-and-fast rule or uniformity

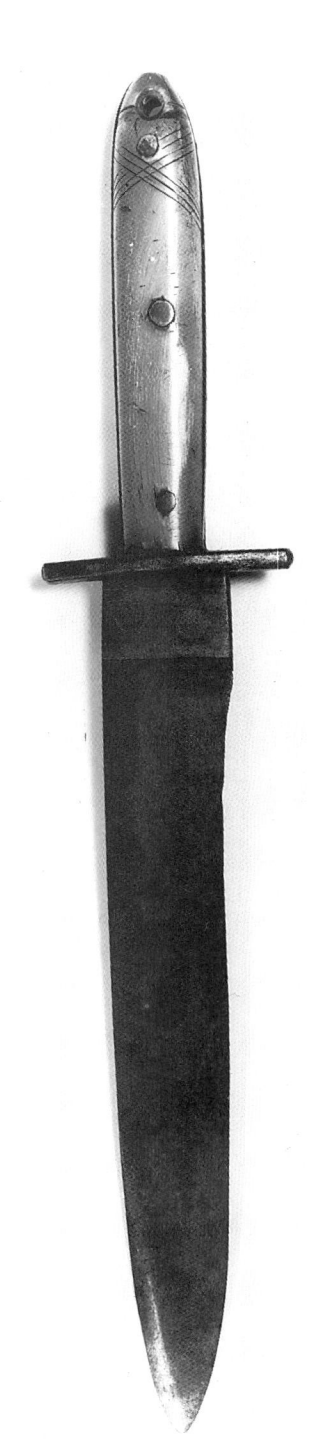

Von Tempsky's bowie knife of the Mediterranean dirk design. It is believed to be missing about one inch from its tip. John Higginson, while serving in the Armed Constabulary, acted as von Tempsky's batman. The knife came into his possession and was later gifted to the Waikato Museum of Art and History by his family.

required as to how the Rangers carried their packs, or even if they carried any at all; in fact the only uniformity required was the blue jumper and carbine, all the rest was left to the man himself, who could go as he darned well pleased. Boots were not considered essential, nor was the pattern of shirt or shawl [kilt] taken into consideration, very many men, like Pierre and George, never wearing boots nor carrying blankets during the summer months.

Of the Forest Rangers' equipment and supplies Hamilton-Browne wrote:

> The expedition was to be made on foot, so discarding our trousers we donned the shawls and were instructed how to wear them. Flannel shirts, our blue jumpers, smasher hats, strong laced boots and worsted socks completed our garbs. Then the blankets were packed. Pierre had drawn four days' rations for each man, and proceeded to distribute them; mine consisted of four pounds of cooked salt pork, four pounds of biscuits, a small tin of tea and sugar mixed, and a smaller tin of pepper and salt mixed. A spare shirt, a pair of socks and a few odds and ends completed my outfit. All these, with the exception of the pork and one day's biscuit, which went into the haversack, were rolled up tightly in the blanket, and the pekau straps (shoulder straps) carefully adjusted; then after we had some food and tea we lay down to get what rest we could before the fall-in went.

It is probable that the men were also issued with a knife, fork, spoon, tin plate and pannikin. These items were probably left in camp when the unit went on expedition.

Some Forest Rangers carried a **tomahawk**, a multi-use tool and weapon in the bush.

Weapons, uniform and equipment

Bowie knife of type used during the New Zealand Wars. Made from waggon spring steel, the riveted grips are of whale bone with Maori patterns tooled into the surface. Along the square-section top are notches similar to those caused by tomahawks.

Bowie Knife (bush knife). The No. 2 Company also carried a bowie knife. Von Tempsky learned the benefits of bowie knife fighting in California while working in the gold fields. He possessed a fine knife of American manufacture for his own use, but had about 60 bowie knives made to his recommendations in Auckland for distribution to his men. These are believed to be crudely made of waggon spring steel – being one of the few sources of suitable steel available to blacksmiths in Auckland at the time. A cutler in Shortland Street, Auckland, was commissioned to manufacture the knives. But due to the short time given to manufacture them, it is possible that the knives came from more than one source (including blacksmiths) resulting in variations of design and length. Most are believed to have blades between 10 and 12 inches long, cross guards and bone or whalebone grips. In practice the knife was held in a thrusting grip with the main edge towards the holder allowing the back of the blade to fend overhead blows from Maori tomahawks (kakauroa and patiti) while the revolver in the other hand could be fired up into the body of the attacker. They were also used to clear tracks through bush, dig defensive positions, cut fire wood and for general use about camp.

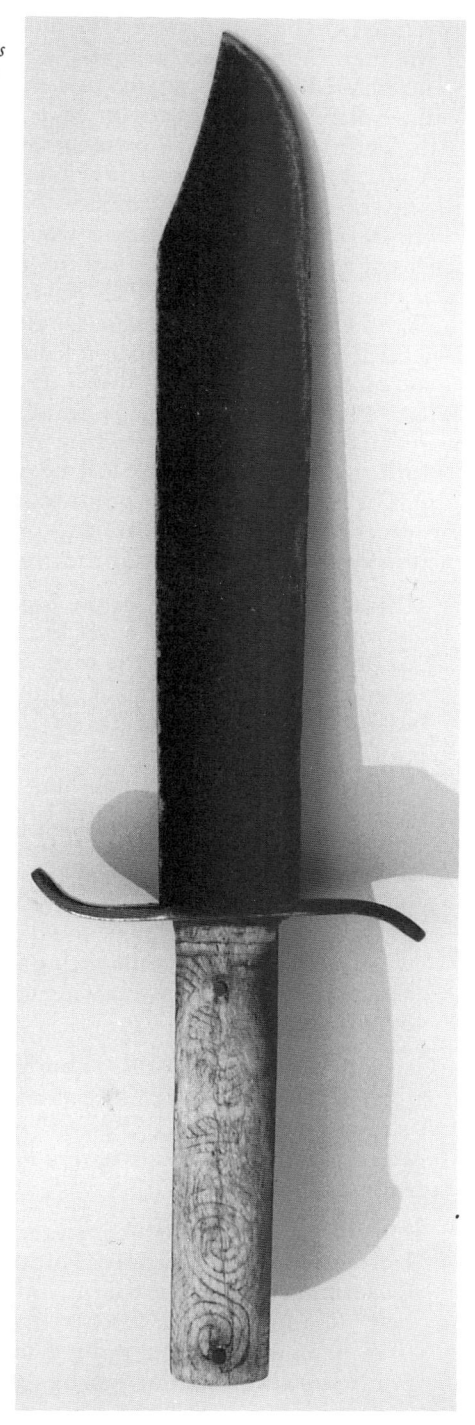

For his own use, von Tempsky preferred the knife he brought from North America. This knife was more of the Mediterranean dirk design that was prevalent in Latin and South America at the time. The design incorporated a cross guard and the blade was a simple design with a near straight top and sloping bottom edge (with no "third edge" usually associated with bowie knives). Other members of his company may also have used a knife of similar design, enjoying its refined qualities as opposed the more probable robust design used by the majority of the men. Many men reshaped their blades and replaced handles. It is possible men removed the cross guards or reduced their size. These practices and variations could explain the different examples of bowie knives existing today that are attributed to the Forest Rangers. All bowie knives were carried in locally-made leather sheaths.

A possible Forest Ranger bowie knife was examined by a collector of militaria during the 1960's in the Waikato.

His description is: The blade was narrowed to a shaft which passed through the centre of a one-piece oak or walnut grip. At the hilt a oval shaped pommel of $1/4$" steel passed over the shaft which was rounded to a tang with a riveting snap. Between the handle and blade was a vertical guard of extended oval shape made of $1/8$" steel. The blade's cross-section tapered from a square back to the cutting edge. To the left of the blade (when looking down upon the knife) and close to the guard were the letters "FR" in 8mm high caps, stamped into the side of the blade. This must have been stamped during manufacture as the steel would be too hard after tempering. Unfortunately the knife tip had been broken and reshaped, but it still was 8-9" long. The blade at its widest point was 2" deep. When considering mass production, this description seems realistic and practicable.

John Roberts, a member of the 2nd Company, described the uses of the knife:

> It was rather awkward in the bush sometimes for it was nearly as long as a bayonet, but it certainly was very handy for cutting tracks. We were taught to hold the knife with the blade pointing inward and upward [with the hilt nearer the small finger], laid along the inner arm [bending the wrist inward with the blade out of harm's way]. With the arm held out, knife-defended thus, a blow [from a tomahawk] could be warded off, and then out would flash the blade in a stab. When we were in camp at Paterangi in 1864 my fellow-subaltern Westrup and I frequently went out in the manuka together and practised the fighting drill. At Orakau we found the knife very useful – not for fighting, but for digging in. Our position was on the east side of the pa, a cultivation-ground bordered with low fern – a place very much exposed to the Maoris' fire. We lay down on the edge of this cultivation and went to work as hard as we could with our long knives, each man digging a shallow shelter for himself and throwing up the earth in front; the bullets were coming over thick that day.

Captain Jackson did not issue bowie knives to his company, but allowed the few members who enjoyed the knife as a weapon to carry them.

A short article signed "Tangiwai" in a 1935 issue of *The New Zealand Railways Magazine*, described an old Forest Ranger (possibly John Toovey) still using his blade about the year 1900:

> One of my old soldier acquaintances in the Waikato had been a corporal in Jackson's and von Tempsky's Forest Rangers. He had a farm near Te Awamutu. Customarily, out on the farm and in the bush, he wore a sheath-knife on his belt. The knife was a veteran like himself. It had been nine or ten inches long of blade, but the point had been broken off, and he re-ground and pointed it; even then it was like a young bayonet. He told its story.

Weapons, uniform and equipment   285

"That's one of old Von's bowie knives," he said. "He had a lot made for us at a blacksmith's in Auckland when the Forest Rangers were divided into two companies and he had command of me. You know, old Von was a terror with the bowie knife. He had learned to use it in Mexico and Central America. Certainly it came in handy in the bush, and as we had no bayonets it was comforting to know you had a good sticker on your hip for a scrimmage. I've had that knife more than thirty years. See how it's worn down.
"I've used it for all sorts of jobs, hacking bush tracks, pig-sticking, skinning sheep, cutting up my tobacco and my loaf of bread. It'll last my day, my boy!"
Old John the Ranger told of one of his warpath mates, a Jamaica Negro who had been sailor and gold-digger, like himself before he became a Ranger. At meal-times he used to apostrophise his bowie knife thus "You old son of a gun, you've dug into a Maori's vitals, you have, at Waiari, you know you have! Come on now, you're going to cut up me vittles!"

A staunch friend of von Tempsky, Sam Nicholls, described von Tempsky's weapons in the goldfields of Coromandel on the eve of his sailing to Auckland in 1863:

That Mexican blade [sword], forged by a Spanish sword-maker from famous Toledo. It was a semi-scimitar in shape, fitting into a curving scabbard.
... His habit on short expeditions was to leave the scabbard in camp and carry the sword naked, as if prepared – as he was – to cut his way through all obstacles.
Another weapon the old campaigner took out of his bundle was a long bowie knife in a leather sheath. This was on a belt, which he buckled around him in place of his sash of red silk, the one touch of flashiness in the goldfields dress. This frontier weapon had a blade nine inches long; a young bayonet. Then there were the two six-shot revolvers [1851 Navy Colt], with their cartridge pouches.
Von Tempsky handled his war-gear lovingly. He packed sword and revolvers in his blanket-roll, and strapped up his spare clothes and other necessaries in a waterproof-covered pack.

What exactly the Forest Rangers took with them on General Chute's march around Taranaki starting late December 1865 is listed in the fascinating inventory below.
The list is headed "Return of Arms, Accoutrements and Ammunition in Possession of the Forest Rangers under Command of Major von Tempsky – 31st December 1865."
From this list one can determine exactly what each Forest Ranger carried.

Sword Rifles 1
[Enfield rifle capable of holding a bayonet. This rifle was probably taken for long range sniping, if needed.]
Breech Loading Carbines 55
[Callisher and Terry carbines. One carbine was left in the Militia Store before leaving Wanganui.]
Revolvers 47
[One revolver was left in the Militia Store before leaving Wanganui

and one un-serviceable revolver left at Patea en route. There being eight fewer revolvers than carbines indicates that the eight Maori guides did not carry revolvers.]

Ramrods [for the Enfield]	1
Swords [bayonet for the Enfield]	1
Scabbards [bayonet scabbard for the Enfield]	1
Muzzle Stoppers [for Callisher and Terrys]	54
Snap Caps & Chains [for Callisher and Terrys]	54
Large Pouches	54
Pouch Belts	54
Waist Belts	2
Ball Bags	2
Frogs [probably for Enfield bayonet]	1
Oil Bottles	0
Slings [probably for Enfield]	1
Cap Pockets [for revolvers]	54
Carbine Pouches [to carry Callisher and Terry ammunition]	55
Waist Belts	55
Carbine Cap Pockets [for Callisher and Terrys]	55
Slings for Carbines [for Callisher and Terrys]	55
Revolver Pouches [to carry revolver ammunition]	50
Revolver Holsters	47
Revolver Belts	0
Bullet Mould – Iron	24
Bullet Mould – Brass	4
Powder Flasks [for revolvers]	38
Wad Cutters	0
Cartridge Frames	0
Breech Wrenches	3
Cleaning Rods	4
Spare Nipples [percussion]	0
Snap & Cap Leathers	0
Nipple Keys	5
Ball Drawers	0
Cramp	0
Breech Brushes [for Callisher & Terrys]	54

[An indication of the problem of fouling around the breech on Callisher and Terrys.]

Large Knives [bowie knifs probably carried by members of the No. 2 Company]	30
Large Knife Sheaths	30
Tomahawks	11
Tomahawk Sheaths	5

Ammunition:

Large Caps [percussion caps for the Callisher and Terrys and Enfield]	37,000

[2000 of these were left at Patea en route, un-serviceable]

Small Caps [percussion caps for the revolvers]	5000

Enfield [cartridges] 2100
Breech Loading [cartridges for Callisher and Terrys] 20,000
[1000 of these were left at Patea en route, un-serviceable.]
Revolver [Bullets for revolvers] 2600

It is not known why they were carrying so many Enfield cartridges. They may have been for volunteers that joined the unit en route or for accompanying Maori who did not belong to the unit but possessed Enfield rifles. Also if a Callisher and Terry carbine became un-serviceable en route, it was probably simpler to acquire an Enfield rifle from the British quartermaster in the field.

While the Forest Rangers were in the Wanganui district many different items were returned to the quartermaster's store in Wanganui between 12 December 1865 and 19 February 1866. Some of the more interesting items mentioned are: blue serge shirts, blue cloth caps, trousers, ankle boots, blue blankets, great coats, worsted socks, tobacco, soap, valises (small leather bags), circular tents, poles for the tents, pegs for the tents, mallets, camp kettles, buckets, tomahawks, large knives (bowie knives), butcher knives, Meat sacks, weights and scales. After Chute's expedition, 12 bell tents were returned to stores, indicating that five or six men may have shared each tent.

Forest Ranger facts

New Zealand Medals issued and unit size

There are 84 known recipients of New Zealand Medals named to the Forest Rangers. Octavus Pierce received two medals. A few replacement medals were issued. A further known 33 medals were issued to Forest Rangers but named to other colonial or imperial units.

The total number of men who enlisted in the Forest Rangers is approximately 365 with about 100 men belonging at any one time. At least eight applications for medals claiming service in the Forest Rangers are known to be false or in error.

Nationalities

At time of enlistment with Forest Rangers, known details of country of birth are: England (62); Ireland (44); Scotland (31); Germany (9); Australia (7); New Zealand (7); Wales (5); Jersey (3); Denmark (2); United States of America (2), both Negroes; At sea (1); Canada (1); India (1), European parents. A further ten Maori and one "half-caste" Maori (Southey) are known to have served.

Occupations

At time of enlistment with Forest Rangers, known details of occupation are: Miner (26); Labourer (20); Farmer (19); Seaman (18); Bushman (7); Settler (6); Gentleman (5); Blacksmith (3); Clerk (3); Butcher (2); Engineer (2); Grocer (2); Soldier (2), many more are known to have seen earlier service with British regiments; Surgeon (2); Baker (1); Carter (1); Filesmith (1); Gardener (1); Horse breaker (1); Lawyer (1); Miller (1); Millwright (1); Platelayer (1); Saddler (1); Sawyer (1); Storekeeper (1); Student (1); Telegraphist (1); Watchmaker (1).

Religions

At time of enlistment with Forest Rangers, known details of religion are: Episcopalian (40); Presbyterian (26); Roman Catholic (22); Church of England (2); Wesleyan (1).

Land grants

At least 130 Forest Rangers received land from the Colonial Government for services rendered while with the Forest Rangers or other units.

Casualties while with Forest Rangers and with later units

Killed in action or died of wounds (9): John Ballenden; Francis Eldred Best; Charles Coghlan; George Lewis Cole; John N. McBain; Spain; William Taylor, Gustavus Ferdinand von Tempsky; Robert Whitfield.

Wounded (9): Allister Henry Campbell; Alexander Davidson; Robert Goldsmith; James Robert Malcolm; James O'Brien (accidentally shot); Edward Ogilvie Ross; James Ryan; James Taylor; John Toovey.

Died during service (4): John R. Dearlove (died of disease); John Duggan (accidentally shot); Frederick Higgins (possibly drowned in service); Robert Patterson Hollister (died in camp); Robert Napier (possibly died of disease).

Deserters

A few Forest Rangers deserted. The circumstances for their absences are not known but the wait for titles of land grants and disillusionment over their land grants may have been contributing factors. The eight known deserters were Thomas Anderson, William Bourke, William Cochrane, James Dunn, William Hartland, William Humphries, Moses McDonald, John Murray and possibly George Vart.

Bibliography

Alexander, Sir J.E., *Bush Fighting*, London, Sampson Low, Marston, Low & Searle, 1873
Alexander, Sir J.E., *Incidents of the Maori War*, London, 1863
Anon, *A Campaign on the West Coast... under the command of Major-General Chute*, Wanganui, 1866
Barton, L.L., *Australians in the Waikato War*, Sydney, Library of Australia History, 1979
Bellich, J., *I Shall Not Die, Titokowaru's War, New Zealand, 1868-9*, Wellington, Allen & Urwin, 1989
Bellich, J., *The New Zealand Wars*, Auckland University Press, Auckland, 1986; Penguin, Auckland, 1988
Cowan, J., *Hero Stories of New Zealand*, Wellington, 1935
Cowan, J., *The Old Frontier*, Te Awamutu, Waipa Post Printing & Publishing Co., 1922
Cowan, J., *The New Zealand Wars and the Pioneering Period*, (2 volumes), Wellington, Government Printer, 1923 and 1955
Featon, J., *The Waikato War 1863-1864*, Auckland, John H. Field, 1879
Gascoyne, F.J.W., *Soldiering in New Zealand*, London, T.J.S. Guilford & Co. Ltd, 1916
Gudgeon, T.W., *Defenders of New Zealand*, Auckland, H. Brett, 1887
Gudgeon, T.W., *Reminiscences of the War in New Zealand*, Sampson Low, Marston, Searle & Rivington, London, 1879
Hamilton-Browne, G., *With the Lost Legion in New Zealand*, London, T. Werner Laurie, circa 1910
Lennard, M., *The Road to War*, Whakatane & District Historical Society, Whakatane, 1986
McDonnell, T., *Incidents of the War*, Auckland, H. Brett, 1887
Morris, N. (Editor), *The Journal of William Morgan*, Auckland, 1963
Parham, W.T., *John Roberts NZC – A Man in his Time*, Whakatane, Whakatane & District Historical Society, 1983
Parham, W.T., *Von Tempsky – Adventurer*, Auckland, Hodder & Stoughton, 1969
Ryan, T. & Parham, W.T., *The Colonial New Zealand Wars*, Wellington, Grantham House, 1986
Tonson, A.E., *Old Manukau*, Auckland, Tonson Publishing House, 1966
Vennell, C.W., *Such Things Were*, Dunedin, Waikato Independent, 1939
Young, R. (Waikato Art Museum), *Gustavus Ferdinand Von Tempsky – The Man and the Artist*, Hamilton, 1978
Young, R. *G. F. Von Tempsky Artist and Adventurer*, Alister Taylor, 1981

Manuscripts

Race, W., *Under the Flag*, circa 1900
Von Tempsky, G.F., *Memoranda of the New Zealand Campaign*, circa 1867

Other sources

Appendices to the Journals of the House of Representatives, 1863-69
Daily Southern Cross, 1863-68
National Archives, Army Department Archives, AD32/0-4999, New Zealand War Medal application files
New Zealand Gazette, 1863-68

Index

Photographs are indicated by page numbers in italic text.

FOREST RANGER ROLLS

(for campaigns, engagements and specific dates)

Original Company
September 1863, 11-12

No. 1 Company
November 1863, 34-35
December 1863, 43
At Waiari, 11 February 1864, 65
At Rangiaowhia and Hairini, 21-22 February 1864, 86
At Orakau, 31 March-2 April 1864, 115
Remain in Te Awamutu district, May 1865, 169

No. 2 Company
November 1863, 35
December 1863, 43
January 1864, 43
At Waiari, 11 February 1864, 65
At Rangiaowhia and Hairini, 21-22 February 1864, 87
At Orakau, 31 March-2 April 1864, 115
Remain in Te Awamutu district, May 1865, 169

No. 1 and No. 2 Companies combined
Present at Paparata, 13 December 1863, 37
Detachment to Maketu, 1864, 118
Travel to Wanganui, April 1865, 131
With Westrup on East Coast, 145
Extra 11 men with Westrup on East Coast, 145
At Camp Abraham, November 1865, 157
In Wanganui and South Taranaki districts (includes Maori guides), December 1865-February 1866, 167
Return from Wanganui to Te Awamutu district, February 1866, 168
On fuel allowance at Camp Alexandra, 9 June 1866, 171
Former Forest Rangers in No. 5 Division Armed Constabulary, 173
Former Forest Rangers in Te Awamutu Cavalry Volunteers, 194
Forest Ranger deserters, 197

ARMED CONSTABULARY ROLLS

No. 5 Division, 172-173
Whitmore's roll of No. 5 Division after Te Ngutu o te Manu, 190

TROOP DEPLOYMENTS AND LISTS

(for campaigns and engagements)
Marched from Te Rore to Te Awamutu and Rangiaowhia, 20/21 February 1864, 84
Hairini, 22 February 1864, 85
March on Orakau (3 columns), 31 March 1864, 95-96, 108-109
Reinforcements at Orakau, 1 April 1864, 101, 110
At Waerengaahika, November 1865, 148
With Chute, 30 December 1865, 158
At Okotuku, 4 January 1866, 158-159
At Te Putahi, 7 January 1866, 159
At Otapawa, 14 January 1866, 163
Leave Ketemarae, 17 January 1866, 166
At Waikoko, 1 February 1866, 166-167
At Te Ngutu o te Manu, 7 September 1868, 176-177
Casualties at Te Ngutu o te Manu, 7 September 1868, 186-187

FOREST RANGER WEAPONS

Bowie knife 8, 38, 44, 99, 270, *282, 283,* 283-285, 286
Callisher and Terry carbines 10, 19, 37, 44, 59, 89, 103, 107, 137, 153, 158, 273-276, *274,* 281, 285-287
Revolvers 10, 21, 25, 36-37, 41, 44, 56, 89, 99, 142, 157, 270-273, *271, 272,* 285-287

FOREST RANGERS

Albin, T. 198
Alexander, R. 198
Allen, T.W. 147, 198
Anderson, J.R. 198
Anderson, T. 198
Arnold, M. 198
Appleyard, W. 198
Argue, G. 199
Aroreta, H. 199
Atkins, R. 199
Babington, W. Hugh 199
Babington, W. Henry 199
Ballenden, J. 75, 79, 101, 200
Bannister, J. 200
Barron, J. 200
Beckham, W. 200
Beckwith, H. 200
Beetham, F.W. 157, 200
Bell, J. 201
Bell, R. 19, 29, 191, 201
Bell, W. 147, 201
Benson, W. 201
Bertram, A.J. 169, 202
Best, F.E. 136-137, 202
Bidgood, J. 202
Bindon, H.W. 202
Birchfield, W.J. 202
Bisland, W. 203
Black, H. 203
Blackey, J. 203
Bochow, E.L. 203
Bond, J. 203
Bond, P. 203
Bond, T. 204
Bond, W. 204
Bourke, J. 204
Bourke, W. 204

Appendices

Boyd, J. 204
Brayley, G. 204
Brassey 12, 204
Brerton, H. 205
Brooking, H.L.S.C. 205
Bruce, A. 205
Bruce, D. Junior 205
Bruce, D. Senior 205
Bruce, G. 205
Bruce, R. 205
Bruce, W. Junior 206
Bruce, W. Senior 206
Buchanan, J. 206
Bulow, B. 206
Burley, P. 157, 206
Burns, J. 206
Burns, J. 206
Burns, L.B. 43, 206
Burns, W. 207
Burry, W. 207
Butter, A. 147, 207
Buttle, T. 207
Bygum, H. 207
Cain, O. 207
Campbell, A.H. 159, 207
Campbell, J. 208
Carran, H. 35, 55, 75, 88, 104-105, 208
Carrol, J. 208
Carter, J. 118, 208
Castin, L. 208
Caughey, D. 208
Chapman, E. 208
Clayforth, C. 208
Clifford, H.G. 209
Clinton, P.J. 209
Clotworthy, G. 138, 209
Cochrane, W. 209
Codling, E. 131, 210
Coghlan, C. 40, 101, 111, 210
Cole, G.L. 13-15, 17, 210
Collins, H. 210
Colston, G. 210
Colton, G.W. 210
Conrad, L. 210
Corboy, W. 211
Cornes, C.A. 211
Costello, J. 211
Crawford, J. 211
Crommelin, J. 211
Crowe, M. 211
Crymble, W. 211
Cullinan, R. 157, 211
Cunningham, J. 211

Cunningham, R. 212
Curran, P. 212
Daley, C. 212
Darrow, J. 212
Davidson, A. 167, 168, 212
Davidson, G. 213
Davis, E. 213
Dearlove, J.R. 213
Devlin, W.H. 213
Donald, M. 213
Donovan, J. 213
Drew, J. 213
Drury, V. 214
Duesbury, H. 214
Duffy, P. 157, 214
Duggan, J. 142, 214
Dunckley, J.W. 214
Dunn, J. 214
Elston, H. 214
Elvin, R. 215
Erskine, R. 215
Evans, W. 216
Evans, W. 216
Fahey, J. 216
Fallon, J. 216
Ferris, J.B. 216
Findlay, R.D. 216
Finlay, J. 216
Fischer, C.F.T. 217
Fisher, H. 217
Fitzgerald, R. 43, 217
Flanagan, E. 217
Foster, F.A.C. 217
Fraser, W. 218
Freeman, J. 218
Frost, R. 218
Gallie, P. 218
Gardiner, J. 218
Garvey, R.E. 218
Gibb, R. 218
Gillanders, J. 157, 218
Goldsmith, R. 219
Grigg, J.J. 219
Guning, E. 219
Haines, A.W. 219
Hannah, W. 219
Hannay, J. 219
Hardy, A.F. 147, 220
Harkin, R. 220
Harris, J. 220
Hartland, W. 220
Harvey, T. 220
Hay, W.McG. 11, 14-19, 22, 24, 29, 34, 123, 220

Healas, R. 221
Hearfield, J.G. 157, 221
Heffernan, M. 221
Hellkessel, P. 221
Hendry, C.F.H. 221
Hennessey, M. 221
Henshaw, T.J. 221
Hewson, H.H. 221
Higgins, F. 221
Hill, A. 22, 222
Hill, G.R. 222
Hinchcliffe, E. 223
Holden, T. 118, 223
Hollister, R.P. 223
Howell, W.J. 224
Huddleston, A. 224
Humphries, W. 224
Husband, E. 225
Jackson, H.B. 225
Jackson, J.H. 225
Jackson, W. *(Throughout book.)* 3, 225, 225, 277
Jacob, S. 226
Jeffares, H. 157, 227
Jennings, J. 227
Johns, W. 38-39, 79, 227, 280
Jolley, A. 227
Jones, W. 227
Kaiwhakataka, H. 227
Kawiti, R. 228
Keena, T. 35, 104, 228
Kenealy, D. 228
Kiely, J. 229
Knight, R.C. 229
Knowles, J. 229
Lander, A.A. 229
Laurensen, L. 229
Lee, W. 229
Liebig, C. 5, 137, 157, 229
Lindsay, J. 230
Lloyd, H.H. 157, 230
Long, H. 230
Lott, J.R. 231
Lynch, J. 231
Lysaught, F. 231
Lysaught, G. 231
McBain, J.N. 135-136, 231
McCarthy, P. 231
McClymont, A.G. 231
McCulloch, J. 232
McDonald, H. 43, 232
McDonald, M. 232
McDonnell, C. 232
McEnaney, J. 232

McGrath, E. 232
McGregor, J. 232
McGuirk, J. 233
McHerron, J.R. 233
McKelson, P. 233
McKenna, E. 168, 233
McKenzie, D. 169, 234
McKenzie, W. 234
McMinn, E.G. 116, 131, 169-170, 189, 191, 234
McNamara, A.F. 43, 234
Madigan, P. 9, *196*, 235
Magill, P. 104, 235
Mahoney, S. 235
Maki, R. 236
Malcolm, J.R. 159, 236
Manning, D. 236
Marsh, N. 236
Martin, J.W. 237
Matheson, R.A. 237
Medex, J. 237
Mellon, E. 237
Methven, W. 237
Mitchell, E.M. 237
Mitchell, L.B. 145, 161, 238
Mohr, J. 238
Morgan, J. 238
Morton, J.A. 238
Moylan, A. 238
Mulligan, J. 239
Munroe, C. 239
Murray, J. 239
Murray, R.W. 239
Muskett, J.H. 239
Mutton, D.J. 239
Napier, R. 239
Napper, H.W. 240
Neil, R. 240
Newcastle, J. 240
Newman, W.J. 240
Newton, J.E. 240
Nolan, J.C. 240
Nolan, M. 241
O'Brien, J. 157, 241
O'Connell, P. 241
O'Connor, P. 241
Osborne, J. 241
Osborne, W. 242
Owens, J. 242
Parr, D. 242
Parsons, J.D. 242
Parsons, W.D. 242
Penamina, 243
Te Pene, 243

Peters, J. 43, 243
Pierce, O. 243
Pilmer, A.A.G. 161, 168, 244
Pohlen, W.H. 244
Pollock, T.McD. 244
Preston, G. 244
Quinlan, J. 245
Quinn, J. 245
Race, W. 13, 40, 42, 44, 49, 55, 56, 58, 67, 69, 71-72, 75, 77, 79-80, 83, 88, 115, 245
Ramsay, A. 245
Ramsay, G. 245
Ramsay, R. 245
Raven, W.J. 245
Ray, T. 246
Reihana 166, 246
Reynolds, W. 246
Richards, W. 246
Roberts, H. 246
Roberts, J.M. 11, 13, 35, 36, 44, 55, 57-58, 71, 73, 89, 93, 95-97, 99, 106-107, 116, 123, 127, 131, 138, 171, 172, 175-177, 182-185, *183*, 190, *192*, 194, 246, 284
Robinson, T.W. 247
Rogers, P. 247
Roper, T. 247
Rose, J. 247
Ross, E.O. 136-137, 140, 147-148, 151, 247
Rowden, J. 247
Rowland, H. 17, 248
Ruhstein, F. 248
Rush, C.A. 248
Russell, F.N. 248
Ryan, J. 151, 248
Ryan, J.McD. 157, 159, 249
Ryan, W. 249
Scally, J. 249
Scanlan, T. 249
Schacht, C.L.A. 249
Schumacher, A. 249
Shaddock, T. 250
Sherret, A.S. 116, 127, 250
Sherret, J. 250
Shine, J. 250
Shuker, W. 250
Sibley, H.T. 251
Sibley, J. 251
Sibley, W.H. 145, 251

Simmons, J.K. 251
Skinner, W.H. 14, 251
Smith, C.B. 157, 252
Smith, E. 252, *252*
Smith, J. 252
Smith, James H. 43, 252
Smith, John H. 36, 39, 43, 252
Smith, P.J.L. 253
Smith, P. 253
Smith, T.J.L. 253
Smith, W. 253
Smith, W. 253
Southey, H. 17-18, 35, 82-83, 105, 107, 191, 254
Spain *162*, 165, 254
Spencer, G. 254
Stanley, W. 255
Steenson, W. 255
Stephenson, J. 255
Stephenson, W.F. 255
Strong, J. 256
Sturmer, E. 169, 256
Sullivan, J. 256
Sullivan, W. 256
Sumsion, C. 256
Taylor, A. 257
Taylor, J. 81, 84, 257
Taylor, J. 257
Taylor, W. 104, 111, 257
Temple, C. 257
Third, A. 258
Thomas, B. 258
Thompson, J.H. 258
Thomson, W.M. 258
Thomson, W. 259
Thornton, H. 259
Thorpe, J. 43, 259
Thurston, F.W. 259
Toovey, J. 96, 104, 175, 259, 284
Torpey, D. 43, 106, 259
Treadwell, C.H. 259
Trelawney, T. 259
Tristram, J.Q. 260
Tubby, J. 260
Tucker, S. 260
Turner, W. 260
Tyrell, L. 260
Usher, J. 131, 260
Varette, E. 260
Vart, G. 260
Vaughan, M. 261
Vincent, W. 261

Appendices

Von Tempsky, G. F.
   (*Throughout book*) *4*, 261,
   174, 180, 262, 277
Waka, T. 166, 263
Wakeford, H.J. 263
Walker, J. 263
Wallace, J. 263
Wallace, T.W. 157, 263
Walsh, J. 264
Warbey, J. 264
Ward, G. 36, 40, 264
Ward, J.P. 264
Warden, M. 265
Warford, 265
Watene, H. 265
Watson, W.F. 265
Watters, J. 40, 118, 265
Watts, J.R. 265
Weal, J. 265
Wells, W. 266
Westrup, C. 36, 39, 58, 67,
   70, 83, 93, 106, 135-137,
   144, 144-145, 147-155,
   266
Wheeler, T. 266
Whitfield, R. 41, 67, 99, 104,
   134-136, 266
Williams, J.P. 267
Williams, T.W. 267
Williams, W. 267
Wilson, G. 267
Winmill, C.G. 267
Woods, W.S. 267
Wright, J.H.A. 142, 267

GENERAL INDEX

Alexander 45
Alexandra Redoubt 20, 30
Anderson, Sergeant 190
Aotearoa flag 38-39, *39*
Areiahi 140
Armed Constabulary 3, 171-
   193, *192*
Atkinson, Major 121, 125,
   143, 158
Auckland Militia 8-9, 13, 34-
   35, 197
Avon 45, 47
Baker, Captain J.D. 63-65,
   103, 105, 108-109, 111
Bald Hills 24, 28, 269
Biggs, Lieutenant R. 147-148,
   153

Blewitt, Captain 96, 108
Blyth, Major 108-109, 115-
   116
Bowdler, 64-65
Brassey, Major W. 141-143,
   145
Brisk 143, 145, 147

British Regiments:
12th: 110
14th: 159, 163
18th: 85, 96, 101, 159, 161
40th: 27-28, 47, 58-59, 63,
   85, 97, 109
43rd: 166
50th: 58-59, *76*, 79-81, 85-86,
   91, 159, 161
57th: 163, 165
65th: 27-28, 71, 73, 75, 80,
   85
68th: 165
70th: 27-28, 47, 80, 82, 85,
   91, 101, 115

Buck, Captain G. 176, 182,
   184, 188
Burtt's farm 25, 27, 29-30
Cambridge *124,* 125
Cameron, Lieutenant-General
   Sir D. 7-8, 42, 44-45, 49,
   51, 53, 57-58, 67, 70-72,
   77, 79, 82-84, 89, 91, 95,
   103, 110, 113, 115-118,
   132, 134, 139-140, 177
Camerontown 25, 28, 31
Carey, General 82, 95, 97, 99,
   108, 111, 129, 131
Chute, Major-General T. 155-
   167, 285
Clare, Captain 9, 21
Colonial Defence Force 10-12,
   20, 27, 29-30, 33, 44, 51,
   70-71, 73, 75, 80-81, 85-
   86, 91, 103, 106, 111,
   118-120, 145, 148, 151,
   154
Cooper, George 15
Daily Southern Cross 7-9, 12,
   15, 19, 41, 49, 79,
Esk 147
Falcon 120
Fisher, Captain 60-61
Flying Column 27-31, 41
Fraser, Major J. 143-144, 147-
   154, *149*

Galloway, General 47
Gascoyne, Lieutenant F. 147
Gentle Annie 137, 269
George, Captain F.N. 129,
   134-137, 141-142, 145
Gorton, Lieutenant-Colonel E.
   156-158, 167
Great South Road 7, *8*, 20, 29,
   47
Grey, Governor Sir G. 6-7, 10,
   19, 53, 84, 103, 116-117,
   139-140, 144
Gudgeon, T. 105, 165
Gundagai 159
Hairini 2, 80-87, 108, 169, 269
Harapepe *126, 128*, 129, *130*,
   131, 138, 169-170
Haultain, Colonel 95, 108-
   109, 127, 144, 155, 168,
   187-188, 190-191
Hamilton-Browne 3-4, 281-
   282
Hastings, Lieutenant 176, 182,
   184
Havelock, Colonel 59, 63-64,
   107, 110, 115
Hawke's Bay Military Settlers
   147-148, 151, 154
Heaphy, Captain C. 28-29, 58,
   60-61, 63-64, 191
Herford, Captain 111
Hill's Clearing 22
Hungahunga-toroa 147
Hunter, Major W. 173, 176,
   181-182, 189
Hunua Ranges 2, 8, 12-21, 36-
   42
Hurst, Lieutenant 97, 109-110
Inman, Captain 99, 110
Kakaramea 132, 134-137, 139,
   161, 269
Kangaroo 45
Kapamahunga Range 45, 47,
   125
Karaponia 94, 97
Kemp, Major (Kepa te
   Rangihiwinui) 165, 177,
   182, 185
Ketemarae 165, 166, 269
Kihikihi 85, 88-89, 92-93, 95,
   108-109, *112,* 125, 129,
   169-170
Kingite 9, 14, 92
Kirikiri 10, 20-21, 41, 269

Kohanga Karearea *152*, 153-154
Koheroa 7
Logan, Lieutenant-Colonel 139
Lord Ashley 145
Lusk, Lieutenant 22, 24, 26, 95
Lusk's Clearing 22-24, 269
McDonnell, T. 31-32, 36, 73, 118-120, 139-140, 143, 156, 159, 163, 168, 173, 175-193
McDonnell, W. 163, 177, 182-183
MacNeil, Colonel 115
Mair, Ensign William G. 73, 102-103
Mataitawa stockade 166
Maketu (Bay of Plenty) 118-120, 269
Maketu pa (south Auckland) 20
Malone, Lieutenant 135-136
Mangapiko 58-67
Mangatawhiri River 7
Maniapoto, Rewi 92, *93*, 94, 101, 107
Manu-rau 1
Marion 103
Martyn's clearing 20
Matata 118-120
Mauku Rifles 22, 24, 26, 195
Meremere 30, 32, *46*, 49
Morgan W. 8, 10, 28
Moule, Lieutenant-Colonel 168, 170, 172
Mounted Artillery 10, 49, 70-71, 80, 85-86, 106, 111
Ngahinapouri 125, 127
Ngaruawahia 45, *45*, 47
Nixon, Colonel 11, 27-29, 51, 70, 73, 79, 85-86
Ohaupo 91, 99, *114*, 115-116, 125
Okotuku 158-159, 195, 269
Orakau 91-117, *100, 102,* 186, 269
Otapawa 161-165, *162*, 269
Pai Marire 134-135, 148-149
Papakura Valley Rifle Volunteers 9
Paparata 13-15, 17, 30, 32, 36-41, 101, 140, 269

Patea Field Force 173
Patea Rangers 141, 143
Paterangi 51, 53, 57-59, 61, *66*, 67, 70, 80, 83, 85-86, 91
Pekapekarau swamp 81
Perekama 140
Pikopiko 49, 51, 53, 55, 70, 86
Pioneer 127
Pipiriki 139-142, 269
Pukekohe stockade 27
Pukekura 91-92, 115
Pukemaire 147-148, 269
Pukerimu *90*, 91, 103, 113, 115, 118, 125, 127
Pye, Captain 27, 30, 81, 111
Queen's Redoubt 7, 31, 79
Raglan 45, 47, 127, 129, 170
Rait, Lieutenant 10, 51, 70-71, 86, 101, 106, 111
Ramarama 35-36, 47
Rangiaowhia 53, 70-87, *74, 76,* 88, 92, 97, 108, 113, 122, 169, 269
Rangiriri 44-45, 47, 49, 61, 70, 95, 103, 186, 269
Rangiriri 45
Ring, Captain 10, 96, 109, 111
Rixon, Lieutenant 18
Ropata 147
Rotorua 123
Ruaruru 176-177, 179, 181
Russell, T. 10-11, 14, 18-19, 21, 25, 33-34, 89, 121
Rutherford, Captain 27, 29, 31
Sandfly 120
Selwyn, Bishop 77, 80, 83-84
Smith, B. 12, 14, 21
Spencer, Surgeon 111, 116
St Kilda 145
Steele, Lieutenant 13, 15
Stoney River 166
Stormbird 157-158, 168
Sturt 147, 149, 173, 191
Surrey Redoubt 36
Tamehana, Wiremu 139
Te Awamutu 70, 79-80, 82-85, 88-93, 95, 97, 104, 108-109, 113, 116, 129, 131, 154, 169
Te Awamutu Cavalry Volunteers 194

Te Kooti 149
Te Ngutu o te Manu 42, 57, 176-189, *178, 180,* 191, 269
Te Putahi 159-161, *160*, 167, 269
Te Rore 53, *54*, 55-59, 70, 84-86, 88, 125, 127, 170
Titokowaru 173, 175-187
Travellers' Rest inn 12, 14-15, 21
Tuhikaramea 47, 49, *50*, 51, Turuturu Mokai 173, 175, 187, 269
Volkner Reverend C.S. 143
Waerengaahika 147-154, *150*, 269
Waddy, Colonel 49, 58-59, 81, 85-86, 88, 92, 137
Waiapu 143-145, 147-148
Waiari 58-67, *62*, 70, 191, 269
Waihi (South Taranaki) 165, 173, 175, 179, 184, 188-189
Waikato Cavalry Volunteers 194
Waikato Militia 6, 33-35, 41-42, 45, 47, 89, 104, 111, 117, 121-122, 125, 129, 131-132, 135, 137-138, 145, 170, 172, 197
Waikato River 91, 115
Waikoko 167, 269
Waipa River 45, 47, *52*, 53, 55, 56, 92, 125
Wairoa Ranges 8, 13, 36
Wairoa Rifle Volunteers 9, 13
Waitetuna River 47, 170
Walmsley, Captain 27, 81, 86
Wanganui 144
Weare, Colonel 82, 85-86
Weraroa 139-141, 161, 269
Wharepapa 93
Whatawhata *48*, 49, 51, 125
Whitmore, Colonel 187, 189
Williamson's clearing 20
Wilson, Captain 70, 73
Wilson, Lieutenant 148, 151, 153-154
Woodall's Redoubt 139, 144, 157, 167
York Redoubt 20